Railways Restored 2006

Edited by
Alan C. Butcher

Ian Allan PUBLISHING

Contents

Front cover: Although ex-GWR No 1450 is privately-owned it can be seen visiting railways around the country, usually with this GWR auto-trailer, No 178, in tow. The consist is seen here at on the Dean Forest Railway. *Alan Barnes*

Previous page: One locomotive that is currently touring a number of heritage railways is GWR 4-4-0 *City of Truro*, No 3440 is seen at Ropley on the Mid-Hants Railway during the 2005 spring gala. *Phil Barnes*

First published 1980
Twenty seventh edition 2006

ISBN (10) 0 7110 3122 3
ISBN (13) 978 0 7110 3122 7

Published by Ian Allan Publishing

an imprint of Ian Allan Publishing Ltd, Hersham, Surrey KT12 4RG
Printed by Ian Allan Printing Ltd, Hersham, Surrey KT12 4RG

Code: 0603/C3

National Railway Heritage Awards

The Awards have been made annually since 1979 and were granted charitable status in 2004. The object remains the same: encouraging high standards of restoration of buildings, structures and signalling installations and of their environmental care, thus promoting public recognition and awareness of our historic railway and tramway heritage and its place in the environment. We aim to promote careful design and quality workmanship in restoration, modernisation, adaptation and maintenance, taking proper account of all relevant factors, particularly manpower and funding. In this way we encourage both public and heritage railways and tramways to present their operational premises as attractive 'shop-windows'. We also encourage owners and occupiers of former railway or tramway premises now used for other purposes to retain as much as possible of their original character.

The awards are organised by the National Railway Awards Committee. Our main sponsors are Ian Allan Publishing together with Westinghouse Invensys, Network Rail, London Underground and the Railway Heritage Trust. Judging is done from the beginning of May through to the end of August and those short listed are notified at the beginning of October. The Awards are presented in early December at a prestigious location by a well-known public figure, with full media coverage.

1992 saw the inclusion of Ireland in the Awards initially with the addition of a special Premier Award and up to three Certificates of Commendation in each sector.

The following projects are eligible:

1 Any building, structure or signalling installation, associated with railways or tramways since their inception in the United Kingdom, the Isle of Man and the Republic of Ireland.

2 An entry may comprise a whole station or any single structure or group of structures, which form, or once formed, part of railway or tramway premises.

3 Certain types of replica are eligible. These include:

- An historic building, structure or signalling installation re-erected at a new site
- An accurate reconstruction of a specfic building, structure or signalling installation, the original of which has been removed or demolished, rebuilt on or very close to its original site
- A completely new but authentic replica of a specific historic building, structure or signalling installation on a new site
- An entry comprising a combination of restored or adapted historic building, structure or signalling installation with modern additions
- Construction of a building in the general style of an historic building, structure or signalling installation with no specific or authentic basis for its design or location, would not be eligible.

Who can enter?

Entries are invited from the following:

Train and tram operating companies.

Companies owning track, structures and stations.

Urban underground and passenger transport authorities and companies.

Operators of preserved, tourist and private railways and tramways.

Residual property owning bodies.

Owners of eligible infrastructure, whether of not still in railway or tramway use.

Architects, engineers and contractors involved in restoration, new or maintenance work.

Local Amenity groups.

Private individuals.

Any group in Great Britain and Ireland involved in railway preservation, whether as a private railway company or as a less formal organisation. Railtrack, Irish Rail, Northern Ireland Railways (NIR). Other public or commercial organisations. Private individuals.

For application forms apply to:
Robin Leleux
12 Bilsdale Way
Baildon
Shipley
West Yorkshire
BD17 5DG

The HRA Annual Award

This, the premier award made by the HRA, is for a group or organisation making an outstanding contribution to railway preservation during the year of the Award.

The Award takes the form of a Royal Train Headboard from the London, Brighton & South Coast Railway, which is on loan to the HRA from the National Railway Museum. The Award is held for one year and the winning group also receives a commemorative plaque. The Award is announced and presented at the Association's Annual General Meeting which is held on the last weekend of January each year.

Editor's Notes

On the following pages will be found a guide to the major preserved railways, railway museums and preservation centres in the British Isles. Information for visitors has been set out in tabular form for easy reference, together with a locomotive stocklist for most centres.

Many preservation centres and operating lines provide facilities for other groups and organisations to restore locomotives and equipment on their premises. It has not been possible to include full details of these groups, but organisations which own locomotives are shown under the centres at which they operate. In addition, a full list of member societies of the HRA is given elsewhere. In the case of most operating lines their length is given, but there is no guarantee that services are operated over the entire length.

Within the heading to each entry a heading block has been incorporated for easy reference as to what each site offers in the way of passenger service to visitors. These are as follows:

Timetable Service: Railways providing a passenger service between two or more stations with public access; eg Mid-Hants Railway.

Steam Centre: A railway or preservation site offering a passenger service on a short length of line, on a regular basis, with public access at only one point; eg Lavender Line.

Museum: A museum or site that does not offer a passenger service on a regular basis, if at all; eg Science Museum, London. Some sites may however offer rides on miniature railways.

Railway Centre: A catch-all for those centres which do not fall clearly into any of the other brackets. Generally those offering rides over short distances using non-steam motive power.

Attraction: Where the railway is an addition to the main attraction of the location (eg Bicton Woodland Railway).

As well as a guide as to what to expect on each site, this year's *Railways Restored* shows what, if any, particular professional body the Companies or Societies belong to. These are:

HRA: Indicates that the organisation is a member of the Heritage Railway Association (HRA).

TT: Indicates that the organisation is a member of the Transport Trust (TT).

Membership of the HRA and TT is open to both organisations and private individuals. Private members are able to take advantage of concessions offered to them by the organisations that subscribe to these two bodies.

The concessions range from a discount on the admission price to free entry. The TT's Travel Back leaflet provides details.

Details given under **Access by public transport** should be checked beforehand to ensure services shown are operating. Unless the Heritage Railway, Steam Centre or Museum has identified the privatised train company operating the service, the phrase 'by rail', or 'main line', has been used to identify access by train.

Visitors wishing to see specific items of rolling stock or locomotives are advised to check before their visit that the exhibit is available for inspection. It should be stressed that not all items are usually available for inspection due to restoration, operating or other restrictions.

Editor's Comment

Welcome to the 27th edition of *Railways Restored*. A number of heritage lines have reported records being broken during 2005, both in terms of visitors and turnover. *Railways Restored* now echoes the achievements of the heritage movement, this edition sees a number of new entries, the addition of colour and even more pages, 240 this year including the 20 page timetable supplement.

For this edition the miniature railway entries have been 'promoted' to the main section, together with the addition of a few more. The popularity of these new lines is a way of encouraging the younger generation to become interested in preserving our transport heritage.

Two sites have been lost over the last year, the Cadeby Railway having closed, although at the time of writing (5 February) the former Rectory, railway and model railway are for sale. The Foyle Valley Railway is moved to the closed section more by default than design. At the time of writing the local council has still not advised of any approved scheme to reopen the museum and adjacent line. The Weardale Railway is still in administration, although it now looks more hopeful of a successful reopening during summer 2006. No doubt details will be revealed in the railway press in due course.

Returning to the fold is Tiverton Museum following a period of refurbishment, and with the London's Transport Museum closed for refurbishment the LT Museum Depot is now included. With the development of the Cambrian Heritage Railway, the Cambrian Railways Society at Oswestry is now included as the Oswestry Railway Centre. As usual a selection of 'new' locations are included including Astley Green Colliery Museum.

If you have enjoyed your visit to any of the attractions in *Railways Restored* why not join in the pleasure of becoming a member and may be volunteering. Not every 'job' entails years of training or physical work. Most operations now have a 'new volunteer' officer or hold an 'open weekend' when a behind the scenes tour gives an idea of how the prospective volunteer can get involved.

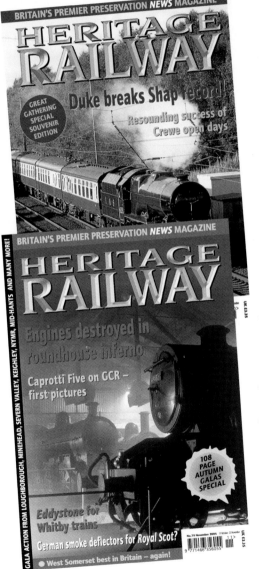

Standard Abbreviations

AEC	Associated Equipment Co
AEG	Allgemeine Elektrizitaets Gesellschaft
A/Barclay	Andrew Barclay
A/Porter	Aveling & Porter Ltd
A/Whitworth	Armstrong Whitworth
B/Drewry	Baguley/Drewry
B/Peacock	Beyer Peacock & Co
B/Hawthorn	Black, Hawthorn & Co
BRCW	Birmingham Railway, Carriage & Wagon
BTH	British Thomson Houston
Buch	23 August Locomotive Works
D/Metcalfe	Davies & Metcalfe
E/Electric	English Electric Ltd
F/Jennings	Fletcher Jennings & Co
F/Walker	Fox Walker
G&S	G. & S. Light Engineering Co
G/England	George England & Co
GRCW	Gloucester Railway, Carriage & Wagon
H/Barclay	Hunslet Barclay
H/Clarke	Hudswell Clarke & Co Ltd
H/Hunslet	Hudson-Hunslet
H/Leslie	Hawthorn Leslie & Co
K/Stuart	Kerr Stuart & Co Ltd
L/Blackstone	Lister Blackstone
M/Cam	Metropolitan Cammell
M/Rail	Motor Rail Ltd
M/Vick	Metrovick (Metropolitan-Vickers)
M/Wardle	Manning Wardle & Co Ltd
N/British	North British Locomotive Co Ltd
N/Wilson	Nasmyth Wilson & Co Ltd
O&K	Orenstein & Koppel
P/Steel	Pressed Steel Co Ltd
RSH	Robert Stephenson & Hawthorn Ltd
R/Hornsby	Ruston Hornsby
R/Proctor	Ruston Proctor
S. F. Belge	Société Franco Belge
SMH	Simplex Mechanical Handling
YEC	Yorkshire Engine Co
W&M	Waggon & Maschinenbau
W/Rogers	Wingrove & Rogers

Company abbreviations

BR	British Railways
DB	German Federal Railway
DSB	Danish State Railways
GWR	Great Western Railway
JZ	Yugoslav Railways
LBSCR	London, Brighton & South Coast Railway
LMS	London, Midland & Scottish Railway
LNER	London & North Eastern Railway
LSWR	London & South Western Railway
MoS	Ministry of Supply
MR	Midland Railway
NLR	North London Railway
NS	Netherlands State Railways
NSB	Norwegian State Railways
RR	Rhodesia Railways
S&DJR	Somerset & Dorset Joint Railway
SAR	South African Railways
SECR	South Eastern & Chatham Railway
SER	South Eastern Railway
SJ	Swedish Railways
SNCF	French National Railways
SR	Southern Railway
USATC	United States Army Transportation Corps
WD	War Department

Other abbreviations

BE	Battery-electric
DE	Diesel-electric
DH	Diesel-hydraulic
DM	Diesel-mechanical
DMU	Diesel multiple-unit
E	Overhead electric
EMU	Electric multiple-unit
F	Fireless
G	Geared
GH	Gas-hydraulic
IST	Inverted saddle tank
LRO	Light Railway Order
ParM	Paraffin-mechanical
PH	Petrol-hydraulic
PM	Petrol-mechanical
PT	Pannier tank
R	Railcar
ST	Saddle tank
STT	Saddle tank and tender
T	Side tank
VB	Vertical boiler
WT	Well tank
4w	Four-wheel

Multiple-unit Type abbreviations

B	Brake
C	Composite (First/Standard class seating)
D	Driving
F	First class
K	Corridor
LV	Luggage Van
M	Motor
O	Open (seating arrangement)
P	Pullman (ex-'Brighton Belle')
R	Restaurant
S	Standard ([or Second] class)
T	Trailer

Added together these give the vehicle designation, for example: DMBS — Driving Motor Brake Second.

The addition of an L indicates that the vehicle has a lavatory (may not be operational on some vehicles).

Some lines operate a Standard class only policy and the First class facility is downgraded. This may result in some vehicles having a different designation to that originally applied.

The first of the Nottingham Trams loaded onto our specialist transporters ready for delivery.

Allelys Heavy Haulage Ltd is part of the Allely Group running approximately 50 vehicles in total.

The Heavy Haulage side have been specialists in the movement of railway vehicles for the last 20 years and has undertaken numerous large contracts.

We offer a full service for movement of railway rolling stock and trackwork and will consider any rail contracts.

We have extensive knowledge of all types of rolling stock and many rail locations in the UK.

Contact Robert Ford
Telephone 01527 857 621

THE SLOUGH, STUDLEY
WARWICKSHIRE B80 7EN

Telephone **01527 857623**
Fax **01527 857623**
Email **enquiries@allelys.co.uk**

Kidlington Railwayana Auctions

At Exeter Hall, Kidlington Nr. Oxford

Entries now accepted for sales on 22nd April and 7th October

LADY GODIVA

ENTRIES ARE NOW BEING ACCEPTED FOR OUR SALES IN 2006

Contact us for a sample catalogue and results of our last sale

10% COMMISSION + VAT (TOTAL 11.75% OF HAMMER PRICE)

LONDON NORTH EASTERN
Nº 2030
DONCASTER
1948
RAILWAY Cº

Worksplate from A2 Class "Bronzino", sold in Sale 103, 8th October 2005, realised **£3,600**

99% OF ENTRIES ILLUSTRATED IN FULL COLOUR
SECURE, INSURED STORAGE AND TRANSPORT
GUARANTEED PAYMENT DATE FOR VENDORS (7 WORKING DAYS AFTER AUCTION)
PROFESSIONAL FULL-TIME STAFF
LARGEST CATALOGUE CIRCULATION (1800+)
20 YEARS' PROVEN TRACK RECORD WITH MANY WORLD RECORD PRICES
MAXIMUM ADVERTISING OF YOUR ENTRIES IN MAGAZINES
AVOID THE UNCERTAINTY OF PRIVATE SALES
COLLECTION SERVICE AVAILABLE

"Talisman" headboard, sold in Sale 103, 8th October 2005, realised **£4,400**

GWR
31

LONDON NORTH EASTERN
1930
DARLINGTON
1944
RAILWAY Cº

TELEPHONE OR WRITE FOR A COMPLEMENTARY CATALOGUE FOR OUR NEXT SALE

EALING BROADWAY

Company Reg. 5405235

Kidlington Railwayana Auctions

Operated by Great Central Railwayana Ltd
14 School Street, Woodford Halse, Daventry, Northants NN11 3RL
Tel: 01327 263633 (Monday to Saturday 10.30 – 7.00)
Personal callers by appointment only please.

Keith & Dufftown
Strathspey
Alford
Royal Deeside
Caledonian Rly (Brechin)
Kerrs
Mull Rail
Almond
Prestongrange
PSPS
Bo'ness & Kinneil
EDINBURGH
Glasgow Museum
Summerlee
Scottish Ind
Leadhills
Giant's Causeway
County Donegal
RPSI
Ulster
BELFAST
Downpatrick
Cavan & Leitrim
DUBLIN
West Clare
Irish Steam
ITG
Waterford
North Tyneside/Stephenson
Bowes
Tanfield
South Tynedale
Beamish
Monkwearmouth
Weardale
Locomotion
Darlington
North Bay
Haig
Eden
Wensleydale
North Yorkshire Moors
Ravenglass & Eskdale
Lightwater
Snaefell Mountain
Great Laxey
Groudle Glen
Manx Electric
I.O.M. Steam Railway
Lakeside & Haverthwaite
Embsay & Bolton Abbey
Keighley & Worth Valley
National Railway Museum
Abbey Light
Derwent
VCT
Blackpool
West Lancashire
Ribble
Middleton
Leeds Museum
Elsecar
Windmill Farm
Lakeside
East Lancashire
Kirklees
Cleethorpes Coast
Astley Green
Museum (Manchester)
Brookside
Penrhyn
Rheilffordd Eryri
Rhyl
Peak Rail
Lincolnshire Wolds
North Inge
Great Orme
Barrow Hill
Crich
Poppy Line
Llanberis Lake
Churnet Valley
Midland/Golden Valley
Snowdon Mountain
Conwy
Railway Age
Ecclesbourne
Wells & Walsingham
Bure Valley
Llangollen
Rudyard
Foxfield
Nottingham
Welsh Highland
Ffestiniog
Oswestry
Cambrian
Amerton
Silk Mill
Great Central
Mid Norfolk
Chasewater
Abbey
Bala Lake
Battlefield Line
Fairbourne & Barmouth
Ironbridge
Snibston
Rutland
Railworld
Corris
Telford
Nene Valley
EATM
Welshpool & Llanfair
Tyseley
Northampton & Lamport
Bressingham
Talyllyn
Vale of Rheidol
Kidderminster
Irchester
Severn Valley
Coventry
Northants Ironstone
Mid-Suffolk
Evesham
Great Whipsnade
Leighton Buzzard
Audley End
Teifi
Gloucestershire Warwickshire
Winchcombe
Brecon Mountain
Colne Valley
EARM
Gwili
Buckinghamshire
Mangapps Farm
Perrygrove
National Waterways
Didcot
Chinnor
Ruislip
Epping
North Woolwich
Swansea Vale
Dean Forest
Pontypool
Cholsey
LONDON
Barry
Swindon & Cricklade
Steam
Sittingbourne & Kemsley
Great Cockcrow
CARDIFF
Bristol
Bredgar
East Kent
Avon Valley
Kew Bridge, LT Depot
Science Museum, Southall
West Somerset
Midsomer Norton
Spa Valley
Kent & East Sussex
Lynton
Longleat
S&DJRT
East Somerset
Mid-Hants
Bluebell
Romney, Hythe & Dymchurch
Bideford
Hollycombe
Rother Valley
Lavender
Yeovil
Gartell
Amberley
Volks
Hayling
Devon Railway Centre
Moors
Dobwalls
Launceston
Seaton
Royal Victoria
Swanage
Beer
Dartmoor
Bicton
Exbury
Eastleigh
Isle of Wight
Bodmin & Wenford
South Devon
Lappa
Paignton & Dartmouth
Alderney
Plym Valley

Above: Steam returned to the Somerset & Dorset Joint Railway in 2005 when ex-LMS Class 3F No 47496 renumbered Spa Valley-based No 47493 visited Midsomer Norton station.

England

Abbey Light Railway

Timetable Service | West Yorkshire

Member: HRA, TT
The Abbey Light Railway was founded in 1976. It is a family run operation supported by volunteers to restore and maintain vintage narrow gauge locomotives and stock. The railway takes visitors to the 11th century Cistercian Monastery of Kirkstall Abbey
Propriator : Mr P. N. Lowe
Location: Bridge Road, Kirkstall, Leeds LS5 3BW
Telephone: (0113) 267 5087
Main station: Kirkstall Abbey
Other public station: Bridge Road (OS ref: SE 262356)
Car park: At Abbey and Bridge Road
Access by public transport: By train to Headingley station. Buses from City Square
Refreshment facilities: At nearby Morrisons supermarket
Souvenir shop: Badges on sale on the train

Industrial locomotives
Narrow gauge:

Name	*No*	*Builder*	*Type*	*Built*
Loweco	1	Lister (20779)	4wDM	1942
Atlas	2	Hunslet (2465)	4wDM	1943
Odin	3	Simplex (5859)	4wDM	1934
Vulcan	4	R/Hornsby (198287)	4wDM	1942
—	5	R/Hornsby (235654)	4wDM	1946
Druid	6	Simplex (8644)	4wDM	1941
—	7	O&K (5926)	4wDM	1935
Go-Go	8	Hudson (39924	4wPM	1924
—	9	Muir Hill (110)	4wPM	1925
—	10	Baguley (736)	0-4-0PM	1917
—	11	Baguley (760)	0-4-0PM	1917
—	12	Greenbat (2848)	4wBE	1957

Depot: Workshops at Bridge Road
Length of line/gauge: Quarter mile, 2ft gauge
Period of public operation: Sundays and Bank Holidays (Sundays 13.00-17.00)
Special events: Kirkstall Gala in Abbey grounds — 8 July

Facilities for disabled: In Abbey grounds
Membership details: As above

Abbey Pumping Station

Museum | Leicester

Member: TT
Narrow gauge site railway (2ft gauge) formerly part of a sewage pumping station that now forms museum site. Railway relaid in concrete by MSC scheme during early 1980s to original track layout. New track layout as an extension to original laid with 35lb rail on wooden sleepers. All the railway system is now run by volunteers. Original Simplex locomotive kept on site in operational condition. Line originally used for transferring solid material from screens to tip

Industrial locomotives
Narrow gauge:

Name	*No*	*Builder*	*Type*	*Built*
Leonard	—	Bagnall (2087)	0-4-0ST	1919
—	—	Motor Rail (5260)	4wPM	1931
—	—	Hibberd (1776)	4wPM	1931
—	—	R/Hornsby (223700)	4wDM	1944
—	—	SMH (40SD515)	4wDM	1979

Stock
3 new passenger vehicles based on Leicester & Swannington coaches.
10 skip wagons, 2 mine tubs, 2 flats, bomb wagon, various miscellaneous.
All locomotives are restored to working order; *Leonard* returned to service in 2005 when restoration work was completed

(about 100yd). Demonstration skip wagon trains as well as passenger trains are run when the railway is operating
Location: Abbey Pumping Station, Corporation Road, off Abbey Lane, Leicester LE4 5XP
Operating group: Leicester City Council Museum, Leicester Museums Technology Association
Telephone: 0116 299 5111
Fax: 0116 299 5125
Car park: Free on site
Access by public transport: Main line Leicester (London Road). First Bus route 54 from city centre (alight at Beaumont Leys Lane)
Length of line/gauge: About 300yd, 2ft gauge. Passenger carrying on special event days and railway running days (small fare payable on free-entry days)
Period of public opening: Daily 1 February to 31 November, Saturdays-Thursdays 11.00 to 16.30, Sundays 13.00 to 16.30. Open for special events only all year
On site facilities: Museum/shop/toilets/car park. Refreshments only on special event days
Facilities for disabled: Access to museum lower floor and grounds. Lift to Engine House and refreshments on event days. Wheelchair access to railway
Volunteer contact: Tony Kendal, c/o Abbey Pumping Station
Museum contact: Mr C. Stevens, c/o Abbey Pumping Station (Tel: 0116 299 5111)
Other attractions: Museum holds various transport, steam navvy, beam engines. Some items only viewable by appointment or on special event days
Special events: Lenny the Loco railway running day — 1 April; Little & Large, steam day — 9 April; Classics and railway running day — 6 May; Train rides and Teddy Bears' Picnic, railway running day — 3 June; Urban Rally and steam day— 24/25 June; Lenny the Loco railway running day — 1 July; Preserved vehicles and railway running day — 5 August; Lenny the Loco railway running day — 2 September; Arts and Crafts, steam day — 10 September; Smelly Railways, railway running day — 7 October; Christmas Toys, steam day — 10 December;
2007 dates include: Meccano Day — 14 January, Steam Toys in Action — 4 February

Steam Centre

Amberley Working Museum

West Sussex

Member: HRA, TT

Narrow Gauge & Industrial Railway Collection (incorporating the Brockham Museum of Narrow Gauge Railways)
The NG&IR Collection is part of an open air industrial museum set in 36 acres of the former Pepper & Co chalk pits. A 2ft gauge line has been constructed and this is used for carrying passengers in genuine workmen's vehicles
Museum Director: Howard Stenning
Location: Houghton Bridge, Amberley, West Sussex (3 miles north of Arundel) on B2139. Adjacent to Amberley main line station
OS reference: TQ 030122
Operating society/organisation: Amberley Museum Trust, Amberley Museum, Houghton Bridge, Amberley, Arundel, West Sussex BN18 9LT
Telephone: Bury (01798) 831370 (Museum office)
Internet address: *Web site:* www.amberleymuseum.co.uk
e-mail (general museum enquiries): office@amberleymuseum.co.uk
e-mail (specific railway enquiries): info@amberleynarrowgauge.co.uk
Car park: Adjacent to Amberley station
On site facilities: Shop and audio-visual show. The 'Limeburners Restaurant' opened in 2004 (event booking details from 01798 839240)
Public opening: Wednesday to Sunday (inclusive) each week, and Bank Holiday Mondays, (open all week in school holidays) 10.00-last entry 17.00, 20 March-3 November
Special events: Railway Gala Weekend — 8/9 July; Miniature Steam & Model Weekend — 23/24 September.
A steam locomotive is scheduled for use on 2, 16/17, 30 April, 1, 7, 14, 21, 28/29 May, 17/18 June, 2, 8/9, 16, 23, 30 July, 6, 13, 27/28, 30 August, 3, 10, 17, 23/24 September, 8 October.
Please see press for details of further activities
Special notes: Displays include working potter, blacksmith, boatbuilder and printer, stationary engines, historic radio collection and vintage Southdown garage and buses. A 2ft 0in gauge industrial railway system is demonstrated when possible, and a 3ft 2.25in gauge line. In addition, a 2ft 0in gauge 'main line' has been constructed. The 500yd line was officially opened by HRH Prince Michael of Kent on 5 June 1984. The railway is operated every day the museum is open (subject to mechanical availability), with steam locomotive haulage on certain days — for details contact the museum office. Wheelchairs can normally be accommodated on the train.
The 'Limeburners Restaurant' features a timber frame, cedar cladding and floored with hand-made clay tiles
Membership details: Friends of Amberley Museum, c/o above address
Membership journal: *Wheelbarrow* — bi-monthly

Locomotives

(2ft or 60cm unless otherwise indicated)

Name	*No*	*Builder*	*Type*	*Built*	
Polar Bear	—	Bagnall (1781)	2-4-0T	1905	
Peter	—	Bagnall (2067)	0-4-0ST	1918	
Townsend Hook	4	F/Jennings (172L)	0-4-0T	1880	(3ft 2.25in gauge)
Scaldwell	—	Peckett (1316)	0-6-0ST	1913	(3ft 0in gauge)
—	23†	Spence	0-4-0T	1921	(1ft 10in gauge)
—	—	Decauville (1126)	0-4-0WT	1947	
—**	—	Baldwin (44656)	4-6-0T	1917	
Monty	(6)	O&K (7269)	4wDM	1936	(3ft 2.25in gauge)
The Major	(7)	O&K (7741)	4wDM	1937	
—	2	Ransomes & Rapier (80)	4wDM	1937	
—	—	Hudson-Hunslet (3097)	4wDM	1944	
—	2	R/Hornsby (166024)	4wDM	1933	
—	3101	M/Rail (Simplex) (1381)	4wPM	1918	(Armoured)
Peldon	—	John Fowler (21295)	4wDM	1936	
Redland	—	O&K (6193)	4wDM	1937	
—	—	Lister (35421)	4wPM	1949	
—	—	M/Rail (Simplex) (872)	4wPM	1918	
—	27	M/Rail (Simplex) (5863)	4wDM	1934	
—	—	M/Rail (Simplex) (10161)	4wDM	1950	(2ft 11in gauge)
Ibstock	—	M/Rail (Simplex) (11001)	4wDM	1951	
*Burt**	—	Simplex 9019))	4wDM	1959	
CCSW	—	Hibberd (1980)	4wDM	1936	
Thakeham Tiles	No 3	Hudson-Hunslet (2208)	4wDM	1941	
Thakeham Tiles	No 4	Hudson-Hunslet (3653)	4wDM	1948	
—	—	Hudson (45913)	4wP/ParM	1932	(2ft 6in gauge)
—	—	H/Clarke (DM686)	0-4-0DM	1948	
Star Construction	—	Hudson-Hunslet	4wDm	c1941	
—	18	R/Hornsby (187081)	4wDM	1937	
—	—	Lister (33937)	4wPM	1949	
—	—††	Hibberd 'Y-type Planet' (3627)	4wPM	1953	
—	WD 904	Wickham (3403/04)	2w-2PMR	1943	
—	2	Wingrove & Rogers (5031)	4wBE	1953	
—	—	Wingrove & Rogers (5034)	4wBE	1953	
—	—	Wingrove & Rogers (4998)	4wBE	1953	
—	—	Wingrove & Rogers (T8033)	0-4-0BE	1979	

†† not on site

** on loan to Leighton Buzzard Railway for restoration

* standard gauge

†includes hoist and 'haulage truck' for conversion to 5ft 3in gauge from Guinness Brewery

Stock

2 Penrhyn Quarry Railway 4-wheel coaches (2ft gauge, ex-1ft 10.75in gauge); RAF Fauld bogie coach (1940) (2ft gauge); Rye & Camber Tramway bogie (incomplete) (1895) (3ft gauge); Post Office Railway unit No 808 of 1930; 4 Groudle Glen Railway 4-wheel coaches (1896 and 1905) (2ft gauge); 60 other varied pieces of rolling stock of 12 different gauges ranging from 1ft 6in to 3ft 2.25in plus numerous miscellaneous exhibits including track, signals, etc

Steam Centre

Amerton Railway

Staffordshire

The Amerton Railway is the home of the famous 1897-built Bagnall saddletank *Isabel*, the line having been built for it in the early 1990s. The railway has developed considerably over the years and now consists of a mile-long line run

Industrial locomotives (2ft gauge)

Name	*No*	*Builder*	*Type*	*Built*
Isabel	—	Bagnall (1491)	0-4-0ST	1897
Lorna Doone	—	K/Stuart (4250)	0-4-0ST	1922
—	526	Henschel (14019)	0-8-0T	1916
—	746	M/Rail (40SD501)	4wDM	1975
—	—	M/Rail (7471)	4wDM	1940

Above: Leonard poses for the camera on the Abbey Pumping Station's demonstartion line. *APS*

Below: Amerton Railway with Bagnall 0-4-0ST *Isabell* working round the circuit. *Phil Barnes*

through the countryside via a passing loop at Chartley Road. At Amerton station there is the locomotive shed, where items of rolling stock can be seen under restoration, the carriage shed and yard, the former GNR station building from Stowe and the Leek & Manifold Railway signalbox from Waterhouses, now under restoration
Location: Amerton Railway, Amerton Farm, Stowe-by-Chartley, Stafford ST18 0LA (situated between Stafford and Uttoxeter, signposted off A51 at Weston)
Operating company: Staffordshire Narrow Gauge Railway Ltd, c/o above address
Telephone:
(Railway only) (01785) 850965; Farm (01889) 270294
OS reference: SJ 993278
On site facilities: Car park at Working Farm. Museum under construction; licensed tea room and bakery (not operated by railway). Souvenir shop in railway ticket office. The railway is one of the main attractions at the farm, admission to most other attractions is free

Name	*No*	*Builder*	*Type*	*Built*
Oakeley	—	Baguley (774)	0-4-0PM	1919
Golspie	—	Baguley (2085)	0-4-0DM/SO	1935
Dreadnought	—	Baguley (3024)	0-4-0DM/SO	1939
—	Yard No 70	R/Hornsby (221623)	4wDM	1943
—	—	R/Hornsby (506491)	4wDM	1964
Gordon	—	Hunslet (8561)	4wDH	1978

Rolling stock
4 toastrack coaches, 3 by Baguley, 1 ex-WHR, SNGRS-built passenger brake van and various wagons

Owner
Lorna Doone on loan from Birmingham Museum of Science & Industry

Access by public transport: By rail to Stafford, then Stevenson's of Uttoxeter Ltd bus to Weston, then a mile walk to Amerton (no Sunday service)
Facilities for disabled:
Wheelchairs can be accommodated in our 'Highland' coach where a wide door and access ramp is available
Period of public operation:
Sundays from mid-March to end of October. Saturdays from Easter until August Bank Holiday. Bank Holiday Mondays. Trains run 12.00 until 17.00. Subject to availability *Isabel* will be in steam Sundays and Bank Holidays. Diesel haulage generally on Saturdays
Special events: Summer Steam Gala, with visiting locomotives — provisionally 17/18 June (with at least two visiting locomotives); Santa Specials — December
Membership details: Membership Secretary, c/o above address
Membership journal: *Isabel Gazette,* quarterly

Steam Centre — Astley Green Colliery Museum — Lancashire

The museum occupies some 15 acres south of the Astley Green colliery site. The low-lying landscape ensures that the museum's 98ft high lattice steel headgear can be seen for many miles. Apart from the steam winding engine and headgear the museum houses many exhibits, not least of which is the collection of over 20 colliery locomotives, the largest collection of its type in the UK. The museum is now run and maintained, on behalf of the community, by the Red Rose Steam Society Ltd, a registered charity based in Lancashire
Location: Between the A580 and Bridgewater Canal in Higher Green Lane, Astley Green, Tyldersley
Operating company: The Secretary, Astley Green Colliery Museum, Higher Green Lane, Astley Green, Tyldersley,

Industrial locomotives

Name	*No*	*Builder*	*Type*	*Built*
(standard gauge)				
—	—	R/Hornsby (244580)	4wDM	1946
(3ft gauge)				
—	17	H/Clarke (DM781)	0-6-0DMF	1953
—	—	Hunslet (4816)	0-6-0DMF	1955
—	11	H/Clarke (DM1058)	0-6-0DMF	1957
—	20	H/Clarke (DM1120)	0-6-0DMF	1957
—	18	H/Clarke (DM1270)	0-6-0DMF	1961
—	BL/107	H/Clarke (DM1295)	0-6-0DMF	1962
—	DM1439	H/Clarke (DM1439)	0-6-0DMF	1978
(2ft 6in gauge)				
—	—	Hunslet (3411)	0-4-0DMF	1947
—	3	E/Electric (7936)	4wBEF	1957
—	4	H/Clarke (DM1173)	0-6-0DMF	1959
—	5	H/Clarke (DM1352)	0-6-0DMF	1967
—	6	H/Clarke (DM1413)	0-6-0DMF	1970
—	7	H/Clarke (DM1414)	0-6-0DMF	1970
—	1-44-170	Hunslet (8575)	0-6-0DMF	1978
—	1-44-174	Hunslet (8577)	0-6-0DMF	1978
Newton	—	Hunslet (8975)	0-6-0DMF	1979
Foggwell Flyer	—	Hunslet (8567)	0-6-0DMF	1981
Bullfrogs Bullet	—	Hunslet (8568)	0-6-0DMF	1981

Manchester M29 7JB
Internet address: *e-mail:* info@agcm.org.uk
For school parties *e-mail*: school.visits@agcm.org.uk
For other groups *e-mail*: group.visits@agcm.org.uk
Period of public operation:
Sundays — 14.00-17.00
Tuesdays — 13.00-17.00
Thursdays — 13.00-17.00.
Closed Christmas and Boxing Days
Membership details: Membership Secretary, Red Rose Steam Society, Higher Green Lane, Astley Green, Tyldersley, Manchester M29 7JB.
E-mail: membership@rrss.agcm.org.uk

Name	*No*	*Builder*	*Type*	*Built*
(2ft 4in gauge)				
—	6	H/Clarke (DM??)	0-6-0DMF	??
(2ft 1in gauge)				
Kestrel	2	H/Clarke (DM674)	0-6-0DMF	1954
(2ft gauge)				
Stacey	—	H/Clarke (DM804)	0-6-0DMF	1951
—	T1	H/Clarke (DM840)	0-6-0DMF	1954
George	14	H/Clarke (DM929)	0-6-0DMF	1955
—	8	M/Vickers (892)	4wBEF	1955
Warrior	14	H/Clarke (DM933)	0-6-0DMF	1956
—	—	H/Clarke (DM1164)	0-4-0DMF	1959
—	—	Hunslet (6048)	0-4-0DMF	1961
Sandy		M/Rail (11218)	4wDM	1962
Point of Ayr	—	R/Hornsby (497547)	4wDMF	1963
Roger Bowen	—	Hunslet (7375)	0-4-0DHF	1973
Calverton	9	Hunslet (7519)	4wDHF	1977
Mole	—	Hunslet (8834)	4wDHF	1978
Lionheart	—	Hunslet (8909)	4wDHF	1979
—	—R4	H/Clarke (DM1443)	0-6-0DMF	1980

Rolling stock (standard gauge)
1 Smith & Rodley steam crane, 1 Coles diesel crane

Miniature Railway

Audley End Railway

Essex

The Audley End miniature railway is a delightful ride on Lord Braybrooke's 10.25in gauge railway through estate woodland
Location: Audley End, Saffron Walden, Essex.
Headquarters: (Postal address) Audley End Estate Office, Brunketts, Wendens Ambo, Saffron Walden, Essex CB11 4JL
Contact: General Manager: H. T. White
Telephone: (01799) 541354 or 541956
Internet address: *e-mail:* aee@farming.co.uk
Web site: www.audley-end-railway.co.uk
Car parking: On site
Access by public transport: Rail to Audley End (1 mile)
On site facilities: Ticket office, shop and light refreshments, toilets, large picnic area
Length of line: 10.25in gauge; 1.5 miles long
Period of public operation: Weekends 18 March-29 October and 2-17 December.
Daily 1-17 April, 1, 29 May-4 June, 22 May-3 September, 21-29 October, 9-17 December
Trains from 14.00 to 16.00, except bank holidays, special events and Santa Specials when first train is 11.00
Special events: Santa Specials — 11-15 December (these can be booked by prior arrangement)
Facilities for disabled: Carriage built in 2002 to enable wheelchair access

Timetable Service

Avon Valley Railway

South Glos

Member: HRA
The Avon Valley Railway has now completed the first phase of its long-term aim to return steam trains, along the former Midland Railway line, to the city of Bath. In May 2004 Avon Riverside station was opened in the heart of the Avon Valley, providing visitors with the opportunity to enjoy the riverside walks, picnic areas and links to the River Avon scenic boat trips. For 2006 the rail/river trips will be operating every steam open day from April to the end of September, except for 6/7 May and 30 July
Headquarters: Avon Valley Railway Company Limited, Bitton Station, Bath Road, Bitton, Bristol BS30 6HD
Telephone: (0117) 932 7296 for timetable information. (0117) 932 5538 enquiries
Internet address: *Web site:* www.avonvalleyrailway.org
Main station: Bitton
OS reference: ST 670705

Car park: Bitton
Access by public transport: Main line train service to Keynsham. Badgerline service No 332 (Bristol-Bath), No 558 (Bristol-North Common)
Access by bike: Bitton station is on the Bristol/Bath Railway Path (route 4 of the National Cycle Network)
Catering facilities: Buffet is able to provide hot and cold snacks, confectionery, hot and cold drinks and ice creams
On site facilities: Station buffet is open every day when the site is open; toilets, picnic area, children's play area close by
Public opening: Bitton station is open daily for viewing of its static collection of locomotives and rolling stock, except for the period between Christmas and New Year. Trains operate:26 March; 2, 4-6, 8*/9, 11-17, 23, 29*/30 April; 1, 6/7, 14, 20*/21, 27*/28, 29-31 May; 1, 4, 10*/11, 17*/18, 25 June; 2, 9, 15*/16, 22*/23, 26/27, 28*/29 July; 1-3, 4*/5, 8-10. 12*/13, 15-17, 19*/20, 22-24, 26*-31 August; 2*/3, 10, 17, 24 September; 1, 7/8, 15, 22, 24-26, 29 October; 26 November; 2/3, 9/10, 16/17, 22-24 December; 1/2 January 2007
*diesel-hauled
Special events: *Advance booking is essential for some of these events. Details from Bitton station — 0117 932 5538*
Mother's Day Lunch — 26 March; Easter Steaming — 11-17 April; Day out with Thomas — 6/7 May; 3rd Bitton Beer Festival — 10/11 June; Father's Day Lunch — 18 June; 1940s Day — 25 June; Polish Day — 16 July; Vintage Bus Rally — 13 August; Art Exhibition — 26-28 August; Railway Relics Valuation Day — 3 September; Murder Mystery Evening — 16 September; Themed Teddy Bears' Picnic — 17 September; Day out with Thomas — 7/8 October; Murder Mystery Evening — 21, 28 October; Wizard Specials — 24-26 October; Santa Specials — 26 November; 2-4, 9/10, 16/17, 22-24 December; Carol Train — 9 December; Sherry and Mince Pie Specials — 1/2 January 2007.

Steam 'N Cuisine (3 course) Luncheon Dining Trains — 26 March, 23 April, 21 May, 18 June, 23 July, 20 August, 24 September, 15 October.

Bitton Bistro (2 course) Luncheon Dining Trains — 9 April, 14 May, 4 June, 9 July, 10 September
Facilities for disabled: Coach converted for disabled use (no toilet facilities)
Membership details: Membership Secretary, c/o Bitton station
Membership journal: *Semaphore* — every 6 months; *Ground Signal* newsletter every 2 months

Locomotives

Name	No	Origin	Class	Type	Built
Sir Frederick Pile	34058	SR	BB	4-6-2	1947
—	44123	LMS	4F	0-6-0	1925
—	48173	LMS	8F	2-8-0	1943
—	D2994	BR	07	0-6-0DE	1962
*—	51909	BR	108	DMBS	1958
*—	56271	BR	108	DTC	1958

*stored off-site
Locomotive notes: D2994 in service

Industrial locomotives

Name	No	Builder	Type	Built
Edwin Hulse	—	Avonside (1798)	0-6-0ST	1918
Karel	—	Chrzanow (4015)	0-6-0T	1954
Phoenix	70	H/Clarke (1464)	0-6-0T	1921
Littleton No 5	—	M/Wardle (2018)	0-6-0ST	1922
—	7151	RSH (7151)	0-6-0T	1944
Meteor	1	RSH (7609)	0-6-0T	1950
Grumpy	WD70031	B/Drewry (2158)	0-4-0DM	1941
—*	Army 200	Barclay (358)	0-4-0DM	1941
Kingswood	—	Barclay (446)	0-4-0DM	1959
*Western Pride**	D1171	H/Clarke (D1171)	0-6-0DM	1951
—†*	—	R/Hornsby (210481)	4wDM	1941
*Basil**	—	R/Hornsby (235519)	4wDM	1945
—†*	—	R/Hornsby (252823)	4wDM	1947
—	429	R/Hornsby (466618)	0-6-0DH	1961
General Lord Robertson	610	Sentinel (10143)	0-8-0DH	1961

*stored/undergoing restoration off-site
†chassis only

Locomotive notes: *Kingswood, Karel, Phoenix* and 7151 are in service

Stock
22 ex-BR Mk 1 coaches (10 stored off-site); 1 ex-BR Mk 1 Restaurant coach; 1 ex-BR Mk 1 sleeper; 2 cranes; 1 Wickham trolley; numerous assorted wagons

Owners
44123 the London Midland Society
48173 the Bitton 8F Locomotive Group

Steam Centre

Barrow Hill Roundhouse Railway Centre

Derbyshire

Member: HRA

In 1839 the North Midland Railway devised an arrangement of stabling locomotives around a turntable within a polygonal building with a conical roof, hence roundhouse. In 1864 locomotives began to be housed in buildings of a square nature (retaining the name) and in 1870 Barrow Hill was built to this design. Retained following the end of steam, Barrow Hill remained in use until 1991. Saved from demolition at the 11th hour, the Grade 2 listed building is unique in Great Britain as the last surviving working roundhouse.

The roundhouse can accommodate up to 24 main line locomotives, and includes maintenance pits and ancillary services

Location/headquarters: Barrow Hill Roundhouse Engine Shed, Campbell Drive, Barrow Hill, Nr Staveley, Chesterfield, Derbyshire S43 2PR.

Locomotives

Name	*No*	*Origin*	*Class*	*Type*	*Built*
Butler Henderson	506	GCR	'Director'	4-4-0	1920
Kolhapur	45593	LMS	'Jubilee'	4-6-0	1934
—	41708	MR	1F	0-6-0T	1880
Britannia	70000	BR	7MT	4-6-2	1951
—	D2853	BR	02	0-4-0DM	1960
—	D2868	BR	02	0-4-0DM	1961
—	03066	BR	03	0-6-0DM	1959
—	D2302	BR	04	0-6-0DM	1960
—	D3000	BR	08	0-6-0DE	1952
—	08827	BR	08	0-6-0DE	1960
—	08869	BR	08	0-6-0DE	1960
—	08928	BR	08	0-6-0DE	1962
Christine	D4092	BR	10	0-6-0DE	1962
—	D9500*	BR	14	0-6-0DH	1965
—	20056	BR	20	Bo-Bo	1961
—	20066	BR	20	Bo-Bo	1961
—	20096	BR	20	Bo-Bo	1961
—	20119	BR	20	Bo-Bo	1962
—	20121	BR	20	Bo-Bo	1962
—	D8132	BR	20	Bo-Bo	1966
—	20168	BR	20	Bo-Bo	1966
—	20901*	BR	20	Bo-Bo	1959
—	20902	BR	20	Bo-Bo	1961
—	20904*	BR	20	Bo-Bo	1961

Situated near junctions 29/30 on M1
OS reference: SK 4175
Project manager: Mervyn Allcock
Contact address: Barrow Hill Engine Shed Society, address as above
Telephone: 01246 472450
Fax: 01246 472450
Internet address: *Web site:* www.barrowhill.org.uk
Car park: Adjacent to site
Access by public transport: Train to Chesterfield, Stagecoach bus Nos 80/90/56
On site facilities: Refreshments, souvenir shop and museum. Toilets
Refreshment facilities: Drinks and light refreshments
Public opening: Open most weekends — 4 major open weekends a year
Special events: Easter, summer, autumn and Christmas open weekends
Membership details: Martyn Brailsford, 18 Queen Street, Brimington, Chesterfield, Derbyshire S43 1HT
Society journal: *The Roundhouse* — three times a year

Name	*No*	*Origin*	*Class*	*Type*	*Built*
—	20905	BR	20	Bo-Bo	1961
—	25067	BR	25	Bo-Bo	1963
—	D5300	BR	26	Bo-Bo	1958
—	26011	BR	26	Bo-Bo	1959
—	31110	BR	31	A1A-A1A	1959
—	31524†	BR	31	A1A-A1A	1959
—	31407†	BR	31	A1A-A1A	1960
—	31412†	BR	31	A1A-A1A	1961
—	31433†	BR	31	A1A-A1A	1960
—	31460†	BR	31	A1A-A1A	1961
Spitfire	33035	BR	33	Bo-Bo	1960
—	33053	BR	33	Bo-Bo	1961
—	33111	BR	33	Bo-Bo	1960
—	37079*	BR	37	Co-Co	1962
—	37201	BR	37	Co-Co	1963
Andania	40013	BR	40	1Co-Co1	1959
—	47053†	BR	47	Co-Co	1964
—	47229†	BR	47	Co-Co	1965
—	47488†	BR	47	Co-Co	1964
—	47628†	BR	47	Co-Co	1965
—	47707†	BR	47	Co-Co	1966
—	47717	BR	47	Co-Co	1966
—	47769	BR	47	Co-Co	1966
—	47780	BR	47	Co-Co	1966
Sherwood Forester	45060	BR	45	1Co-Co1	1961
—	45105	BR	45	1Co-Co1	1961
Alycidon	D9009	BR	55	Co-Co	1961
Tulyar	55015	BR	55	Co-Co	1961
Royal Highland Fusilier	55019	BR	55	Co-Co	1961
Royal Scots Grey	55022	BR	55	Co-Co	1961
—	56006	BR	56	Co-Co	1977
—	56128*	BR	56	Co-Co	1983
—	58001	BR	58	Co-Co	1983
—	73138	BR	73	Bo-Bo	1966
—	E3003	BR	81	Bo-Bo	1960
—	82008	BR	82	Bo-Bo	1961
—	E3035	BR	83	Bo-Bo	1961
—	84001	BR	84	Bo-Bo	1960
Doncaster Plant150 1853-2003	85101	BR	85	Bo-Bo	1961
—	89001	BR	89	Co-Co	1986

D2094 away on loan

Industrial locomotives

Name	*No*	*Builder*	*Type*	*Built*
Henry	—	H/Leslie (2491)	0-4-0ST	1901
The Welshman	—	M/Wardle (1207)	0-6-0ST	1890
—	—	Peckett (2000)	0-6-0ST	1941
—	1	GEC	0-6-0	
—	9	YEC (2521)	0-4-0ST	1952
Marstons	—	— (2553)	0-4-0	—
Harry	—	Drewry (2589)	0-4-0	1956
—	NCB 20	Barclay	0-4-0DE	—
—	RMS 10	GEC	0-6-0DE	—
—	—	Hunslet (63000316)	0-4-0DE	—
Coalite 7	—	Sentinel	0-6-0	—
Coalite 9	—	Vanguard	0-6-0	—

Stock

2 ex-BR Mk 1 BSK coach, 1 ex-BR Mk 2 coach, 1 ex-MR brake van, 1 Tunny wagon, 2 ex-BR bogie vans, 1 dynamometer car,

2 ex-BR Lowmac, 1 ex-LMS brake van, 2 ex-BR brake van, 1 ex-SR brake van, 1 ex-GWR Toad brake van,

Owners
*Harry Needle Railroad Co (for overhaul or stored)
†FM Rail
§stored off site
506, 55002 and 84001 on loan from the National Railway Museum
D3000 and D9500 Ian Goddard
03066, 03094, and 20096 Trevor Dean
33035, 45060 and 45105 the Pioneer Diesel Group
33111 the Class 33111 Group
55009 and 55019 the Deltic Preservation Society
73138, E3003, 82008, 83012, 85101 and 86401 the AC Loco Group
The Welshman and 9 the National Mining Museum
89001 on loan to the AC Loco Group from the Great North Eastern Railway
41708 the Waterman Heritage Trust
47769 Riviera Trains

Timetable Service

The Battlefield Line Railway

Leicestershire

Member: HRA, TT
A quiet country railway operated by the Shackerstone Railway Society Ltd
Headquarters: Shackerstone station (3 miles north of Market Bosworth in Leicestershire)
Address: Shackerstone Station, Shackerstone, Nuneaton CV13 6NW
Telephone: Timetable enquiries: (01827) 880754
Internet address: *Web site*: www.battlefield-line-railway.co.uk
Operating Manager: D. Weightman
Main station: Shackerstone
Other public station: Shenton
OS reference: SK 379066
Car park: Shackerstone (free), Shenton (council car park)
Access by public transport: Bus service from Nuneaton weekends only. Ring Traveline 0870 6082608 for details
Refreshment facilities: Tea rooms on Shackerstone station. Buffet/bar on most trains
Souvenir shop: Shackerstone
Museum: Shackerstone
Depot: Shackerstone
Length of line: 4.75 miles (8km)
Passenger trains: Shackerstone-Shenton
Period of public operation: Easter to October

Locomotives and multiple-units

Name	*No*	*Origin*	*Class*	*Type*	*Built*
Diane	D2867	BR	02	0-4-0DH	1961
—	03170	BR	03	0-6-0DM	1960
—	03180	BR	03	0-6-0DM	1962
—	11215	BR	04	0-6-0DM	1956
—	D2310	BR	04	0-6-0DM	1960
—	08576	BR	08	0-6-0DE	1959
—	08818	BR	08	0-6-0DE	1960
—	08825	BR	08	0-6-0DE	1960
—	12083	BR	11	0-6-0DE	1953
—	D9529	BR	14	0-6-0DE	1965
—	20105	BR	20	Bo-Bo	1961
Brush Veteran	D5518	BR	31	A1A-A1A	1958
Calder Hall Power Station	31130	BR	31	A1A-A1A	1959
Griffon	33019	BR	33	Bo-Bo	1960
—	37227	BR	37	Co-Co	1964
—	45015	BR	45	1Co-Co1	1960
—	47640	BR	47	Co-Co	1966
—	73105	BR	73	Bo-Bo	1965
—	73114	BR	73	Bo-Bo	1966
—	51131	BR	116	DMBS	1958
—	51321	BRCW	116	DMS	1959
—	55005	GRCW	122	DMBS	1958
—	59522	P/Steel	117	TC(L)	1959

Industrial locomotives

Name	*No*	*Builder*	*Type*	*Built*
Linda	—	Bagnall (2648)	0-4-0ST	1941
Waleswood	—	H/Clarke (750)	0-4-0ST	1906
Sir Gomer	—	Peckett (1859)	0-6-0ST	1932
Dunlop No 7	—	Peckett (2130)	0-4-0ST	1951
Richard III	—	RSH (7537)	0-6-0T	1949
Lamport No 3	—	Bagnall (2670)	0-6-0ST	1942
William	—	Sentinel (9656)	4wVBT	1956

Special events: See leaflet and press for further details
Facilities for disabled: Special car park and toilets
Special notes: Family tickets available. Scenic countryside views including Ashby Canal. Shenton station is adjacent to Bosworth Battlefield (1485) Country Park. 20 minute walk along 'Battlefield Trail' to visitor centre, return by later train
Operating company/ preservation society contact: The Secretary, Shackerstone Railway Society, Shackerstone Station, Shackerstone, Nuneaton CV13 6NW
Membership journal: *Shackerstone News* — 2/3 times/year

Name	*No*	*Builder*	*Type*	*Built*
—	—	Barclay (422)	0-6-0DM	1958
—	19	Barclay (594)	0-6-0DM	1974
—	—	E/Electric (8431)	0-4-0DH	1963
—	890445	GEC (5402)	0-6-0DM	1975
—	47	T/Hill (249V)	0-6-0DH	1974
—	—	R/Hornsby (263001)	4wDM	1949
—	44	Hunslet (6684)	0-6-0DH	1968
—	—	R/Royce (10254)	0-4-0DE	1966
—	—	Simplex (9921)	4wDM	1955

Stock
8 ex-BR Mk 1 coaches (including Griddle Car), 2 ex-BR Mk 2 coaches, 1 ex-BR Mk 3 sleeper; 5 passenger-rated vans; 1 rail-mounted steam crane; 2 rail-mounted diesel cranes; 35 wagons (inc 3 goods brake vans SR, MR, BR)

Owners
33019, 73105, 73114 and 47640 on loan from FM Rail
20105, A/Barclay (594) and GEC (5904) on loan from Harry Needle Railroad Co

Museum

Beamish

County Durham

The railway station, signalbox and goods shed have been completely re-created along with the other exhibits to show a way of life long past. There are some very old locomotives in the collection
Location: The North of England Open Air Museum, Beamish, County Durham DH9 0RG
OS reference: NZ 214548
Telephone: 0191 370 4000
Fax: 0191 370 4001
Internet address: *e-mail:* museum@beamish.org.uk
Web site: www.beamish.org.uk
Car park: At museum
Access by public transport: Bus service from Eldon Square, Newcastle upon Tyne; bus service Nos 775 and 778 from Sunderland via Chester-le-Street; bus service 720 from Milburngate, Durham City
On site facilities: This 300-acre open air museum vividly re-creates life in the North of England in the early 1800s and 1900s. The Town has dentist's surgery, solicitor's office, Co-op shops, garage, sweet shop and bank. The Colliery Village has pit cottages, village school and chapel, 'drift' mine and

Locomotives

Name	*No*	*Origin*	*Class*	*Type*	*Built*
—	65033	NER	C	0-6-0	1889

On loan to Poppy Line until 2025

Industrial locomotives

Name	*No*	*Builder*	*Type*	*Built*
*Locomotion**	1	LE (1)	0-4-0	1975
Twizell†	3	Stephenson (2730)	0-6-0T	1891
—††	14	H/Leslie (3056)	0-4-0ST	1914
South Durham Malleable††	No 5	Grange Ironworks	0-4-0ST	c1880
Coffee Pot§	—	Head Wrightson	0-4-0VB	1871
—††	E1	Black, Hawthorn (897)	2-4-0CT	1883
Jacob§	680	McEwan Pratt	0-4-0P	1916
—**	18	Lewin (693)	0-4-0WT	1877
Steam Elephant	—*	Wallsend Colliery	0-6-0G	1815/2000
—	17	Head Wrightson (33)	0-4-0VB	1873
—	—	R/Hornsby (476140)	4wDM	1963
Puffing Billy	—	A/Keef (71)	0-4-0	2005

†on long-term loan to Tanfield ††on static display
§under repair **undergoing major rebuild
*replica

Locomotive notes: E1, 680 and R/Hornsby not usually on display. Others usually on display

Owners
Locomotion the Locomotion Trust

Note
Not all exhibits on display
Twizell on long-term loan to Tanfield Railway

Above: Memories of the days of a traditional steam shed at Barrow Hill as locomotives are lined up around the turntable. The main differnce is the cleanliness of both locomotives and atmosphere. *Alan Barnes*

Below: The 14.00 is seen at Shenton, on the Battlefield Line Railway, following arrival from Shackerstone behind Class 31 No D5518. *Phil Barnes*

Above: Most of the locomotive fleet on display at the Beer Heights Light Railway. *Peco*

Below: Although looking like a steam locomotive *Sir Walter Raleigh* on the Bicton Railway a diesel-powered. *Phil Barnes*

pithead. Home Farm with farm house, livestock and exhibitions. Railway station complete with goods yard and signalbox, rolling stock on static display. Pockerley Manor illustrates the lifestyle of a yeoman farming family in the early 1800s.

Early Railways — opened in 1999, near Pockerley Manor, a large stone engine shed with displays illustrating the development of railways in the early 1800s. New at Pockerley Waggonway in late May 2006 — a working replica of William Hedley's 1813 *Puffing Billy*. Visitors take a short ride in re-created carriages of the period pulled by the replica *Locomotion* or *Steam Elephant*

Public opening:
Summer (1 April-29 October) daily 10.00-17.00, last admission 15.00. Winter (30 October-23 March 2007) 10.00-16.00, last admission 15.00, closed Mondays and Fridays. Also closed 11 December 2006 to 1 January 2007

NB: A winter visit to Beamish is centred on the Town and Tramway; other areas of the museum are closed and admission charges are, consequently, reduced

Length of line:
Pockerley Waggonway, ¼-mile — operational daily in summer. Rebuilt NER station, colliery sidings

Facilities for disabled: One carriage at 1825 Railway suitable for wheelchairs. Advance notice for parties to Bookings Officer preferred

Miniature Railway

Beer Heights Light Railway

Devon

An extensive railway in the landscaped grounds of publisher and model railway ranufacturing group

Location: Underleys, near Beer, South Devon

Headquarters: Pecorama, Underleys, Beer, Devon EX12 3NA

Managing Director:
C. M . Pritchard,

Telephone: 01297 21542

Fax: 01297 20229

Internet address: *E-mail:* pecorama@btconnect.co,
Web site: www.peco-uk.com

OS reference: CSY 223891

Car parking: Ample on site, free for our visitors

Access by public transport: By rail to Axminster station, then Axe Valley Bus to Beer. By rail to Exeter station, then First Bus to Weymouth via Beer.

On site facilities: Restaurant, shop, model railway exhibition and fully restored Pullman car 'Orion'

Length of line: 1 mile, 7.25in gauge

Period of public operation:
Easter to end October — Monday to Friday 10.00-17.30; Saturdays 10.00-13.00; Sundays open at Easter and then from Whitsun to start of September 10.00-17.30

Locomotives

Name	*No*	*Builder*	*Type*	*Built*
Dickie	—	—	0-4-2	1976
Thomas II	—	—	0-4-2ST+T	1979
Linda	—	—	2-4-0ST+T	1983
Jimmy	—	—	Bo-Bo	1986
Mr P	—	Macdougall	0-6-0	1997
Gem	—	Peco	0-6-0T+T	1999
Alfred	—	Macdougall / Nation	0-4-0Tram	2003
Otter	—	WNG*	2-4-2	2004
Claudine	—	Macdougall	2-4-4	2005

*built byWestern Narrow Gauge, privately owned

Rolling stock — coaches
3 4-seat bogie open coaches built by Cromar White; 9 4-seat bogie open 'Pullman' coaches built by BHLR; 8 4-seat quad-articulated coaches built by BHLR

Rolling stock — wagons
6 4-wheeled wagons; 1 bogie open wagon; 2 4-wheel bolster wagons, 2 4-wheeled tipper wagons; 1 generator wagon

Special events: Peco Loco Week — 30 July-4 August (entire Peco locomotive fleet plus guest locomotives in operation daily); Peco Diamond Jubilee — 27/28 August (weekend of special events to mark the Company's 60th Anniversary

Facilities for disabled: All toilet blocks with facilities for disabled, wheelchair access to Model Exhibition, gardens and restaurant (Note: some paths in the gardens are steep and wheelchair bound will need assistance)

Membership details: Season ticket to Pecorama available, apply to above address

Attraction

Bicton Woodland Railway

Devon

A passenger-carrying line of 18in gauge with stock mainly from the Woolwich Arsenal Railway and of World War 1 vintage
Location: Bicton Park, near Budleigh Salterton
OS reference: SY 074862
Operating society/organisation: Bicton Woodland Railway, Bicton Gardens, East Budleigh, Budleigh Salterton, Devon EX9 7BS
Telephone: Colaton Raleigh (01395) 568465
Car park: On site
Access by public transport: Buses pass half-hourly from Exeter, Exmouth, Sidmouth in season
On site facilities: Indoor and outdoor play areas, Glass Houses, Palm House, Grade 1 gardens, museum and restaurant
Length of line: 3,250yd
Public opening: Open all year, winter 10.00-17.00, summer 10.00-18.00
Trains operate: Winter 12.15 and 14.30, summer 6-8 trains a day
Facilities for disabled: Toilets, wheelchairs available. Special carriage for wheelchairs

Locomotives (1ft 6in gauge)

Name	*No*	*Builder*	*Type*	*Built*
Bicton	2	R/Hornsby (213839)	4wDM	1942
Clinton	4	H/Hunslet (2290)	0-4-0	1941
Sir Walter Raleigh	—	Keef	4wDM	2000

Stock
5 closed bogie coaches

Museum

Bideford Railway Heritage Centre

Devon

Member: HRA
Based at the former LSWR/SR station on the now closed Barnstaple-Torrington line, the site is undergoing restoration. The former signalbox has been rebuilt, double track laid throughout and signals erected. A growing collection of rolling stock is being gathered. Passenger railway rides returned to Bideford station during summer 2001 after a gap of 36 years. Diesel-hauled brake van rides on selected weekends during summer months. Long term aim of the Group is to reinstate the railway back to Barnstaple (9 miles)
Headquarters: Bideford Station, Railway Terrace, East-the-Water, Bideford, Devon EX39 4BB
Telephone: 01237 429072
Internet address: *Web site:* www.bidefordrailway.co.uk
OS reference: SS 456263
Operating society: Bideford & Instow Railway Group
Access by public transport: By train — Barnstaple 9 miles. Station is within walking distance of the town of Bideford and its bus stops
On site facilities: Museum, souvenir shop, book shop, refreshments, visitor centre, rolling stock under restoration
Period of public opening: Easter to end October — Sundays, Tuesdays, Thursdays and Bank Holidays 14.00-17.00; November to Easter — Sundays and Bank Holidays only
Special events: Annual open day — 13 August; Santa Specials — 9, 16 December
Disabled facilities: Limited
Membership details: Mr C. Fairchild, 4 Crichton Road, Carshalton Beeches, Surrey SM5 3LS
Membership journal: *Atlantic Coast Express* (quarterly)
Special note: The group also manage Instow Signalbox, some three miles north. This all-equipped former LSWR box is open on Sundays, 14.00-17.00, throughout the year

Multiple-units

Name	*No*	*Origin*	*Class*	*Type*	*Built*
—	76350	BR	423 / 4VEP	DTSO	1967

Industrial locomotives

Name	*No*	*Builder*	*Type*	*Built*
Kingsley	—	Hibberd (3832)	0-4-0DM	1957

Rolling stock
BR Mk 1 TSO No 4489, ex-SR Parcels Van No S2142, ex-BR brake van, ex-LMS closed box van, platelayers' trolley
2 18in gauge skip (ex Peters Marland Clay Works)

Owner
Kingsley the Torridge Diesel Loco Co Ltd

Timetable Service

Blackpool & Fleetwood Tramway

Lancashire

The Blackpool & Fleetwood Tramway is the sole surviving traditional street tramway system in the United Kingdom and attracts visitors from all over the country. During the autumn the streets are illuminated and tours are available by historic or illuminated tram.

Operating organisation: Blackpool Transport Services Ltd, Rigby Road, Blackpool, Lancashire FY1 5DD

Telephone: (01253) 473001

Managing Director: Steve Burd

Operations Director: David Eaves

Customer Services Officer: Jean Cox

Length of line: 11.5 miles, standard gauge

Period of public operation: Daily throughout the year, except Christmas Day, Boxing Day and New Year's Day

Number of trams: 78 double and single-deck trams.

Trams

No	*Trucks*	*Builder*	*Date*
Boat Cars			
§600	E/Electric	E/Electric	1930
602	E/Electric	E/Electric	1934
604	E/Electric	E/Electric	1934
605	E/Electric	E/Electric	1934
607	E/Electric	E/Electric	1934
Brush Cars			
§621	EMB	Brush	1937
622	EMB	Brush	1937
§623	EMB	Brush	1937
§625	EMB	Brush	1937
626	EMB	Brush	1937
§627	EMB	Brush	1937
630	EMB	Brush	1937
631	EMB	Brush	1937
§632	EMB	Brush	1937
§634	EMB	Brush	1937
636	EMB	Brush	1937
§637	EMB	Brush	1937
Centenary Cars			
641	Blackpool	East Lancs	1984
642	Blackpool	East Lancs	1986
643	Blackpool	East Lancs	1986
644	Blackpool	East Lancs	1986
645	Blackpool	East Lancs	1987
646	Blackpool	East Lancs	1987
647	Blackpool	East Lancs	1988
648	Blackpool	East Lancs	1990
Towing Cars			
671	E/Electric	E/Electric / Blackpool	1960
672	E/Electric	E/Electric / Blackpool	1960
673	E/Electric	E/Electric / Blackpool	1961
674	E/Electric	E/Electric / Blackpool	1962
675	E/Electric	E/Electric / Blackpool	1958
§676	E/Electric	E/Electric / Blackpool	1958
§677	E/Electric	E/Electric / Blackpool	1960
Ex-Towing Railcoaches			
678	E/Electric	E/Electric / Blackpool	1961
§679	E/Electric	E/Electric / Blackpool	1961
680	E/Electric	E/Electric / Blackpool	1960
Trailer Cars			
681	Maley & Taunton	MCW	1960
682	Maley & Taunton	MCW	1960
683	Maley & Taunton	MCW	1960
684	Maley & Taunton	MCW	1960
685	Maley & Taunton	MCW	1960
§686	Maley & Taunton	MCW	1960
§687	Maley & Taunton	MCW	1960
Balloon Cars			
700	E/Electric	E/Electric	1934
701	E/Electric	E/Electric	1934
702	E/Electric	E/Electric	1934
703	E/Electric	E/Electric	1934
*704	E/Electric	E/Electric	1934
705	E/Electric	E/Electric	1934
706	E/Electric	E/Electric	1934

No	*Trucks*	*Builder*	*Date*
707	E/Electric	E/Electric	1934
708	E/Electric	E/Electric	1934
709	E/Electric	E/Electric	1934
710	E/Electric	E/Electric	1934
711	E/Electric	E/Electric	1934
712	E/Electric	E/Electric	1935
713	E/Electric	E/Electric	1934
715	E/Electric	E/Electric	1935
*716	E/Electric	E/Electric	1935
*717	E/Electric	E/Electric	1934
718	E/Electric	E/Electric	1934
719	E/Electric	E/Electric	1935
720	E/Electric	E/Electric	1935
721	E/Electric	E/Electric	1935
722	E/Electric	E/Electric	1935
723	E/Electric	E/Electric	1935
724	E/Electric	E/Electric	1935
726	E/Electric	E/Electric	1935
Jubilee Cars			
761	Blackpool	E/Electric / Blackpool	1979
762	Blackpool	E/Electric / Blackpool	1982
Illuminated Trams			
*632	EMB	from Brush 632	2001
*633	EMB	from Brush 633	2001
*734	E/Electric	from Pantograph 174	1962
*735	E/Electric	from Railcoach 222	1963
736	E/Electric	from Pantograph 170	1965
Engineering Vehicles			
259	EMB	Blackpool	1937
260	EMB	Blackpool	1973
750	MRCW	Blackpool	1907
752	MRCW	Blackpool	1928
754	E/Electric	Blackpool	1992
Preserved Trams			
5	?	D/Kerr	1901
40	Preston McGuire	United Electric Co	1914
66	Brill	Electric Railway & Carriage	1901
147	Preston McGuire	Hurst Nelson	1924
304	Maley & Taunton	Hurst Nelson	1952
§513	Maley & Taunton	Charles Roberts	1950
§619	E/Electric	Bolton Trams	1987
660	Maley & Taunton	Charles Roberts	1953

*out of service
§currently mothballed

Owners

5 the Stockport 5 Trust
40 the Tramway Museum Society
66 the Bolton 66 Group
304 and 632 the Lancastrian Transport Trust
513 Beamish Open Air Museum

Timetable Service

Bluebell Railway

East Sussex

Member: HRA, TT
This famous steam railway was the first standard gauge passenger line to be taken over by enthusiasts. It derives its name from the bluebells which proliferate in the woodlands adjoining the line. A strong Victorian atmosphere pervades this branch line which has a large collection of Southern and pre-Grouping locomotives and coaches
Operations Manager: Mr Chris Knibbs
Headquarters: Bluebell Railway Preservation Society, Sheffield Park Station, Uckfield, East Sussex TN22 3QL
Telephone: Uckfield (01825) 720825 for travel information (24hr talking timetable); (01825) 720800 for general enquiries etc during office hours; (01825) 720801 – Golden Arrow Pullman (reservations and Catering Department)
Internet address: *Web site:* www.bluebell-railway.co.uk
Main station: Sheffield Park
Other public stations: Horsted Keynes and Kingscote
Car parks: Sheffield Park, Horsted Keynes
OS reference:
Sheffield Park TQ 403238,
Horsted Keynes TQ 372293
Access by public transport: Bus service 473 between main line East Grinstead and Kingscote (2 miles). See timetable brochure for details of operation
Refreshment facilities: Sheffield Park restaurant/bar/self-service; Horsted Keynes – Victorian bar/buffet. The line's 'Golden Arrow' Pullman operates a dinner service most Saturday evenings and Pullman luncheon service most Sundays.
Telephone (01825) 720801 during normal office hours for details.
Souvenir shops: Sheffield Park, Horsted Keynes
Museum: Sheffield Park
Depots: Sheffield Park (locomotives), Horsted Keynes (stock)
Length of line: 9 miles
Passenger trains: Sheffield Park-

Locomotives and multiple-unit

Name	*No*	*Origin*	*Class*	*Type*	*Built*
Stepney	55	LBSCR	A1X	0-6-0T	1875
Fenchurch	72	LBSCR	A1X	0-6-0T	1872
Birch Grove	32473	LBSCR	E4	0-6-2T	1898
—	27	SECR	P	0-6-0T	1910
—	65	SECR	O1	0-6-0	1896
—	263	SECR	H	0-4-4T	1905
—	323	SECR	P	0-6-0T	1910
—	592	SECR	C	0-6-0	1902
—	1178	SECR	P	0-6-0T	1910
—	96	LSWR	B4	0-4-0T	1893
—	120	LSWR	T9	4-4-0	1898
—	488	LSWR	0415	4-4-2T	1885
—	27505	NLR	2F	0-6-0T	1880
Earl of Berkeley	9017	GWR	9000	4-4-0	1938
—	541	SR	Q	0-6-0	1939
—	847	SR	S15	4-6-0	1937
Stowe	928	SR	V	4-4-0	1934
—	1618	SR	U	2-6-0	1928
—	1638	SR	U	2-6-0	1931
—	30064	SR	USA	0-6-0T	1943
Blackmoor Vale	21C123	SR	WC	4-6-2	1946
Sir Archibald Sinclair	34059	SR	BB	4-6-2	1947
Camelot	73082	BR	5MT	4-6-0	1955
—	75027	BR	4MT	4-6-0	1954
—	78059†	BR	2MT	2-6-0	1956
—	80064	BR	4MT	2-6-4T	1953
—	80100	BR	4MT	2-6-4T	1954
—	80151	BR	4MT	2-6-4T	1957
—	92240	BR	9F	2-10-0	1958
—	11201*	BR	4COR	DMBSO	1937

†purchased without tender, for conversion to tank engine, work in hand
*on static display at Horsted Keynes

Industrial locomotives

Name	*No*	*Builder*	*Type*	*Built*
Baxter	3	F/Jennings (158)	0-4-0T	1877
†*Stamford*	24	Avonside (1972)	0-6-0ST	1927
Sharpthorn	4*	M/Wardle (641)	0-6-0ST	1877
Britannia	—	Howard (957)	4wPM	1936

*On static display
†On long-term loan to the Rutland Railway Museum

Stock
Substantial collection of pre-Nationalisation coaches including SECR, LSWR, Bulleid, Maunsell and Chesham vehicles. Also freight stock and engineers' vehicles plus 45-ton steam crane

Owners
592 the Wainwright C Class Preservation Society
541, 847, 928 and 1618 the Maunsell Locomotive Society Ltd
96 and 21C123 the Bulleid Society Ltd
263 the H Class Trust
73082 the Camelot Locomotive Society
120 on loan from the National Railway Museum
1178 Southern Locomotives Ltd

Horsted Keynes-Kingscote
Period of public operation: Weekends all year round; daily 13-17 February (half term), 3 April-27 October; Santa Specials 2/3, 9/10, 16/17, 21-24 December, daily 26-31 December; 1 January 2007. Closed 25 December. Museum, locomotive sheds, buffet and shop at Sheffield Park open daily except Christmas Day
Special events: Goods Train Day — 9 April; Southern at War — 13/14 May; Day out with Thomas — 24/25 June, 1/2 July; Sussex Bus Day — 3 July; Giants of Steam — 21/22 October; Wizard Weekend — 28/29 October. Santa Specials — 2/3, 9/10, 16/17, 21-24 December. Further details of events available on request
Facilities for disabled: All station facilities are on the level and ramps available for placing wheelchair visitors into trains. Special toilets in buffet at Sheffield Park and at Kingscote, 'multi-purpose vehicle' for use by groups, please telephone to confirm availability
Membership details: Membership Secretary, c/o above address
Membership journal: *Bluebell News* — quarterly

80064 the 80064 Group
80151 the 80151 Group
11201 the Southern Electric Group

Timetable Service

Bodmin & Wenford Railway

Cornwall

Member: HRA
The Bodmin & Wenford Railway typifies the bygone branch railways of Cornwall. The terminus, close to Bodmin town centre, has an interesting collection of standard gauge locomotives and rolling stock, and the operating line winds down to a junction with main line rail services at Bodmin Parkway. Passengers can alight at the intermediate Colesloggett Halt from where a footpath (not suitable for wheelchairs or the infirm) leads to Cardinham Woods (FC) with waymarked trails, picnic areas and a café. From the train there are scenic views across the beautiful valley of the River Fowey. A second line circles Bodmin to Boscarne Junction where it meets the Camel Trail, a recreational path for cyclists and walkers. A visit can be made to the nearby Camel Valley Vineyard (July and August only). Most trains are steam-hauled except Saturday
Location: Bodmin General station, on B3268
General Manager: Mr R. Webster
Operating society/organisation: Bodmin & Wenford Railway, Bodmin General Station, Bodmin, Cornwall PL31 1AQ
Telephone: All enquiries (01208) 73666
Internet address: *e-mail:* enquiries@bodminandwenfordrailway.co.uk
Web site:

Locomotives and multiple-units

Name	*No*	*Origin*	*Class*	*Type*	*Built*
—	30587	LSWR	0298	2-4-0WT	1874
—	4612	GWR	5700	0-6-PT	1942
—	4247	GWR	4200	2-8-0T	1916
—	5552	GWR	4575	2-6-2T	1928
Wadebridge	34007	SR	WC	4-6-2	1945
Triumph	50042	BR	50	Co-Co	1968
River Fowey	20166	BR	20	Bo-Bo	1966
—	20197	BR	20	Bo-Bo	1967
—	33110	BR	33	Bo-Bo	1960
—	37142	BR	37	Co-Co	1963
—	D3452	BR	10	0-6-0DE	1957
—	08444	BR	08	0-6-0DE	1958
—	51947*	BR	108	DMBS	1960
—	52054	BR	108	DMCL	1960
—	53980	BR	108	DMBS	1960

*for spares

Industrial locomotives

Name	*No*	*Builder*	*Type*	*Built*
—	—	Bagnall (2766)	0-6-0ST	1944
—	19	Bagnall (2962)	0-4-0ST	1950
Judy	—	Bagnall (2572)	0-4-0ST	1934
Alfred	—	Bagnall (3058)	0-4-0ST	1953
—	—	Bagnall (3121)	0-4-0F	1957
Peter	—	Fowler (22928)	0-4-0DM	1940
Progress	—	Fowler (4000001)	0-4-0DM	1945
Swiftsure	—*	Hunslet (2857)	0-6-0ST	1943
Lec	—	R/Hornsby (443642)	4wDM	1960

*may not be on site for all of 2006

Stock
12 BR Mk 1 coaches; 1 BR Mk 2 coach; 1 Mk 3 Sleeper; 6-wheel 10-ton steam crane; 1 GWR coach; 1 GWR Siphon G; various freight wagons

Owners
34007 the Wadebridge 34007 Ltd
30587 on loan from the National Railway Museum
37142 the B&W Main Line Diesel Group

www.bodminandwenfordrailway.co.uk
Car park: Bodmin General and Bodmin Parkway
Access by public transport: Interchange at Bodmin Parkway arrivals by main line train; through tickets available from most stations. Local bus services to Bodmin
Refreshment facilities: Light refreshments at Bodmin General and bar on most trains. Café open daily at Bodmin Parkway
On site facilities: Railway shop, limited display of historic artefacts, toilets
Length of lines: 3.5 miles General-Parkway; 3 miles General-Boscarne
Passenger trains: 22, 26, 29 March; 2, 4/5, 9-23, 25/26, 29/30 April; 1-3, 6/7, 9/10, 14, 16/17, 21, 23/24, 27-31 May; daily — 1 June-30 September; 1, 4, 8, 11, 15, 17/18, 21-29 October; 1, 8 November. Santa Specials 2/3, 9/10, 16/17, 23/24 December; Mince Pie Specials 26/27, 30/31 December and 1 January 2007
Special events: Diesel Weekend — 18/19 March; Easter 'Family Fun Weekend' — 14-17 April; Steam at War Weekend — 29 April-1 May; Day out with Thomas — 27 May-2 June, 2-7 August; Steam Gala — 1-3 September; Diesel Gala — 23/24 September; Ghost Night 28 October.
Murder Mystery Evening Specials most Tuesdays (and Fridays in August) from June to September; Vineyard Special — 8 July; Dining coaches on selected dates including 26 March, Mothering Sunday and 18 June, Father's Day. Please enquire for dates or see leaflet
Driving experience courses: Courses held in spring and autumn. Please apply for details
Facilities for disabled: Level access to platform, shop and buffet. Disabled toilet. Disabled section on train. Registered disabled travel at child fare, carers conveyed *free*
Membership details: Mr R. Holmes, Bodmin Railway Preservation Society, c/o above address
Special notes: Reduced fares for families. Bicycles and dogs conveyed *free*
Membership journal: *Bodmin & Wenford News* — 3 issues/year

Steam Centre

Bowes Railway

County Durham

Member: HRA
The railway includes the only preserved rope-hauled standard gauge inclines, whose operation requires considerable skill and dexterity. You should not miss the opportunity of inspecting the inclines and winding house and haulage engine when you can. The Engineering Workshop has just been restored
Chairman: Phillip Dawe
Location: Bowes Railway, Springwell Village, near Gateshead (on B1288)
OS reference: NZ 285589
Operating society/organisation: Bowes Railway Co Ltd
Telephone: Tyneside (0191) 416 1847
Internet address: *Web site:* www.bowesrailway.co.uk
Car park: Springwell
Access by public transport: Northern Buses services Nos 184 Washington/Birtley, 187/188 Gateshead Metro/Sunderland, 189 Washington (Brady Sq)-Gateshead 638 Ryton/Sunderland
On site facilities: Exhibition of Railway's history, wagon exhibition, workshop displays. On operating days — shop, refreshments and guided tours. One

Industrial locomotives

Name	*No*	*Builder*	*Type*	*Built*
WST	—	Barclay (2361)	0-4-0ST	1954
—	22	Barclay (2274)	0-4-0ST	1949
—	20/110/709	Barclay (613)	0-6-0DH	1977
—	—	Hunslet (6263)	0-4-0DH	1964
—	503	Hunslet (6614)	0-6-0DH	1965
—	101	Planet (3922)	4wDM	1959
—	2207/456†	E/Electric (2476)	4wBE	1958
Victoria	2216/286†	H/Clarke (DM842)	0-6-0DMF	1954
BO3	20/122/514*	Hunslet (8515)	Bo-BoDMF	1981
—	—*	EIMCO (LD2163)	Rockershovel	1959
—	—§	Clayton (5921)	4wBE	1971
—	—§	Clayton (B3060)	4wBE	1983

†2ft gauge
*2ft 6in gauge
§3ft gauge

Owners
WST on loan from British Gypsum Ltd and loaned to National Railway Museum
Barclay 0-6-0DH on loan from Mr P. Dawe

Stock
20 ordinary 10-ton wooden hopper wagons (Springwell built); 16 other wooden hopper wagons (of various pedigrees); 3 steel 14-ton hopper, 2 steel 16-ton hopper wagons; 7 wagons; 7 steel 21-ton hopper wagons; 1 reel bogie (for rope replacement); 1 drift bogie (for shunting by rope); 1 loco coal wagon; 7 material wagons; 2 tool vans; 3 brake vans; 4 flat wagons; 1 18-ton wooden hopper (ex-Ashington); 1 21-ton wooden hopper (ex-Seaham); 2 steel ballast hopper wagons; 1 tank wagon; 1 wooden side door coal wagon; 3 Londonderry Chaldron wagons, 2ft gauge 4-wheel manrider, 2ft 6in gauge R. B. Bolton-type bogie manrider, Easington Colliery weights wagon, 1 Pontop & Jarrow Railway flat bogie, 1 Dandy cart

of the last operational Strowger mechanical telephone exchanges still in daily use. Steam-hauled brake van rides. Rope haulage demonstration trains. Tarmac car park available for helicopter visitors (prior permission required, phone site)
Public opening: Site open Mondays to Fridays for static viewing. Please contact for operating details during 2006. Santa Specials week prior to Christmas. Guided tours Saturdays, out of season can be accommodated with prior notice (not trains)
Length of line: 1.25 miles of rope haulage incline railway.
1.5 mile line used for passenger trains as the Wreckenton extension is now open

Stationary haulage
Met-Vick/Wild, 300bhp electric (Blackham's Hill) 1950
BTH/Robey, 500bhp electric (Black Fell) 1950
Clarke Chapman, 22hp electric (Springwell Yard)
14ft diam, Gravity Dilly Wheel (Springwell)

Special notes: Preserved section of the Pontop & Jarrow Railway; designed G. Stephenson; opened 1826; largest collection of colliery wagons in country, the only preserved standard gauge rope-hauled incline railway in the world; Railway's own historic workshops preserved, with examples of all of the Railway's wagon types
Facilities for disabled: Toilet and refreshment room
Membership details: John Young, Railway Secretary, c/o above address
Disclaimer: The Bowes Railway Co Ltd wish to point out that all advertised facilities are subject to alteration without prior notice. The company can therefore not be held responsible for any loss or expense incurred

Steam Centre

Bredgar & Wormshill Light Railway

Kent

Member: HRA
A short, 2ft gauge, private railway constructed and operated to a very high standard
Location/headquarters: The Bredgar & Wormshill Light Railway, The Warren, Bredgar, Nr Sittingbourne, Kent ME9 8AT
Contact: Bill Best, David Best
Telephone: (01622) 884254
Fax: (01622) 884668
Internet address: *Web site:* www.bwlr.co.uk
Access by public transport: Main line trains to Sittingbourne (5 miles) and Hollingbourne (3.5 miles). No taxis from Hollingbourne
OS reference: TQ 868579
Car park: On site (300 places)
On site facilities: Souvenir shop, museum, light refreshments, toilets, picnic sites, traction engines, 7.25in and 15in gauge model locomotives, working beam engine, model railway. Largest UK collection of Bean motor cars. Steam-hauled train rides from Warren Wood to Stony Shaw (1km).
Public opening: First Sunday in each month May to October (11.00-17.00). Also Easter Sunday. Admission: Adults £6, children £3
Special events: Steam locomotive driving courses, enthusiast days
Facilities for disabled: Generally good including toilets
Note: A private site with no 'out of hours' access, but groups by arrangement

Industrial locomotives

Name	*No*	*Builder*	*Type*	*Built*
(2ft gauge)				
Bronhilde	1	Schwartzkopf (9124)	0-4-0WT	1927
Katie	2	Arn Jung (3872)	0-6-0WT	1931
Armistice	4	Bagnall (2088)	0-4-0ST	1919
Bredgar	5	B/Drewry (3775)	0-4-0DH	1983
Eigiau	6	O&K (5668)	0-4-0WT	1912
Victory	7	Decauville (246)	0-4-2ST	1897
—	8	O&K (12722)	0-4-0WT	1936
No 1	—	Hunslet (1429)	0-4-0ST	1922
—	—	Fowler (13573)	0-4-2T	1912
Limpopo	—	Fowler (18800)	0-6-0T	1930
(2ft 6in gauge)				
—	105	Henschel (29582)	0-6-0WT	1956

Stock
3 bogie coaches, 1 four-wheel coach, 6 four-wheel wagons, 2 four-wheel tank wagon, 4 four-wheel works trucks, 1 open bogie coach

Steam Centre

Bressingham Steam Experience

Norfolk

Member: TT
Five miles of various gauges of railway running through extensive gardens, and a collection of well-maintained and impressive main line locomotives. All the fun of the fair, with something for everyone, a great day out for all the family
Location: Two miles west of Diss on the A1066
OS reference: TM 080806
Operating society/organisation: Bressingham Steam Preservation Co Ltd, Bressingham Hall, Diss, Norfolk IP22 2AB
Telephone: Bressingham (01379) 686900. Infoline (01379) 687382
Fax: (01379) 686907
Internet address: *Web site:* www.bressingham.co.uk
Car park: Steam Centre (free)
Access by public transport: Diss main line station (3 miles)
On site facilities: 10.25/15/24in and standard gauge lines, totalling nearly 5 miles. Museum, steam roundabout, souvenir shop and restaurant, extensive gardens and plant centre. 'Dad's Army' permanent exhibition open all year
Public opening: Open every day between Easter and end of October. Steam every day with narrow gauge rides and the Gallopers. 10.30-17.30. Education services for schools are available with pre-booking in March-October period
Special events: Please telephone (01379) 686900 for details
Facilities for disabled: Wheelchair access to majority of site including toilets. Able to take wheelchairs on Nursery Line Railway and Waveney Line
Special notes: Reduced rates for coach parties. Prices on application

Locomotives and multiple-unit

Name	*No*	*Origin*	*Class*	*Type*	*Built*
Martello	662	LBSCR	A1X	0-6-0T	1875
Thundersley	80	LTSR	3P	4-4-2T	1909
Granville	102	LSWR	B4	0-4-0T	1893
—	490	GER	E4	2-4-0	1894
Henry Oakley	990*	GNR	C2	4-4-2	1898
Royal Scot	6100*	LMS	7P	4-6-0	1927
Peer Gynt	5865	NSB	52	2-10-0	1944
King Haakon VII	377	NSB	21c	2-6-0	1919
—	54347	Met-Cam	101	DTCL	1959

*undergoing restoration

Industrial locomotives

Name	*No*	*Builder*	*Type*	*Built*
Beckton	1	Neilson (4444)	0-4-0ST	1892
Beckton	25	Neilson (5087)	0-4-0ST	1896
William Francis	6841	B/Peacock (6841)	0-4-0+0-4-0T	1937
Millfield	—	RSH (7070)	0-4-0CT	1942
Bluebottle	—	Barclay (1472)	0-4-0F	1916
County School	GET 1	R/Hornsby (497753)	0-4-0DE	1963

2ft gauge locomotives

Name	*No*	*Builder*	*Type*	*Built*
Gwynedd	—	Hunslet (316)	0-4-0ST	1883
George Sholto	—	Hunslet (994)	0-4-0ST	1909
Bronllwyd	—	H/Clarke (1643)	0-6-0WT	1930
Toby	—	M/Rail (22120)	4wDM	1964

15in gauge locomotives

Name	*No*	*Builder*	*Type*	*Built*
Rosenkavalier	—	Krupp (1662)	4-6-2	1937
Mannertreu	—	Krupp (1663)	4-6-2	1937
Flying Scotsman	4472	W. Stewart (4472)	4-6-2	1976
Works Loco	—	Diss	0-4-0DM	1992
Replica	6353	—	Bo-Bo	—

10.25in gauge locomotives

Name	*No*	*Builder*	*Type*	*Built*
Alan Bloom	1	BSM	0-4-0ST	1995

Owner
80, 490 and 990 on loan from the National Railway Museum
GET 1 the Great Eastern Traction Group

Steam Centre

Bristol Industrial Museum

Bristol

Member: HRA
The Museum houses machinery and vehicles associated with Bristol's industrial past, from horse-drawn vehicles to aircraft
Location: Princes Wharf, Bristol
OS reference: ST 585722
Operating society/organisation: Bristol Industrial Museum, Princes

Wharf, Bristol BS1 4RN
Telephone: (0117) 925 1470
Fax: (0117) 929 7318
Car parks: Available nearby
Access by public transport: Buses to centre of city, 1km from Temple Meads station
On site facilities: Shop
Length of line: Half-mile, extension of one-mile open for a.m. trips
Public opening: Open all year Saturday to Wednesday 10.00-17.00
Facilities for disabled: Reasonable access

Industrial locomotives

Name	No	Builder	Type	Built
Portbury	34†	Avonside (1764)	0-6-0ST	1917
Henbury	—†	Peckett (1940)	0-6-0ST	1937
—	3*	F/Walker (242)	0-6-0ST	1874
—	—	R/Hornsby (418792)	0-4-0DM	1958

*not on public display
†only on view when in steam

Special notes: Operation of railway on advertised weekends only, 11.30-17.00
Membership details: Officer in charge — D. Martin, Bristol Harbour Railway c/o above address

Miniature Railway

Brookside Miniature Railway

Cheshire

Member: Britain's Great Little Railways
Location: Brookside Garden Centre
Headquarters: Brookside Garden Centre Ltd, Macclesfield Road, Poynton, Cheshire
Contact: Chief Executive Mr C Halsall
Telephone: (01625) 872919
Fax: (01625) 859119
Internet address: *Web site:* www.brookside-miniature-railway.co.uk
Car parking: On site
Access by public transport: Main line stations: Hazel Grove (2.5 miles, Poynton (2 miles).
Bus No 191 stops outside the Centre
On site facilities: Full restaurant/café facilities. Extensive museum of railwayana, large display of totems (c200) and advertising enamels
Depots: On site and visits may be made by prior arrangement
Length of line: 7.25in gauge, half mile
Period of public operation: Weekends throughout the year, plus Wednesdays April to September; every day mid-July and August. Summer — 11.00-16.30; winter — 11.00-16.00

Steam Centre

Buckinghamshire Railway Centre

Bucks

Member: HRA
The Buckinghamshire Railway Centre is situated at Quainton Road on the freight-only Aylesbury-Calvert line, once part of the Metropolitan and Great Central line from London to Verney Junction. Quainton Road station is also the old junction for the Brill Tramway closed in 1935. The Centre is now home to the former LNWR Rewley Road station moved brick-by-brick from the centre of Oxford. Opened in 1851, this Grade 2* listed building is built in the same manner as the Crystal Palace Great Exhibition building of 1881 destroyed by fire in the 1930s. It is unique in its construction and

Locomotives and multiple-units

Name	No	Origin	Class	Type	Built
—	1	Met Rly	E	0-4-4T	1898
—	0314	LSWR	0298	2-4-0WT	1874
Defiant	5080	GWR	'Castle'	4-6-0	1939
Wightwick Hall	6989	GWR	'Hall'	4-6-0	1948
—	7200	GWR	7200	2-8-2T	1934
—	7715	GWR	5700	0-6-0PT	1930
—	9466	GWR	9400	0-6-0PT	1952
—	41298	LMS	2MT	2-6-2T	1951
—	41313	LMS	2MT	2-6-2T	1952
—	46447	LMS	2MT	2-6-0	1950
—	D2298	BR	04	0-6-0DM	1960
—	3405*	SAR	25NC	4-8-4	1958
—	51886	BR	115	DMBS	1960
—	51899	BR	115	DMBS	1960
—	59761	BR	115	TCL	1960

*3ft 6in gauge

provides a superb setting in which the pick of the Centre's locomotives and carriages are now displayed
Location: Adjacent to goods-only line to Aylesbury. Turn off A41 at Waddesdon 6 miles NW of Aylesbury, Bucks
OS reference: SP 738190
Operating society/organisation: Quainton Railway Society Ltd, The Railway Station, Quainton, Nr Aylesbury, Bucks HP22 4BY
Telephone: Quainton (01296) 655450
Internet address:
Web site: www.bucksrailcentre.org
Car park: Quainton Road — Free parking
Access by public transport: Main line Aylesbury station. Local bus Monday-Saturday only
On site facilities: Souvenir bookshop, light refreshments, toilets, steam-hauled train rides. Museum of small relics, secondhand bookshop, miniature railway
Catering facilities: Hot snacks and light refreshments available
Length of line: Two half-mile demonstration lines
Public opening: Open Wednesday to Sunday inclusive from April to October. Steaming days each Sunday and Wednesdays during school holidays.
Opening times: 10.30-16.30 as well as Bank Holidays
Special events: Day out with Thomas — 12, 14-17 April; May Day Weekend & Model Collectors Fair — 30 April-1 May; Heritage Building Works at the Visitor Centre — 17 May; Spring Bank Holiday Weekend — 28/29 May; Miniature Traction Engine Rally — 3/4 June; Stephen's Rocket Fortnight — 17-30 June; Summer Steam & Diesel Gala — 2 July; Day out with Thomas — 7-9 July; Cuddle Toy Day & Children's Day — 6, 14, 21 August; August Bank Holiday Weekend — 27/28 August; Day out with Thomas — 9/10 September; Grand Traction Engine Show — 23/24 September; Autumn Steam & Diesel gala — 8 October; Magical Wizard Show — 29 October.
Facilities for disabled: Access to most of site including special toilets

Industrial locomotives

Name	*No*	*Builder*	*Type*	*Built*
Scott	—	Bagnall (2469)	0-4-0ST	1932
—	—	Baguley (2161)	0-4-0DM	1941
Swanscombe	—	Barclay (699)	0-4-0ST	1891
—	—	GF3 Barclay (1477)	0-4-0F	1916
—	—	Barclay (2243)	0-4-0F	1948
Osram	—	Fowler (20067)	0-4-0DM	1933
—	3	H/Leslie (3717)	0-4-0ST	1928
Sir Thomas	—	H/Clarke (1334)	0-6-0T	1918
—	—	H/Clarke (1742)	0-4-0ST	1946
—	—	Hunslet (2067)	0-4-0DM	1940
Arthur	—	Hunslet (3782)	0-6-0ST	1953
Juno	—	Hunslet (3850)	0-6-0ST	1958
—	65	Hunslet (3889)	0-6-0ST	1964
—	66	Hunslet (3890)	0-6-0ST	1964
—	26	Hunslet (7016)	0-6-0DH	1971
Redland	—	K/Stuart (K4428)	0-4-0DM	1929
Coventry No 1	—	NBL (24564)	0-6-0ST	1939
—	—	Peckett (1900)	0-4-0T	1936
Gibraltar	—	Peckett (2087)	0-4-0ST	1948
—	—	Peckett (2104)	0-4-0ST	1948
—	—	Peckett (2105)	0-4-0ST	1948
—	T1	Hibberd (2102)	4wD	1937
Tarmac	—	Hibberd (3765)	0-4-0DM	1955
—	11	Sentinel (9366)	4wVBTG	1945
—	7	Sentinel (9376)	4wVBTG	1947
—	—	Sentinel (9537)	4wVBTG	1947
Chislet	9	Yorkshire (2498)	0-6-0ST	1951

Stock: *Coaches —*
1 LCDR 1st Class 4-wheeler; 1 MSLR 3rd Class 6-wheeler; 4 LNWR coach bodies; 2 GNR 6-wheelers; 3 LNWR; 3 LMSR; 1 BR(W) Hawksworth brake 3rd; 2 BR Mk 1; 1 BR Mk 2; 1 BR Suburban brake; 3 LNER; 1 LNWR full brake 6-wheeler; 1 LMSR passenger brake van; 1 GWR passenger brake van; 1 GCR Robinson brake third
Wagons —
A large and varied collection including 1 LNWR combination truck; 1 LSWR ventilated fruit van; 1 SR PMV; 1 BR(W) Siphon G; 1 BR horse box; 1 BR CCT

3 ex-London Underground coaches
1 2ft gauge post office mailbag car 803
Sentinel/Cammell 3-car steam railcar unit 5208 (ex-Egyptian National)
Numerous goods vehicles/wagons/vans

Owners
41298, 41313, 46447 and *Juno* the Ivatt Locomotive Trust
9466 the 9466 Group
Defiant on loan from Tyseley Locomotive Works

Special notes: One of the largest collection of standard gauge locomotives, together with a most interesting collection of vintage coaching stock, much of which was built in the 19th century
General: The public area of the centre covers some 25 acres of land with views across the Buckinghamshire countryside. A picnic area is available at the miniature railway

Above: The driver of this Sandy River & Rangeley Lakes Railroad locomotive poses for the photographer at the Brookside Miniature Railway. *BMR*

Below: This 1948-built Peckett 0-4-0ST is painted in British Railways mixed traffic livery although it was only ever used in industrial service. No 2087 is seen in action on one of the Buckinghamshire Railway Centre's demonstration lines. *Phil Barnes*

Bure Valley Railway

Member: HRA, TT
Opened in 1990, the BVR runs over the old Great Eastern Wroxham-Aylsham line. It is paralleled throughout the entire 9 miles by the Bure Valley Walk and cycle path which offers excellent photographic opportunities
Headquarters: Bure Valley Railway (1991) Ltd, Aylsham Station, Norwich Road, Aylsham, Norfolk NR11 6BW
Chairman: Andrew Barnes
Telephone: (01263) 733858
Fax: (01263) 733814
Internet address: *e-mail:* info@bvrw.co.uk
Web site: www.bvrw.co.uk
Main public station: Aylsham (Norwich Road); Wroxham (Coltishall Road)
Other public stations: Coltishall, Brampton and Buxton
Car and coach parks: Aylsham and Wroxham

Locomotives

Name	*No*	*Builder*	*Type*	*Built*
Wroxham Broad	1	G&S/Winson	2-6-4T	1992
2nd Air Division USAAF	3	BVR	4w-4wDH	1989
—	4	H/Hunslet	0-4-0DH	1996
—	5	Lister	4wDM	
Blickling Hall	6	Winson*	2-6-2	1994
Spitfire	7	Winson*	2-6-2	1994
Thunder	8	BVR/Winson	2-6-2T	1997
Mark Timothy	10	Winson/Keef§	2-6-4T	2003

*based on Indian Railways 2ft 6in gauge 'ZB' class
§based on Leek & Manifold Railway design

Stock
20 fully enclosed saloons, 2 fully enclosed compartment coaches, 1 fully enclosed brake saloon, 6 enclosed saloons designed to carry wheelchairs, 2 guard's vans, generator car, miscellaneous wagons including a rail-mounted flail and weedkilling unit and purpose-built p-way tool vehicle

OS reference:
Aylsham — TG 195264
Wroxham — TG 303186
Access by public transport: By rail – Wroxham station is adjacent to main line Hoveton & Wroxham station (Norwich-Cromer/ Sheringham line). By bus – Eastern

Counties buses run between Norwich and Aylsham
Refreshment facilities: Restaurant at Aylsham with picnic area, light refreshments at Wroxham
Souvenir shops: Aylsham and Wroxham
Journey time: Approximately 45min each way plus turnround time
Length of line: 9 miles; 15in gauge
Passenger trains: Frequency depends on time of year, maximum frequency one per hour
Period of public operation: Weekends in March, 30 September to 15 October. Daily 1April to 24 September and 21-29 October
Facilities for disabled: Toilets at Aylsham and Wroxham, special rolling stock to carry wheelchairs; advance notice would be appreciated
Special events: Please contact for full details, Day out with Thomas — 27-29 May and 23/24 September; Santa Specials —25/26 November, 2/3, 9/10, 16-24 December (advance booking essential); Mince Pie Specials 27 December to 2 January 2007
Special notes: Steam locomotive driving courses. Group discounts available. Frequent Travellers Railcards. Children's Birthday Parties. Private charters by arrangement. Special combined train and Broads boat excursions run most days during the summer
Membership details: Friends of the Bure Valley Railway, Membership Secretary, c/o above address

Diesel Centre

Cambrian Heritage Railway

Shropshire

Member: HRA
It was announced in December that Shropshire County Council has agreed in principle to purchase the currently mothballed Gobowen-Blodwell line from Network Rail. This is planned to be used as a cycle way and for the operation of a heritage railway.
Location: Llynclys is situated on the B4396 about 5 miles south of Oswestry, just off the A483 Welshpool-Oswestry road
Telephone: 01691 831569
Internet address: *e-mail:* admin@cambrianrailwaystrust.com
Web site: www.cambrianrailwaystrust.com
OS reference: SJ284239
Operating society: Cambrian Railways Trust, c/o Llynclys House, Llynclys, Oswestry, Shropshire SY10, 8LL
Access by public transport: Bus approx hourly from Oswestry to White Lion Inn, Llynclys crossroads (200yd from site), with connecting buses from Gobowen station and Shrewsbury. Also buses from Welshpool and llanfyllin (Arriva Midlands / Tanat Valley Coaches)
On site facilities: Buffet and shop
Period of public opening: Generally weekends and bank holidays — 14 April-5 November, but visitors welcome at other times
Disabled facilities: Level access to platforms, ramps onto trains
Membership details: c/o above address

Locomotives and Multiple-units

Name	*No*	*Origin*	*Class*	*Type*	*Built*
Cogan Hall	5952	GWR	Hall	4-6-0	1935
Ditcheat Manor	7821	GWR	'Manor'	4-6-0	1950
—	D2094	BR	08	0-6-0DE	1953
—	D3019	BR	03	0-6-0DM	1960
—	51187	Met-Cam	101	DMBS	1958
—	51205	Met-Cam	101	DMBS	1958
—	51512	Met-Cam	101	DMC	1959
—	54055	Met-Cam	101	DTSL	1957

Rolling stock
7 ex-BR Mk 1 coaches, 1 ex-BR courier coach, 3 ex-GWR vans, small selection of wagons

Steam Centre

Chasewater Railway

Staffordshire

Member: HRA, TT
Founded in 1959 as the Railway Preservation Society (West Midlands District), the Chasewater Railway was re-formed in 1985 as a Registered Charity. The railway operates as 'The Colliery Line' to reflect its origins and location in the heart of the Cannock Chase coalfield. A regular timetabled service operates between Brownhills West station and Chasetown (Church Street), with intermediate stations at Norton Lakeside (which adjoins Chasewater's Wildfowl Reserve) and Chasewater Heaths.
Location: Chasewater Park, Brownhills (off A5 southbound, nr jct A452 Chester Road). Brown tourism signs are provided on A5
OS Reference: SK 034070
Operating society/organisation: Chasewater Light Railway & Museum Co
Telephone: 01543 452623
Internet address: *e-mail:*

info@ChasewaterRailway.co.uk
Web site:
www.ChasewaterRailway.co.uk
Car park: Ample car parking within Chasewater Park
Access by public transport: *Nearest railway stations* — Walsall and Birmingham New Street.
Sunday bus services from Walsall Bus Station (St Paul's Street) — Saturdays: 396A (Stand L) and 396C (Stand K), alight at Poole Crescent
Sundays: 362 (Stand K) and 394A (Stand L) to Brownhills West (Rising Sun Inn).
Bus services from Birmingham (Carrs Lane)
Saturdays and Sundays: 156 (Stand DJ) to Brownhills West (Rising Sun Inn).
Brownhills West station is approx 15min walk from the Rising Sun Inn, 10min walk from Poole Crescent
For timetable information and details of services, contact Traveline 0870 608 2608
On site facilities: Refreshments, shop, lakeside walks and large grassed areas
Catering facilities: Hot and cold buffets at Brownhills West and Chasewater Heath stations
Length of line: Approx 2 miles
Public opening: Sundays and Bank Holiday Mondays throughout the year.

Trains run approx hourly from Brownhills West station, 11.00-17.00. Check web site for running dates and timetables.

Most services are with steam traction (subject to availability). Industrial diesel locomotives are normally used once a month and at off-peak periods.

All tickets give unlimited rides on day of issue

Diesel locomotive and multiple-units

Name	*No*	*Builder*	*Class*	*Type*	*Built*
—	31203	BR	31	A1A-A1A	1960
—	37219	BR	37	Co-Co	1964
—*	73128	BR	73	Bo-Bo	1966
—	W51370	Pressed Steel	117	DMBS	1960
—	W51372	Pressed Steel	117	DMBS	1960
—	W51412	Pressed Steel	117	DMS	1960
—	W59444	BR Derby	116	TS	1958
—	W55922	Pressed Steel	117	TCL	1960
—	W59603	Pressed Steel	127	TSL	1959

*named *O. V. S. Bulleid CBE*

Industrial locomotives

Name	*No*	*Builder*	*Type*	*Built*
Colin McAndrew	3	Barclay (1223)	0-4-0ST	1911
Sheepbridge No 15	—	H/Clarke (431)	0-6-0T	1895
Whit No 4	—	H/Clarke (1822)	0-6-0T	1949
Asbestos	4	H/Leslie (2780)	0-4-0ST	1909
Alfred Paget	11	Neilson (2937)	0-4-0ST	1882
—	6	Peckett (917)	0-4-0ST	1902
Sentinel	5	Sentinel (9632)	4wVBT	1957
Bass No 5	—	Baguley (3027)	0-4-0DM	1939
—	—	Bagnall (3119)	0-6-0DM	1956
Dealer	—	Brush (3097)	0-4-0DE	1956
—	—	Fowler (4100013)	0-4-0DM	1948
Toad	37	Fowler (4220015)	0-4-0DH	1962
—	462	Hibberd (1891)	4wDM	1934
—	—	Hibberd (3906)	4wDM	1959
—	6678	Hunslet (6678)	0-4-0DH	1968
—	21	Kent Constr (1612)	4wDM	1929
—	1*	M/Rail (1947)	4wPM	1919
Ryan	—	R/Hornsby (305306)	0-4-0DM	1952
Fleet	11517	R/Hornsby (458641)	0-4-0DE	1963

*currently dismantled

Rolling stock
A variety of passenger and freight vehicles are housed on site, including a number of considerable historical importance, together with an ex-LNER steam crane

Special events: Spring Gala — 1/2 April; Kids Easter Eggstravaganza — 9 April; Bus Rally (Chasewater Heaths) — 18 June; Steam & Diesel Gala — 9/10 September; Halloween Specials — 29 October; Santa Specials —throughout December

Facilities for disabled: Disabled access to stations, trains and buffet
Membership details: Membership Secretary, Brownhills West Station, Chasewater Country Park, Pool Road, Nr Brownhills, Staffs WS8 7NL

Steam Centre

Chinnor & Princes Risborough Railway — 'The Icknield Line'

Oxfordshire

Member: HRA
The Chinnor & Princes Risborough Railway runs from Chinnor station, close to the beautiful Chiltern Hills and to the Vale of Aylesbury. Originally built in 1872 to connect the towns of Watlington in Oxfordshire to Princes Risborough in Buckinghamshire. The line was closed to all traffic by British Railways in 1989. Since then a team of volunteers has rebuilt Chinnor

station to its Victorian glory. The railway operates the 3.5-mile ex-Great Western Railway branch line as a tourist attraction for both families and railway enthusiasts. A regular steam-hauled service is provided every Sunday from the end of March to October. Special events are a feature of the programme including Day out with Thomas weekends and Santa Specials. Cream teas are served on selected afternoon trains during the summer months
Location: M40 Junction 6 then B4009 north 4 miles towards Princes Risborough to village of Chinnor. Once in village follow brown tourist signs to station
Operating society/organisation: Chinnor & Princes Risborough Railway Co Ltd, Chinnor Station, Station Road, Chinnor, Oxon OX39 4ER
Contact: Brian Dickson, Press & Publicity Officer, 58 Grenville Avenue, Wendover, Bucks HP22 6AL. Tel: 01296 622569
Telephone: Talking Timetable 01844 353535. Thomas Booking Line: 01844 354117 (Weekends 10.00-17.00 only)
Internet address: *e-mail:* brian@dicksons.screaming.net
Web site: www.cprra.co.uk
OS reference: SP 756003
Access by public transport: Nearest main line station — Princes Risborough (4 miles) Chiltern Railways
By car: M40 junction 6 then B4009 north towards Princes Risborough to village of Chinnor, then follow brown tourist signs to station
Length of line: 3.5 miles
Journey time: 45min, steam and heritage diesel trains
On site facilities: Souvenir shop, small buffet on Chinnor station. Bar/buffet on most trains (cream teas on selected trains on summer Sunday afternoons). Toilets, free car park, picnic area
Passenger trains: Chinnor-Thame Junction-Chinnor
Public opening: 26 March; 2, 9, 14-17, 23, 29/30 April; 1, 7, 14, 21, 28/29 May; 4, 11, 18, 25 June; 1/2, 9, 15/16, 22/23 July; 5/6, 13, 20, 26-28 August; 3, 10, 17, 24, 30 September; 1, 8, 15, 22, 29 October; 3, 9/10, 16/17, 23/24, 30/31 December (Santa Specials); 2 January 2007
Special events: Mother's Day — 26 March; Easter Steam Specials — 14-17 April; St George's Day — 23 April; Day out with Thomas — 29/30 April, 1 May; Teddy Bear Weekend — 29/30 May; Summer Gala — 11 June; Father's Day — 18 June; Strawberries & Cream — 265 June; Commercial Vehicles Weekend — 1/2 July; Senior Citizens' Half Price — 9 July; Summer Diesel Weekend — 15/16 July; Heritage Traction Weekend — 22/23 July; Day out with Thomas — 5/6 August; Vintage Vehicle Weekend — 26-28 August; Grandparents' Half Price — 24 September; Day out with Thomas — 30 September/1 October; Teddy Bear Day — 15 October; Halloween Spooks Express — 29 October; Santa Specials — 3, 9/10, 16/17, 23/24 December; Mince Pie Specials — 30/31 December, 2 January 2007.
Afternoon Crean Teas — 26 March, 9 April, 7, 21 May, 4, 18 June, 9, 30 July, 13, 20 August, 10, 24 September, 8, 22 October. Other dates available for party bookings
Special note: Group charter hire and film and photographic facilities. For group bookings contact: 01844 353535.
Advance booking is necessary for Day out with Thomas and Santa Specials
Driver Experience Courses: The railway will be offering steam driver experience courses throughout the year. Gift vouchers are also available for these courses. Please telephone in the first instance Brian Dickson on 01296 622569 for details
Facilities for disabled: Ramp, toilet, accessible parking area. All public areas accessible. Guide dogs welcome
Membership details: Mr Peter Harris, 12 Ann's Close, Aylesbury, Bucks HP21 9XG
Membership journal: *The Watlington Flyer* — quarterly

Locomotives

Name	No	Origin	Class	Type	Built
Haversham	13018	BR	08	0-6-0DE	1953
—	D8568	BR	17	Bo-Bo	1963
—	31113	BR	31	A1A-A1A	1959
—	D5581	BR	31	A1A-A1A	1961
—	55023	BR	121	DMBS	1958
—*	9682	GWR	57xx	0-6-0PT	1949

*on loan from GWR Preservation Group, Southall

Industrial locomotives

Name	No	Builder	Type	Built
Blue Circle	—	A/Porter (9449)	2-2-0TG	1926
Iris	459515	R/Hornsby (459515)	0-6-0DH	1952
Brill	14	M/Wardle (1795)	0-4-0ST	1912

Stock - coaches
1 ex-LNWR Mess coach, 1 ex-BR Mk 1 NDV, 1 ex-BR Mk 1 RMB, 1 ex-BR Mk 1 CK, 1 ex-BR Mk 1 BSK, 1 ex-BR Mk 2 FK, 16 various wagons, 1 Coles self-propelled crane

Owners
D8568 the Diesel Traction Group

Timetable Service

Cholsey & Wallingford Railway

Oxfordshire

Member: HRA
The Barclay has now returned to steam and has been restored in the guise of GWR 701, a former Swansea Harbour Trust locomotive. Due to ongoing alterations/ improvements to Wallingford station and upgrading of the line to Cholsey during 2006, the timetable is subject to revision without notice. Please check the web site or 24hr answerphone for up-to-date information
Location: 5 Hithercroft Road, Wallingford, Oxfordshire
Sales & Marketing: Denis Strange
Operating Society: Cholsey & Wallingford Railway Preservation Society, 5 Hithercroft Road, Wallingford, Oxon OX10 9GQ
Telephone: (01491) 835067 (24hr information line)
Internet address: *e-mail:* cwrail@yahoo.co.uk
Web site: www.cholsey-wallingford-railway.com
Disabled Access: Access direct to Wallingford station from adjoining car park, access ramp to shop, platform and train, disabled toilet on site. No disabled facilities at Cholsey station
Access by public transport: Thames Travel Buses — X39 from Oxford, X40 from Reading. First Great Western Link trains to Cholsey station
Public opening: Trains run depart every hour from Wallingford, 11.10-16.10; and from Cholsey platform 11.35-16.35
Length of line: 2.5 miles from Wallingford
Journey time: Approximately 14min (one way), 50min (return)
On site facilities: Souvenir shop, café and museum
Special events: Ivor the Engine — 15-17 April; C&W 25th Anniversary Celebrations— 30 April, 1, 6/7, 13/14, 20/21 May; Teddy Bears' Picnic — 24/25 June; Real Ale Weekend — 8/9 July; Ivor the Engine — 19/20 August; BunkFest — 2/3 September; Guinness Weekend — 16/17 September; Halloween Wizard Weekend — 28/29 October; Santa Specials — 2/3, 9/10, 17/18 December; Evening Carol Trains — 10 December
Special notes: Railway crosses new bypass (A4130) at a level crossing. The Society is running into Cholsey bay platform.
Membership details: Alan Saunders, at above address
Membership journal: *The Bunk* — 3 issues/year

Locomotives

Name	*No*	*Origin*	*Class*	*Type*	*Built*
Unicorn	D3074	BR	08	0-6-0DE	1953
Lion	D3030	BR	08	0-6-0DE	1953
George Mason	D3190	BR	08	0-6-0DE	1955

Industrial locomotives

Name	*No*	*Builder*	*Type*	*Built*
—	701	Barclay (1964)	0-4-0ST	1929
Carpenter	3271	Planet (3270)	0-4-0DM	1949
—	803	Alco (77777)	Bo-Bo	1950

Rolling stock — coaches: GWR autocoach, Hawksworth brake coach, GWR full brake, 2 BR Mk 1 coaches

Timetable Service

Churnet Valley Railway

Staffordshire

Member: HRA
This heritage railway is situated deep in the heart of the Staffordshire moorlands. Cheddleton is an original Victorian country station set in picturesque countryside complete with riverside parking and picnic island. The journey takes you to the idyllic hamlet of Consall Forge and onwards to the reinstated station Kingsley & Froghall
Main station/location: Cheddleton Station, Station Road, Cheddleton,

Locomotives and multiple-units

Name	*No*	*Origin*	*Class*	*Type*	*Built*
—	1	NSR	—	0-4-0BE	1917
—	44422*	LMS	4F	0-6-0	1927
—	5197	USATC	S160	2-8-0	1942
—	92134	BR	9F	2-10-0	1957
—	D2334	BR	04	0-6-0DM	1961
—	D3991	BR	08	0-6-0DE	1960
—	20007	BR	20	Bo-Bo	1957
—	D8154	BR	20	Bo-Bo	1966
Tamworth Castle	D7672	BR	25	Bo-Bo	1967
—	33102	BR	33	Bo-Bo	1960
—	37009	BR	37	Co-Co	1961
—	37211	BR	37	Co-Co	1961

Nr Leek, Staffs ST13 7EE
OS reference: SJ 983519
Operating society/organisation: Churnet Valley Railway (1992) plc
Telephone: 01538 360522
Fax: 01538 361848
Internet address: *e-mail:* mgtcvr@onetel.com
Web site: www.churnetvalleyrailway.co.uk
Other stations: Consall, Kingsley & Froghall
Car parks: Adjacent to Cheddleton and Froghall stations
Access by public transport: Main line Stoke-on-Trent (10 miles). A regular bus service (No 16) runs from Hanley and Leek to Cheddleton village
On site facilities: Refreshment facilities on all trains and at Cheddleton and Froghall
Souvenir shop: Cheddleton and Froghall
Museum: Small relics museum and locomotive display hall at Cheddleton
Length of line: 5.25 miles
Tickets: Day rover tickets available
Public opening: Steam trains March-October inclusive: weekends and bank holidays. Wednesdays in June and July. Daily in August.
Special events: Station at War, Day out with Thomas, Ghost Train and Santa Specials
Facilities for disabled: Access to station areas is possible by wheelchair, train travel by arrangement. Disabled toilet facilities at Consall and Froghall
Membership details: North Staffordshire Railway Co (1978) Ltd, Membership Secretary, c/o above address
Special notes: Party bookings by arrangement, footplate experience courses, wine & dine dates on application. Licensed for weddings

Name	*No*	*Origin*	*Class*	*Type*	*Built*
—	47192	BR	47	Co-Co	1965
—	47524	BR	47	Co-Co	1967
—	73110	BR	73	Bo-Bo	1966
—	53455	BRCW	104	DMBS	1957
—	53437	BRCW	104	DMBS	1957
—	53494	BRCW	104	DMCL	1957
—	53517	BRCW	104	DMCL	1957
—	59137	BRCW	104	TSL	1957
—	62351	BR	423	MBSO	
—	71032	BR	423	MTSO	
—	76529	BR	423	DTC	
—	76712	BR	423	DTS	

*on loan to East Lancashire Railway

Industrial locomotives

Name	*No*	*Builder*	*Type*	*Built*
—	68030	Hunslet (3777)	0-6-0ST	1952
Cammell	—	YEC	0-4-0DH	1960
Brightside	—	YEC	0-4-0DH	1960

Locomotive notes: Locos expected to be in service: 5197, 48305, 68030, D2334, D3991, 20007, 20154 and 33102

Stock
Ex-BR Mk 1 coaches: CK (1), BSK (2), SO (3), TSO (2), FK (3), RMB (1), RK (1) and BG (2); ex-BR Mk 2 coaches: BFK (1) and BSO (1); ex-BR suburban coaches: S (1), BS (2), SLO (1); 1 ex-NSR coach body; 1 ex-LMS 6-wheel full brake; 2 ex-LMS goods brake vans; 1 ex-LMS 6-wheel CCT; 2 ex-LMS box vans; 3 ex-BR box vans; 2 ex-LMS five-plank wagons; 1 ex-LMS hopper wagon; 1 Esso tank wagon; 1 ex-BR standard brake van; 1 ex-BR Oyster; 5 ex-BR General Utility Vans; 2 ex-BR Medfits; 2 ex-BR Catfish; 1 ex-GWR bogie bolster; 2 Flatrols; 1 Lowmac; 7-ton diesel rail-mounted crane; 75-ton rail-mounted diesel crane; 3 ex-BR QQX tool vans; 1 ex-BR QPX staff and dormitory

Owners
NSR 1 and 44422 the 4F Locomotive Fund and the National Railway Museum
68030 the Standard Class 4 Preservation Trust
33102 and D7672 the NSR Diesel Group
20007, D8154, 37009, 37211, 73110, D3991 and *Brightside* the Churnet Traction & Rolling Stock Group
47192 and 47524 the Staffordshire Type 4 Ltd

Timetable Service

Cleethorpes Coast Light Railway

North East Lincolnshire

Member: HRA
The East Coast's award winning seaside 15in gauge steam railway. Built in 1948 as a 10.25in line, it was converted in 1972 to 14.25in and then to 15in gauge in 1994.

The railway has a good reputation for galas and events, and facilities continue to improve year on year. In 2005 a new 'Griffon Hall' museumwas officially opened.

The railway is supported by the

Light Railway Association, whose members assist in running the line, undertaking a wide range of duties. This small group provides volunteers from station staff to engine drivers.

2006 will again feature a spring gala, the 'Bakers Dozen' with other events planned throughout the year; two additional visiting engines are planned to visit the line for the main summer season

Operating society/organisation: Cleethorpes Coast Light Railway Ltd, Lakeside Station, Kings Road, Cleethorpes, Lincolnshire DN35 0AG
Telephone: (01472) 604657
Fax: (01472) 291903
Internet address: *e-mail:* genoffcclrltd.freeserve.co.uk
Access by public transport: By rail to Cleethorpes station (First Transpennine South). Local bus service Stagecoach services 9 (all year) and 17 (summer only). Or Coopers Seafront Open Top service (summer only).
Alternative seafront roadtrain from the pier to CCLR Kingsway station. By car, Kings Road is the main resort road, follow brown tourist signs for Lakeside (look for the train symbol)
On site facilities: Large 500 space car park at Lakeside station (pay & display, local authority operated). Lakeside station — Brief Encounters tea room; Model Box model shop; Griffon Hall museum; 4-ways café. Kingsway station — Station Masters gift shop.
Period of public opening: Please contact for details

Locomotives (15in gauge)

Name	*No*	*Built/rebuilt*	*Type*	*Date*
—	7	Lister	4wDH Tram	—
The Cub/John	3	Minirail/CCLR	4w4DM	1993
—	24	Fairbourne	2-6-2	1989
—	—	A. Moss	4wDM	1995
Battison	—	Battison	2-6-4DH S/O	1958
Yvette	1	—	2-6-0	1946

Rolling stock
10 coaches, 2 x 4-wheel wagons, 2 x 4-wheel box vans, 1 x 4-wheel goods brake van, 4 bogie flat wagons, 2 x 4-wheel ballast wagon

15in gauge Sutton Collection

Locomotives

Name	*No*	*Built/rebuilt*	*Type*	*Date*
Sutton Belle	1	BL/Cannon Ironfoundries/Hunt	4-4-2	1933
Sutton Flyer	2	Bassett Lowke/Hunt	4-4-2	1950
—	4	G&S Light Engineering	Bo-Bo	1946

Rolling stock
6 closed coaches, 4 open coaches, 4-wheel coal truck

20in gauge Hudswell Collection

Name	*No*	*Built/rebuilt*	*Type*	*Date*
Robin Hood	—	H/Clarke (D570)	4-6-4DH S/O	1932
May Thompson	—	H/Clarke (D582)	4-6-2DH S/O	1933

Rolling stock
4 x toastrack coaches

Note
During the year visiting locomotives are based on the CCLR, and locomotives and rolling stock are under repair for other operators

Steam Centre — Colne Valley Railway — Essex

Member: HRA, TT
A completely reconstructed country station and railway within sight of a 12th century castle and specialising in entertainment and education. A complementary Farm Park provides interest for all the family (May to September)
Location: Castle Hedingham Station, Yeldham Road, Castle Hedingham, Halstead, Essex CO9 3DZ
OS reference: TL 774362
Operating society/organisation:

Locomotives and multiple-units

Name	*No*	*Origin*	*Class*	*Type*	*Built*
Blue Star	35010	SR	MN	4-6-2	1942
—	45163	LMS	5	4-6-0	1935
—	45293	LMS	5	4-6-0	1936
—	D2041	BR	03	0-6-0DM	1959
—	D2184	BR	03	0-6-0DM	1962
—	D3476	BR	10	0-6-0DE	1957
—	31255	BR	31	A1A-A1A	1961
—	47771	BR	47	Co-Co	19??
—	54287	P/Steel	121	DTS	1961
—	55033	P/Steel	121	DTC	1960
—	68009	BR	MLV / 419	DMVL	1961
—	69318	BR	4-BIG / 422	TRBS	1965

Colne Valley Railway Preservation Society Ltd
Telephone: Hedingham (01787) 461174
Internet address:
Web site:
www.colnevalleyrailway.co.uk
Car park: At the site (access from A1017 road between Castle Hedingham and Great Yeldham)
Access by public transport: Eastern National bus services 88 Colchester-Halstead, 89 Halstead-Hedingham and Hedingham Omnibuses 4 Braintree-Hedingham, 5 Sudbury-Hedingham. Nearest main line station — Braintree (7 miles)
On site facilities: Depot, museum, souvenir shop, buffet, 4-acre riverside picnic area, toilets, video carriage, exhibition centre, 30 acre farm park (May to September)
Catering facilities: Buffet carriage when trains operating. Pullman on-train service on selected days for Sunday lunch, private hire and evening wine and dine (pre-booking essential for all Pullman services)
Length of line: 1 mile
Public opening: Steam trains operate every Sunday from 14 April to 8 October, also Wednesdays and Thursdays during school summer holidays, every Bank Holiday (except Christmas & New Year), Wednesdays during other school holidays (except February). Diesel railcar on many other days. Phone for free timetable or visit web site
Special events: A Day out with Thomas, Santa Specials
Educational events: Diesel trains available every day for school visits (steam on certain days). Special steam school days in June. Victorian Special in October. All educational events must be pre-booked
Family tickets: Available — 2 adults and up to 4 children, giving unlimited train rides except on special events
Facilities for disabled: Access to most areas. Ramps to trains, staff will help. Special carriage available
Special notes: The railway has been completely rebuilt on part of the original Colne Valley & Halstead Railway trackbed. It offers much of educational value specialising in school party visits by appointment at any time of the year
Membership details: Membership Secretary, c/o Castle Hedingham Station

Name	*No*	*Origin*	*Class*	*Type*	*Built*
—	W79976	AC Cars	—	Railbus	1958
—	E79978	AC Cars	—	Railbus	1958
—	55508	BR	141	DMS	1983
—	55528	BR	141	DMS(L)	1983

Industrial locomotives

Name	*No*	*Builder*	*Type*	*Built*
Victory	8	Barclay (2199)	0-4-0ST	1945
—	WD190	Hunslet (3790)	0-6-0ST	1952
—	68072	Vulcan (5309)	0-6-0ST	1945
Jupiter	60	RSH (7671)	0-6-0ST	1950
—	40	RSH (7765)	0-6-0T	1954
Barrington	—	Avonside (1875)	0-4-0ST	1921
—	1	H/Leslie (3715)	0-4-0ST	1928
—	—	Barclay (349)	0-4-0DM	1941
—	YD43	R/Hornsby (221639)	4wDM	1943
—	—	Hibberd (3147)	4wDM	1947
—	—	Unilok (2109)	4wDM R/R	1982
—	—	Lake & Elliot (1)	4wPM	1924
—	—	R/Hornsby (281266)	4wDM	1950

Locomotive notes: 40, *Barrington* and 190 will be operational during 2005. Diesels 31255 and 55033 also operational

Stock
2 ex-Pullman cars, *Aquila* and *Hermione;* 9 ex-BR Mk 1 coaches (2xTSO, SO, 2xCK, SK, 2xBSK); 1 ex-BR Mk 3 SLEP; 9 BR NPCCS, 2 ex-LNER — 1xBTO (16551) 1xTK (42240); 1 LMS BG, 1 GER BTK;
4 goods brake vans (GWR, LNER & 2 BR), 3 oil tank wagons, BR steam crane, LT ballast wagon, BR Sturgeon, BR Conflat, GER van, BR van, BR Medfit, LNER tube wagon, BR diesel crane, BR Flatrol, BR Lowmac

Owners
35010 and 45293 the British Engineman's Steam Preservation Society
54287 and 55033 Pressed Steel Heritage Ltd
31255 and 68009 the Colne Valley Railway Diesel Group
47771 the Class 47 Preservation Project
45163 the 45163 Preservation Group

Museum — Coventry Electric Railway Centre — Warwickshire

Member: HRA
Originally commenced in 1983 as the Coventry Steam Railway Centre which was (and still is) is the only standard gauge line in the county of Warwickshire, The Centre has been

Electric multiple-units (complete)

Unit Nos	*No*	*Origin*	*Class*	*Type*	*Built*
4732	12795	BR	4SUB / 405	DMBSO	1951
	12354	BR	4SUB / 405	TS	1948
	10239	BR	4SUB / 405	TOS	1948
	12796	BR	4SUB / 405	DMBSO	1951

developed on a six acre greenfield site with no prior railway use. In 2000 the Suburban Electric Railway Association (SERA) bought controlling interest in the operating company and used the site to locate its collection of vintage electric multiple-units (EMUs); with the SERA collection and some privately owned EMU vehicles and electric locomotives on site it has become home to the largest collection of DC electric traction in preservation. This has prompted a change of name and direction in 2006 for the development of the site as the UK's only Electric Railway Heritage Centre. The site has witnessed some extensive development over the last couple of years with a demonstration line of just over a third of a mile under construction and new improved fencing. The full development of the Centre is an on-going process but at long last DC traction has a dedicated 'home' in UK preservvation

Location: At the boundary of Coventry Airport, south of the city centre and adjacent to the East Midlands Air Museum. Reached via Rowley Road, junction with A45/A46, Coventry Eastern Bypass — M6/M69/M1 link road. Follow signs to Coventry Airport and the entrance is on Rowley Road

Internet address: *e-mail:* info@emus.co.uk

Web site: http:/www.emus.co.uk

OS reference: SP 349750

Access by public transport: National Rail services to Coventry, West Midlands bus route 1 from overbridge at north end of station to Tollbar End — 10-15min walk up Rowley Roadto site

Operating society/organisation: Coventry Railway Centre/Suburban Electric Railway Association

Length of line: Third of a mile (under construction)

Public opening: Due to ongoing construction work at the site there is no regular opening, but groups or parties can be accommodated by prior arrangement. Some open days are planned for 2006, please check web site and railway press for details.

Please note that many items are tarpaulined for protection

Car park: On site, at main access gate

Unit Nos	*No*	*Origin*	*Class*	*Type*	*Built*
—	28690	LMS	503	DMBSO	1938
	29298	LMS	503	DTTO	1938
	29720	LMS	503	TCO	1938
5791/93	65321	BR	2EPB / 416/2	DMBSO	1954
	77112	BR	2EPB / 416/2	DTC	1954
4311	61287	BR	2HAP / 414	DMBSO	1959
	75407	BR	2HAP / 414	DTCL	1959
6307	14573	BR	2EPB / 416/3	DMBSO	1959
	16117	BR	2EPB / 416/3	DTS	1959
—	68008†	BR	MLV / 419	DMVL	1961

Electric multiple-units (from incomplete units)

From Unit No	*No*	*Origin*	*Class*	*Type*	*Built*
—	(7)	LOR*	—	TFO	1895
5176	15345	BR	415 / 4EPB	TSO	1954
1523	61383†	BR	4CEP / 411	DMSO	1958
1500	70302	BR	4CEP / 411	TSO	1958
1500	70345	BR	4CEP / 411	TBCK	1958
2205	69339†	BR	4BIG / 411	TSRB	1970
7001	67300	BR	457	DMSO	1981

*Liverpool Overhead Railway, built by Brown Marshall & Co

Electric locomotives

Name	*No*	*Builder*	*Type*	*Built*
—	(1)	E/Electric (EE905)	4wBE/WE	1935
—	1	H/Leslie	Bo-Bo	1928

Main line diesel locomotive

Name	*No*	*Origin*	*Class*	*Type*	*Built*
(Leviathan)	50040	BR	50	Co-Co	1968

Diesel multiple-units

Unit No	*No*	*Origin*	*Class*	*Type*	*Built*
—	50397†	P/Royal	103	DMBSO	1958
—	68007	BR	MLV / 419	DMVL	1961
210002	67301	BR	210	DTSO	1981

,

Diesel locomotives

Name	*No*	*Builder*	*Type*	*Built*
—	(L14)†	R/Hornsby (235515)	4wDM	1945
Mazda	—	R/Hornsby (268881)	0-4-0DE	1950
(Crabtree)	—	R/Hornsby (338416)	4wDM	1953
—	(L7)†	R/Hornsby (349038)	4wDM	1954

Petrol locomotives

Name	*No*	*Builder*	*Type*	*Built*
(C. P. May)	—	Hibberd (2895)	4wPM	1944

Steam locomotives

Name	*No*	*Builder*	*Type*	*Built*
—	(1)†	A/Barclay (1772)	0-4-0F	1922

†may not be on site for all of 2006

Rolling stock

Coaches — Ex-City & South London Railway trailers Nos 135 and 163 1 BR Mk 1 TSO

Wagons — 1 bogie tool van (converted from Maunsell Ironclad coach), 1 LNER brake van, 2 BR 12ton van fits, 1 MoD (SR design) brake van, 1 MoD 3,000gal 4-wheel tanker

Rail-mounted cranes — 1 steam crane, 1 hand crane

Facilities for disabled: Site is relatively flat, assistance will be given if requested by prior notice, there are no toilets on site

Tram Service | **Crich Tramway Village** | Derbyshire

Member: HRA, TT
An experience of living transport history with vintage horse-drawn, steam and electric trams running through a re-created townscape of authentic buildings, stone setts, iron railings and historic street furniture. The heart of the Museum is its collection of over 70 vintage trams and you can enjoy the thrill of travelling on the scenic mile-long track
Location: Crich, Nr Matlock, Derbyshire DE4 5DP
OS reference: SK 345549
Manager: Vacant
Operating society/organisation: Tramway Museum Society
Telephone: 01773 854321
Internet address: *Web site:* www.tramway.co.uk
Car park: Site; coach parking also available
Access by public transport: By rail, nearest main line stations: Cromford or Alfreton then by bus; or Whatstandwell and steep uphill walk
On site facilities: Souvenir shop, play areas, bookshop and picnic areas. 1-mile electric tramway. Tramway period street, depots, displays, exhibitions and video theatre. Large exhibition hall with new interpretive display depicting the history of the tram and Turn of the Century Trade Exhibition plus other exhibitions/displays
Refreshment facilities: Hot and cold snacks and meals
Public opening: Daily 11-26 February (10.30-16.00).
Weekends in March (10.30-16.00).
Daily 1 April until 29 October (10.00-17.30).
Weekends in November and December (10.30-16.00).
Special events: Battle of Britain — 16/17 April; Morris Minor Day — 23 April; 1950s Rock n' Roll Weekend — 30 April/1 May; Models Weekend plus Teddy Bears' Outing — 13/14 May; Folk Festival — 28/29 May; Tramathon

Locomotives

Name	*No*	*Builder*	*Type*	*Built*
—	—	B/Peacock (2464)	0-4-0VB tram loco	1885
—	—	E/Electric (717)	4wE	1927
*Rupert**	—	R/Hornsby (223741)	4wDM	1944
*GMJ**	—	R/Hornsby (326058)	4wDM	1952
—*	—	R/Hornsby (373363)	4wDM	1954

*not on display

Trams

No	*Operator*	*Built*
1	Derby	1904
1	Douglas Head Marine Drive	1896
1	Leamington & Warwick	1881
1	London Transport	1932
2	Blackpool & Fleetwood	1898
4	Blackpool Corp	1885
5	Blackpool	*1972
5	Gateshead & District	1927
7	Chesterfield	1904
8	Chesterfield	1899
9	Oporto	1873
10	Hill of Howth	1902
14	Grimsby & Immingham	1915
15	Sheffield	1874
21	Dundee & District	1894
22	Glasgow	1922
35	Edinburgh	1948
40	Blackpool & Fleetwood	†1914
40	Blackpool	1926
45	Southampton	1903
46	Sheffield	1899
(47)	New South Wales Govt	1885
49	Blackpool	1926
52	Gateshead & District	*1901
59	Blackpool	*1902
60	Johannesburg	1905
68	Paisley & District	1919
74	Sheffield	1900
76	Leicester	1904
102	Newcastle	1901
106	London County Council	1903
132	Kingston-upon-Hull	§1910
166	Blackpool	1927
167	Blackpool	1928
180	Leeds	1931
180	Prague	1908
189	Sheffield	1934
264	Sheffield	1937
273	Oporto	—
298	Blackpool	*1937

These two images show a contrast in preserved rail traction. On the left is a scene on the Colne Valley Railway as a single car DMU leaves the station whilst below Glasgow No 22 passes through the Bowes Lyon Bridge at Crich Tramway Village.
Both Phil Barnes

— 11 June; Emergency Vehicles Day — 25 June; MiniMeet — 16 July; The Jazz Years - 1920s and 1930s — 28/29 July; Austin Seven Day — 29 July; Lancashire & Yorkshire Day — 6 August; 1940s Weekend — 12/13 August; Transport Extravaganza — 27/28 August; Ford Capri Day — 3 September; Classic Ford Day — 10 September; Beetle Drive — 17 September; Enthusiasts' Day — 30 September; Treasure Trail — 21-29 October; Starlight Halloween — 28 October; East German Day — 5 November; Santa Special/ Christmas Street Fair — 9/10 December
Family tickets: Available
Facilities for disabled: Access to all public facilities, Braille guide book available, 1969 Berlin tram specially adapted to lift and carry people in wheelchairs. Also a 'wheelway', a smooth path routeing around and through cobbled areas
Special notes: Crich houses the largest collection of preserved trams in Europe and has a 1-mile working tramway on which restored electric trams are regularly operated. Special events are arranged at weekends and Bank Holidays throughout the season. Part of tram line occupies route of narrow gauge mineral railway built by George Stephenson

No	*Operator*	*Built*
331	Metropolitan Electric	1930
345	Leeds	*—
399	Leeds	1926
510	Sheffield	1950
600	Leeds	1931/54
602	Leeds	1953
674	New York 3rd Avenue Transit	1939
812	Glasgow	1900
869	Liverpool	1936
902	Halle	
1100	Glasgow	1928
1105	Glasgow	1929
1147	Hague	1957
1282	Glasgow	1940
1297	Glasgow	1948
1622	London Transport	1912
3006	Berlin	1969
—	London Tramways	c1895

*stored off-site
†on loan to Blackpool
§on loan to Hull Museum of Transport

Note: In addition to the trams (including examples from Czechoslovakia, Germany, The Netherlands, Portugal, USA and South Africa) — about a third of which have been restored to working order — there are a number of Works Cars not listed

Membership details: From above address
Membership journal: *The Journal* — quarterly

Museum

Darlington Railway Centre & Museum

County Durham

Member: HRA
The site as a whole is known as the Darlington Railway Centre and Museum, and is owned by Darlington Borough Council. Within the site are four separate buildings. The former North Road Station is run as a museum by the council. Darlington Railway Preservation Society occupies the former Stockton & Darlington Railway North Road Goods and the former S&DR Hopetown Carriage Works is divided between the A1 Steam Locomotive Trust and the North Eastern Locomotive Preservation Group. Darlington Model Railway Club occupies the former Goods Offices.

Locomotives

Name	*No*	*Origin*	*Class*	*Type*	*Built*
Locomotion	1	S&DR	—	0-4-0	1825
Derwent	25	S&DR	—	0-6-0	1845
—	1463	NER	1463	2-4-0	1885
—	910	NER	901	2-4-0	1875
Blue Peter	60532	LNER	A2	4-6-2	1948

Stock
1 Stockton & Darlington Rly passenger coach (1846)
1 North Eastern Railway Coach body (c1860)
1 NER 20-ton mineral wagon
1 Chaldron wagon

Owners
Locomotion, Derwent, 1463 and 910 are all on loan from the National Railway Museum
60532 on loan via the North Eastern Locomotive Preservation Group

All organisations except the Model Railway Club are members of the HRA.

The Ken Hoole Study Centre houses a collection of reference material on the railways of north-east England including the library of the North Eastern Railway Association (access by appointment).
Northern train services provide a link to Darlington's main line station and to Shildon, for 'Locomotion' and the Timothy Hackworth Museum
Museum Manager: Bob Clark
Location: North Road Station, Darlington, County Durham DL3 6ST. Approximately three-quarters of a mile north of town centre, off North Road (A167)
OS reference: NZ 289157
Telephone: (01325) 460532
Internet address: *Web site:* www.drcm.org.uk
Car park: At museum site
Access by public transport: Rail services to Darlington North Road station. Local bus services along North Road
Catering facilities: Buffet open 11.00-14.30 daily. Vending machines at other times
On site facilities: Souvenir and bookshop, toilets, meeting room
Public opening: Daily 10.00-17.00 (except 25/26 December and 1 January). Days and times may be subject to amendment
Special events: Contact for details, details will appear on the web site, or write or telephone
Facilities for disabled: Access to main museum building for wheelchairs. Disabled person's toilet. Parking spaces for disabled in forecourt
Membership details: Friends of Darlington Railway Museum, Darlington Railway Preservation Society, A1 Steam Locomotive Trust and North Eastern Locomotive Preservation Group. All can be contacted via the museum. Members of these organisations and registered supporters of the A1 Trust, members of the Museums Association and holders of HRA InterRail pases all receive free admission except on Thomas and Santa days
Note: The A1 Steam Locomotive Trust's part of the Carriage Works, where they are building a new Peppercorn Pacific, *Tornado*, is generally open to the public on Saturdays. The Goods Shed, and part of the Carriage Works occupied by the North Eastern Locomotive Preservation Group, where during 2006 they will be rebuilding their J72 and J27, are open only by appointment. Visitors are welcome at all buildings on the site, but are strongly advised to make arrangements in advance for all buildings other than the main station itself.

Darlington Railway Preservation Society

Member: HRA
Internet address: *Web site:* www.drps.visit.ws

Locomotives

Name	*No*	*Origin*	*Class*	*Type*	*Built*
—	78018	BR	2MT	2-6-0	1954

Industrial locomotives

Name	*No*	*Builder*	*Type*	*Built*
—	—	Bagnall (2898)	0-4-0F	1948
—	2	RSH (7925)	0-4-0DM	1959
—	1	Peckett (2142)	0-4-0ST	1953
David Payne	185	Fowler (4110006)	0-4-0DM	1950
Smiths Dock Co Ltd	—	Fowler (4200018)	0-4-0DM	1947
—	—	GEC	4wE	1928
—	—	R/Hornsby (279591)	0-4-0DM	1949
—	—	R/Hornsby*	4wDM	—
—	—	R/Hornsby*	4wDM	—
—	—	R/Hornsby*	4wDM	—

*1ft 6in gauge

Stock

Various wagons, steam and diesel cranes

A1 Steam Locomotive Trust

Member: HRA

Locomotives

Name	*No*	*Origin*	*Class*	*Type*	*Built*
Tornado	60163	A1SLT	8P6F	4-6-2	Under construction

Timetable Service

Dartmoor Railway

Devon

Member: HRA
Dartmoor Railway is a very young railway as far as tourism is concerned although the railway has been in existence for 140 years as the Southern Railway main line from Waterloo to Plymouth. The line only survived because of ballast supplies from Meldon Quarry. Dartmoor Railway is now part of the ECT Group offering a unique experience which encompasses access to Dartmoor National Park for everyone including the disabled, the less energetic and cyclists. Views of Meldon Quarry and workings. Meldon has expanded its visitor centre to include a history of

the Dartmoor railways and tramways. The Meldon Quarry station as well as Okehampton have been restored to the 1950s style
Headquarters: Dartmoor Railway Ltd, Okehampton Station, Okehampton, Devon EX20 1EJ
Telephone: 01837 55637
Fax: 01837 54588
Internet addresses:
Web site: www.dartmoorrailway.co.uk
Managing Director: John Hummel
General Manager: Stuart Farmer
Project Manager: Robin Townshend
Main station: Okehampton
Other public stations: Meldon Quarry for Meldon Viaduct, access only by rail and National Cyclepath. Sampford Courtenay has access by road and rail, free parking
Access by public transport: Main line trains on Sundays from end of May to end of September. Bus on Sundays all year round
Refreshment facilities: Fully licensed buffets at Okehampton and Meldon
Model & Gift shops: Extensive model and gift shop at Okehampton. Books and souvenirs also available at Meldon
Depot: Meldon Quarry, access only by rail and National Cyclepath
Length of line: 15.5 miles from Coleford Junction-Meldon Quarry
Passenger trains: Services between Sampford Courtenay-Okehampton-Meldon operate every weekend and Bank Holiday, except Christmas Day and Boxing Day, throughout the year. Open daily during the summer holidays and extended days opening at Easter, May Bank Holiday and school half terms. Sunday Rover trains operate between Exeter and Okehampton from May to September. Call for further information
Special events: Sunday lunches and evening special trains aboard the new 'Dartmoor Belle' First Class wine and dine train throughout the year
Special notes: All trains have provision for bicycles. Visits for interest groups and education tours. Trains are available for private hire. Special function coach can be added to train for both corporate and special functions. 'Dartmoor Pony' available for private short

Locomotives and multiple-units (in use as hauled stock)

Name	*No*	*Origin*	*Class*	*Type*	*Built*
Bluebell Mel	08937	BR	08	0-6-0DE	1962
—	31301*	BR	31	A1A-A1A	1962
—	31415*	BR	31	A1A-A1A	1961
—	31423*	BR	31	A1A-A1A	1960
—	31426*	BR	31	A1A-A1A	1960
—	31437*	BR	31	A1A-A1A	1960
—	31439*	BR	31	A1A-A1A	1960
—	47348*	BR	47	Co-Co	1965
—	47716*	BR	47	Co-Co	1966
—	73103*	BR	73	Bo-Bo	1965
—	73117*	BR	73	Bo-Bo	1966
—	73134*	BR	73	Bo-Bo	1966
—	663	NSR	600	0-6-0DE	1956
—	61743	BR	411	DMSO	1956
unit 412	70826	BR	438 / 4TC	DTSO	1967
unit 412	70860	BR	438 / 4TC	DTSO	1967
unit 412	76301	BR	438 / 4TC	DTSO	1967
unit 412	76302	BR	438 / 4TC	DTSO	1967
unit 205028	60146	BR	205	DMBS	1957
unit 205028	60673	BR	205	DMBS	1957
unit 205028	60827	BR	205	DTC	1957
unit 205032	60150	BR	205	DMBS	1957
unit 205032	60677	BR	205	DMBS	1957
unit 205032	60831	BR	205	DTC	1957
unit 1198	61736	BR	411 / 3CEP	DMSO	
unit 1198	61737	BR	411 / 3CEP	DMSO	
unit 1198	70573	BR	411 / 3CEP	DBC	
unit 1399	62385	BR	421 / 4CIG	MBSO	
unit 1399	70508	BR	421 / 4CIG	TSOL	
unit 1399	76747	BR	421 / 4CIG	DTCSOL	
unit 1399	76818	BR	421 / 4CIG	DTCSOL	
—	69332	BR	423 / 4VEP	TRB	1969
—	69310†	BR	422	TRBS	1965

†static buffet at Meldon
*owned by FM Rail

Locomotive notes:
FM Rail locomotives on scheduled service workings: 47716, 73117, 73134

Industrial locomotives

Name	*No*	*Builder*	*Type*	*Built*
—	S103*	H/Clarke (1864)	0-6-0T	1952
Flying Falcon	MSC 0256*	Fowler	0-6-0DE	

*undergoing restoration, expected to enter service in 2006

Stock
Courier vehicle NXX No 80225;
ex-BR Mk 1s RBR: 1691, 1697; FO 3125 (leased from Riviera Trains); BSK 21224 (leased from Riviera Trains)
ex-BR Mk 2s TSO 5920, 6002, 6181; FO 3353, 3354, 3411, 3387, 3402, 3425; RBF 1213
ex-BR Mk 3 sleeping cars 10518, 10595, 10611, 10727;
1 ex-BR sleeping car 10000; function coach, converted from 99622;
Generator coach, DB977335 (FM Rail owned). Former 'Queen of Scots' saloon No 10000. CCT van and Ferrywagon
Following EMU vehicles for spares reclamation only: 61742, 70812
Selection of maintenance vehicles including horse box S96300 converted to Generator coach for 'Dartmoor Belle'

Owners
Class 31s, 47 and 73s — FM Rail
Class 205 units stored on behalf of Porterbrook Leasing Co

excursions
Facilities for disabled: Facilities on train and buffets for disabled and accessible by wheelchair
Membership details: Friends of Dartmoor Railway c/o above address. Gives discount to members for train rides, gifts, etc

663 Andy Mills
Unit 1198 the EMU Preservation Society
Unit 1399 Edward lloyd

Membership journal: Three times a year

Timetable Service

Dean Forest Railway

Glos

Member: HRA, TT
Passenger services operate between Norchard and Lydney Junction (Severn & Wye Joint), and Norchard and Parkend.The line boasts five level crossings, three of which are manually operated
Location: Headquarters at Norchard station on the B4234. Signposted off the A48 Lydney bypass to town centre whence B4234 commences
OS reference: SO 629044
Operating society/organisation: Dean Forest Railway Society in conjunction with owning company, Forest of Dean Railway Ltd
Telephone: (01594) 843423 information line; (01594) 845840 (daytime)
Internet address: *Web site:* www.deanforestrailway.co.uk
Car park: Norchard only, adequate for cars and coaches. No parking at other stations
Access by public transport: Main line station at Lydney. Stagecoach Red & White buses (service 73 Monday-Saturday) Gloucester-Lydney-Newport
On site facilities: Shop at Norchard with museum, riverside walk and forest walks
Catering facilities: Hot and cold meals at Coaches Café on Norchard platform on service days. Parties catered for by appointment. Sunday lunchtime service by 'Royal Forester' first class dining car service, runs on selected Sundays in season, advance booking essential
Length of line: 4.25 miles
Public opening: Daily for static display — shop and museum, open every Saturday and Sunday 11.00-

Locomotives and multiple-units

Name	*No*	*Origin*	*Class*	*Type*	*Built*
—	28	TVR	O1	0-6-2T	1897
—	5541	GWR	4575	2-6-2T	1928
—	9681	GWR	5700	0-6-0PT	1949
—	03128	BR	03	0-6-0DM	1960
Charlie	13308	BR	08	0-6-0DE	1956
—	08734	BR	08	0-6-0DE	1960
Gladys§	D3937	BR	08	0-6-0DE	1960
—	D9555	BR	14	0-6-0DH	1965
—	5386	BR	27	Bo-Bo	1962
—	D7633	BR	25	Bo-Bo	1965
—	D5634	BR	31	A1A-A1A	1960
—	37263	BR	37	Co-Co	1965
—	73901	BR	73	Bo-Bo	1962
—*	73002	BR	73	Bo-Bo	1962
—§	E6005	BR	73	Bo-Bo	1962
—§	E6006	BR	73	Bo-Bo	1962
The Royal Alex	73101	BR	73	Bo-Bo	1965
—	50619	BR	108	DMBS	1958
—	51914	BR	108	DMS	1960
—	56492	BR	108	DTC	1960
—	56495	BR	108	DTC	1960
—	62364	BR	421	MBSO	
—	62378	BR	421	MBSO	
—	70273	BR	411	TSOL	
—	76726	BR	421	DTCSoL	
—	76740	BR	421	DTCSoL	
—	76797	BR	421	DTCSoL	
—	76811	BR	421	DTCSoL	

§on loan to Severn Valley Railway
*mobile stores vehicle

Industrial locomotives

Name	*No*	*Builder*	*Type*	*Built*
—	—	Barclay (2221)	0-4-0ST	1946
Uskmouth No 1	—	Peckett (2147)	0-4-0ST	1952
Wilbert	—	Hunslet (3806)	0-6-0ST	1953
Warrior	—	Hunslet (3823)	0-6-0ST	1954
—	—	Hunslet (2145)	0-4-0DM	1940
—	—	Fowler (4210127)	0-4-0DM	1957
—	—	Hibberd (3947)	4wPM	1960

Stock
2 ex-GWR coaches; 12 ex-BR coaches; 1 DFR constructed Cafeteria coach

17.00 and weekdays late March to Christmas.

Steam train rides supported by heritage DMUs: All Sundays 26 March to 30 October; Good Friday, Easter Saturday and all Bank Holiday Sundays and Mondays (Christmas excepted). Wednesdays June to September. Thursdays in August.

Heritage DMU service operates alone most Saturdays June, July and September

Special events: Day out with Thomas — 7-10 April, 1-4 June, 1-3 September; Forces Military Weekend — 23/24 September; Halloween Ghost Trains — 28 October; Carol Service Special (to St Mary's Church, Lydney) — tbc; Santa Specials — 3, 9/10, 16/17, 22-24 December

(static at Norchard), 3 Wickham trolleys; 1 steam crane Thos Smith (Rodley) TS 5027 (10ton); Booth 15-24 tonne diesel-hydraulic crane, Cowans & Sheldon 30-ton diesel crane (ADRC 96101), Schöma p-way tram and trailer

Owners

28 the National Railway Museum
5541 the Forest Prairie Fund
9681 the Dean Forest Locomotive Group
03128, 13308, D3937, 08734, 5386, D5634, D7633, 73901, 73002, E6005, E6006 and 73101 the Dean Forest Diesel Association
37263 the Virgin CrossCountry Class 37 Group
Class 108 DMUs the Dean Forest DMU Group

Facilities for disabled: Access to museum, shop, toilets and trains
Membership details: Mr R. Bramwell, 4 Poole Ground, Highnam, Gloucester GL2 8NA and web site
Membership journal: *Forest Venturer* — half yearly
Marketing name: The Friendly Forest Line — re-creating the railway heritage of the Royal Forest of Dean

Steam Centre | Derwent Valley Light Railway | North Yorkshire

Member: TT
The DVR's most notable fact about its history is that it was never nationalised. Private from its inception until the final section was closed in the late 1980s. The line was mothballed until 1989 when it was transformed into a cycleway by Sustrans. A half-mile section adjacent to the Yorkshire Museum of Farming was donated to the museum along with the most necessary Light Railway Order.
Location: Murton Park, Murton Lane, Murton, Nr York YO19 5UF
Operating society/organisation: Derwent Valley Light Railway Society
Telephone: (01904) 489966
Internet address: *e-mail:* jdunn@murphysden.karoo.co.uk
web site: www.dvlr.org.uk
OS reference: SE 651537
On site facilities: Refreshments, souvenir shop (Yorkshire Museum of Farming)
Car park: Free, on site
Length of line: Half-mile
Access by public transport: York-Stamford Bridge and York-Hull bus services from York main line station. (Tel: 0870 608 2608 or www.yorkshiretravel.net)
Souvenir shops: Within the Yorkshire Museum of Farming, and a railway souvenir shop within the station (open when trains running). Once the entrance fee to the Yorkshire Museum of Farming has been paid train rides are free
Facilities for disabled: Toilets, ramped ways, etc
Public opening: Open daily mid-February-end October, for the Yorkshire Museum of Farming, Danelaw (Viking) Village and the Derwent Valley Light Railway. Trains operate Sundays and Bank Holidays Easter-end September and for Santa Specials
Special events: Santa Special — weekends and certain weekdays in December
Membership details: 64 Wolfreton Lane, Willerby, East Yorkshire HU10 6PT
Society journal: *DVLR News* (quarterly)

Locomotives

Name	*No*	*Origin*	*Class*	*Type*	*Built*
—	03079	BR	03	0-6-0DM	1960

Industrial locomotives

Name	*No*	*Builder*	*Type*	*Built*
—	8	A/Barclay (2369)	0-4-0ST	1955
—	65	H/Clarke (1631)	0-6-0T	1929
—	—	Fowler (4200022)	0-4-0DM	1948
Churchill	—	Fowler (410005)	0-4-0DM	1947
Jim	—	R/Hornsby (417892)	4wDM	1959
—	97088	R/Hornsby (466630)	4wDM	1962
British Sugar York	—	R/Hornsby (327964)	0-4-0DM	1953

Rolling stock

1 NER coach, 1 NER coach body, 1 Swiss-style coach (built in 2003), 12 various freight wagons, and 1 steam rail crane

Devon Railway Centre

The Devon Railway Centre features a lovingly restored Victorian Great Western Railway station together with historic locomotives, carriages and wagons as featured on TV. Unlimited passenger rides can be taken on the 2ft gauge railway and miniature railways. There is also a large model railway exhibition featuring 15 working layouts including Polchester and Chiltern Green. All-inclusive admission price

Location: Alongside Bickleigh Bridge over the River Exe on the A396, four miles south of Tiverton and 10 miles north of Exeter

General Manager: Matthew Gicquel

Contact address: Devon Railway Centre, Bickleigh, Nr Tiverton, Devon EX16 8RG

Telephone: 01884 855671

Internet address: *Web site:* www.devonrailwaycentre.co.uk

OS reference: SS 938074

Car park: On site

Access by public transport: Regular bus service from Tiverton and Exeter, routes 55 and 55A

On site facilities: Passenger-carrying line, large model railway exhibition, restored GWR station, standard gauge static display, historic narrow gauge collection, miniature railway, refreshments and souvenirs, crazy golf, drive your own miniature railway

Length of line: Half mile, 2ft gauge; half mile 7.25in gauge, 200yd standard gauge demonstration line; 100yd 7.25in gauge drive your own train

Opening times: 10.30-17.00. 8 April until 29 October. Daily 8-23 April, 28 May-10 September, 21-29 October (closed Mondays in June). Wednesdays to Sundays 3-27 May, 13 September-1 October. Saturdays/Sundays in October. Also open 1 May.

Special events: Gala weekend — 5/6 August; Santa Specials — 9/10, 16/17 December. Phone for further details

Industrial locomotives (2ft gauge)

Name	*No*	*Builder*	*Type*	*Built*
—	—	O&K (5744)	0-4-0WT	1912
Horatio	—	R/Hornsby (217967)	4wDM	1942
Pen-yr-Orsedd	—	R/Hornsby (235711)	4wDM	1945
Ruston	—	R/Hornsby (418770)	4wDM	1957
Claude W. Lane	—†	R/Hornsby (435398)	4wDM	1959
Planet	—	Planet (2201)	4wDM	1939
Lister	—	Lister (6299)	4wPM	1935
—	—	Lister (34025)	4wDM	1949
—	—	Planet (2025)	4wDM	1937
—	—	Kent (1747)	4wPM	1931
Ivor	—	M/Rail (8877)	4wDM	1944
—	—	M/Rail (20073)	4wDM	1950
Sir Tom	—	M/Rail (40s273)	4wDM	1966
—	—*	M/Rail (105H006)	4wDM	1919
—	—	BEV	0-4-0BE	c1970

†2ft 9in gauge
*3ft gauge

Industrial locomotives (standard gauge)

Name	*No*	*Builder*	*Type*	*Built*
Boris	1	Baguley (3357)	0-4-0DM	1952

Locomotive notes: All locomotives are expected to be working in 2006, except for *Claude,* Kent and Planet 2025

Rolling stock: All 2ft gauge unless indicated. Two Alan Keef bogie passenger coaches, Two Hudson bogie passenger coaches, Hudson 4-wheel coach, Dinorwic Yellow Coach, 2 slate slab wagons, GWR slate wagon, 7 skip wagons, 4 mine tubs, RAF bomb wagon, Hudson 3-plank wagon, 2 bogie coach chassis. Lochaber incline wagon (3ft gauge), copper mine tub (20in gauge), Cattybrook brickworks wagon (2ft 10in gauge), assorted works wagons. Standard gauge: 2 ex-BR Mk 1 coaches, 1 ex-BR BG

Miniature railway locomotives (7.25in gauge)

Name	*No*	*Builder*	*Type*	*Built*
—	D7011*	Cromar White	Bo-BoBE	1969
—	D7029	Cromar White	Bo-BoPM	1972
(Intercity)	—	—	Bo-BoBE	c1995
—	—	Pfeiferbahn	4wPH	1993
—	—	Chandler	4wBE	1978
—	7	Parkside	4WBER S/O	2002

*rebuilt from petrol to battery power by DRC during 2002
7 is a drive your own train operated by coin in the slot

Rolling stock: 2 sit-in coaches built by DRC, 1 sit-astride coach

Right: No 8, a Barclay-built 0-4-0ST in action on one of the Derwent Valley Railway's Santa Specials. *DVLR*

Below: A new arrival at the Devon Railway Centre during 2005 was this Orenstein & Koppel 0-4-0WT imported from Argentina. The other steam locomotive that can be seen is *Pixie*, on loan during 2005 from the Leighton Buzzard Railway. *Phil Barnes*

Steam Centre

Didcot Railway Centre

Oxfordshire

Member: HRA, TT
The Great Western Railway was incorporated in 1835 to build the railway from Bristol to London and it was designed and engineered by Isambard Kingdom Brunel to be the finest in the land. At Didcot, half way between Bristol and London, members of the Great Western Society have created a living museum of the GWR. It is based around the original engine shed and depot, to which has been added a typical branch line with a country station, signalling demonstrations and re-creation of Brunel's broad gauge trackwork and newly built replica of the locomotive *Fire Fly* dating from 1840. There is a large collection of GWR steam locomotives, carriages and wagons. On steamdays the locomotives come to life and you can ride in the 1930s trains on one or both of the demonstration lines
General Manager: Michael Dean
Location: Adjacent to main line station, Didcot, Oxfordshire. Access via station subway
OS reference: SU 525907
Operating society/organisation: Great Western Society Ltd, Didcot Railway Centre, Didcot, Oxon OX11 7NJ
Telephone: Didcot (01235) 817200
Internet address: *Web site:* www.didcotrailwaycentre.org.uk
Car park: Didcot station
Access by public transport: Entry is at Didcot Parkway rail station served by First Great Western trains from London (Paddington), the Thames Valley, Oxford, Birmingham, Bristol, etc.

On the A4130 road signed from the M4 motorway (jct 13) and A34
Refreshment facilities: Refreshment room open all days centre is open (lunches, snacks). Picnic area.

Lunch is available in the GWR super-saloon carriages on Mother's Day 26 March, Father's Day 18 June, or Victorian Pudding Evenings 19, 26 July (please contact the centre in advance)
On site facilities: GWR locomotive depot, replica GWR station, museum and broad gauge demonstration. Souvenir sales. Rides are available on the demonstration lines on Steamdays.

Admission prices vary according to events and include train rides on Steamdays. Party rates available for more than 15 persons, guided tours, evening visits and special menus for lunch or tea can be arranged. Private steamings when visitors can try their hand at driving locomotives can be arranged
Length of line: 1,000yd
Public opening: Saturdays and Sundays all year. Daily 1-17 April,

Locomotives

Name	*No*	*Origin*	*Class//Bilder*	*Type*	*Built*
Fire Fly	—†	GWR	'Fire Fly'	2-2-2	2005
—	22	GWR	Diesel Railcar	1A-A1	1940
—	1338	GWR (Cardiff Rly)	Kitson (3799)	0-4-0ST	1898
Trojan	1340	GWR	Avonside (1380)	0-4-0ST	1897
—	1363	GWR	1361	0-6-0ST	1910
—	3650	GWR	5700	0-6-0PT	1939
—	3738	GWR	5700	0-6-0PT	1937
—	3822	GWR	2884	2-8-0	1940
Pendennis Castle	4079	GWR	'Castle'	4-6-0	1924
—	4144	GWR	5101	2-6-2T	1946
—	4866	GWR	4800	0-4-2T	1936
*Lady of Legend**	2999	GWR	'Saint'	4-6-0	1929
Earl Bathurst	5051	GWR	'Castle'	4-6-0	1936
—	5322	GWR	4300	2-6-0	1917
—	5572	GWR	4575	2-6-2T	1927
Hinderton Hall	5900	GWR	'Hall'	4-6-0	1931
King Edward II	6023	GWR	'King'	4-6-0	1930
—	6106	GWR	6100	2-6-2T	1931
—	6697	GWR	5600	0-6-2T	1928
Burton Agnes Hall	6998	GWR	'Hall'	4-6-0	1949
—	7202	GWR	7200	2-8-2T	1934
Cookham Manor	7808	GWR	'Manor'	4-6-0	1938
—	D3771	BR	08	0-6-0DE	1959
Pontyberem	2	Burry Port & Gwendraeth Valley Rly		0-6-0ST	1900
Shannon	5	Wantage Tramway		0-4-0WT	1857

†broad gauge reconstruction of 1840 design
*under construction using frames of No 4942 *Maindy Hall*

Industrial locomotives

Name	*No*	*Builder*	*Type*	*Built*
Bonnie Prince Charlie	1	RSH (7544)	0-4-0ST	1949
—	26	Hunslet (5238)	0-6-0DH	1962

Locomotive notes: Locomotives available in 2006 should be: 22, 1338, 1340, 3822, 4144, 5051. Locomotives under restoration include: 3650, 4079, 5322, 6023, 7202. 4079 was repatriated from Australia in 2000

Stock
Over 40 ex-GWR coaches are preserved along with numerous ex-GWR freight wagons

Owner
5 on loan from the National Railway Museum

27 May-4 June, 24 June-September, 21-29 October, 27 December to 1 January 2007. Steamdays 2, 9, 14-17 April, all Saturdays, Sundays and Bank Holidays 29 April-3 September, All Wednesdays 12 July-30 August, 25, 28/29 October. Open 10.00-16.00 (weekends and Steamdays March-October 10.00-17.00)
Train rides: On Steamdays there is normally continuous operation of the passenger train, interrupted by Travelling Post Office demonstrations and turning of the locomotives on some days
Special events: Brunel Bicentennial with *Fire Fly* — 9 April; Day out with Thomas — 6-8 October; Family Activity Steamdays — 27-29 May, 29/30 July; Broad gauge steamings with *Fire Fly* — 2/3 June; 1/2 July, 5/6 August; Little & Large Weekend (with Pendon Museum) — 23/24 September; An audience with *Fire Fly* — 28/29 October; Thomas Santa Special — 8-10, 15-17, 22-24 December; New Year Steamings — 31 December, January 2007
Facilities for disabled: Visitors are advised that there is an awkward flight of steps at the entrance, with level access within the centre (help can normally be given with prior advice)
Membership details: Charles Roberts, at above address
Membership journals: *Great Western Echo* — quarterly; *National Newsletter* — seven times annually
Note: Children under 12 must be accompanied by an adult

Miniature Railway

Dobwalls Family Adventure Park

Cornwall

Location: Just off the A38 at Liskeard
Headquarters: Dobwalls, Nr Liskeard, Cornwall PL14 6HB
Contact: General Manager: Lyn Southern
Telephone: (01579) 320325/321129
Fax: (01579) 321345
Internet address:
Web site: www.dobwalls adventurepark.co.uk
Access by public transport: By train to Liskeard — 3 miles; by bus — National Express coaches to/from Cornwall via Plymouth stop in Dobwalls village; By car — signposted off A38
On site facilities: Refreshments, picnic areas, souvenirs and gift shop, children's indoor and outdoor adventure playground, wildlife art gallery, steam back in time. Toilets inc disabled, mother & baby facilities
Length of line: 7.25in gauge; two 1-mile long routese
Period of public operation: Daily Easter-end of October. 10.30-17.00. Closed some days in early/late season
Facilities for disabled: Wheelchair access throughout (free loan, subject to availability), toilets

Locomotives (7.25in gauge)

Name	*No*	*Builder*	*Type*	*Built*
General Palmer	488	Curwen	2-8-2	1971
Queen of Wyoming	818	S/Lamb	4-8-4	1974
William Jeffers	4008	S/Lamb	4-8-8-4	1978
Centennial	6908	S/Lamb	Do-Do	1979
Otto Mears	498	Curwen	2-8-2	1980
Mathias Baldwin	3008	S/Lamb	Bo-Bo	1980
Queen of Nebraska	838	S/Lamb	4-8-4	1981
Spirit of America	248	S/Lamb	Co-Co+Co-Co	1983
Pioneer	5908	S/Lamb	Co-Co	1989

Operating Museum

East Anglia Transport Museum

Suffolk

Member: TT
The East Suffolk Light Railway is the title given to the 2ft gauge railway, which winds its way 300yd or so along the northern perimeter of the museum site, between the stations of Chapel Road and Woodside. The railway commenced operation in 1973 and aims to re-create a typical passenger-carrying light railway of years gone by. Many aspects of railway interest can be found along its length. The track came from Leziate sand quarry and Canvey Island, as well as from the Southwold Railway, and signals from various local locations; all of which help to set the overall scene
Location: Carlton Colville, three miles south-west of Lowestoft in Suffolk
OS reference: TM 505903
Operating society/organisation: East Anglia Transport Museum Society Ltd, Chapel Road, Carlton Colville, Lowestoft, Suffolk NR33 8BL
Telephone: (01502) 518459
Internet address: *Web site:* www.eatm.org.uk

Car park: Adjacent
Access by public transport: First Eastern Counties 111, 112 and X2 (Monday-Saturday); First Eastern Counties X71 (Sundays and Bank Holidays) from Lowestoft. Main line rail, Oulton Broad South (1.5 miles) then Ambassador bus 606, 607, 608 or 609
On site facilities: Refreshments, picnic areas, souvenir and bookshop, toilets (including disabled), working transport museum, including trams, narrow gauge railway, trolleybuses, steamrollers and other commercial and public transport vehicles. Unlimited free rides
Public opening: Sundays and Bank Holidays (11.00-17.00) April until end of September. Also Saturdays (14.00-17.00) June to September. Midsummer opening, daily (except Mondays) 18 July to 1 September (14.00-17.00).
Last admission 1 hour before closing

Industrial locomotives

Name	No	Builder	Type	Built
Aldeburgh	2	M/Rail (5912)	4wDM	1934
Leiston	4	R/Hornsby (177604)	4wDM	1936
Orfordness	5	M/Rail (22209)	4wDM	1964
Thorpeness	6	M/Rail (22211)	4wDM	1964

Trams

No	Trucks	Body	Date	Operator
11	Maley & Taunton	E/Electric	1939	Blackpool Corp
14	Brill	Milnes	1904	Lowestoft Corp
159	Preston McGuire	Blackpool Corp	1927	Blackpool Corp
474	Beijnes	Beijnes	1929	Amsterdam
1858	EMB	E/Electric	1930	London Transport

Stock
Locally designed and built covered coach, plus combined coach and brake van, suitable for wheelchairs. Small selection of wagons. Van body ex-Southwold Railway

Special events: Please phone for details
Special notes: Limited facilities for the disabled. Pre-booked party rates
Membership details: From the above address

Steam Centre

East Anglian Railway Museum

Essex

Member: HRA, TT, AIM, EETB, EATL
Adjacent to Chappel Viaduct which is the most spectacular railway structure in East Anglia
Location: Chappel & Wakes Colne Station, near Colchester
OS reference: TL 898289
Chairman: Mike Stanbury
Operating society/organisation: East Anglian Railway Museum, Chappel & Wakes Colne Station, Station Road, Wakes Colne, Essex CO6 2DS. Registered charity No 1001579
Telephone: Colchester (01206) 242524
Fax: 0870 1258315
Internet address: *e-mail:* information@earm.co.uk
Web site: www.earm.co.uk
Car park: On site
Access by public transport: 'one' Great Eastern Chappel & Wakes Colne station. Also Eastern National/Hedingham Omnibus service No 88 Colchester-Halstead (hourly). Sundays Eastern National

Locomotives and multiple-units

Name	No	Origin	Class	Type	Built
A. J. Hill	69621†	GER	N7	0-6-2T	1924
—	D2279	BR	04	0-6-0DM	1960
—	50599	BR	108	DMBS	1958
—	54223	BR	108	DTCL	1959
—	51213	BR	101	DMBS	1959
—	51505	BR	101	DMC	1959
—	56358	BR	101	DTC	1959
—	54365	BR	101	DTCL	1958

† on loan to North Norfolk Railway

Industrial locomotives

Name	No	Builder	Type	Built
Jubilee	—	Bagnall (2542)	0-4-0ST	1936
—	11	Barclay (1047)	0-4-0ST	1905
Belvoir	—	Barclay (2350)	0-6-0ST	1954
Jeffery	2039	Peckett (2039)	0-4-0ST	1943
Penn Green	54	RSH (7031)	0-6-0ST	1941
—	AMW144	Barclay (333)	0-4-0DM	1938
—	23	Fowler (4220039)	0-4-0DH	1965
—	2029	Simplex (2029)	0-4-0PM	1920

Stock
1 ex-LNER TSO coach; 1 fully restored GER 6-wheel full brake; 1 GER fully restored 4-wheel coach; 1 ex-GER bogie coach; 1 SR PMV; 1 ex-BR 13-ton open wagon; 2 ex-BR 16-ton mineral wagons; 1 Lo-mac wagon; 1 ex-LMS 12-ton open wagon; 1 Wickham Trolley; 1 GWR Toad brake van;

No 88C Colchester-Halstead (every 2 hours)
On site facilities: Refreshments, bookshop, museum, signalboxes, souvenir shop, picnic area, miniature railway and toilets
Public opening: Daily 10.00-16.30
Special events: Day out with Thomas — 14-17 April, 25-29 August; 7th Cider Festival — 8-11 June; Chappel Beer Festival — 5-9 September; Gauge One Exhibition and Steam Day — 1 October; Halloween Evening Steam — 27 October; Steam and Diesel Day — 29 October; Day out with Thomas and Santa Steamings — 9/10, 16/17, 20 December

Other dates include:
Diesel Days — 16 July, 13 August; MiniRail Days — 26 July, 2, 9 August, 25 October;
Railway Experience Courses — 29 April, 27 May, 3 June, 1, 29 July, 30 October;
Steam Days — 30 April, 1, 28/29 May, 4 June, 2, 30 July, 6, 13 August, 24 September
Family tickets: Available on all days (unlimited rides on steam days)
Special notes: Steam days as in Special Events list. Driver experience courses available on a number of dates throughout 2006; please phone for details or book online at http://www.earm.co.uk

Three restored signalboxes, large goods shed and restoration shed. Original Victorian country junction station. Schools days and Santa Steamings. Disabled visitors welcome — prior advice appreciated. Guided tours by prior arrangement. Light refreshments daily, Signals café on event days
Membership details: Membership Secretary, 50 Ayr Way, Rise Park, Romford, Essex RM1 4UH
Membership journal: *Stour Valley Steam* — 3 times/year

1 ex-BR brake van; Somersham 'pump' trolley, 1 Grafton steam crane, 1 LMS 5 plank wagon, 1 BR cattle van (on loan ex-NRM), 1 BR special tank wagons, 1 Molasses tank wagon

Timetable Service

East Kent Railway

Kent

Member: HRA
The East Kent Light Railway Society was formed in 1985 with the aim of preserving the remaining 3-mile section of the Colonel Stephens light railway which originally ran from Shepherdswell to Wingham. Passenger-carrying operations between Shepherdswell and Eythorne started during 1995, and 1996 saw the first steam on the line for over 30 years. The extension to Wigmore Lane opened in August 2005 and is used on some special events
Location: Station Road, Shepherdswell, Dover, Kent CT15 7PD
Internet address: *Web site:* www.eastkentrailway.com
OS reference: TR 258483
Operating organisation: East Kent Railway Trust
Car park: Shepherdswell and Eythorne stations
Access by public transport: Main line trains to Shepherdswell station (adjacent) tel: 08457 484950
On site facilities: Light refreshments, book and souvenir shop, museum, plus 3.5/5in gauge steam railway. Picnic area and toilets. Restored signalbox visitor.

Locomotives and multiple-units

Name	*No*	*Origin*	*Class*	*Type*	*Built*
—	09025	BR	09	0-6-0DE	1961
—	53256	M/Cam	101	DMBS	1957
—	54343	M/Cam	101	DTC(L)	1958
—	65373*	BR	2EPB/416	DMBS	1953
—	77558*	BR	2EPB/416	DTS	1953
—	68001	BR	MLV/419	MLV	1959
—	68002	BR	MLV/419	MLV	1959
—	61229†	BR	412/CEP	DMSO(A)	c1956
—	61230†	BR	412/CEP	DMSO(A)	c1956
—	69345†	BR	412/BEP	TSRB	c1956
—	70235†	BR	412/CEP	TBCK	c1956
—	60154§	BR	205	DMBS	1957
—	60800§	BR	205	DTCL	1957

§unit No 1101
*unit No 5759
†unit No 7105

Industrial locomotives

Name	*No*	*Builder*	*Type*	*Built*
Richborough Castle	—	E/Electric (D1197)	0-6-0D	1967
The Buffs	—	R/Hornsby (466616)	0-6-0DH	1961
Snowdon	—	Fowler (416002)	0-4-0DM	1952
St Dunstan	—	Avonside (2004)	0-6-0ST	1927

Rolling stock
Leyland Experimental coach, LMS brake third, LMS full brake (BG), BR Mk 1s TSO, BR Mk 2 TSO and a selection of freight vehicles including an SR GUV

Owners
St Dunstan and diesel multiple-units the East Kent Railway Trust
LMS brake third the Walmer Model Railway Group

Leyland Experimental Coach the Nene Valley Railway
EMU vehicles the EPB Preservation Group

Eythorne: Signalbox and small shop
Public opening: Most weekends throughout the year for static displays. Passenger trains — Easter to September Sundays and Bank Holidays
Special events: Mother's Day — 26 March; Easter Bunny Specials — 14-17 April; Tedies Picnin — 27-29 May; Father's Day — 18 June; Senior Citizens Day (£1 day rover fare for senior citizens) — 16 July; August Gala Weekend (intensive timetable using all avaliable stock) — 26-28 August; Bus Rally (including local vintage bus tours) — 10 September; Ghost Trains (please dress for the occasion) — 28/29 October; Santa by Train — 3, 9/10, 16/17, 22-24 December
Events & site answerphone: 01304 832042
Facilities for disabled: Limited access to buffet, and platforms at both stations
Membership details: EKR Membership Secretary, Shepherdswell Station, Dover, Kent CT15 7PD
Membership journal: *East Kent Railway News,* 3 times a year

Timetable Service

East Lancashire Railway

Lancashire

Member: HRA, TT
A very popular railway run by the East Lancs Railway Society in close co-operation with local authorities, the line won the 1987 ARPS award. Visit the line to find out the cause of the line's popularity and success
Location: Bolton Street Station, Bury, Lancashire BL9 0EY
OS reference: SD 803109
Publicity Director: Graham Vevers
Operating society/organisation: East Lancashire Railway Preservation Society
Telephone: 0161 764 7790
Internet address: *Web site:* www.east-lancs-rly.co.uk
Access by public transport: Main line services to Manchester, Bolton, Rochdale and Burnley. Metrolink from central Manchester to Bury Interchange. Various bus services also operate to Bury, Ramsbottom or Rawtenstall from the main line stations listed
On site facilities: Refreshments normally available when trains are running. Buffet car service on most trains. Souvenir shop, transport museum
Length of line: Approximately 12 miles
Public opening: Steam- and diesel-hauled services operate on Saturdays, Sundays and Bank Holidays throughout the year. Santa Specials (advance booking only) in December
Special events: Steam Event — 1/2 April; Day out with Thomas —

Locomotives and multiple-units

Name	*No*	*Origin*	*Class*	*Type*	*Built*
—	7229	GWR	7200	2-8-2T	1935
—	52322	L&Y	27	0-6-0	1896
—	42765	LMS	5P4F	2-6-0	1927
—	44871	LMS	5MT	4-6-0	1945
—	45337	LMS	5MT	4-6-0	1937
The Lancashire Fusilier	45407*	LMS	5MT	4-6-0	1937
Leander	5690	LMS	'Jubilee'	4-6-0	1936
Princess Elizabeth	6201	LMS	'Princess'	4-6-2	1933
—	46428	LMS	2MT	2-6-0	1948
—	47324	LMS	3F	0-6-0T	1926
Shaw Savill	35009	SR	MN	4-6-2	1945
Duke of Gloucester	71000	BR	8P	4-6-2	1954
—	76079*	BR	4MT	2-6-0	1957
—	80097	BR	4MT	2-6-4T	1954
—	11506	BR	01	0-4-0DM	1956
—	D2062	BR	03	0-6-0DM	1959
—	D3232	BR	08	0-6-0DE	1956
—	08445	BR	08	0-6-0DE	1958
—	08479	BR	08	0-6-0DE	1958
—	08944	BR	08	0-6-0DE	1962
—	D9531	BR	14	0-6-0DH	1965
—	D8233	BR	15	Bo-Bo	1959
—	20087	BR	20	Bo-Bo	1961
—	D5054	BR	24	Bo-Bo	1960
—	D5705	BR	28	Co-Bo	1958
—	D5600	BR	31	A1A-A1A	1959
—	31467	BR	31	A1A-A1A	1960
—	31556	BR	31	A1A-A1A	1961
—	D7076	BR	35	B-B	1963
—	33117	BR	33	Bo-Bo	1960
—	D335	BR	40	1Co-Co1	1961
—	D345	BR	40	1Co-Co1	1961
Onslaught	D832	BR	42	B-B	1961
3rd Carabinier	45135	BR	45	1Co-Co1	1961
Gateshead	47402	BR	47	Co-Co	1962
Valiant	50015	BR	50	Co-Co	1967
Western Prince	D1041	BR	52	C-C	1962
—	51192	M/Cam	101	DMBS	1958
—	54352	M/Cam	101	DTC (L)	1959

29/30 April, 1 May; War Weekend — 27-29 May; Morris Minor Day at Heywood station — 18 June; Steam Event — 24/25 June; Diesel Event — 5-9 July; Rover Car Ralley at Bury station — 23 July; Day out with Thomas — 4-6 August; Teddy Bears' Picnic — 28 August; Diesel Event — 1-3 September; LMS Theme Day (all steam) — 9/10 September; Vintage Vehicle Day at Bury station — 10 September; Rossendale Valley Motorbike Show at Rawtenstall station — 24 September; Day out with Thomas — 7/8 October; Steam Event — 28/29 October; English Electric Theme Day (all diesel) — 11 November; Santa Specials — weekends in December; Irwell Valley Diner, Wine & Dine Trains (advance booking only — please apply for details)
Special Notes: The Society re-opened the Bury-Summerseat-Ramsbottom section in 1987 and the Ramsbottom-Irwell-Rawtenstall section in 1991 with the Bury-Heywood section following in September 2003
Membership details: D. Layland
Membership journal: *The East Lancashire Railway News* — twice yearly
Marketing name: East Lancs

Name	*No*	*Origin*	*Class*	*Type*	*Built*
—	51485	Cravens	105	DMBC	1958
—	56121	Cravens	105	DTC	1956
—	60130†	BR	207	DMBS	1962
—	60904†	BR	207	DTS	1962
—	65451	BR	504	DMBS	1958
—	70549	BR	207	TS	1958
—	77172	BR	504	DTS	1958

†unit 207202
†at Riley & Sons Ltd for restoration
*on loan to North Yorkshire Moors Railway for 2006

Industrial locomotives

Name	*No*	*Builder*	*Type*	*Built*
Gothenburg	32	H/Clarke (680)	0-6-0T	1903
—	1	Barclay (1927)	0-4-0ST	1927
—	—	Sentinel (10204)	4wDH	1964
MR Mercury	1	Hibberd (3438)	4wDM	1950
Winfield	—	M/Rail (9009)	4wDM	1948
—	4002	H/Clarke (D1076)	6wDM	1959

Stock
44 BR Mk 1 coaches; 11 BR Mk 2 coaches, 1 GWR coach; 1 Bogie guard's coach; Cravens 50-ton steam crane RS1013/50 (1930), NER 5-ton hand crane DB915390 (1880) and Smiths 5-ton diesel crane (1939) plus over 80 goods vehicles

Owners
D335 and D345 the Class 40 Preservation Society
D99 and D5705 the Pioneer Diesel Group
6201 the 6201 Princess Elizabeth Locomotive Trust
65451 and 77172 The Class 504 Group
35009, 45407 and 76079 Riley & Sons (Railways)
D5054 the East Lancs Type 2 Group
47402 the Waterman Heritage Trust
50015 the Manchester Class 50 Group
Class 101 on loan from the National Railway Museum
D8233 the Class 15 Preservation Society

Timetable Service

East Somerset Railway

Somerset

Member: HRA
The ESRwas created byDavid Shepherd and his friends in the early 1970s. Cranmore is still one of the few preserved railways offering only steam-hauled trains. The railway seeks to portray a country branch line, and offers a warm and personal welcome to all visitors who want to experience the sights and sounds of the steam era
Contact: Booking Office
Headquarters: East Somerset Railway, Cranmore, Shepton Mallet, Somerset BA4 4QP
OS reference: ST 664429
Telephone: Cranmore (01749) 880417

Locomotives

Name	*No*	*Origin*	*Class*	*Type*	*Built*
—	5637	GWR	5600	0-6-2T	1924
—*	B110	LBSCR	E1	0-6-0T	1877
—	30075	JZ	USA	0-6-0T	1950s
—	47365	BR	47	Co-Co	1965

Industrial locomotives

Name	*No*	*Builder*	*Type*	*Built*
Lord Fisher	1398	Barclay (1398)	0-4-0ST	1915
—	705	Barclay (2047)	0-4-0ST	1937
*Lady Nan**	1719	Barclay (1719)	0-4-0ST	1920
—	39	Sentinel (10204)	0-4-0DH	1965

*undergoing overhaul

Stock
Numerous ex-BR Mk 1 coaches; 25 assorted wagons, mostly LMS and SR

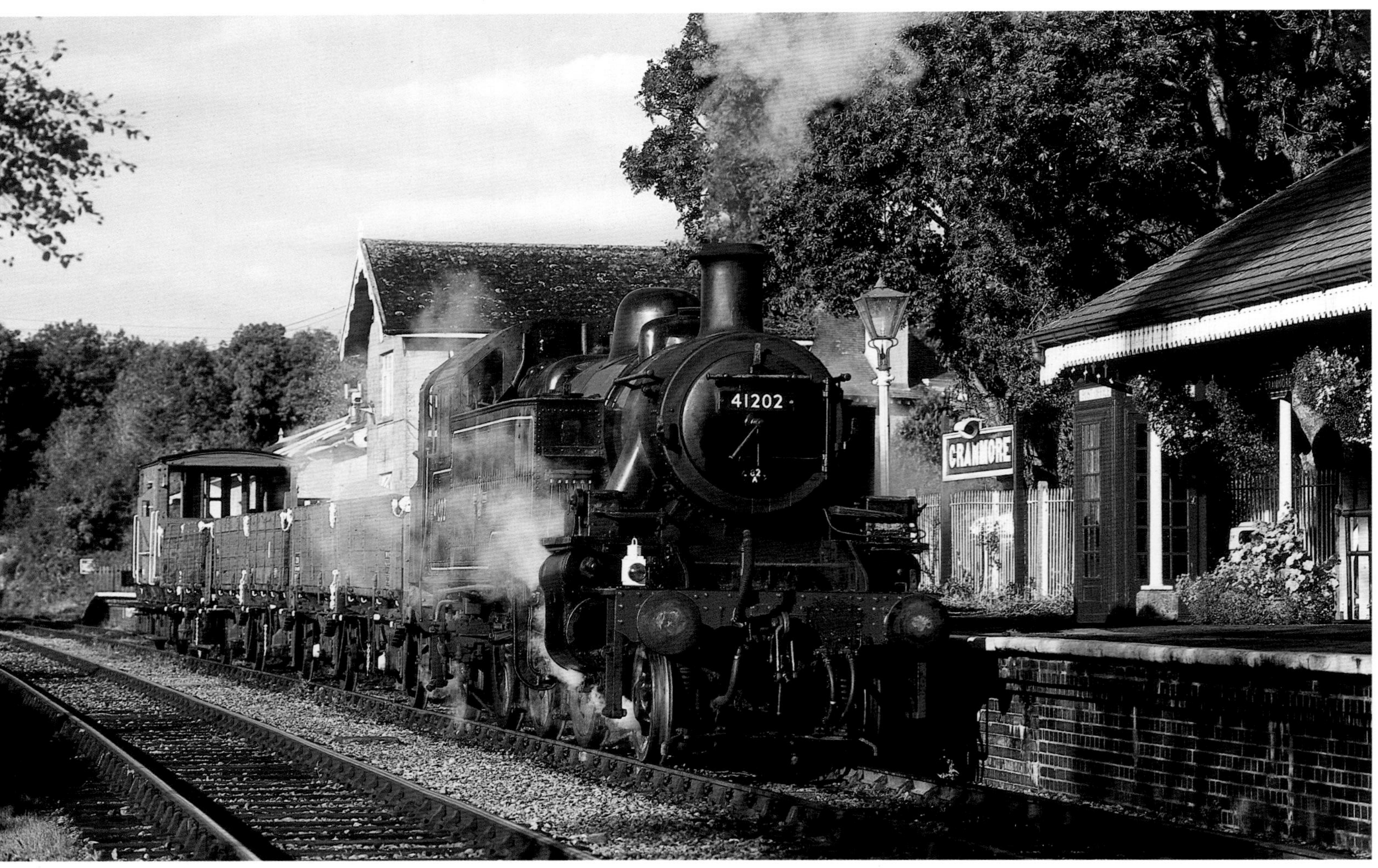

Locomotives are often renumbered during special events or when hired for a photographic charter. Here we see Mid-Hants Railway-based No 41312, as No 41202, during such an event at Cranmore on the East Somerset Railway. *Alan Barnes*

Fax: (01749) 880764
Internet address: *e-mail:* info@eastsomersetrailway.com
Web site: www.eastsomersetrailway.com
Main station: Cranmore
Car park: Cranmore — free
Refreshment facilities: The Whistlestop Restaurant at Cranmore offers lunches, snacks, teas, etc. Group catering by arrangement. Picnic areas at Cranmore. Public and private Wine & Dine trains
Souvenir shop: Cranmore
On site facilities: Station shop. David Shepherd Gallery with railway and wildlife prints for sale. Children's play area. Engine shed and workshops open for viewing. Small railway museum
Depot: Engine shed and workshop at Cranmore West (0.25-mile from Cranmore)
Length of line: 2 miles
Passenger trains: Cranmore to Mendip Vale via Cranmore West and Merryfield Lane. Return trip takes c35min. Ticket allows unlimited travel on normal operating days. All trains are steam-hauled
Period of public operation: Sundays in March; weekends and bank holidays in April, May; Wednesdays and weekends in June and July; Wednesdays, Thursdays and weekends in August; weekends in September and October; Sundays, plus 11th, in November. Please call for details and train times. Last admission 30min before closing time
Special events: Spring Gala — 1/2 April; Santa Specials — 2/3, 9/10, 16/17, 22-24 December
Wine & Dine trains:
Lunchtime — 26 M arch, 23 April, 21 May, 18 June, 16 July, 20 August, 17 September, 15 October, 19 November.
Evening — 6 may, 8 July, 7, 28 October, 11 November, 15 December.
Booking required for all Wine & Dine trains and Santa Specials
Facilities for disabled: All public areas and trains are accessible
Special Notes: Footplate experience courses available, both half day and full day. Please call for availability, prices and brochure. School groups, children's parties, private parties and Wine & Dine by arrangement — please call to discuss your requirements
Membership details: Please call for leaflet
Membership journal: *Cuttings* — 4 per year

Owners
5637 the 5637 loco Group
30075 the Project 62 Group
D3032 on loan from Foster Yeoman
Sentinel (10204)Stratford Railway Society

Miniature Railway

Eastleigh Lakeside Steam Railway

Hampshire

Location: Lakeside Country Park, Eastleigh
Headquarters: Eastleigh Lakeside Steam Railway, Lakeside Country Park, Wide Lane, Eastleigh Hants SO24 5PE
Telephone: 023 8061 2020
Internet address: *e-mail:* clive@steamtrain.co.uk
Web site: www.steamtrain.co.uk
Car parking: On site
Access by public transport: xx
Length of line: Over 1 mile, 7.25in and 10.25in gauges
Period of public operation: Every weekend, daily July, August and September and all school holidays
Special events: Day out with Thomas — 27 May-4 June, 9/10 September, 26 December-1 January 2007;
Visiting Locomotives Weekends — 11/12 March, 7/8 October; Double-headed Weekends — 11/12 March, 8/9 July, 11/12 November; Lakeside Fireworks Spectacular — 4 November (trains 18.00-17.30 and after display; Santa Specials — 10, 16/17, 22/23 December

Locomotives (10.25/7.25in gauge)

Name	*No*	*Builder*	*Type*	*Built*
Sandy River	7		2-4-2	1982
The Monarch	1001	Bullock	4-6-2	1932
The Empress	1002	Bullock	4-6-2	1933
Rob Roy	70055	Pullen	4-6-2	1948
Sir Nigel Gresley	4498	Kirkland	4-6-2	1964
Sir Arthur Heywood	7	Williamson	2-6-2*	1990
Ernest Henry Upton	1908	G&S Engineering	4-4-2	1937
Eastleigh	D1994	Millard/Mattingley	B-B*	1994
William Baker	4789	Baker	4-4-2*	1947
Francis Henry Lloyd	3	Guest	4-8-4*	1959
Saint-Leonard	1A		0-4-0-0-4-0*	2001
Sgt Murphy	—		0-6-0T*	
Florence	92		0-6-0DH	1999
Eurostar	3221	Southampton Uni	Bo-BoBE	
Sanjo	—		0-4-0*	

*7.25in gauge, remainder 10.25in

Steam Centre

Ecclesbourne Railway

Derbyshire

Pasenger services commenced on the Ecclesbourne Valley Railway on 24 August 2004. The initial length was just half-a-mile between Wirksworth and Gorsey Bank level crossing, but the plan is to reach Duffield with a main line connection in a few years. The track is in situ but requires work to bring it up to operational standard. Meanwhile the section from Wirksworth to Ravenstor, a further half-mile, opened on 1 September 2005. This incorporates a grade of 1 in 30 and provides access to the High Peak Trail

Managing Director: Martin S. Miller

Headquarters: Wirksworth Station, Coldwell Street, Wirksworth, Derbyshire DE4 4FB

Telephone: 01629 823076

Fax: 01629 825922

Internet adresses: *e-mail:* station@wyvernrail.co.uk

Web sites: www.wyvernrail.co.uk www.evra.org.uk and www.mytesttrack.com

Main station: Wirksworth

Other stations: Ravenstor, Idridgehay (opening 2006?), Shottle (opening 2007?), Duffield (opening 2008?)

OS references: Wirksworth (SK 290541), Ravenstor (SK 287548), Gorsey Bank (SK 288533), Idridgehay (SK 290489), Shottle (SK 304469), Hazelwood (SK 319449), Duffield (North) (SK 337439)

Car parking: Wirksworth station

Access by public transport: Bus – Derby/Belper/Wirksworth/Matlock/Bakewell

Location of refreshment facilities: Wirksworth station

Souvenir shops & museum: Wirksworth station

Length of line: Approx. 1 mile (2 miles in 2005)

Opening times: Wirksworth station – daily (except Xmas day) 10.00-16.00

Public operation: Sats & Suns all year round over all or part of the line. Tuesdays, Wednesdays and Thursdays May-September Wirksworth to Ravenstor

Facilities for the disabled: Specially equipped toilets

Membership details: Ecclesbourne Valley Railway Association, 530 Kedleston Road, Derby DE22 2NG

Membership Journal: *Ecclesbourne Express* – quarterly

Locomotive and multiple-units

Name	*No*	*Origin*	*Class*	*Type*	*Built*
–	03084	BR	03	0-6-0DM	1959
Margaret-Ann	D2158	BR	03	0-6-0DM	1960
–	31414	BR	31	A1A-A1A	1961
–	37075	BR	37	Co-Co	1962
–	51360	BR	117	DMBS	1959
–	55006	Gloucester	122	DMBS	1958
–	56224	BR	108	DTC(L)	1959
–	68500*	BR	489	GLV	1959
–	68506*	BR	489	GLV	1959
–	72632*	BR	491	TSH	1973
–	72633*	BR	491	TSH	1973
–	72716*	BR	491	TS	1973

*former Gatwick Express hauled-stock

Industrial locomotives

Name	*No*	*Builder*	*Type*	*Built*
–	–	Barclay (2212)	0-4-0ST	1947
–	3	Barclay (2360)	0-4-0ST	1954
–	11520	R/Hornsby (319284)	0-4-0DM	1952
Sir Peter & Lady Hilton	–	R/Hornsby (402803)	0-4-0DE	1956
–	–	R/Hornsby (432479)	0-6-0DE	1958
–	–	R/Hornsby (421037)	0-6-0DE	1958
–	–	R/Hornsby (421435)	0-6-0DE	1958
–	–	Sentinel (10194)	0-4-0DH	1964

Stock

1 BR Newspaper van (used as DMU support vehicle); 1 Taylor Hubbard crane and runner wagon. Around 20 wagons for use in maintaining the line, including examples of Grampus and Dogfish hopper wagons, plus 2 Road/Rail vehicles. 5 Permaquip trolleys, 3 Ultra Light Rail vehicles

Owners

37075 the 5C Locomotive Group
DMUs by Railcar Enterprises

Eden Valley Railway

Cumbria

Member: HRA

The mothballed Eden Valley Railway between Appleby and Warcop in Cumbria is one step closer to carrying passengers again. The EVR has plans to reopen the 6-mile railway which still connects with the famous Settle and Carlisle line at Appleby.

Please contact or see web site for further details

Headquarters: Eden Valley Railway Co and Eden Valley Railway Trust, 1 Victoria Road, Barnard Castle, Co Durham DL12 8HW

Internet address:
e-mail: admin@evr.org.uk
Web site: www.evr.org.uk

Secretary: Gillian Boyd

Main station: Appleby

OS reference: NY 687208

Car park: Appleby

Access by public transport: By bus: Stagecoach services from Penrith to Brough (stops at Warcop station (0870 6082608 for details); K. & B. Bainbridge services from Penrith to Appleby (01768 865446). By rail: Appleby. By road: M6 jct 40, A66 east to Warcop (23 miles); M6 jct 38, A685, B6260 to Appleby (20 miles); A1 Scotch Corner, A66 west to Warcop (40 miles)

Refreshment facilities: Light refreshments available on open weekends, picnic area

Membership details: Membership Secretary, EVR Trust, 60 Brisco Meadows, Upperby, Carlisle, Cumbria CA2 4NY

Membership journal: *Shackerstone News* — 2/3 times/year

Locomotives and multiple-units

Name	*No*	*Origin*	*Class*	*Type*	*Built*
—	68003	BR	419	MLV	1960
—	68005	BR	419	MLV	1960
—	60108†	BR	205	DMBS	1957
—	60658†	BR	205	DMBS	1957
—	60808†	BR	205	DTC	1957
—	31410*	BR	31	A1A-A1A	1960
—	20169*	BR	20	B0-B0	1966
—	37897	BR	37	Co-Co	1963
—	61798	BR	412	DMSO	1956
—	61799	BR	412	DMSO	1956
—	61804	BR	412	DMSO	1956
—	61805	BR	412	DMSO	1956
—	70229	BR	412	TSOL	1956
—	70539	BR	412	TSOL	1956
—	70354	BR	412	TBCK	1956
—	70607	BR	412	TBCK	1956

†unit 205009
*stored at Kirkby Stephen East station

Industrial locomotives

Name	*No*	*Builder*	*Type*	*Built*
—	21	Fowler (4220045)	0-4-0DH	1967

Stock

2 ex-BR Mk 1 coaches; 2 passenger-rated van; 1 rail-mounted 15-ton diesel cranes; selection of wagons for maintenance work

Elsecar Railway Preservation Group

Steam Centre

South Yorkshire

Member: HRA

The Elsecar Railway runs between Elsecar Heritage Centre and the canal basin at Hemingfield, through a scenic conservation area alongside the Elsecar branch of the Dearne & Dove Canal

Location/headquarters: Elsecar Heritage Centre, Wath Road, Elsecar, Barnsley, South Yorkshire S74 8HJ

Telephone: (01226) 746746

Fax: (01226) 350239

Multiple-units

Name	*No*	*Origin*	*Class*	*Type*	*Built*
—	53160	BR	101	DMC	1956
—	53164	BR	101	DMBS	1957

Industrial locomotives

Name	*No*	*Builder*	*Type*	*Built*
Countess Fitzwilliam	544996	R/Hornsby (382808)	4wDM	1968
Earl Fitzwilliam	1917	Avonside (1917)	0-6-0ST	1923
Earl of Stafford	2895	YEC (2895)	0-6-0DH	1963
Jenny	7	H/Clarke (1689)	0-4-0	1937
Catherine	—	H/Clarke (1884)	0-6-0T	1955
Mardy Monster	2150	Peckett (2150)	0-6-0ST	1954

Internet address: *e-mail:* elsecarheritagecentre@barnsley.gov.uk
Web site: www.barnsley.gov.uk/leisure/elsecar
Main station: Elsecar
Length of line: 1-mile, 20min journey
Car park location: On site, free
Access by public transport: Main rail line Elsecar from Sheffield, Huddersfield, Leeds
Refreshment facilities: On site
Souvenir shops: On site
On site facilities: Refreshments, antiques centres, crafts and souvenir shop, toilets
Museum: Attractions include Educational Workshops, 'Living History Centre', Bottle Collection, Hot Metal Press, Newcomen Beam Engine, working crafts people, various special events. Antiques centre open 7 days a week
Facilities for disabled: There are four disabled persons' toilets at different locations on the site. All buildings are fully wheelchair accessible at ground floor level
Public opening: Site open daily 10.00-17.00. Living History Centre open Tuesday to Sunday 10.30-16.30 (closed Monday except Bank Holidays). Please check for Christmas and New Year openings

The railway operates a public service on Sundays 12.00-16.00 from March to October, also Halloween and Christmas events, special event days and Bank Holidays
Special events: Include Thomas the Tank Engine, Vintage Weekend, Noddy Family Fun Event, Christmas Fair, Halloween Hauntings and Santa Specials on the railway
Special notes: Free admission to site. Charges apply to Living History Centre, railway and special events

Name	*No*	*Builder*	*Type*	*Built*
—	10432	Drewry	0-4-0DH	1955
—	—	V/Foundry	0-4-0DM	1945

Stock
4 ex-BR Mk 1 coaches, 1 Wickham trolley

Owners
Class 101 unit the East Pennine Class 101 Double Power Car Group
Catherine and *Jenny* the Brian Harrison Trust

Timetable Service

Embsay & Bolton Abbey Steam Railway

North Yorkshire

Member: HRA, TT
Yorkshire's 'Friendly Line' operates from Embsay station built in 1888. The railway is very family-orientated with many events for children. The enthusiast is not forgotten, with one of the finest collections of ex-industrial tank engines in Britain. The railway is currently constructing a new museum and workshop complex, and the line's extension to Bolton Abbey opened in 1997. Bolton Abbey station has been built to the original Midland Railway style. An atmosphere of the rural branch line prevails, which is operated by ex-industrial locomotives
Operating Committee: Vacant
Business & Marketing Manager: Stephen Walker. Tel: 01756 710614 (ext 3). Fax: 01756 710720
Internet address: *Web site:* www.embsayboltonabbeyrailway.org.uk
Location: Bolton Abbey Station, Bolton Abbey, Skipton, Yorkshire BD23 6AF
OS reference: SE 007533
Operating society/organisation:

Locomotives and multiple-units

Name	*No*	*Origin*	*Class*	*Type*	*Built*
—	D2203	BR	04	0-6-0DM	1952
—	08700	BR	08	0-6-0DE	1960
—	NCB 38 (D9513)	BR	14	0-6-0DH	1964
—	52005	BR	107	DMBS	1960
—	52012	BR	107	DMC	1960
—	52031	BR	107	DMCL	1960

Industrial locomotives

Name	*No*	*Builder*	*Type*	*Built*
Annie	9	Peckett (1159)	0-4-0ST	1908
Gladiator	8	H/Clarke (1450)	0-6-0ST	1922
Slough Estates No 5	—	H/Clarke (1709)	0-6-0ST	1939
Primrose No 2	S121	Hunslet (3715)	0-6-0ST	1952
Ann	—	Sentinel (7232)	4wVB	1927
Beatrice	7	Hunslet (2705)	0-6-0ST	1945
Airedale	3	Hunslet (1440)	0-6-0ST	1923
York No 1	—	Yorkshire (2474)	0-4-0ST	1949
Illingworth	—	H/Clarke (1208)	0-6-0ST	1916
—	140	H/Clarke (1821)	0-6-0T	1948
Spitfire	S112	Hunslet (2414)	0-6-0ST	1942
Wheldale	S134	Hunslet (3168)	0-6-0ST	1944
Sir Robert Peel	8	Hunslet (3776)	0-6-0ST	1952
—	69	Hunslet (3785)	0-6-0ST	1953
Monkton No 1	—	Hunslet (3788)	0-6-0ST	1953
—	22	Barclay (2320)	0-4-0ST	1952
—	68005	RSH (7169)	0-6-0ST	1945
Thomas	4	RSH (7661)	0-4-0ST	1950

Yorkshire Dales Railway Museum Trust
Telephone: 01756 710614, 24hr Talking Timetable 01756 795189
Car parks: Embsay and Bolton Abbey
Access by public transport: Pennine bus from Skipton, National Park bus from Ilkley
On site facilities: Souvenir shop at Bolton Abbey and Embsay — transport and industrial archaeological bookshop at Embsay
Catering facilities: Buffet and bar on most trains. Buffet at both Bolton Abbey and Embsay stations. Special charters can be arranged, meals for parties can be arranged on normal service trains, subject to advance booking, please write for further details
Length of line: 4.5 miles
Public opening: Steam trains run every Sunday throughout the year, weekends from 25 March to end October, Tuesdays in June, early July, September and 26 December. Wednesdays and Thursdays in July. Daily 14-23 April, 1-31 August and 21-29 October.
Special events: Diesel weekend — 25/26 March; Day out with Thomas — 14-17 April; May Day Children Travel Free Weekend — 29 April-1 May; Day out with Thomas — 27-29 May; Teddy Bears' Picnic — 29/30 July; Day out with Thomas — 26-28 August; 1940s Weekend — 16/17 September; White Rose Historic Vehicles Rally — 1, 8 October; Harvest of Steam Weekend — 14/15 October; Santa' Special Trains — Sundays 19, 26 November, 2/3, 9/10, 16/17, 23 December; New Year's Day Specials — 31 December 2006. Summer Sundays from June to September will be designated Stately Train days when in addition to a normal passenger train service a vintage train will operate using historic coaches (excluding 27 August and 17 September)
Special notes: Steam rides are on the 4.5-mile line to the new station and picnic area at Bolton Abbey. Old Midland Railway buildings, fine collection of industrial locomotives
Membership details: Membership Secretary at above address
Membership journal: *Dale Steam YDR News* — 4 times/year

Name	*No*	*Builder*	*Type*	*Built*
H. W. Robinson	—	Fowler (4100003)	0-4-0DM	1946
—	—	Fowler (4200003)	0-4-0DM	1948
—	MDE15	B/Drewry (2136)	4wDM	1938
—	887	R/Hornsby (394009)	4wDM	1955
—	—	Wickham (7610)	2w-2PMR	1957
—	—	Lister (9993)*	4wPM	1938
—	—	Lister (10225)*	4wPM	1938
—	—	R/Hornsby (175418)*	4wDM	1936
—	—	R/Hornsby*	4wDM	—
—	—	M/Rail (8979)*	4wDM	1946
—	—	M/Rail (5213)*	4wDM	1930
—	—	R/Hornsby	4wDM	1957
Meaford	—	Barclay (440)	0-4-0DH	1958
—	36	H/Clarke (D1037)	0-6-0DM	1958

*2ft gauge

Stock
18 ex-BR Mk 1 coaches (SK, CK, 2xBCK, 5xTSO, 2xRMB, 1xBSO(T), 1xRBR and 1xSLS), 4 ex-LNER coaches; 2 SR parcels vans; Freight stock and service vehicles, SR and GW brakes
Stephen Middleton collection of vintage coaches

Owners
Class 107 DMU vehicles the Class 107 Ltd

Note
Items on display may vary

Timetable Service — Epping-Ongar Railway — Essex

A preserved section at the northern end of the former London Underground Central Line. The section between Ongar and North Weald opened in autumn 2004. 2006 will be the second full season of the nearest heritage railway to London
Operating society/organisation: Epping Ongar Railway, Station House, High Street, Ongar, Essex CM5 9BN

Locomotives

Name	*No*	*Origin*	*Class*	*Type*	*Built*
—	(1008)	Finnish*		4-6-2	1948
—	1060	Finnish*		2-8-2	1954
—	794	Finnish*		0-6-0T	1925
—	531	Finnish*	TK3	2-8-0	1919
—	1134	Finnish*		2-8-0	1946
—	51342	P/Steel	117	DMS	1959
—	51384	P/Steel	117	DMS	1959
—	L11	LT	—	—	1964

*1,524mm gauge, on static display

Contact: Mark Dewell
Telephone: 01277 366616
Internet address: *Web site:* http://eorailway.co.uk
Main station: Ongar
Other station: North Weald
OS references: Ongar TL 551035, North Weald TL 49603)
Access by public transport: Use London Underground Central Line to Epping, then local bus service to Ongar or North Weald. Local buses also available from Harlow and Brentwood
On site facilities: Light refreshments only at Ongar
Length of line: 6 miles (4.5 miles operational)
Public opening: DMU service on Sundays 11-00-17.00
Special events: Please see web site

Industrial locomotives

Name	No	Builder	Type	Built
—	—*	Ruston (398616)	4wDM	1956
—	—	Ruston (512572)	4wDM	1965
Heather	D1995	Drewry (2566)	4wDM	1955

*for spares only

Stock

2 Finnish Railway wooden-bodied carriages (1,524mm gauge). Brake van, well wagon, Dogfish ballast hopper and box van

Owner

L11 Cravens Heritage Trains

Facilities for disabled: Level access to platforms. Ramp available for wheelchair access to guard's compartment
Membership details: Epping Ongar Railway Volunteer Society, c/o above address
Membership journal: *Mixed Traffic* — quarterly

Evesham Vale Light Railway

Steam Centre — Worcestershire

Member: BGLR

The Evesham Vale Light Railway takes you through the old apple orchards to a picnic and viewing area overlooking some of the most picturesque scenery in the Vale of Evesham. Steam locomotives are used on most days and it is possible to break your journey and walk to the river, returning on a later train. The railway is situated within Evesham Country Park, 1 mile to the north of the historic town of Evesham. Enjoy a day out and stroll around the 130 acre estate, including a mile and quarter of the River Avon. Visit the Ark Animal Sanctuary, browse in the relaxed atmosphere of the courtyard shops or try some of the freshly prepared lunches and snacks in the licensed Apple Barn restaurant
Location/headquarters: Evesham Vale Light Railway, Evesham Country Park, Twyford, Nr Evesham, Worcestershire WR11 4TP
Contact: Jim Shackell
Telephone: 01386 422282
Internet address: *e-mail:* enquiries@evlr.co.uk
Web site: www.evlr.co.uk

Locomotives

Name	No	Builder	Type	Built
Prince William	5751	G&S	4-6-2	1949
Sludge	—	Lister (41545)	4wDM	1955
Bessie	—	Eddy/Nowell	4wDM	2002
St Egwin	312	Exmoor Steam Rly	0-4-0T+T	2003
Dougal	3	Severn-Lamb	0-6-2T	1970
Scooter	—	Eddy/Nowell	4wPM	2004
R. H. Morse	712*	Morse	0-4-0	1950
John	103	Barnes	4-4-2	1921

*off-site for overhaul

Main station: Twyford (adjacent to Evesham Country Park car park)
Other station: Evesham Vale (in the country park)
OS reference: SP 0446
On site facilities: Large car and coach park, licensed restaurant within park shopping complex. Small souvenir shop at Twyford station
Length of line: 1.25 miles, 15in gauge
Locomotive and carriage depots: Adjacent to Twyford station — viewing avaiable on request
Access by public transport: By train to Evesham main line station then bus — Stagecoach No 28 — from Evesham bus station, hourly service will stop close to park entrance, then 15min walk to Twyford station
Public opening: Weekends and Bank Holidays throughout the year and also the following inclusive dates: 13-17 February (half term), 19-21 April (Easter), 1 May, 29 May-2 June (half term), 24 July-1 September (summer), 23-27 October (half term), 20 December-2 January 2007 (excluding Christmas Day and Boxing Day). Please ring information line (01386 422282) for more details. Trains run every half-hour from 10.30 to 17.00 (16.00 November to March)
Facilities for disabled: Wheelchair facilities on all trains

Above: St Egwin built in 2003 by the Exmoor Steam Railway and now on the Evesham Valley Light Railway is based on a Krauss-built 0-4-0T+T on the Romney, Hythe & Dymchurch Railway. *EVLR*.

Below: The Exbury Gardens Railway's locomotives were also built by the Exmoor Steam Railway. Here 2001-built *Rosemary* has just arrived back at Exbury Central. Both these lines have been built new as tourist attractions and have proved very popular. *Phil Barnes*

Steam Centre

Exbury Gardens Railway

Hampshire

Member: BGLR
A comparatively new line with purpose-built locomotives and rolling stock around part of Exbury Gardens. Train fare is in addition to entrance fee
Location/headquarters: Exbury Gardens, Exbury, Southampton SO45 1AZ
Contact: Ian Wilson (railway foreman). Tel: 023 8089 2898
Telephone: 023 8089 1203
Internet address: *Web site:* www.exbury.co.uk
Access by public transport: Main line trains to Brockenhurst
Car park: On site, free
On site facilities: Souvenir shop, refreshments and toilets adjacent to main car park
Length of line: 1.25 miles, 12.25in gauge
Public opening: 1 March to 5 November. Limited winter opening.

Available for 2006 are driver experience courses and Railwayman's Packages for groups of 15 or more people (unlimited train rides, engine shed tour, guided walk around wood yard, footplate rides [limited numbers], and much more)
Special events: Spring Train — 26 March; Easter Bunny Trains — 15-17 April; 'We'll Meet Again' wartime memories — 3/4 June; Narrow Gauge in the Gardens — 17/18 June; Teddy on the Train — 5/6 August; Exbury Scarecrow Festival — 26-28 August; Steam in the Gardens — 7/8 October; Exbury Ghost Train — 24-29 October; Santa Steam Specials — 9/10, 16/17, 20/21 December
Facilities for disabled: Yes, access to 4 coaches
Tickets:
High season (20 March to 4 June) entrance prices include a free voucher for a return to Exbury in October/November to see the autumn colours.

Discount for OAPs in high season available Mondays to Fridays. Other concessions available.

Season tickets are available for access to gardens only or gardens plus trains, additional on site discounts are available to season ticket holders

Industrial locomotives

Name	*No*	*Builder*	*Type*	*Built*
Rosemary	—	Exmoor (315)	0-6-2T	2001
Naomi	—	Exmoor (316)	0-6-2T	2002
—	—	Exmoor	0-4-0DH	2001

Stock
8 coaches

Timetable Service

Foxfield Steam Railway

Staffordshire

Member: HRA
The railway was built in 1893 to carry coal from Foxfield Colliery to the North Staffordshire Railway at Blythe Bridge. Following closure of the colliery in 1965 the line was rescued for preservation. The Society is working towards rebuilding the railway a further 0.75 mile down the famous Foxfield Bank to the site of Foxfield Colliery as part of a half million pound lottery grant
Chairman: S. Sutton
Headquarters: Foxfield Steam Railway, Blythe Bridge, Stoke-on-Trent
Postal address: P. O. Box 1967, Stoke-on-Trent ST4 8YT
Telephone:
01782 396210 or 01782 643507

Industrial locomotives

Name	*No*	*Builder*	*Type*	*Built*
*Bellerophon**	—	Haydock Foundry (C)	0-6-0WT	1874
—	1827	B/Peacock (1827)	0-4-0ST	1879
—	6	R/Heath	0-4-0ST	1886
—	4101	Dübs (4101)	0-4-0CT	1901†
Henry Cort	—	Peckett (933)	0-4-0ST	1903††
Millom	—	Avonside (1563)	0-4-0ST	1908†
Moss Bay	—	K/Stuart (4167)	0-4-0ST	1920††
Cranford	—	Avonside (1919)	0-6-0ST	1924†
Helen	—	Simplex (2262)	4wDM	1924
Marston No 3	—	H/Leslie (3581)	0-6-0ST	1924†
—	—	K/Stuart (4388)	0-4-0ST	1926•
Lewisham	—	Bagnall (2221)	0-6-0ST	1927
Rom River	—	K/Stuart (4421)	6wDM	1929
Boots No 1	—	Barclay (1984)	0-4-0F	1930††
Ironbridge No 1	—	Peckett (1803)	0-4-0ST	1933††
Spondon No 2	—	E/Electric (1130)	4wBE	1939††
Roker	—	RSH (7006)	0-4-0CT	1940††
Hawarden	—	Bagnall (2623)	0-4-0ST	1940
—	WD820	B/Drewry (2157)	0-4-0DM	1942

Above: Although of only 2ft gauge the Gartell Light Railway runs for part of its length along the trackbed of the well-known Somerset & Dorset Joint Railway. Here GLR No 1 *Amanda* approaches Pinesway Junction station where the line joins the S&DJR route. *Mike Lucas*

Below: The Foxfield Railway relies on former industrial locomotives to operate its passenger trains, fortunately the passenger accommodation is lot more comfortable than the traditional 'industrial passenger' stock would be. *Phil Barnes*

Fax: 01782 396210
Internet address: *Web site:* www.foxfieldrailway.co.uk
Main station: Blythe Bridge (Caverswall Road)
OS reference: SJ 957421
Car park: Blythe Bridge
Access by public transport: Main line railway Blythe Bridge (400yd). PMT bus service to Blythe Bridge
Refreshment facilities: Buffet and real ale bar at Blythe Bridge
Souvenir shop: Blythe Bridge
Passenger trains: Steam-hauled trains operate from Blythe Bridge (Caverswall Road) to Dilhorne Park and return
Family ticket: Available (2 adults + 2 children or 1 adult + 4 children)
Length of line: 3.5 miles. Current operation over 2.5 miles of line
Period of public operation: Steam trains operate Sundays and Bank Holiday Mondays Easter-end October inclusive between Blythe Bridge and Dilhorne Park.
Special events: Steam Gala — 16/17 July; Halloween and Santa Specials, weekends in December (both pre-booked events). Please contact for details
Facilities for disabled: Access to majority of Caverswall Road station is on the level; disabled toilets.

Name	*No*	*Builder*	*Type*	*Built*
(Hercules)	242915	R/Hornsby (242915)	4wDM	1946
—	11	Peckett (2081)	0-4-0ST	1947•
Whiston	—	Hunslet (3694)	0-6-0ST	1950
—	9535	Sentinel (9535)	4wVBGT	1952•
Florence No 2	—	Bagnall (3059)	0-6-0ST	1953†
Meaford No 2	—	RSH (7684)	0-6-0T	1951
Wimblebury	—	Hunslet (3839)	0-6-0ST	1956
(Gas-oil)	88DS	R/Hornsby (408496)	4wDM	1957†
Wolstanton No 3	—	Bagnall (3150)	0-6-0DM	1960
B. R. C. (Megan)	—	Thomas Hill (103C)	0-4-0DH	1957
Rachel	—	R/Hornsby (423637)	0-4-0DE	1958
(Roman)	165DS	R/Hornsby (424841)	0-4-0DE	1960
Ludstone	—	YEC (3207)	0-4-0DH	1961
Leys	—	Bagnall (2868)	0-6-0DE	1962
Meaford No 4	—	Barclay (486)	0-6-0DH	1964

†under overhaul
††static exhibit
•awaiting overhaul
*on loan for ten years

Stock
3 ex-BR Mk 1 CK coaches; 1 ex-BR Mk 2a TSO coach; 4 other coaches; 3 scenery vans (converted for other uses); 79 assorted wagons, 16-ton mineral wagons; 1 rail-mounted self-propelled diesel-electric crane

Owner
Bellerophon the Vintage Carriages Trust

Advance notice essential for those wishing to travel on the train
Membership journal: *Foxfield News* — quarterly

Timetable Service

Gartell Light Railway

Somerset

Owned and operated by three generations of the Gartell family, the Gartell Light Railway offers visitors the chance to travel by train along the route of the old Somerset & Dorset Joint Railway. A half-mile section of the line from Pinesway Junction to Park Lane runs along the old S&D trackbed, while work has started on an extension northwards from Pinesway Junction along the S&D formation towards Templecombe. A flyover has been constructed to carry the extension over the existing line to the terminus at Common Lane and tracklaying has begun. On most open days a three train service is operated, with departures every 15min and trains crossing at Pinesway Junction. The GLR is fully signalled using a variety of upper and lower quadrant, colour light and shunt signals controlled by two full size signalboxes. The GLR's first steam locomotive, a locally built 0-4-2T, specially designed to cope with the steep gradients and sharp curves of the section from Common Lane up to Pinesway Junction, entered service in 1998.
Location/headquarters: Gartell Light Railway, Common Lane, Yenston, Nr Templecombe, Somerset BA8 0NB
Telephone: 01963 370752
Internet address: *Web site:* http://www.glr.co.uk
General Manager: John Gartell
Main station: Common Lane
Other stations: Pinesway Junction, Park Lane
Car park: Large free car park at Common Lane
OS reference: ST 718218
Access by public transport: 1.5 miles south-east of Templecombe railway station
Refreshment facilities: Refreshment room at Common Lane serving a range of hot and cold snacks and drinks. Lakeside picnic area at Pinesway Junction
Visitor centre: Common Lane
Souvenir shop: Common Lane
Depot: Common Lane (not open to public)
Length of line: 0.75-mile
Facilities for disabled: Two of the three trains in service have accommodation for a disabled visitor in a wheelchair
Period of public operation:

17 April; 1, 29 May; 25 June; 30 July; 6, 13, 20, 27/28 August; 24 September, 29 October. 10.30-16.30
Special events: Santa Specials (must be pre-booked) — 16/17 December

Industrial locomotives

2ft gauge:

Name	No	Builder	Type	Built
Amanda	1	GLR	Bo-BoDH	2003
Andrew	2	R/Hornsby	4wDH	1964/5
Alison	5	A/Keef (10)	4wDH	1983
Mr G	6	N. Dorset Loco Wks	0-4-2T	1998

Rolling stock — coaches: 9 fully enclosed bogie coaches

Rolling stock — wagons: goods guard's van, tool van, open wagon, bogie PW gang/tool van, bogie hopper, bogie open, bogie well, bogie flat and bogie crane

Timetable Service

Gloucestershire Warwickshire Railway

Glos

Member: HRA
Part of an ambitious project to link Cheltenham with Stratford, much has been done to re-create the railway and buildings that made up this cross-country route. The railway is home to many owners of private locomotives and rolling stock, so from time to time the items on display may vary. The extension from Gotherington to Cheltenham Racecourse opened in April 2003.

2006 sees the centenary of the opening of the line and the 25th anniversary of the GWR Ltd
Location: Toddington station, Toddington
OS reference: SO 050322
Operating society/organisation: Gloucestershire Warwickshire Steam Railway plc, The Station, Toddington, Cheltenham, Glos GL54 5DT
Telephone: Toddington (01242) 621405
Internet address:
e-mail: enquiries@gwsr.com
Web site: www.gwsr.com
Main station: Toddington
Other public stations: Winchcombe, Cheltenham Racecourse, Gotherington (request halt, off-peak only)
Access by public transport: Hourly service from Cheltenham to Greet for Winchcombe station. Local bus service Castleways will answer timetable queries on (01242) 602949. Regular Stagecoach service to Cheltenham station. Racecourse Park & Ride

Locomotives and multiple-units

Name	No	Origin	Class	Type	Built
—	2807	GWR	2800	2-8-0	1905
—	4270	GWR	4200	2-8-0T	1919
Raveningham Hall	6960*	GWR	6959	4-6-0	1944
Owsden Hall	6984	GWR	6959	4-6-0	1948
Foremarke Hall	7903	GWR	6959	4-6-0	1949
—	7069	LMS	—	0-6-0DE	1939
Peninsular & Oriental SNCo	35006	SR	MN	4-6-2	1941
—	8274	LMS	8F	2-8-0	1941
—	76077	BR	4MT	2-6-0	1956
Black Prince	92203	BR	9F	2-10-0	1959
—	03069	BR	03	0-6-0DM	1959
—	D2182	BR	03	0-6-0DM	1952
—	D9553	BR	14	0-6-0DH	1965
—	D8137	BR	20	Bo-Bo	1966
—	24081	BR	24	Bo-Bo	1960
—	26043	BR	26	Bo-Bo	1959
—	37215	BR	37	Co-Co	1964
Clydebridge	37324	BR	37	Co-Co	1962
Phaeton	45149	BR	45	1Co-Co1	1961
Sparrowhawk	D1705	BR	47	Co-Co	1963
—	47105	BR	47	Co-Co	1963
Freightliner 1995	47376	BR	47	Co-Co	1965
—	56003	BR	56	Co-Co	1977
—	73129	BR	73	Bo-Bo	1966
—	51950	BR	108	DMBS	1960
—	52062	BR	108	DMC	1960

*off-site under repair

Industrial locomotives

Name	No	Builder	Type	Built
Wemyss Private Rly	15	Barclay (2138)	0-6-0ST	1945
—	19	Fowler (4240016)	0-6-0DH	1964
—	21	Fowler (4210130)	0-4-0DM	1957
John	—	Peckett (1976)	0-4-0ST	1939
King George	—	Hunslet (2409)	0-6-0ST	1942
—	1	Drewry/RSH (2573/7859)	0-6-0DM	1956
—	2	Drewry/RSH (2574/7860)	0-6-0DM	1956
—	—	Hunslet (5511)	0-6-0DM	1957

(approx half mile to GWR station)
Car park: All stations
On site facilities: Sales, catering, narrow gauge rides, toilets, new children's play area
Length of line:
Standard gauge 10 miles
Narrow gauge 1 mile
Public opening: On non-operating mid weekdays the station is closed. Public services: weekends, Bank Holiday Mondays, between March and November, some summer weekdays
Special events: Spring Diesel Gala — 31 March, 1/2 April; Anniversary Steam Gala* — 27 May-4 June; Transport Nostalgia Day — 11 June; Day out with Thomas — 24/25 June; Transport Nostalgia Day — 9 July; Autumn Diesel Gala— 9/10 September; Transport Nostalgia Day — 24 September; Day out with Thomas — 30 September/1 October; Winter Diesel Gala— 4/5 November; Christmas Diesel Day — 27 December
*A gala to celebrate 100 years since the line was opened throughout and 25 years of the GWR Ltd
Special notes: The site is being developed as the headquarters of the railway between Cheltenham and Stratford. The GWR owns the railway land between Cheltenham and Broadway and operates over 10 miles from Toddington to Cheltenham Racecourse with an intermediate station at Winchcombe.

No public access to restoration area or sheds except on guided tours. Please ring for details.

Guest locomotives will be operating during the year with special guest *City of Truro* expected.

Wine & Dine train 'Elegant Excursions' at www.excursions@freeserve.co.uk

Round trip tickets give unlimited travel on day of purchase.

Family tickets available
Facilities for disabled: Visitors with impaired mobility welcomed. Please advise in advance if assistance required. Wheelchairs can be accommodated in specially converted carriages
Membership details: From above address
Membership journal: *The Cornishman* — quarterly

Stock
4 ex-GWR coaches; 55 ex-BR coaches; 4 ex-LMS coaches; Baguley/Drewry inspection vehicle; 2 Wickham trolleys; plus numerous wagons (including 10 brake vans, 45-ton steam crane, 18-ton diesel crane)

Owners
2807 the Cotswold Steam Preservation Ltd (www.gwr2807.co.uk)
35006 the P&O Locomotive Society
8274 and 7069 the Churchill (8F) Locomotive Co
92203 David Shepherd
26043 and 45149 the Cotswold Mainline Diesel Group
D9553 Cotswold Diesel Preservation Group
37215 and 37324 the Growler Group
47105 and 47376 the Brush Type 4 Fund
D8137 the English Electric Type 1 Group

North Gloucestershire Railway

Industrial narrow gauge locomotives (2ft gauge)

Name	*No*	*Builder*	*Type*	*Built*
Isibutu	5	Bagnall (2820)	4-4-0T	1946
George B	—	Hunslet (680)	0-4-0ST	1898
Chaka	—	Hunslet (2075)	0-4-2T	1940
Justine	—	Jung (939)	0-4-0WT	1906
Brigadelok	—	Henschel (15968)	0-8-0T	1918
—	2	Lister (34523)	4wDM	1949
—	3	M/Rail (4565)	4wPM	1928
Spitfire	—	M/Rail (7053)	4wPM	1937
—	1	R/Hornsby (166010)	4wDM	1932
—	L5	R/Hornsby (181820)	4wDM	1936
—	—	R/Hornsby (354028)	4wDM	1953

Stock
3 coaches; 11 wagons

Timetable Service

Great Central Railway

Leicestershire

Member: HRA, TT
The original Great Central Railway's extension to London in 1899 was the last main line to be built in this country, most of which was closed in the 1960s. Steam-hauled services operate through attractive rolling Leicestershire countryside, crossing the picturesque Swithland reservoir. The railway's aim is to re-create the experience of British main line railway operation in the days of steam. The images of a main line are backed up by a double track line with long trains hauled by large locomotives
Headquarters: Great Central Railway plc, Loughborough Central Station, Great Central Road, Loughborough, Leicestershire LE11 1RW
Telephone: Loughborough (01509) 230726
Fax: 01509 239791
Internet address: *e-mail:* sales@gcrailway.co.uk
Web site: www.gcrailway.co.uk
Main stations: Loughborough Central, Leicester North

Former LMS Class 5 No 45305 is seen at Loughborough on the Great Central Railway. *Alan Barnes*

Other public stations: Quorn & Woodhouse, Rothley
OS reference: SK 543194
Car park: Quorn, Rothley
Access by public transport: Loughborough Midland station (0.75-mile). Add-on ticket from any National Rail station includes unlimited travel on day of visit. Arriva Fox County, Barton, Kinch, South Notts and Trent Buses serve Loughborough Baxtergate (0.5 mile). Arriva Fox County Nos 126/7 pass end of Great Central Road (A6 Leicester Road, 300yd)
Refreshment facilities: Licensed Griddle Car with hot and cold drinks on majority of trains and at Loughborough Central station. Light refreshment facilities available at all other stations. Luxurious First Class Restaurant Car, for which advance booking is obligatory, is provided on 13.15 train every Saturday and Sunday. Also provided on 19.30 train every Saturday and every Friday (June-September). Additional service may run at peak times. Private charter trains available, along with more details of all the above, on request
Souvenir shop: Loughborough
Museum: Loughborough
Depot: Loughborough
Length of line: 8 miles
Passenger trains: Loughborough-Leicester North
Period of public operation: Weekends and Bank Holidays throughout the year. Daily between 17 July and 30 August with additional services at times of peak demand
Special events: 1960s Weekend—25/26 March; Day out with Thomas — 28-30 May; Wizards & Witches — 29 April-1 May; Diesel Gala — 12-14 May; Day out with Thomas — 27-29 May; Railwayana Swapmeet at Quorn — 4 June; Wartime Weekend 'Operation Big Foot' — 10/11 June; 'Seaside Specials' — 1/2 July; Edwardian Experience at Rothley — 9 July; Mail by Rail — 29/30 July; Day out with Thomas — 25-28 August; Railwayana Swapmeet at Quorn — 3 September; Diesel Gala — 15-17 September; Summer Railway Gala — 7/8 October; Day out with Thomas — 21/22 October; Halloween — 31 October; Bonfire & Firework Display at Quorn — 3 November; Edwardian

Locomotives and multiple-units

Name	*No*	*Origin*	*Class*	*Type*	*Built*
—	4141	GWR	41xx	2-6-2T	1946
*Witherslack Hall**	6990	GWR	'Hall'	4-6-0	1948
Sir Lamiel	30777	SR	N15	4-6-0	1925
Boscastle	34039	SR	WC	4-6-2	1946
Brocklebank Line	35025**	SR	MN	4-6-2	1948
Alderman A. E. Draper	45305	LMS	5MT	4-6-0	1936
—	46521	LMS	2MT	2-6-0	1953
—	47406	LMS	3F	0-6-0T	1926
—	48305	LMS	8F	2-8-0	1943
—	63601	GCR	8K	2-8-0	1919
—	69523	GNR	N2	0-6-2T	1921
Oliver Cromwell	70013	BR	7MT	4-6-2	1951
—	73156	BR	5MT	4-6-0	1956
—	78019	BR	2MT	2-6-0	1954
—	D3101	BR	08	0-6-0DE	1955
§—	D4067	BR	10	0-6-0DE	1961
—	D8048	BR	20	Bo-Bo	1959
—	D8098	BR	20	Bo-Bo	1961
—	D5185	BR	25	Bo-Bo	1960
Harlech Castle	25265	BR	25	Bo-Bo	1963
—	D5830	BR	31	A1A-A1A	1962
—	33116	BR	33	Bo-Bo	1960
—	37255	BR	37	Co-Co	1965
†—	D123	BR	45	1Co-Co1	1961
Sparrowhawk	D1705	BR	47	Co-Co	1965
Sir Herbert Walker	E6003	BR	73	Bo-Bo	1966
—	51427	BR	101	DMBS	1959
—	51616	BR	127	DMBS	1959
—	51622	BR	127	DMBS	1959
—	53193	BR	101	DMC	1959
—	53203	BR	101	DMBS	1957
—	53266	BR	101	DMC	1957
—	53321	BR	101	DMC	1958
—	59276	BR	120	TS	1958
—	62384	BR	421	MBSO	
—	76746	BR	421	DTCSO	
—	76817	BR	421	DTCSO	
—	70527	BR	411	TSOL	

*undergoing overhaul at Tyseley Locomotive Works
§ named *Alfred Thomas & Margaret Ethel Naylor*
† named *Leicestershire & Derbyshire Yeomanry*
**expected to leave during 2006

Industrial locomotives

Name	*No*	*Builder*	*Type*	*Built*
(Arthur Wright)	D4279	Fowler (4210079)	0-4-0DE	1952
Duke of Edinburgh	28	A/Barclay (400)	0-4-0DM	1956

Owners
6990 the David Clarke Railway Trust
7821 the Great Western Steam Locomotives
34039 the Boscastle Locomotive Syndicate
35025 the Brocklebank Line Association
45305 the 5305 Locomotive Association
46521, 73156 and 78019 Loughborough Standard Locomotives Group
47406, D3101, D4067 private
30777, 63601, 70013 and 33116 on loan from the National Railway Museum
69523 the Gresley Society
D5830, D8098 and D1705 the Type 1 Locomotive Co
E6003 the ED Locomotive Group

Experience at Rothley — 11 November; Santa Specials — weekends 24 November-24 December; Christmas Day — 25 December; Mince Pie Specials — 26 December-1 January. Other events include All Aboard for Murder, Murder by the Book, Murder on the Loughborough Express.
For additional information phone 08708 308298
Facilities for disabled: Special carriage for wheelchair/disabled persons (advance notice required). Wheelchair access good at Quorn and Rothley, can be arranged at Loughborough with advance notification. Boarding ramps at all stations
Membership & share details: Share enquiries: Company Secretary, Great Central Railway plc
Membership: Membership Secretary, Main Line Steam Trust Ltd. Both c/o above address. Friends of Great Central Railway, Friends Co-ordinator c/o above address

Class 101s Renaissance Railcars
37255 on loan from Fragonset Railways
D1705 the Type One Locomotive Co

Miniature Railway

Great Cockcrow Railway

Surrey

Emanating from the private Greywood Central Railway, built from 1946, the Great Cockcrow Railway opened in 1968 in the small village of Lyne near Chertsey. This is a 7.25in gauge system with a signalling system worked from four signalboxes
Headquarters: Hardwick Lane, Lyne, Chertsey, Surrey
Contact: Jill Wright
Telephone:
Mon-Fri (01932) 255514;
Sun (01932) 565474
Internet address: *e-mail:* jill.wright@ianallan.co.uk
Web site: www.cockcrow.co.uk
Main station: Hardwick Central
Car parking: On site
Access by public transport: Chertsey railway station (1.25 miles); London Buslines 561, 586 Holloway Hill (half-mile)
On site facilities: Toilet, light refreshments, picnic area
Depots: Hardwick Central
Length of line: 1.75 miles, 7.25in gauge
Period of public operation: Every Sunday Easter to October inclusive, 14.00-17.30
Journey time: Journey time about 15-20min
Facilities for disabled: Limited, but staff are happy to co-operate
Special note: Sponsored by Ian Allan Group. Send second class SAE for brochure to Terminal House, Shepperton, TW17 8AS. Fare £2.50 adult, £2 child. Gladesman £4 per person

Locomotives (7.25in gauge)

Name	*No*	*Prototype*	*Builder*	*Type*	*Built*
—	206	LNER K5	D. Simmonds	2-6-0	1956
—	837	SR S15	D. Curwen	4-6-0	1947
—	1239	NER R1	F. Baldwin	0-6-2T	1913
—	1249	NER T2	R. Sills	0-8-0	1986
—	1401	GWR 14xx	R. Sills	0-4-2T	1980
—	1442	NER C1	—	4-4-2	1989
Eureka	—	GCR	L. Shaw	4-6-2	1927
North Foreland	2422	LBCSR H2	J. Lester	4-4-2	1981
Sister Dora	5000	LMS 5P5F	A. Glaze	4-6-0	1989
—	5145	LMS 5P5F	—	4-6-0	1989
—	5241	LMS 5P5F	—	4-6-0	1989
The Glasgow Highlander	45157	LMS 5P5F	D. Grant	4-6-0	1996
Royal Scot	6100	LMS 6P	Barnet & Willoughby	4-6-0	1947
Royal Scot	6100	LMS 6P	J. Butt	4-6-0	1982
Scots Guardsman	6115	LMS 6P	P. Ormand	4-6-0	1989
—	8200	LMS 8F	P. Pownall	2-8-0	
—	8374	LMS 8F	Glaze, Hancock & York	2-8-0	1993
—	30541	SR Q	J. Butt	0-6-0	2000
—	30542	SR Q	J. Butt	0-6-0	2000
—	3151	GWR 31xx	K. Wilson	2-6-2T	1990
Winston Churchill	34051	SR BoB	N. Sleet	4-6-2	1995
General Steam Navigation	21C11	SR MN	N. Sleet & M. Lester	4-6-2	1993
Mercury	70020	BR 7MT	N. Sleet	4-6-2	1985
Lady of the Lake	70047	BR 7MT	J. Butt	4-6-2	1995
Grand Parade	2744	LNER A3	R. Warren	4-6-2	1990
Longmoor	73755	WD 8F	J. Liversedge	2-10-0	1951
A. B. Macleod	7028	BR Hymek	A. Glaze	Bo-Bo	1983
Faraday	11	BR 08	Jennings & Marden	0-6-0P	1958
—	40106	BR 40	N. Sleet	1Co-Co1	1992

Steam Centre

Great Whipsnade Railway

Bedfordshire

Member: HRA
Location: Whipsnade Wild Animal Park, Dunstable, Bedfordshire LU6 2LF
Telephone: (01582) 871332 (extension 2270)
Fax: (01582) 873748
Internet address: *e-mail:* whipsnade-operations@2sl.org
Railway Engineer: Kevin Edwins
Main station: Whipsnade Central
Length: 2 miles (2ft 6in gauge)
On site facilities: Car park (100yd), souvenir shop, refreshments (30yd)
Period of public operation: January — no trains; February — half term; March — weekends only; April to July — daily (steam at weekends); August daily steam trains; September/October — daily (steam at weekends); November — school half term; December — no trains
Facilities for disabled: Carriage designed for wheelchairs

Locomotives

Name	*No*	*Builder*	*Type*	*Built*
Excelsior	2	K/Stuart (1049)	0-4-2T	1908
Superior	4	K/Stuart (4034)	0-6-2T	1920
Victor	—	Fowler (4160004)	0-6-0DM	1951
Hector	—	Fowler (4160005)	0-6-0DM	1951
Mr Bill	10	R/Hornsby (221625)	0-4-0DM	1944
Hercules	—*	23rd August Works (Bucharest)	0-6-0DH	1981
The Brick	—	Ruhrthaler	0-4-0DH	

*Polish State Railways Class LYD2

Rolling stock: 10 carriages, 9 wagons

Museum

Haig Colliery Mining Museum

Cumbria

Member: HRA
Haig Colliery Mining Museum, Whitehaven, is an educational and informative museum under development based on local and social mining history. The Museum is situated in Cumbria's last deep coal mine that closed in March 1986. It houses the world's only Bever Dorling & Co Ltd winding engines, one of which is restored and operated daily
Location: Kells, half-mile south of Whitehaven, take the road to St Bees and follow brown tourist signs
OS reference: NX 967176
Operating society/organisation: The Haig Colliery Mining Museum Ltd, Solway Road, Kells, Whitehaven, Cunbria CA26 9BG
Telephone/Fax: 01946 599949 (general information)
Internet address: *e-mail:* museum@haigpit.com
Car park: On site
Access by public transport: By rail: Whitehaven is on the Barrow-Carlisle line
By bus: No 01 bus from bus station (opposite railway station) — 9min journey
On site facilities: Small gift shop, gardened area suitable for picnics. Toilets. Meet and Greet by museum guides. Locomotives viewable on request to the guides.
Length of lines: Standard gauge – under construction
Public opening: Daily except Wednesdays (09.30-16.30). Free entry
Facilities for disabled: Parking area, toilets, wheelchair access to all areas

Industrial locomotives

Name	*No*	*Builder*	*Type*	*Built*
Askham Hall	—	Avonside (1772)	0-4-0ST	1917
—	226	V/Foundry (5262)	0-4-0DM	
—	ND 3815	Hunslet (2389)	0-4-0DM	1941
—	244	Fowler (22971) rebuilt T/Hill (130C/1963)	0-4-0DH	1942

Rolling stock
Coles 10-ton diesel crane, 4 16-top open wagons, 2 flat bed wagons

Timetable Service

Hayling Seaside Railway

Hampshire

There are three stations on the line: Beachlands, the main station/ storage/workshop building located seaward of the funfair; Eastoke Corner 1-mile to the east is the other end of the line; Hornby Halt (sponsored by Hornby the modelmakers) with passing loop is between. All stations are provided with ample (Council) pay & display car parking and (private) refreshment facilities
Headquarters: 20 Jasmond Road, Cosham, Portsmouth PO6 2SY
Managing Director: Bob Haddock
Telephone: 023 9237 2427
Main public station: Beachlands
Other public stations: Eastoke Corner, Hornby Halt
Car parks: Pay & display at all stations
Access by public transport: Regular buses from Havant railway station
Refreshment facilities: At all stations

Locomotives

Name	*No*	*Builder*	*Type*	*Built*
Jack	—	A/Keef (23)	0-4-0DH s/o	1988
Alister	—	Ruston (201790)	4wDH	1940
Alan B	—	M/Rail (7199)	4wDM	1937
—	—	EHLR	0-4-0T	*
Edwin	—	R/Hornsby (1002-0967-5)	4wDH	1967

*under construction

Stock
2 4-wheel enclosed coaches built 1992/1997, 2 4-wheel balcony coaches built 1996, 1 enclosed bogie coach built 2004, 1 toastrack bogie coach built 2004. All built by East Hayling Light Railway at its works

Journey time: Departures every 45 minutes
Length of line: 1 mile, 2ft gauge
Period of public operation: Every weekend and Wednesday (market day) all year round, plus school holidays
Facilities for disabled: All platforms and coaches built to latest mobility standards
Special events: Please contact for full details; Pirates of Beachlands — May half term; Spooky Specials — October half term; Santa Specials
Special notes: On display are the original BR station signs Hayling Island and Havant for Hayling
Membership details: Terry Mercer 023 9271 7550
Membership journal: *The Hayling Billy* — quarterly

Steam Centre

Hollycombe Steam Collection

West Sussex

Member: HRA, TT
An extensive collection of working steam, including railways, traction engines, fairground rides, Bioscope, organs, the oldest Burrell Showman's engine *Emperor*, sawmill and engine from the paddle steamer *Caledonia*, set in woodlands and gardens
Location: Iron Hill, Hollycombe, near Liphook, Hants
OS reference: SU 852295
Operating society/organisation: Hollycombe Steam & Woodland Garden Society, Iron Hill, Midhurst Road, Liphook, Hants GU30 7LP
Telephone: Liphook (01428) 724900 (24hr answerphone)
Fax: (01428) 723682
Internet address: *Web site:* www.hollycombe.co.uk

Industrial locomotives

Name	*No*	*Builder*	*Type*	*Built*
Caledonia	70	Barclay (1995)	0-4-0WT	1931*
Jerry M	38	Hunslet (638)	0-4-0ST	1895*
Commander B	50	H/Leslie (2450)	0-4-0ST	1899
—	16	R/Hornsby	4wDM	1941*

*2ft gauge

Car park: On site
Access by public transport: Liphook main line station (1 mile)
On site facilities: Shop and refreshments, toilets, car park, *dogs allowed in car park only*
Length of lines: Standard gauge – quarter mile
2ft gauge 'Quarry Railway' – 1.5 miles
7.25in gauge – quarter mile
Public opening: All Easter weekend. Sundays and Bank Holidays 9 April-8 October. Daily 30 July-28 August. 12.00-17.00.
Special events: Railway Weekend — 3/4 June; Festival of Steam — 1/2 July.
Please phone for details of other events

Steam Centre — Irchester Narrow Gauge Railway Museum — Northants

Member: HRA
The aims of the controlling trust are to acquire and preserve narrow gauge railway locomotives, rolling stock and exhibits associated with Northamptonshire and the East Midlands, to display the collection for the benefit of the public and to restore exhibits to working order so they may be demonstrated in a proper manner
Location: Within Irchester Country Park, 2 miles south of Wellingborough
Operating society/organisation: The Irchester Narrow Gauge Railway Trust, 3 St Christopher's Close, Cranwell, Lincs NG34 8XB
On site facilities: Shop, museum, demonstration line, picnic area
Access by public transport: Main line Wellingborough (Midland Road) station, buses to Irchester and Little Irchester

Industrial locomotives

Name	*No*	*Builder*	*Type*	*Built*
—	85*	Peckett (1870	0-6-0ST	1934
—	86*	Peckett (1871)	0-6-0ST	1934
—	87*	Peckett (2029)	0-6-0ST	1942
Cambrai	—*	Corpet (493)	0-6-0T	1888
—	ND3645*	R/Hornsby (211679)	4wDM	1941
—	—†	R/Hornsby (281290)	0-6-0DM	1949
—	ED10*	R/Hornsby (411322	4wDM	1958
—	—†	M/Rail (1363)	4wPM	1918
The Rock	—*	Hunslet (2419)	0-4-0DM	1941

* metre gauge
† 3ft gauge

Car Parks: Main park car parks
Toilets: Main park complex
Public opening: Every Sunday (summer 10.00-17.00, winter 10.00-16.00), at other times by arrangement. Steam and demonstration weekends are held on last full weekend of the month — March-October
Facilities for disabled: Museum and site on level, staff available if required
Membership details: Membership Secretary, 1 Wilby Street, Northampton NN1 5JX

Museum — Ironbridge Gorge Museums — Shropshire

The railway items form only a small part of the displays on two of the museum's main sites: Blists Hill Victorian Town and Coalbrookdale. The Blists Hill site offers an opportunity to see a number of industrial and other activities being operated in meticulously reconstructed period buildings. A working foundry is just one of the exciting exhibits. A full size working replica of Richard Trevithick's 1802 steam locomotive built by the Coalbrookdale Company can also be seen operating at certain times at the Blists Hill site. The Ironbridge Gorge was designated a World Heritage Site in 1987
Location: Ironbridge, Shropshire
OS reference: SJ 694033
Operating society/organisation: Ironbridge Gorge Museum Trust, Coach Road, Coalbrookdale, Telford, Shropshire TF8 7DQ
Telephone: Telford (01952) 433522
Fax: (01952) 432204
Internet address: *Web site:* www.ironbridge.org.uk
Car park: At the sites
Access by public transport: Various operators. Please telephone Telford Travel Link 01952 200005 or 0870 6082608 for further details
Catering facilities: Licensed Victorian pub, sweet shop and tea rooms at the Blists Hill site, serving drinks and mainly cold snacks. Tea, coffee and light refreshments at the Museum of Iron, Coalbrookdale and Coalport China Museum
Public opening: Main sites, including Museum of Iron and Blists Hill, daily (except Christmas Eve, Christmas Day and New Year's Day) 10.00-17.00
Special notes: Tickets for all the sites or just for single sites available. Phone main phone number for special access details

Industrial locomotives

Name	*No*	*Builder*	*Type*	*Built*
—	—	Sentinel/Coalbrookdale (6185)	0-4-0VBT	1925
—	—	Sentinel/M/Wardle (6155)	0-4-0VBT	1925
—	5	Coalbrookdale	0-4-0ST	1865
—	—	A/Barclay	0-6-0ST	1896

All locomotives are at the Museum of Iron site. Phone 01952 432141 for details

Timetable Service

Isle of Wight Steam Railway

Isle of Wight

Member: HRA, TT
Separated from the mainland by the Solent, the line's isolation encouraged the maintenance and retention of Victorian locomotives and coaching stock which still operate on the line today. Its rural charm enhances its attraction for the island's holidaymakers during the summer season
Commercial Director: Jim Loe
Headquarters: Isle of Wight Steam Railway, Haven Street Station, Ryde, Isle of Wight PO33 4DS
Telephone: (01983) 882204
Internet addresses: *e-mail:* ronlee@iwsteamrailway.co.uk
Web site: www.iwsteamrailway.co.uk
Main station: Haven Street
OS reference: SZ 556898
Other public stations: Wootton, Ashey and Smallbrook Junction
Car park: Haven Street
Access by public transport: 'Island Line' service from Ryde or Shanklin to Smallbrook Jct
Refreshment facilities: Light refreshments available (licensed)
Souvenir shop: Haven Street
Museum: Small exhibits museum at Haven Street.
Carriage & Wagon workshop open for viewing most days
Depot: Haven Street
Length of line: 5 miles
Passenger trains: Wootton-Smallbrook Jct
Period of public operation: Daily — June to September. Selected days — March to May and October
Special events: Real Ale Festival — 29 April-1 May; Replica Rocket Week — 27 May-1 June; Austin Car Rally — 18 June; 1940s Weekend — 1/2 July; Island Motor Show— 8/9 July; A Day out with Thomas — 28 July-1 August; Island Steam Show— 25-28 August; Morris Minor Rally — 3 September; Wizard Week — 23-29 October; Ghost Walks — 27-28 October; Santa Specials in December (please contact for details)
Facilities for disabled: Limited facilities, but can be catered for individually, or in groups (by prior arrangement), toilets available
Membership details: Membership Secretary at above address
Membership journal: *Island Rail News* — quarterly

Locomotives

Name	*No*	*Origin*	*Class*	*Type*	*Built*
Freshwater	W8 (32646)	LBSCR	A1X	0-6-0T	1876
Newport	W11 (32640)	LBSCR	A1X	0-6-0T	1878
Calbourne	W24	LSWR	O2	0-4-4T	1891
—	D2554	BR	05	0-6-0DM	1956
—	D2059	BR	03	0-6-0DM	1959

Industrial and Army locomotives

Name	*No*	*Builder*	*Type*	*Built*
Invincible	37	H/Leslie (3135)	0-4-0ST	1915
Ajax	38	Barclay (1605)	0-6-0T	1918
Waggoner	192	Hunslet (3792)	0-6-0ST	1953
Royal Engineer	198	Hunslet (3798)	0-6-0ST	1953

Owners
Royal Engineer and *Waggoner* on loan from The Army Museum

Stock
1 IWR coach; 4 LBSCR coaches; 3 SECR coaches; 2 LCDR coaches; 5 IWR coaches (bodies only); 5 LCDR coaches (bodies only); 1 LBSCR coach (body only); 1 crane; 1 Wickham trolley; 30 wagons; 6 parcels vans; 2 ex-LT hoppers; 1 ex-BR Lowmac; 1 LSWR Road van; 1 cattle van (on loan from the National Railway Museum).
Non-passenger vehicles are not normally acessible for public viewing

Timetable Service

Keighley & Worth Valley Railway

West Yorkshire

Member: HRA
1968 saw the reopening of the Worth Valley branch following the first sale of a standard gauge railway to a preservation society. Qualified volunteers have now managed and operated the KWVR every weekend, summer and winter for three decades. The KWVR is justifiably proud of having led the British independent railway movement in establishing the now ubiquitous late 1950s/early 1960s house style. Many have copied, but few succeed so well as the Worth Valley with totems, A5 handbills, period posters, red uniform ties, hanging baskets, gas lights and coal fires. One of the most community-orientated independent railways, being the first to create a 'Resident's Railcard' discount fares scheme
Chairman, Joint Management Committee: Sam MacDougal
Headquarters: Haworth Station, Keighley, West Yorkshire BD22 8NJ
Telephone: Haworth (01535) 647777 24hr recorded timetable and

Built in 1887 for use by the Lancashire & Yorkshire Railways this locomotive is seen carrying British Railway livery as No 52044. It is seen here leaving Keighley on the Keighley & Worth Valley Railway. *Alan Barnes*

Proudly carrying its somewhat brighter livery is GWR No 1638 which was actually built by British Railways in 1951 and should strictly be in a more sombre black scheme. *Alan Barnes*

information service; Haworth (01535) 645214 (other calls)
Internet address: *Web site:* www.kwvr.co.uk
Main stations: Keighley, Ingrow West, Haworth, Oxenhope
Other public stations: Damems, Oakworth
OS reference: SE 034371
Car parks: Free at Keighley, Ingrow West, Oakworth and Oxenhope. Parking at Haworth (small charge, part refundable if travelling). Coaches at Ingrow West and Oxenhope only
Access by public transport: Fast and frequent electric Metro trains from Leeds, Bradford and Skipton to Keighley (joint station with KWVR). GNER direct services to Leeds and Keighley. Northern Trains through services from Glasgow, Carlisle, Morecambe, Lancaster to Keighley station. Through bookings to 'Oxenhope KWVR' are available from any travel centre throughout Britain and allow one day's unlimited travel on KWVR. Northern Train services from Blackpool, Preston, Blackburn, Accrington, Burnley,

Locomotives and multiple-units

Name	*No*	*Origin*	*Class*	*Type*	*Built*
—	41241	LMS	2MT	2-6-2T	1949
—	43924	MR	4F	0-6-0	1920
—	45212*	LMS	5MT	4-6-0	1935
Bahamas	45596	LMS	'Jubilee'	4-6-0	1935
—	48431	LMS	8F	2-8-0	1944
—	47279	LMS	3F	0-6-0T	1925
—	1054	LNWR	—	0-6-2T	1888
City of Wells	34092	SR	WC	4-6-2	1949
—	80002	BR	4MT	2-6-4T	1952
—	75078	BR	4MT	4-6-0	1956
—	78022	BR	2MT	2-6-0	1953
—	30072	SR	USA	0-6-0T	1943
—	5775	GWR	5700	0-6-0PT	1929
—	52044	L&Y	2F	0-6-0	1887
—	19*	L&Y	Pug	0-4-0ST	1910
—	51218	L&Y	Pug	0-4-0ST	1901
—	752	L&Y	—	0-6-0ST	1881
—	85	TVR	02	0-6-2T	1899
—	5820	USATC	S160	2-8-0	1945
—	90733	MoS	WD	2-8-0	1945
—	D226	BR	—	0-6-0DE	1956
—	D2511	BR	—	0-6-0DM	1961
—	D3336	BR	08	0-6-0DE	1954
—	D5209	BR	25/1	Bo-Bo	1963
—	D8031	BR	20	Bo-Bo	1960
—	50928	BR	108	DMBS	1959
—	51192	BR	101	DMBS	1958
—	51565	BR	108	DMC	1959
—	51803	BR	101	DMCL	1959

Manchester to Hebden Bridge for connection via bus service 500 to Oxenhope (tel 01535 603284 for days of operation and timings)
Refreshment facilities: Buffet facilities at Oxenhope and Keighley (open when train service in operation). The only CAMRA-approved 'Real Ale' bar operates on most steam trains (March-October). Wine and Dine services by prior booking only — the 'White Rose Pullman' and 'West Riding Ltd'
Picnic areas: Keighley Station, Haworth Locomotive Depot, Oxenhope Station
Viewing areas: Keighley (Garsdale) Turntable, Haworth Locomotive Depot
Souvenir shops: Keighley, Haworth and Oxenhope stations; Ingrow Vintage Carriages Museum
Museums: Vintage Carriages Trust's carriage and locomotive museum at Ingrow Railway Centre. Open daily 11.00-16.30
Depots: Carriage and wagon — Oxenhope; Motive power/loco works — Haworth, 'Bahamas Locomotive Society' workshops and museum at Ingrow Railway Centre
Length of line: 4.75 miles
Passenger trains: Early morning local shoppers' services worked by diesel railbus/diesel multiple-unit, otherwise all steam-hauled

Frequent bus service between Haworth station and Haworth village top on Sundays (May-September) and Bank Holidays
Period of public operation: Steam-hauled passenger services every weekend and Bank Holiday throughout the year (in December diesel-hauled). Daily during July and August

Name	*No*	*Origin*	*Class*	*Type*	*Built*
—	79962	W&M	—	Railbus	1958
—	79964	W&M	—	Railbus	1958

Industrial locomotives

Name	*No*	*Builder*	*Type*	*Built*
Hamburg	31	H/Clarke (679)	0-6-0T	1903
Nunlow	—	H/Clarke (1704)	0-6-0T	1938
Brussels	118	H/Clarke (1782)	0-6-0ST	1945
Tiny	—	Barclay (2258)	0-4-0ST	1949
Merlin	231	H/Clarke (D761)	0-6-0DM	1951
—	MDHB No 32	Hunslet (2699)	0-6-0DM	1944

*away on loan

Stock
30 coaches including examples of pre-Grouping types; BR Mk 1 stock including the oldest vehicle in existence, part of the prototype batch; 2 Pullman cars, NER and L&Y observation cars

Owners
19, 752 and 51218 the L&YRPS Trust
75078 and 78022 the Standard 4 Preservation Society
Bahamas, Nunlow, Tiny the Bahamas Locomotive Society
1054 the National Trust
52044 the Bowers 957 Trust
34092 the *City of Wells* Syndicate

Special events: Day out with Thomas — 16/17 September; Steam Gala Weekends — 13-15 October; Beer & Music Festival — 20-22 October; Steam-hauled tours of the line — 20-22, 27-29 June; Vintage Trains Days — 4 June, 2 July, 6 August; Santa Specials — 2/3, 10/11, 16/17, 22/23 December; Mince Pie Specials 26 December-2 January 2007
Facilities for disabled: Level access to all stations.Wheelchair ramps available at all stations. Full disabled toilet facilities at Haworth station. Non-folding wheelchairs can be accommodated in guard's compartments. Staff available to offer assistance and advice at all stations. Museum of Rail Travel at Ingrow offers easy access to wheelchair users (inc toilet facilities). Audio loop and braille facilities available and attention given to those with special needs
Special notes: Accompanied children under 5 years of age free. Children 5-15 and senior citizens at discount rate. Family ticket available (2 adults + 3 children/senior citizen). Free entry to VCT Museum with rover tickets
Membership details: Membership Secretary c/o above address
Membership journal: *Push & Pull* — quarterly
Marketing name: Worth Valley

Timetable Service

Kent & East Sussex Railway

Kent

Member: HRA, TT
The Kent & East Sussex Railway owes much of its charm to its origin as the world's first light railway. The tightly curved line with steep gradients is typical of those country railways that were developed on shoestring budgets to bring the 'iron horse' to sparsely populated areas. Services operate over 10.5 miles of line from the picturesque town of Tenterden to Bodiam.

Pride of the line's coach fleet is the magnificently restored train of vintage carriages built between 1860 and 1901

Company Secretary: Nick Pallant
Headquarters: Kent & East Sussex Railway Co Ltd, Tenterden Town Station, Tenterden, Kent TN30 6HE
Telephone: Tenterden (01580) 762943 (24 hour talking timetable); Tenterden 087 060 060 714 (office)
Internet address: *Web site:*

www.kesr.org.uk
Main station: Tenterden Town
Other public stations: Rolvenden, Wittersham Road, Northiam, Bodiam
Car parks: Tenterden, Northiam
OS reference: Tenterden TQ 882336, Northiam TQ 834266
Access by public transport: Stagecoach No 400 from Ashford (Kent) main line station. Arriva No 12 Maidstone-Headcorn station-Tenterden & Rye
Refreshment facilities: Tenterden Town and Northiam. Also on many trains. Lunch and afternoon teas on many trains (advance booking essential). Picnic areas at Tenterden, Wittersham Road, Northiam and Bodiam
Souvenir shop: Tenterden Town Station
Museum: Colonel Stephens Railway Museum at Tenterden Town
Depot: Rolvenden
Length of line: 10.5 miles
Passenger trains: Tenterden-Bodiam. All Bank Holidays and school holidays. Daily 22 July to 3 September. Most days ring for details, full service in August
Special events: Spring Opening Event (in conjunction with Bodiam Castle) — 25/26 March; All Fools' Day — 1 April; Grandparents' Weekend — 8/9 April; St George's Day — 23 April; Terrier Weekend — 6/7 May; Country Music Weekend — 13/14 May; Artist's Days — 24/25 May; Children's Fun Week — 27 May-2 June; Day out with Thomas* — 10/11, 17/18 June; Victorian Experience — 27-29 June; Family History Day — 1 July; Branch Line Weekend — 8/9 July; MG Car Rally — 29/30 July; Art Exhibition — 19/20 August; The Famous Hoppers Weekend — 9/10 September; Pensioners' Treat (£7.50/seat) — 19-21 September; Day out with Thomas* — 23/24, 30/31 September; Tenterden Folk Festival — 7/8 October; Austin Counties Car Rally — 14/15 October; Halloween* — 23-29 October; Heritage Diesel Weekend — 4/5 November; Santa Specials* — 2/3, 9/10, 15-17, 21-24 December; Post Christmas Running — 27-31 December, 1 January 2007.
*tickets for reserved seats can be booked online
Facilities for disabled: A special coach for disabled people, 'Petros', is conveyed in many trains (telephone for confirmation of availability), reserved parking at Northiam.
Toilets with disabled access at Tenterden, Northiam and Bodiam, also in 'Petros'
Special notes: The Wealden Pullman luxury dining car service operates on most Saturday evenings April to October and selected Fridays in the summer. Roast lunch served most Sundays. Advance booking is essential for these trains. Santa Special services operate on each Saturday and Sunday in December. Advance booking recommended
Membership details: Membership Secretary, c/o above address
Membership journal: *The Tenterden Terrier* — 3 times/year

Locomotives and multiple-units

Name	*No*	*Origin*	*Class*	*Type*	*Built*
Bodiam	3	LBSCR	A1X	0-6-0T	1872*
Tenterden	32678	LBSCR	A1X	0-6-0T	1880*
—	753	SECR	P	0-6-0T	1909*
Wainwright	DS238	SR	USA	0-6-0T	1943*
Maunsell	65	SR	USA	0-6-0T	1943
—	1638	GWR	1600	0-6-0PT	1951
—	20	GWR	AEC	diesel railcar	1940
Norwegian	376	NSB	21c	2-6-0	1919*
—	D2023	BR	03	0-6-0DM	1958
—	D2024	BR	03	0-6-0DM	1958
—	08108	BR	08	0-6-0DE	1955◊
Ashford	D6570	BR	33	Bo-Bo	1961◊
—	51571	BR	108	DMC	1959*
—	53971	BR	108	DMBS	1959*

Industrial locomotives

Name	*No*	*Builder*	*Type*	*Built*
Marcia	12	Peckett (1631)	0-4-0T	1923
Charwelton	14	M/Wardle (1955)	0-6-0ST	1917*
Holman F. Stephens	23	Hunslet (3791)	0-6-0ST	1952
Rolvenden	24	Hunslet (3800)	0-6-0ST	1953*
Northiam	25	Hunslet (3797)	0-6-0ST	1953*
—	40	BTH	Bo-Bo	1932*

*in passenger traffic

Passenger stock in service
SECR family saloon; LNWR 6-wheel director's saloon; SECR 4-wheel full third; SR Maunsell CK; GER 6-wheel composite; District Railway 4-wheel full first; 2 SR Maunsell brake open 1st Class; SR Maunsell non-descript brake-open; BR Mk 1 RU and 5 other BR Mk 1 coaches; 1926 Pullman Parlour Cars *Barbara* and *Theadora*

Stock
2 ex-SECR 'Birdcage' coaches; 2 ex-LSWR coaches; 1 GER observation car; 2 Pullman cars; 3 ex-SR Maunsell coaches; 3 steam cranes; large interesting collection of freight vehicles, totalling 51 vehicles

Steam Centre

Kew Bridge Steam Museum

London

The museum is housed in a magnificent 19th century Pumping Station and centres around the station's five world famous Cornish Beam Engines, three of which can be seen in steam on selected 'Cornish Engine Experience' weekends. Originally used to pump West London's water supply for more than a century, one of them, the 'Grand Junction 90', is the world's largest working beam engine. In surrounding buildings other large engines work at weekends, demonstrating more modern steam and diesel pumping machinery.

The Water For Life Gallery reveals the fascinating history of London's water supply from Roman toilet spoons to the massive 'high-tec' London ring main.

Many Victorian waterworks had their own railway. At Kew Bridge this is demonstrated by a short line, operated by the Hampshire Narrow Gauge Railway Society. 1998 saw the return to steam of *Cloister* for the first time in 22 years

Location: 100yd from the north side of Kew Bridge, next to the tall Victorian tower

Operating group: Kew Bridge Engines Trust, Green Dragon Lane, Brentford, Middx TW8 0EN

Telephone: 020 8568 4757 (information line)

Internet address: *Web site:* www.kbsm.org

Car park: Free on site

Access by public transport: *Rail*: SouthWest Trains, Kew Bridge (from Waterloo via Clapham Junction) and North London Line to Gunnersbury; *Bus:* Nos 65, 237, 267, 391; *Tube:* Gunnersbury (District Line, then 237 or 267 bus), Kew Gardens (District Line, then 391 bus)

Length of line/gauge: About 140yd, 2ft gauge

Public opening: Museum: Tuesdays to Sundays 11.00-17.00. Closed Mondays (except Bank Holidays), Good Friday and 23-26 December 2006. Railway: see below

Special events: Exhibition: 'Wondrously Wacky Gadgets' — until 17 April; Stirling & Hot Air Engine Rally — 2 April; Magic of Meccano Show — 22*/23 April; Historic Fire Engine Rally — 21 May; Kew Bridge Model Boat Show — 10*/11 June; London Open House Weekend — 16/17 September; The Steam Models Show — 1*/2* October; Live Steam Model Railway Show — 18*/19 November.

*The railway is scheduled to operate every Sunday March to November, plus Saturdays marked **

On site facilities: Bookshop/toilets/car park. Refreshments available at weekends only

Facilities for disabled: Wheelchair access to 90% of ground floor areas via ramp and lift. Large print guide available and guide dogs welcome. Wheelchair loan service and wheelchair accessible toilet. Railway carriage can accommodate wheelchairs.

Special note: Groups of 10 or more can be given guided tours and a 10% discount on admission charges. Special steaming can be arranged and touch tours are available for partially sighted groups. All groups must be pre-booked.

Children under 13 must be accompanied by an adult.

Different admission rates apply to selected special events and tower tours. Please contact the museum for details

Museum contact: Kew Bridge Engines Trust, c/o above address

Railway contact: HNGRS, 44 St Thomas' Avenue, Hayling Island, Hants PO11 0EX

Other attractions: Museum displays a selection of stationary steam engines and associated water supply displays

Industrial locomotives

2ft gauge:

Name	*No*	*Builder*	*Type*	*Built*
Cloister	—	Hunslet (542)	0-4-0ST	1891
Alister	2	Lister (44052)	4wDM	1958

Museum

Kidderminster Railway Museum

Worcestershire

Established in an 1878 GWR warehouse, the museum houses an enormous collection of railway relics, photographs and documents, with a number of 'hands-on' exhibits.

Contact address: Station Approach, Comberton Hill, Kidderminster, Worcestershire DY10 1QX

General Manager: David Postle

Telephone: Kidderminster (01562) 825316

Internet address:
e-mail: krm@krm.org.uk
Web site: www.krm.org.uk

OS reference: SO 837763

Location: Adjacent to SVR station

Car park: SVR car park

Access by public transport: Kidderminster main line station, Midland Red bus service X92 to Kidderminster

Facilities for disabled: Ramp access for wheelchairs to ground level

Special events: Practical signalling

courses using Museum and SVR resources. Filmshows, model railway exhibitions, railway art exhibitions, postcard/photograph fairs,

On site facilities: Souvenirs, refreshments
Public opening: Open on SVR operating days

Timetable Service | Kirklees Light Railway | West Yorkshire

Member: HRA
Location/headquarters: Clayton West, A636 Wakefield-Denby Dale road
General Manager: Graham Hurd
Operating society/organisation: Kirklees Light Railway, Park Mill Way, Clayton West, Nr Huddersfield HD8 9XJ
Telephone: (01484) 865727
Internet address: *Web site:* www.kirkleeslightrailway.com
Location: Clayton West, the terminus of the railway, is situated midway between Wakefield, Barnsley, Holmfirth and Huddersfield, on the A636 Wakefield-Denby Dale Road
Main station: Clayton West
Other station: Cuckoos Nest, Skelmanthorpe, Shelley
Length of line: 4 miles, 15in gauge
Car park: Clayton West — free
Access by public transport: By bus: from Holmfirth No 484, from Leeds No 482 (484) from Wakefield No 484. From Barnsley No 235, from Huddersfield Nos 235/240, from Wakefield No 935. Ask driver for Park Mill Way, Clayton West. By rail to Huddersfield, Wakefield or Denby Dale stations
Refreshment facilities: Clayton West, Visitor Centre and Café
Souvenir shop: Clayton West
On site facilities: Toilets, swings, half-scale roundabouts, lake. HQ of Barnsley Society of Model Engineers
Facilities for disabled: Yes
Period of public operation: Winter— weekends & most school holidays. Summer — daily from Spring Bank Holiday to end August
Special events: Please phone or write for details

Locomotives

Name	*No*	*Builder*	*Type*	*Built*
Fox	—	Taylor	2-6-2T	1987
Badger	—	Taylor	0-6-4T	1991
Tram Engine	7	Taylor	0-4-0	1995
Jay	—	Taylor	4wD	1992
Hawk	—	Taylor	0-4-4-0*	1998
Owl	—	Taylor	4w-4wT*	2000

*articulated

Rolling stock
2 rakes of six carriages (some heated in winter), 4-wheel tool van, 4-wheel ballast/stone wagon, heavy bogie flat car for rail carrying

Timetable Service | Lakeside & Haverthwaite Railway | Cumbria

Member: HRA, TT
Originally this Furness Railway branch line carried passengers and freight from Ulverston to Lakeside but now the only part remaining is the 3.5-mile section from Haverthwaite to the terminus at Lakeside where connections are made with the steamers which ply the 10-mile length of Windermere
General Manager: M. A. Maher
Headquarters: Lakeside & Haverthwaite Railway Co Ltd, Haverthwaite Station, Nr

Locomotives and multiple-units

Name	*No*	*Origin*	*Class*	*Type*	*Built*
—	20	FR	A5	0-4-0	1863
—	42073	LMS	4MT	2-6-4T	1950
—	42085	LMS	4MT	2-6-4T	1951
—	17(AD601)	LMS	—	0-6-0DE	1945
—	5643	GWR	5600	0-6-2T	1925
—	8(D2117)	BR	03	0-6-0DM	1959
—	D2072	BR	03	0-6-0DM	1959
—	20214	BR	20	Bo-Bo	1967
—	D5301	BR	26	Bo-Bo	1958
—	52071	BRCW	110	DMBC	1961
—	52077	BRCW	110	DMBC	1961

Ulverston, Cumbria LA12 8AL
Telephone: Newby Bridge (015395) 31594
Internet address: *Web site:* www.lakesiderailway.co.uk
Main station: Haverthwaite
Other public stations: Intermediate station at Newby Bridge. Terminus at Lakeside
OS reference: SD 349843
Car parks: Haverthwaite, Lakeside
Access by public transport: Lakeside steamers on Windermere call at Lakeside. CMS bus to Haverthwaite
Refreshment facilities: Haverthwaite
Souvenir shop: Haverthwaite
On site facilities: Picnic area at Haverthwaite
Depot: All rolling stock at Haverthwaite
Length of line: 3.5 miles
Passenger trains: Steam-hauled Haverthwaite-Lakeside
Period of public operation: 1 April to 29 October 2006 (inclusive)
Special events: Santa Specials (advance booking essential) please contact for details
Special notes: Combined railway/lake steamer tickets available, from the station at Haverthwaite and lake steamer piers at Bowness and Ambleside. Lake steamers are operated by Windermere Lake Cruises Ltd
Membership journal: *The Iron Horse* — quarterly

Industrial locomotives

Name	*No*	*Builder*	*Type*	*Built*
*Caliban**	1	Peckett (1925)	0-4-0ST	1937
Rachel	9	M/Rail (2098)	4wDM	1924
Repulse	11	Hunslet (3698)	0-6-0ST	1950
Princess	14	Bagnall (2682)	0-6-0ST	1942
NCB 10	—	Barclay (1245)	0-6-0T	1911
David	13	Barclay (2333)	0-4-0ST	1953
Cumbria	10	Hunslet (3794)	0-6-0ST	1953
Fluff	16	Hunslet/Fowler	0-4-0DM	1937
—	20	Jones crane	0-4-0DM	1952
Sir James	21	Barclay (1550)	0-6-0F	1917

*under restoration at Steamtown, Carnforth

Stock
10 ex-BR Mk 1 coaches; 1 ex-LNER BG; 1 ex-BR Mk 1 miniature buffet coach, Royal saloon No 5 (built GER, Stratford 1898), North London coach (c1890); selection of freight vehicles

Owner
5643 the Furness Railway Trust

Miniature Railway

Lakeside Miniature Railway

Lancashire

The longest continuously running 15in gauge railway in Great Britain, running during both world wars. The first train ran at 3pm on 25 May 1911. The line was extended in 1948, now running between two stations, Pleasureland and Marine Parade.
Location: Marine Lake, Southport
Headquarters: 1 Wingates, Penwortham, Preston, Lancs PR1 9YN
Name of contact: Mr D. Clark
Telephone: 01772 745511
Fax: xx;
Internet address: *E-mail:* jennifer.clark2@virgin.net
Web site: www.lakesideminiaturerailway.co.uk
On site facilities: Shop (selling ice cream, soft drinks, and Thomas the Tank Engine)
Length of line: 800yd, 15in gauge
Period of public operation: Easter to end of October, and during school holidays (weather permitting). 11.00-16.30. Journet time 5min

Locomotives

Name	*No*	*Builder*	*Type*	*Built*
Duke of Edinburgh	—	Barlow	4-6-2+4-4DE	1947
Prince Charles	—	Barlow	4-6-2+4-4DE	1954
Golden Jubilee	—	Barlow	4-6w+4-4DE	1963
Princess Anne	—	S/Lamb	6w-6DH	1971

A new locomotive is under construction for delivery during 2006

Rolling stock
3 sets of carriages each seating 72 passengers

Steam Centre

Lappa Valley Railway

Cornwall

Member: TT
Location/headquarters: Benny Halt, St Newlyn East, Nr Newquay, Cornwall TR8 5HZ
Telephone: 01872 510317
Internet address: *web site:* www.lappavalley.co.uk
General Manager: Miss Amanda Booth
Main station: Benny Halt
Other station: East Wheal Rose, Newlyn Downs Halt
Car park: Benny Halt
Access by public transport: Bus service, Newquay to Truro and return. Western National and The Cornishman coaches to St Newlyn East. Signposted, half-mile walk from bus stop to railway. No direct bus service
Refreshment facilities: Café at East Wheal Rose serving hot and cold food, snacks, hot and cold drinks; licensed
Souvenir shop: East Wheal Rose and Benny Halt
On site facilities: 15in, 10.25in and 7.25in gauge railways. Canoes, paddle boats, crazy golf, pedal cars, electric motorbikes, children's play area, brick path maze, listed engine house, walks and a video
Depot: Benny Halt
Facilities for disabled: Limited number of reserved parking bays. Toilets at East Wheal Rose and Benny Halt. All buildings are single storey with no steps. Level or gently sloping paths with even surfaces. Main steam train has compartments with doors that will accommodate wheelchairs (only the largest motorised wheelchairs are excluded), ramps and staff available to assist. The smaller train at East Wheal Rose cannot take wheelchairs. Some other attractions are not suitable for wheelchair users (eg canoes, mine building, maze and country walks)
Public opening: Easter to end of October, usually daily but ring for early and late season opening days
Special notes: Entry by one all-in price, except for electric bikes.
Family tickets and reduced afternoon saver fares are available all days. Under 3s free

Locomotives

Name	*No*	*Builder*	*Type*	*Built*
Muffin	2	Berwyn	0-6-0	1967
		rebuilt Tambling		1991
Zebedee	1	S/Lamb	0-6-4T	1974
		rebuilt Tambling		1990
Gladiator	3	Minirail	4w-4wDH	c1960
Pooh	4	Lister (20698)	4wDM	1942

(all 15in gauge)

Rolling stock
15in gauge — 10 passenger coaches
10.25in gauge — 4 passenger coaches, 2 wagons
7.25in gauge — 1 Mardyke APT set

Timetable Service

Launceston Steam Railway

Cornwall

Member: HRA, TT
The railway runs through the beautiful Kensey Valley on a track gauge of 1ft 11.5in, following the trackbed of the old North Cornwall line. The locomotives formerly worked on the Dinorwic and Penrhyn railways in North Wales. Launceston station contains a museum of vintage cars and motorcycles and a collection of stationary steam engines which are demonstrated at work. There are catering, gift shop and bookshop facilities. At the far end of the line there are pleasant riverside walks and a shaded picnic area, adjacent to Newmills Farm Park (a popular separate attraction). The covered rolling stock ensures an enjoyable visit whatever the weather. The station area was once the site of an Augustinian Priory some of which can be seen by visitors to the railway
Location: Newport Industrial Estate, Launceston, Cornwall
OS reference: SX 328850
Operating society/organisation: The Spice Settlement Trust Co Ltd, trading as the Launceston Steam Railway, Newport, Launceston PL15 8DA
Telephone: (01566) 775665
Stations: Launceston-Hunts Crossing-New Mills
Car park: Newport Industrial Estate, Launceston
Length of line: 2.5 miles
Gauge: 1ft 11.5in
Access by public transport: Main line Gunnislake 13 miles, Plymouth or Bodmin 25 miles
On site facilities: Buffet, transport museum, workshop tours, gift and bookshop, all situated at Launceston
Period of public operation: 28 May until 15 September daily except Saturdays
Public opening: Trains run from 11.00-16.30. Departures about every 40min and more frequently if required. Unlimited riding on date of issue of ticket
Family ticket: Available, 2 adults and up to 4 children, £21.
Adults £6.80, children £4.50

Free travel: Children under three years old
Senior citizens: Discounted tickets £5.50
Groups: Discounted tickets
Journey time: Return 35min
Facilities for disabled: Easy access to all areas except bookshop and motorcycle museum. No toilet facilities for disabled. However, public toilets are reasonably accessible
Special events: Double-headed trains on Wednesdays in July and August (whenever possible). Demonstration freight trains (contact for details)

Industrial locomotives

Name	*No*	*Builder*	*Type*	*Built*
Lilian	—	Hunslet (317)	0-4-0ST	1883
Velinheli	—	Hunslet (409)	0-4-0ST	1886
Covertcoat	—	Hunslet (679)	0-4-0ST	1898
Sybil	—	Bagnall (1760)	0-4-0ST	1906
Dorothea	—	Hunslet (763)	0-4-0ST	1901
—	—	M/Rail (5646)	4wDM	1933
—	—	M/Rail (9546)	4wDM	1950

Locomotive notes: All passenger trains are steam-hauled

Stock
1 electric inspection trolley; 4 bogie carriages (2 open, 2 closed), 1 diesel-electric railcar for maintenance staff
2 Post Office Railway 'Mail Train' units

Steam Centre — Lavender Line — East Sussex

Member: HRA
The Lavender Line is centred around a typical country station, which, somewhat untypically, is in the village it was built to serve. The image portrayed is of the transition steam-diesel era of the 1950s/1960s on the Southern Region of British Railways
Location: Isfield Station, Isfield, Nr Uckfield, East Sussex TN22 5XB. Isfield village is off the A26 between Lewes and Uckfield
OS reference: TQ 452171
Operating society/organisation: The Lavender Line Preservation Society
Telephone/Fax:
Information line: 0891 800645
Business/fax: 01825 750515 (24hr answerphone when not manned)
Internet address: *Web site:* www.lavender-line.co.uk
Car park: On site, free to patrons
Access by public transport: By bus: Service 29 calls at Isfield and runs between Brighton and Tunbridge Wells at half-hourly intervals from Mon-Sat and every two hours on Sundays. Tel: 01273 886200 Brighton & Hove Buses
On site facilities: 'Cinders' buffet/ restaurant, gift shop, goods shed museum, picnic area, access to signalbox. Children's parties arranged on operating days. Family area. Private functions, weddings and parties etc catered for

Multiple-unit

Name	*No*	*Origin*	*Class*	*Type*	*Built*
—	69333	BR	422 / 4BIG	TRBS	1965
—*	60151	BR	205	DTC	1962
—*	60678	BR	205	DMBS	1962
—	60822	BR	205	DTC	1957
—*	60832	BR	205	DTC	1962

*unit 205033

Industrial locomotives

Name	*No*	*Builder*	*Type*	*Built*
Blackie	68012	Hunslet (3193)	0-6-0ST	1944
Austin No 1†	—	Kitson (5459)	0-6-0ST	1932
—	15	Barclay	0-4-0DM	1945
—	16	Barclay	0-4-0DM	1945
—	ND 3827	Hibberd (SC2196/3857)	0-4-0DM	1957
—	ND 10022	Hibberd (SC3986/3968)	0-4-0DM	1960
—	—	Planet (3865)	4wDM	1965

*2ft gauge
†on hire from Llangollen Railway for 2006

Stock
3 ex-BR Mk 1 coaches.
A variety of BR and pre-Nationalisation wagons are in service in a vintage goods train, or are under restoration. A GWR Toad brake van is used on most passenger trains, allowing visitors to ride on the veranda or inside by the stove. The engineering vehicle fleet includes examples from London Transport and pre-Grouping companies

Length of line: 1 mile each out and back trip, takes 15min
Public opening: Open Sundays all year, Bank Holidays, weekends in June, July and August.Wednesdays and Thursdays in August. Site open from 10.00-17.00, trains from 11.00
Please note that the Isfield site is not normally open for viewing outside of operating dates
Facilities for disabled: Access to most facilities on site. Toilets with wheelchair access and baby changing facilities. Wheelchair access to most of site except signalbox and trains. A ramp is

available for partially disabled access to the trains
Special events: To be arranged, please ring for details. Santa Specials November/December.

Ticket price is valid for unlimited rides on day of issue; however, on special event days entry prices, and conditions, may vary

Museum

Leeds Industrial Museum

Leeds

Location: The Leeds Industrial Museum, Armley Mills, Canal Road, Leeds LS12 2QF
OS reference: SE 275342
Operating society/organisation: Leeds City Council, Department of Learning & Leisure, The Town Hall, Headrow, Leeds LS1 2QF
Curator of Engineering: N. Dowlan
Telephone: (0113) 263 7861
Car park: Cark park adjacent to the Museum
Access by public transport: Nos 5A, 14, 66 and 67 from City Square, Leeds (outside the railway station)
Public opening: April-September: Tuesdays-Saturdays 10.00-17.00, Sundays 13.00-17.00. October-March: Tuesdays-Saturdays 10.00-17.00, Sundays 13.00-17.00. Closed Mondays (except Bank Holidays). NB: last admission 16.00 on all days
Special events: Pleae contact for details
On site facilities: Museum shop, refreshments (vending machines), picnic area
Special notes: Facilities for the disabled (toilets etc), lifts. Museum can be viewed by visitors in wheelchairs (most areas are accessible)
Details of locomotive and rolling stock: Locomotive collection includes steam, diesel, mines locomotives and a narrow gauge railway and engines

Industrial locomotives

Name	*No*	*Builder*	*Type*	*Built*
1ft 6in gauge				
Jack	—	Hunslet 684)	0-4-0WT	1898
Coffin	—*	G/Bat (1326)	0-4-0BE	1933
2ft gauge				
Barber	—	T/Green (441)	0-6-2ST	1908
Cheetal	—	Fowler (15991)	0-6-0WT	1923
Simplex	—	M/Rail (1369	4wPM	1918
Hudson Fordson	—	Hudson (36863)	4wDM	1928
Layer	—*	Fowler (21294)	4wDM	1936
Hudson Hunslet	—	Hunslet (2959)	4wDM	1944
Resin	—	Hunslet (2008)	0-4-0DM	1939
Nacob	—*	Hunslet (5340)	0-4-0DM	1957
Sharlston	—†	H/Clarke (1164)	0-4-0DM	1959
Demtox	—†*	Hunslet (6048)	0-4-0DM	1961
2ft 1in gauge				
Fricl	—*	Hunslet (4019)	0-4-0DM	1948
Pitpo	—*	Hunslet	0-4-0	1955
Calverton	—*	H/Clarke (1368)	0-4-0DM	1965
2ft 6in gauge				
Junin	—	H/Clarke (D557)	2-6-2DM	1930
Fimyn	—†	Hunslet (3411)	0-4-0DM	1947
2ft 8in gauge				
Ficol	—*	Hunslet (3200)	0-4-0DM	1945
2ft 11in gauge				
Lurch	—	H/Clarke (D571)	4wDM	1932
3ft gauge				
Lord Granby	—*	H/Clarke (633)	0-4-0ST	1902
Cement	—*	Fowler (20685)	2-4-0DM	1935
Lofti	—*	Hunslet (4057)	0-6-0DM	1953
3ft 6in gauge				
Pioneer	—	H/Clarke (D634)	0-6-0DM	1946
Festival of Britain	—*	H/Clarke (D733)	0-6-0DM	1951
Standard gauge				
Hodbarrow	—*	Hunslet (299)	0-4-0ST	1882
Aldwyth	—	M/Wardle (865)	0-6-0ST	1882
Capper	—	Fowler (22060)	0-4-0DM	1938
Fort William	—*	Fowler (22893)	0-4-0DM	1940
Trecwn	—	Hunslet (2390)	0-4-0DM	1941
Elizabeth	—	H/Clarke (1888)	0-4-0ST	1958
Southam No 2	—*	H/Clarke (D625)	0-4-0DM	1942

Name	No	Builder	Type	Built
Luton	—	G/Bat (1210)	0-4-0BE	1930
Smithy Wood	—*	G/Bat (2543)	0-4-0WE	1955

Notes
*not currently on public display
†on loan to Red Rose Steam Society/Astley Green Colliery Museum
Simplex is on loan to Moseley Industrial Railway Museum
Barber is on loan to the South Tynedale Railway Trust from February 2004

Timetable Service

Leighton Buzzard Railway

Bedfordshire

Member: HRA, TT
The LBR enables visitors to take a 70min journey into the vanished world of the English light railway. Sharp curves and steep gradients make the locomotives work hard and it is unique with its roadside running. The LBR possesses one of the largest collection of narrow gauge locomotives in Britain together with a varied selection of coaches and wagons — an important part of the national railway heritage. Many items are on permanent display, and some can be seen in action at special events
General Manager: J. Horsley
Headquarters: Leighton Buzzard Railway, Page's Park Station, Billington Road, Leighton Buzzard, Bedfordshire LU7 4TN
OS reference: Page's Park SP 928242
Telephone: (01525) 373888, 24hr answerphone with service and event details
Fax: (01525) 377814
Internet address: *e-mail:* info@buzzrail.co.uk
Web site: www.buzzrail.co.uk
Main station: Page's Park. The station is on the A4146 to the south of Leighton Buzzard, near its junction with the A505
Other public stations: Stonehenge Works
Car park: Page's Park, free
Access by public transport: Leighton Buzzard main line station, Silverlink County services from London (Euston), Watford, Hemel Hempstead, Milton Keynes and Northampton (Tel: 08457 484950). Nearest bus stops at Morrisons supermarket (5min walk) and Leighton Buzzard town centre

Locomotives

Name	No	Builder	Type	Built
—	740	O&K (2343)	0-6-0T	1907
—	—	O&K (2544)	0-4-0WT	1907
Pedemoura	—	O&K (10808)	0-6-0WT	1924
—	778	Baldwin (44656)	4-6-0T	1917
—	—	Freudenstein (73)	0-4-0WT	1901
Sezela No 4	—	Avonside (1738)	0-4-0T	1915
Peter Pan	114	K/Stuart (4256)	0-4-0ST	1922
Chaloner	1	de Winton	0-4-0VBT	1877
Bluebell	1	Hibberd (2631)	4wDM	1938
Pixie	2	K/Stuart (4260)	0-4-0ST	1922
Rishra	3	Baguley (2007)	0-4-0T	1921
Doll	4	Barclay (1641)	0-6-0T	1919
Elf	5	O&K (12740)	0-6-0WT	1936
Falcon	7	O&K (8986)	4wDM	1938
—	8	Ruston (217999)	4wDM	1943
Madge	9	O&K (7600)	4wDM	1934
Haydn Taylor	10	M/Rail (7956)	4wDM	1945
P. C. Allen	11	O&K (5834)	0-4-0WT	1912
—	12	M/Rail (6012)	4wPM	1930
Arkle	13	M/Rail (7108)	4wDM	1937
—	14	Hunslet (3646)	4wDM	1946
—	15	Hibberd (2514)	4wDM	1941
—	16	Lister (11221)	4wDM	1939
Damredub	17	M/Rail (7036)	4wDM	1936
Feanor	18	M/Rail (11003)	4wDM	1956
—	19	M/Rail (11298)	4wDM	1965
—	20	M/Rail (60s317)	4wDM	1966
Festoon	21	M/Rail (4570)	4wPM	1929
—	22	under construction	4wDM	—
—	23	Ruston (164346)	4wDM	1932
—	25	M/Rail (7214)	4wDM	1938
—	24	M/Rail (11297)	4wDM	1965
Yimkin	26	Ruston (203026)	4wDM	1941
—	27	Ruston (408430)	4wDM	1957
RAF Stanbridge	28	Ruston (200516)	4wDM	1940
Creepy	29	Hunslet (6008)	4wDM	1963
—	30	M/Rail (8695)	4wDM	1941
—	31	Lister (4228)	4wPM	1931
—	32	Ruston (172892)	4wDM	1934
—	33	Hibberd (3582)	4wDM	1954
Red Rum	34	M/Rail (7105)	4wDM	1936
Binky	35	Hunslet (6619)	0-4-0DM	1966
Caravan	36	M/Rail (7129)	4wDM	1938
—	37	Ruston (172901)	4wDM	1934

(205min walk). (Tel: 01234 228337 for details)
Refreshment facilities: Dobbers buffet at Page's Park for hot & cold snacks, drinks and ice creams. Refreshments also at Stonehenge Works
Souvenir shop: Page's Park and Stonehenge Works
Depots: Page's Park and Stonehenge Works
Length of line: 2.85 miles, 2ft gauge
Journey time: Single 25min, return 70min
Passenger trains: Page's Park-Stonehenge Works
Group discounts for pre-booked parties of 10 or more people. Packages such as Birthday Breaks, Schools trains and Sunset Specials available, plus train hire
Period of public operation: Sundays 12 March-29 September; Mondays 17 April, 1, 29 May, 28 August; Tuesdays 1-22 August; Wednesdays 12 April, 31 May-23 August, 25 October; Thursdays 1 June, 3-24 August; Friday 14 April; Saturdays 5, 29 April, 27 May, 3 June, 5-26 August, 9 September, 7 October
Special events: Mothering Sunday — 26 March; Easter Fun — 14-17 April; Indian Holiday — 29 April-1 May; Teddy Bears and Guide Dogs — 14 May; Father's Day — 18 June; Vintage Vehicles Rally — 25 June; Model Railways — 2 July; Family Fun Day — 6 August; Steam Up Weekend — 9/10 September; Steam Glow — 7 October; Halloween Haunting — 29 October
Working Heritage Attractions: Industry Trains — 16 April, 29 May, 18 June, 10 September
Sand Quarry — 16 April, 28 May, 25 June, 9 September
Facilities for disabled: Priority parking at Page's Park. Ramp access to all facilities including dedicated toilet at Page's Park. Wheelchairs are conveyed in specially adapted coaches. Advance notice appreciated. Web site pages and leaflets available in large print on request
Membership details: The line is operated by unpaid volunteers. Membership secretary, c/o above address
Membership journal: *Chaloner* — quarterly
Marketing name: The Leighton Buzzard Slow Train

Name	*No*	*Builder*	*Type*	*Built*
Harry Barnet	38	Lister (37170)	4wDM	1951
T. W. Lewis	39	Ruston (375316)	4wDM	1954
Trent	40	Ruston (283507)	4wDM	1949
Somme	41	Hunslet (2536)	4wDM	1941
Sarah	42	Ruston (223692)	4wDM	1944
—	43	M/Rail (10409)	4wDM	1954
—	44	M/Rail (7933)	4wDM	1941
—	45	M/Rail (21615)	4wDM	1957
—	46	Ruston (209430)	4wDM	1942
—	47	Hudson (38384)	4wDM	1930
MacNamara	48	Hunslet (4351)	4wDM	1952
—	49	Hibberd (2586)	4wDM	1941
—	50	Hibberd (1568)	4wPM	1927
Beaudesert	80	A/Keef (59R)	4wDM	1999
—	3090	M/Rail (1369)	4wPM	1918
—	—	Hunslet (9347)	4wDH	1994
—	2182	M/Rail (461)	4wPM	1917
LOD 758009	—	M/Rail (8641)	4wDM	1941
LOD 758220	—	M/Rail (8745)	4wDM	1942
RTT/767182	—	Wickham (2522)	4wPMR	1938
WD 767139	—	Wickham (3282)	4wPMR	1943

Stock
10 coaches and a wide selection of wagons

A selection of locomotives and rolling stock is on public display at any one time. Viewing of other stock is by prior arrangement

Miniature Railway

Lightwater Valley Theme Park

North Yorkshire

Location: Lightwater Valley Theme Park
Headquarters: North Stainley, Nr Ripon, North Yorkshire
Contact: Operations & Maintenance Dept: P. Walker
Telephone: 0870 458 0060, 0870 458 0040 (administration/party bookings)
Internet address: *Web site:* www.lightwatervalley.net
Car parking: On site
Access by public transport: Main line station Harrogate (12 miles) and Thirsk (9 miles)
On site facilities: 125 acres of country park featuring unique white knuckle rides including Europe's longest rollercoaster, family attractions, go-karting. Wide range of catering facilities and themed shopping malls
Length of line: 15in gauge; 1 mile long
Period of public operation: Easter-October (daily in June/July/August). Telephone for details

Timetable service

Lincolnshire Wolds Railway

Lincolnshire

Members: HRA
The only standard gauge steam railway in Lincolnshire open to the public. The location is part of the original Great Northern Railway, which opened in 1848
Headquarters: The Railway Station, Ludborough, Grimsby, NE Lincs DN36 5SQ
Telephone: 01507 363881
Internet address: *Web site:* www.lincolnshirewoldsrailway.co.uk
Contacts: David Ambler / Frank Street
Main station: Ludborough
OS reference: TF 302986
Car park: Opposite station site
Access by public transport: No access by rail, very limited Grimsby-Louth bus service
Refreshment facilities: Light refreshments available in buffet car in bay platform on diesel and steam days
Souvenir shop: On site
Museum: On site
Depot: On site
Length of line: 1,400yd at present
Period of public operation: Site open for static viewing all weekends except Christmas. April to September 09.00-16.00, October to March 09.00-15.00. First train leaves at 11.00 on following dates

Locomotives and multiple-units

Name	*No*	*Origin*	*Class*	*Type*	*Built*
—	D3167	BR	08	0-6-0DE	1955
—	97650	BR	—	0-6-0DE	1953

Industrial locomotives

Name	*No*	*Builder*	*Type*	*Built*
Lion	—	Peckett (1657)	0-4-0ST	1914
Fulstow	—No 2	RSH (7849)	0-6-0ST	1955
M. F. P. No 1	—	Fowler (4210131)	0-4-0DM	1957
M. O. P. No 8	—	Fowler (4210145)	0-4-0DM	1958
Tioxide No 4	—	R/Hornsby (375713)	0-4-0DM	1954
Tioxide No 6	—	R/Hornsby (414303)	0-4-0DM	1957
Tioxide No 7	7—	R/Hornsby (421418)	0-4-0DM	1958
—	—	Sentinel (10166)	0-6-0DH	1963
Colonel B	—	Hunslet (5308)	4wDH	1963

Stock
6 ex-BR Mk 2 coaches, various wagons

Owner
D3167 and 97650 on loan from Lincoln City Council

Special events: Steam dates for 2006 are: 2, 16, 30 April; 14, 28 May; 4 June; Lincolnshire Louth Motor Club Day — 18 June; 9 July; Teddy Bear Day — 23 July; 13 August; Vintage Fire Engines — 27 August; 1940s Weekend — 9/10 September; Ploughman's Lunches — 15 October; Saturday Halloween — 28 October (15.00-18.00); Christmas Fair — 19 November

Facilities for disabled: Full facilities should be available on site by Easter 2006, coach in process of adaptation for disabled as another buffet car, access to rest of site and train is complete
Membership journal: *On the Line* — 3 times/year
Special note: Unlimited travel on the day

Museum

Locomotion — The NRM at Shildon

County Durham

Member: HRA
Locomotion is an £11 million project, a joint venture between Sedgefield Borough Council and the National Railway Museum at York, the first branch of a national museum in the region. The development includes interactive displays within buildings which are of historical importance in terms of the town's railway heritage and a brand new high quality 6,000 sq ft centre, which houses up to 60

Locomotives and multiple-units

Name	*No*	*Origin*	*Class*	*Type*	*Built*
Sans Pareil		L&MR		0-4-0	1829
Cornwall	3020	LNWR	—	2-2-2	1847
—	563	LSWR	T3	4-4-0	1893
—	75S	W&CR	—	Bo electric	1898
—	68846	GNR	J52	0-6-0ST	1899
	1	NER	BTH	Bo electric	1904
—	901	NER	T3	0-8-0	1919
—	2	NSR	New L	0-6-2T	1923
—	2500	LMS	4P	2-6-4T	1934
—	2700	LMS	5P4F	2-6-0	1934
_	10656	SR	2BIL	DMBSK	1937

vehicles from the national collection.
Museum Manager: Dr George Muirhead
Location/address: Locomotion, Shildon, Co Durham DL4 1PQ
Telephone: 01388 777999
Telephone/Fax: 01388 771448
Internet addresses: *e-mail:* sjoyce@locomotion.uk.com
Web site: www.locomotion.uk.com
Car parking: Available on site, also disabled and coach parking
Access by public transport: Rail – 3min walk from Shildon station. Bus – local bus services (call Traveline on 0870 608 2608). Car – Junction 58 A1M, take A68 and A6072 to Shildon and follow signs
On site facilities: Café, children's playground, picnic area, public art sculpture, shop
Length of line: 1 kilometre
Public opening: 10.00-17.00 every day from Easter to end of October. 10.00-16.00 Wednesday to Sunday from November to Easter. Closed 19 December-4 January
Special events: A full and exciting events programme, contact Locomotion for full details
Access for disabled: All buildings fully accessible. Call Locomotion in advance to book a wheelchair. Bio-bus accommodates disabled visitors to transport from one end of the site to the other.
Special note: Steam train rides on summer Sundays and event days

Name	*No*	*Origin*	*Class*	*Type*	*Built*
—	12123	SR	2BIL	DTCK	1937
—§§	80079	BR	4MT	2-6-4T	1954
Deltic	—	E/Electric	-	Co-Co	1955
—	E5001	BR	71	Bo-Bo	1959
—	03090	BR	03	0-6-0DM	1960
Sans Pareil	—*	L&MR		0-4-0	1980

Industrial and Army locomotives

Name	*No*	*Builder*	*Type*	*Built*
Woolmer	—	Avonside (1572)	0-6-0ST	1910
—	—	Simplex (4217)	4wPM	1925
Hexhamshire	15	A/Whitworth (D21)	0-4-0DE	1933
Merlin	—§	Peckett	0-4-0ST	1939
Hetton Loco	—	G. Stephenson	0-4-0	1851
King Fisal of Iraq	—	Hunslet (3183)	0-6-0ST	1944
—	1	Barclay (2373)	0-4-0F	1956
—	—	H/Clarke (D1345)	0-4-0DH	1970
Eustace Forth	—	R/Hornsby (7063)	0-6-0ST	1942
—	14†	H/Clarke (D1274)	0-6-0DM	1961
—	—	H/Clarke (D1345)	0-6-0DM	1967
MTR	9†	Hunslet (9227	B-BDH	1986

*replica of original Liverpool & Manchester Railway built for the 150th anniversary
§off-site for overhaul
†3ft gauge

Rolling stock powered units – gas turbine
1972 BR Advanced Passenger Train

Rolling stock powered units – electric
1983 BR APT prototype train

Rolling Stock Powered Units — Diesel
1937 SR Driving Motor Brake Third No S10656S
1937 SR Driving Trailer Composite No S12123S

Rolling stock – departmental
1850 GNR 4-wheel hand crane No 112
1891 NER snow plough No DE900566
1904 MR Officers' Saloon No 2234
1949 BR Matisa tamping machine No 74007
1957 BR Track recording trolley No DX 50002 Neptune

Rolling Stock — Passenger
1845 S&DR 1st/3rd Composite No 59
1850 SDR 3rd No 179
1872 NLR Directors' Saloon No 1032
1887 GWR 6-wheel tricomposite No 820
1905 LNWR Corridor 1st Brake 5154 (Royal Train)
1905 LNWR Corridor 1st Brake 5154 (support vehicle)
1908 ECJS Passenger Brake Van No 109
1927 Rhodesian Railways sleeping car
1928 LMS 3rd Sleeping Car No 14241
1962 BR Mk II 1st corridor No 21274

Rolling stock – freight and non passenger carrying
1826 Cramlington Colliery Chaldron Wagon
1870 S&DR Chaldron Wagon (replica)
1870 Seaham Harbour Colliery Chaldron Wagon
1889 Shell-Mex oil tank wagon No 512

1901	Shell/BP Tank Wagon No 3171
1907	NER 16-ton bogie stores van No 041273
1912	NER Sand wagon No DE14974
1920	GCR single bolster wagon
1920	GNR double bolster wagon
1926	GWR Fitted open wagon No 108246
1935	GWR Motor car van No 126438
1936	LMS Tube wagon No 499254
1940	WD Warflat No 161042
1940	LNER Tunnel Van No DE471818
1946	SNCF 16-ton mineral wagon No ADB192437
1946	LNER 20-ton hopper wagon No E270919
1950	BR 24-ton iron ore hopper wagon No B436275
1951	BR(SR) Show cattle wagon No S3733S
1952	BR 30-ton bogie bolster wagon No B943139
1953	Buxton Lime Quarries 23-ton bogie hopper wagon No 19154
1954	BR 27-ton iron ore Tippler No B383560
1954	National Benzole oil tank wagon No 2022
1955	BR china clay tip wagon No B743141
1957	BR Horse box No S96369
1959	BR Conflat No B737725
1960	BR Banana Van No B882593
1961	BR Presflo cement wagon No B873368
1964	Prototype HAA coal hopper wagon, No 350000
1965	BR Boiler Wagon Nos DB902805, DB902806, DB902807, DB902808
1970	Phillips Petroleum 100-ton GLW tank wagon No PP85209
1970	S&D Chaldron Wagon (replica), Shildon

Locomotive tender
SDR 'Collier' class *Etherley*

Powered units
SR 2BIL unit, No 2090

Passenger stock

1850	SDR 3rd No 179
1908	ECJS Passenger brake van LNER No 396
1970	S&D chaldron wagon (replica)

Owners
80079 on loan from Severn Valley Railway
H/Clarke (D1345) private

Museum

London's Transport Museum Depot

London

Member: HRA, TT
The Depot is a working museum store and treasure trove of over 370,000 objects. Attractions include rare road and rail vehicles, station models, signs, ticket machines, posters and original artwork
Contact: Covent Garden, London WC2E 7BB
Depot location: 118-120 Gunnersbury Lane, Acton, London W3 8BQ
Operating society/organisation: Transport for London
Telephone:
020 7565 7299 (24hr recorded)
020 7379 6344 (Administration, education service, group bookings, events and archives, corporate hospitality, mail order enquieries)
Fax: 020 7565 7250
Internet address:
W-mail: enquiry@ltmuseum.co.uk
Web site: www.ltmuseum.co.uk
Access by public transport: Bus or Underground to Acton Town station
Access by car: Parking on site is reserved for blue badge holders and

Locomotives and multiple-units

Name	*No*	*Origin*	*Class*	*Type*	*Built*
—*	23	Met Rly	A	4-4-0T	1866
*John Hampden**	5	Met Rly	—	Bo-Bo	1922
—	13	C&SLR	—		1890
—	ESL107	LT	—	Bo-Bo	1940
—	L35	LT	—	Bo-BoBE	1938
—	10012	LT	1938	DM	1938
—	012256	LT	1938	T	1939
—	12048	LT	1938	M	1939
—	11012	LT	1938	DM	1938
—	11152	LT	1938	DM	1939
—	320	LT	Standard		1925-34
—	846	LT	Standard		1925-34
—	1789	LT	Standard		1925-34
—	3693	LT	Standard		1925-34
—	3328	LT	Standard		1925-34
—	4184	LT	Q	DM	1923
—*	4248	LT	Q23	DM	1923
—	08063	LT	Q35	T	1935
—	4416	LT	Q38	DM	1938
—	4417	LT	Q38	DM	1938
—	22679	LT	R49	DM	1952
—	16	LT	Prototype	DM	1986
—	3530	LT	1972	DM	1972
—	3763	LT	1983	DM	1983

Industrial locomotives

Origin	*Builder*	*Type*	*Built*
Wotton Tramway†	A/Porter (807)	0-4-0TG	1872

must be requested in advance. Limited parking available in local area. Parking available for groups booking a private view
On site facilities: Museum shop (open weekends only), lecture theatre
Public opening: Open weekends: 20/21 May and 21/22 October. Pre-booked guided tours on the last Friday and Saturday of the month (except December). Private views can be arranged for groups.
Open Weekends; Adults £6.95, Concessions £4.95, Friends (of LT Museum) and accompanied children under 16 free.
Guided tours: Adults £10.00, Concessions £8.50.
For group bookings, please contact the Museum in advance, group rates available for pre-booked parties of 10 or more
Facilities for disabled: Disabled toilet, on the ground floor, ramps and wheelchair platforms to some areas and a lift to the first floor. Parking on site for blue badge holders must be booked in advance. The Museum offers a range of British Sign Language tours and talk, as well as object handling sessions. For further information, contact the resource Desk on 020 7379 6344, minicom 0207565 7310 or e-mail enquiry@ltmuseum.co.uk
Special events: Open weekends are themed:
150 Years of the London General Omnibus Co — 20/21 May; Family Weekend — 21/22 October
Membership details: Details from the Friends of London's Transport Museum on 020 7565 7296. Benefits include fre enty to The Depot Open Weekends (whilst the Museum in Covent Garden is undergoing refurbishment), discount on purchases made at London}s Transport Museum shops in Covent Garden and Acton, discounted rate on talks and events. These are just some of the benefits available

Rolling stock: passenger
Metropolitan Railway Jubilee coach body 1899

Rolling stock: freight
City & South London Railway ballast wagon, No 63 of 1921
Metropolitan Railway milk van of 1890

*at Covent Garden and not available for viewing
†on loan to Buckinghamshire Railway Museum

Miniature Railway

Longleat Railway

Wiltshire

Contact: T. Moore
Headquarters: Longleat Railway, Warminster, Wilts BA12 7NW
Telephone: 01985 844400
Internet address: *Web site:* www.longleat.co.uk
Car parking: On site
Access by public transport: Main line stations at Frome or Warminster
On site facilities: Too numerous to list, but include: grounds and gardens, safari park, historic house, Lord Bath's murals, safari boats, pets corner, etc
Souvenir shops: throughout the attraction
Length of line: 1.25 miles, 15in gauge
Opening times: House open all year (except Christmas Day). All attractions open daily from mid-February to early November. Railway operates from March to November 10.00 (up to) 18.00 (might be earlier during off-peak season).
Please contact for opening times/dates of specific attractions.

Locomotives

Name	*No*	*Builder*	*Type*	*Built*
Dougal	3	S/Lamb	0-6-2T	1970
Lenka	4	Longleat	4-4DHR	1984
Ceawlin	5	Longleat*	2-8-2DH	1989

*rebuilt from Severn-Lamb 2-8-0DH dating from 1975

Rolling stock
11 passenger coaches and 2 works wagons

Steam Centre

Lynton & Barnstaple Railway

Devon

Member: HRA
The Lynton & Barnstaple Railway in North Devon is one of the world's most famous and picturesque narrow gauge lines. Passengers can now travel along part of the original route within the Exmoor National Park above the Heddon Valley near Parracombe. Awarded the HRA Annual Award for Small Groups 'for successfully re-creating the ambience of the legendary L&BR and for successfully running trains on the original trackbed at Woody Bay 69 years after the railway closed'
Location/headquarters: Lynton & Barnstaple Railway, Woody Bay Station, Martinhoe Cross, Parracombe, Devon EX31 4RA
Telephone: 01598 763487
Internet address: *Web site:* www.lynton-rail.co.uk
Contact: Tony Nicholson, 10 Castle Heights, Lynton, Devon EX35 6JD
Chairman L&BR Co: Mike Buse
Chairman L&BR Trust: Peter Bowes
Main station: Woody Bay
Other station: Chelfham
OS references: Woody Bay SS 684464
Chelfham SS 610357
Car park: Woody Bay station only
Access by public transport: First Bus service 300 (Taunton-Minehead-Ilfracombe-Barnstaple), 309 and 310 (both Barnstaple-Lynton) all stop at Woody Bay station; the 310 largely follows the original route of the railway and also stops at Chelfham
Length of line: currently 1 mile, 1ft 11.5in gauge
On site facilities: Light refreshments and souvenirs are available at Woody Bay station
Passenger services: most days between Easter and the end of October
Facilities for disabled: Toilets and access to trains and refreshments/ shop
Membership details: Membership Secretary, David Bradbury, Rancourt, Riverside, Temple Gardens, Staines, Middx TW18 3NJ (*e-mail:* dabradbury@aol.co.uk)
Membership journal: *Lynton & Barnstaple Railway Magazine* — three times a year

Locomotives

Name	*No*	*Builder*	*Type*	*Built*
Emmet	—	Haylock	0-4-0T	2003
Pilton	—*	Drewry (2393)	0-6-0DM	1952
—	—	Hunslet (6660)	4wDH	1965
Snapper	—	R/Hornsby (283871)	4wDM	1950
Holwell Castle	—	Simplex	4wDM	1965
Titch	—	M/Rail (8729)	4wDM	1941
Exmoor Ranger	—	Hunslet (6348)	4wDM	1975

*under restoration off-site
Two steam locomotives will also be available

Owners
Exmoor Ranger on loan from Woodhorn Colliery Museum

Steam Centre

Mangapps Farm Railway Museum

Essex

Member: HRA
Mangapps re-creates the atmosphere of a rural light railway, featuring a large museum collection, strong in items of East Anglian interest, railway signalling and goods rolling stock. Other features include original station buildings from Mid-Suffolk Light, Great Eastern and Midland & Great Northern Railways
Superintendent of the Line: John Jolly
Commercial Manager: June Jolly
Location: Mangapps Farm Railway Museum, Southminster Road, Burnham-on-Crouch, Essex

Locomotives and multiple-units

Name	*No*	*Origin*	*Class*	*Type*	*Built*
—	2018	BR	03	0-6-0DM	1958
—	D2089	BR	03	0-6-0DM	1960
—	03081	BR	03	0-6-0DM	1960
—	03399	BR	03	0-6-0DM	1961
—	D2325	BR	04	0-6-0DM	1961
—	51381	BR	117	DTS	1961
—	22624	LT	R38	DMS	1938
—	1030	LT	1959	DM	1959
—	2044	LT	1959	T	1959
—	79963*	W&M	—	Railbus	1958

*on loan from the Poppy Line

Industrial locomotives

Name	*No*	*Builder*	*Type*	*Built*
Minnie	—	F/Walker (358)	0-6-0ST	1878

CM0 8QQ. (Entrance on B1021, 1 mile north of Burnham)
Telephone: (01621) 784898
Fax: (01621) 783833
Internet address: *Web site:* www.mangapps.co.uk
Access by public transport: Burnham station approx 1 mile
On site facilities: Station, car park, souvenir shop, toilets, amenity and picnic areas
Refreshment facilities: Teas and light refreshments
Length of line: Three-quarter-mile
Public opening: Weekends & Bank Holidays all year (except 25/26 December) and daily during Easter and summer school holidays. Closed 2-31 January. Steam trains operate every Sunday in August, Bank Holiday Sundays and Mondays and special event days. Diesel trains run on all other days
Opening times: Weekends (except January), Bank Holidays (except Christmas) daily during Easter fortnight and August school holidays — 11.30-16.30
Special events: Please contact for details

Name	*No*	*Builder*	*Type*	*Built*
Brookfield	—	Bagnall (2613)	0-6-0PT	1940
Empress	—	Bagnall (3061)	0-6-0ST	1954
Toto	—	Barclay (1619)	0-4-0ST	1919
—	47	Barclay (2157)	0-4-0ST	1943
Hastings	—	Hunslet (469)	0-6-0ST	1888
Elland	No 1	H/Clarke (D1153)	0-4-0DM	1959
—	11104	Drewry (2252)	0-6-0DM	1953
—	—	S/Henshaw (7502)	4wDM	1966

Rolling stock
LNER Gresley and BR Mk1 coaching stock, extensive stock of goods wagons)

Timetable Service

Mid-Hants Railway

Hampshire

Member: HRA
Originally built as the Winchester to Alton link, the Mid-Hants Railway became known as the Watercress Line through regularly carrying this local produce to London markets. Now restored, the line runs from its main line connection at Alton through rolling countryside to its terminus at Alresford. Large and powerful locomotives work impressively over the steeply inclined route, known to railwaymen as 'the Alps'. No 41312 entered service early 1999. No 34016 returned to service in summer 2003. Nos 34016 and 73096 have seen considerable use on the main line
Headquarters: Mid-Hants Railway plc, Alresford Station, Alresford, Hants SO24 9JG
Telephone: 01962 733810
Fax: 01962 735448
Talking timetable: 01962 734866
Internet address: *Web site:* www.watercressline.co.uk
Main station: Alresford
Other public stations: Ropley, Medstead & Four Marks, Alton
OS reference: Alresford SU 588325, Ropley SU 629324
Car park: Alresford, pay &

Locomotives

Name	*No*	*Origin*	*Class*	*Type*	*Built*
—	30499	LSWR	S15	4-6-0	1920
—	30506	LSWR	S15	4-6-0	1920
Harry A. Frith	E828	SR	S15	4-6-0	1923
—	31625	SR	U	2-6-0	1929
—	31806	SR	U	2-6-0	1926
—	31874	SR	N	2-6-0	1925
Bodmin	34016	SR	WC	4-6-2	1945
249 Squadron	34073	SR	BB	4-6-2	1948
Swanage	34105	SR	WC	4-6-2	1950
Canadian Pacific	35005	SR	MN	4-6-2	1945
—	41312	LMS	2MT	2-6-2T	1952
—	45379	LMS	5MT	4-6-0	1937
Bittern	60019	LNER	A4	4-6-2	1937
—	73096	BR	5MT	4-6-0	1956
—	76017	BR	4MT	2-6-0	1954
—	D3358	BR	08	0-6-0DE	1957
—	12049	BR	11	0-6-0DE	1948
—	D5353	BR	27	Bo-Bo	1961
—	D6593	BR	33	Bo-Bo	1962
—	45132	BR	45	1Co-Co1	1961
—	51363	BR	117	DMBS	1959
—	51405	BR	117	DMS	1959
—	55003	BR	122	DMBS	1958
—	59505*	BR	117	TC	1959
—	59510*	BR	117	TCL	1959
—	59511*	BR	117	TCL	1959
—†	60124	BR	205	DMBS	1957
—†	60824	BR	205	DTCL	1957

*available for use as locomotive-hauled coaching stock
†unit No 205025

Right: The Mid-Hants Railway has a connection to the national network and over the last few years has been host to a number of visiting locomotives stopping over during a break in main line commitments. Here No 71000 *Duke of Gloucester* runs round its train at Alton on the occasion of an open day for members of the locomotive's supporting Trust. *ACB*

Below: Seen from the platform of the current Wymondham Abbey station the Mid-Norfolk Railway's permanent way department are putting in the final touches to a new loop. This will enable locomotives to run round the train. Class 20 No D8069 provides the motive power. *ACB*

display (free Sundays & Bank Holidays). Alton station pay & display
Access by public transport: *SouthWest Train services* — just over 1hr from London, Waterloo. Alternatively, travel to Winchester station and catch a bus from nearby City Road.
Bus services – operated by Stagecoach 0870 608 2608
Refreshment facilities: Buffet service on most trains; 'West Country' buffet at Alresford; T. Junction picnic area at Ropley; tea/coffee available at Alton when information office open
Catering facilities: The 'Countryman Pullman' pre-booked Sunday lunch trains, Christmas specials, and some evening trains. The 'Watercress Belle' operates on certain Saturday evenings March-December. Early booking is essential, please telephone to confirm seat availability for both trains. Real Ale trains run selected Saturday evenings featuring beers from local breweries and light snacks to purchase
Souvenir shops: Alresford, Alton and Ropley
On site facilities: Picnic area, children's play area and viewing facilities at Ropley. Interpretative display in Alresford shop
Depot: Ropley. Locomotive yard open on operating days 10.30-16.30
Length of line: 10 miles
Passenger trains: Phone Talking Timetable (01962 734866), or visit web site to confirm details. Bank Holidays and weekends January to October; various midweek dates May to September (inc), school half term in February, October half term 'Wizard Week', Steam Galas, Day out with Thomas at Easter and August. Santa Specials in December (bookings commence October)
Journey time: Round trip 1hr 40min max
Special events: Steam Gala — 3-5 March; Day out with Thomas — 8-17 April; War on the Line — 24/25 June; Steam Gala — 22-24 September; Bus Rally — 16 July; Wizard Week — 21-29 October; Santa Specials — December
Facilities for disabled: Toilets at Ropley and the old goodshed at Alresford station. Passengers in fixed wheelchairs can be carried in the brake compartment on most trains. Ramps are provided to ease entry to trains. Ask SouthWest Trains staff at Alton to cross foot crossing
Membership details: Membership Secretary, c/o above address

Industrial locomotives

Name	No	Builder	Type	Built
—	4	Fowler (22889)	0-4-0DM	1939
Thomas	1	Hunslet (3781)	0-6-0T	1954
Douglas	10	Hunslet (2890)	0-6-0	1943

Stock
23 ex-BR Mk 1 coaches; 2 ex-BR Mk 2 coaches used for accommodation; 2 ex-BR Mk 1 Pullman Cars; 3 ex-SR coaches; 1 ex-LSWR coach; 1 ex-LMS coach; 3 steam cranes; Numerous goods vehicles

Owners
30499 and 30506 the Urie Locomotive Society
E828 the Eastleigh Preservation Society
34105 the 34105 Light Pacific Group
35005 Bryherley Ltd
76017 the Standard 4 Locomotive Group
12049 Day Aggregates

Mid-Norfolk Railway

Timetable Service

Norfolk

Member: HRA
A scheme to preserve part of the former Great Eastern line from Wymondham to Wells-next-the-Sea. The section from Wymondham to Dereham has been purchased and opened for passenger and freight traffic since May 1999. Clearance work is now completed on the Dereham-North Elmham section. The Mid-Norfolk Railway Preservation Trust also operates County School station as a tea room and visitor centre during the summer months
Headquarters: The Railway Station, Station Road, Dereham, Norfolk NR19 1DF

Locomotives and multiple-units

Name	No	Origin	Class	Type	Built
—	D8069	BR	20	Bo-Bo	1961
—	31235	BR	31	A1A-A1A	1960
Sister Dora	31530	BR	31	A1A-A1A	1961
—	31538	BR	31	A1A-A1A	1959
Aldeburgh Festival	47596†	BR	47	Co-Co	1966
Ramillies	50019	BR	50	Co-Co	1968
Oystermouth	56040†	BR	56	Co-Co	1978
—	51226	M/Cam	101	DMBS	1958
Matthew Smith	51434	M/Cam	101	MBS	1958
—	51499	M/Cam	101	DMBS	1959
—	51503	M/Cam	101	DMC	1959
—	55009	Gloucester	122	DMBS	1958
—	59117	M/Cam	101	TC	1958
—	56301*	Gloucester	100	DTC	1957
—	68004	BR	MLV / 419	DMVL	1959

Main station: Dereham
Telephone: (01362) 690633
Talking timetable: (01362) 851723 (answerphone)
Fax: (01362) 698487
Internet address:
Web site: www.mnr.org.uk
e-mail: info@mnr.org.uk
Car park: At Dereham
Museum: Small relics museum at Dereham
Souvenir shop: Dereham
Refreshment facilities: Railway Buffet at Dereham (March-December) and tea room at County School station (summer only)
Access by public transport: Bus from Norwich and King's Lynn. 'One' Anglia trains to Wymondham
Period of public operation: Weekends and bank holidays 18 March to 29 October. Wednesdays 10 May to 25 October. Thursdays 27 July to 7 September. Sundays 5-19 November
Special events: Diesel Gala — 18/19 March; Easter Specials —

†expected to arrive during 2006
*in use as static shop and tea room at County School station

Industrial locomotives

Name	*No*	*Builder*	*Type*	*Built*
—§	GET 2	Bagnall (8368)	0-4-0DM	1962
—§	GET 5	Drewry (2566)	0-4-0DM	1955
—§	GET 7	B/Drewry (3733)	4wDE	1977
—§	GET 8	R/Royce (10272)	0-6-0DM	1967
—§	GET 9	R/Hornsby (512842)	0-4-0DE	1965
—§	11103	Drewry (2583)	0-4-0DM	1956

§privately owned, stored at Hardingham and viewable from trains, no public access

Locomotive notes: D8069, 31235, 31538 and 50019, also various DMUs are in service

Rolling stock: 1 BR Mk 1 coach, 9 BR Mk 2 coaches, BR Mk 2 TSO 5536 used as static bar coach, 10-ton rail-mounted crane, selection of freight wagons, operational and stored at Hardingham

Owners
50019 and 68004 the Class 50 Locomotive Association
47596 the Stratford 47 Group
31235 the Colne Valley Enterprises Ltd
D8069 the Type One Association
GET the Great Eastern Traction group
56040 the Class 56 Group

WICKLEWOOD
MORLEY
DEREHAM
WYMONDHAM 2
B1135
QUALITY ASSURED
VISITOR
ATTRACTION
MID-NORFOLK RAILWAY
Station Road, Dereham, NR19 1DF
01362 690633 www.mnr.org.uk
East Anglia's longest heritage railway

16/17 April; 1960s Weekend — 17/18 June; 1970s Weekend — 15/16 July; Autumn Diesel Gala — 23/24 September; Halloween Specials — 28 October; Carol Service Special (to Thuxton) and Santa Specials — 3, 10, 17, 24 December

Membership details: Membership Secretary c/o Dereham Station

Membership journal: *The Blastpipe* (four times a year)

Museum

Mid-Suffolk Light Railway

Suffolk

Member: HRA

The Mid-Suffolk Light Railway, known affectionately as 'The Middy',was a classic case of a railway built late on in the great railway age that never paid its way. It effectively went broke before it opened but still managed to struggle on for 50 years. This example of quirky English history is remembered in Suffolk's only railway museum

Location: Wetheringsett, Nr Stowmarket, Suffolk IP14 5PW

OS reference: TM 129659

Operating organisation: Mid-Suffolk Light Railway Company

Telephone: 01449 766899

Internet address: *Web site:* www.mslr.org.uk

Car park: On site

Access by public transport: Some local buses from Ipswich to Diss set down and pick up on the A140 Ipswich-Norwich road near to the museum. Local buses from Stowmarket to Wetheringsett. Services tend to be infrequent and the timetables are subject to change at short notice. Details of services can be obtained from Traveline 0870 608 2608 or www.traveline.org.uk

On site facilities: Souvenir shop, refreshments, railway walk, railwayana and photographic exhibition, toilets (including disabled) and picnic area

Period of public opening: Usually open on Sundays and Bank Holidays from Easter to end September, plus Wednesday afternoons in August

Special events: Steam event days: Easter Sunday and Monday, early and late May Bank Holiday Sundays and Mondays. 18 June, 2 July. Every Sunday in August. August Bank Holiday Monday, 10 September, 10 and 17 December

Special notes: Museum dedicated to Mid-Suffolk Light Railway. Original MSLR restored buildings and artefacts. Reproduction MSLR ticket on entry. *Railway World* award winner in 1994 and HRA award winner in 2002

Facilities for disabled: Most of the site is accessible for disabled users. A wheelchair is available on request and there is wheelchair access to the demonstration passenger train. Toilets are accessible to wheelchair users

Membership details: Membership Secretary, Poachers Cottage, Church Hill, Stowmarket, Suffolk IP14 4SQ

Society journal: *Making Tracks:* quarterly MSLRS Newsletter

Industrial locomotives

Name	*No*	*Builder*	*Type*	*Built*
Little Barford	—	Barclay	0-4-0ST	1939
—	1604	H/Clarke (1604)	0-6-0ST	1928
—	304470	R/Hornsby (304470)	0-4-0DM	1951

Rolling stock

GER 2-compartment brake third, GER 6-compartment brake third, GER 3-compartment first, 1 GER ventilated van, 1 GER non-ventilated van, private owner coal wagon (rebuilt from BR open wagon), BR tube wagon, LNER brake van, NER milk van body, 2 GER 5 compartment third bodies, GER ventilated van body. GER steel outside frame ventilated van, GER horsebox body, conflat (to provide underframe for horsebox), replica contractor open wagon

Steam Centre

Middleton Railway

Leeds

Member: HRA

This is a preserved section of 'the world's oldest working railway', authorised by the first railway Act of Parliament in 1758, and also the first standard gauge railway to be taken over by volunteers in 1960

Headquarters: Middleton Railway Trust Ltd, Moor Road, Hunslet, Leeds LS10 2JQ

Telephone: 0113 271 0320

Internet addresses: *e-mail:* info@middletonrailway.org.uk *Web site:* www.middletonrailway.org.uk

Main station: Moor Road, Hunslet

OS reference: SE 302309

Car park: Moor Road (free)

Access by public transport: Nearest main line station, Leeds City. Bus service No 61 from Aire Street (next to Leeds City station) to Tunstall Road (then 150yd walk)

Souvenir shop: Moor Road

Above: There is a great contrast between the size of various heritage railways, although the ambitions are just as great. Here at Brockford on the Mid-Suffolk Light Railway volunteers are recreating the 'Middy'. The line's Ruston Hornsby diesel is at the head of a short train. *Phil Barnes*

Below: Moving up the scale we come to the Midland Railway — Butterley. Here Nos 47357 and 80098 raise steam at Swanwick shed. *Phil Barnes*

Museum: In preparation. Depot open weekends and Bank Holidays 10.00 to 16.30 in season
Length of line: 1.25 miles (extension pending)
Passenger trains: Sunday trains, Bank Holidays and special events steam operated. Saturdays usually diesel hauled. Charter trains can be arranged, but see below
Period of public operation: The railway will reopen on Saturday 15 April 2006 then run every Saturday to 28 October between 13.00 and 16.20. On Sundays and Bank Holidays to 26 November trains will run between 11.00 and 16.20. Santa trains will operate on December weekends when an amended timetable will apply
Special events: Walk in the Woods — 7, 14 May; in association with Hunslet Festival (24/25 June; Everything Goes Gala — 23/24 September; Halloween Trains — 28/29 October
Facilities for disabled: Good access with additional assistance by prior arrangement. Disabled toilets, reserved car parking spaces. These may not be available at all times due to the major engineering works
Special notes: Never having closed since 1758 the railway still operates under its original Act of Parliament. The first railway to successfully use steam locomotives commercially from 1812. The first standard gauge railway to be operated by volunteers from June 1960. Conveyed 10,000 tons of freight annually from BR to local works from 1960 to 1983. Part of South Leeds Heritage Trail, highlighting former locomotive works in the area, and other historic places

Locomotives

Name	*No*	*Origin*	*Class*	*Type*	*Built*
—	1310	NER	Y7	0-4-0T	1891
—	68153	LNER	Y1	0-4-0VB	1933
—	385	DSB	HsII	0-4-0WT	1893
John Alcock	7051	LMS	—	0-6-0DM	1932
(Olive)	RDB998901	BR	—	4wDM	1950

Industrial locomotives

Name	*No*	*Builder*	*Type*	*Built*
John Blenkinsop	—	Peckett (2003)	0-4-0ST	1941
—	—	Peckett (2103)	0-4-0ST	1948
—	—	Bagnall (2702)	0-4-0ST	1943
Henry de Lacy II	—	H/Clarke (1309)	0-4-0ST	1917
Mirvale	—	H/Clarke (1882)	0-4-0ST	1955
Manchester Ship Canal No 67	—	H/Clarke (1329)	0-6-0T	1921
—	11	Hunslet (1453)	0-4-0ST	1925
Picton	—	Hunslet (1540)	2-6-2T	1927
—	1684	Hunslet (1684)	0-4-0T	1931
Brookes No 1	—	Hunslet (2387)	0-6-0T	1941
Windle	—	Borrows (53)	0-4-0WT	1909
Matthew Murray	—	M/Wardle (1601)	0-6-0ST	1903
Lucy	—	Cockerill	0-4-0VBT	1890
Sir Berkeley†	—	M/Wardle (1210)	0-6-0ST	1891
—	6	H/Leslie (3860)	0-4-0ST	1935
Carroll	—	H/Clarke (D631)	0-4-0DM	1946
Mary	—	H/Clarke (D577)	0-4-0DM	1932
—	—	Hunslet (1786)	0-4-0DM	1935
—	—	Fowler (3900002)	0-4-0DM	1945
Austin No 1	—	Peckett (5003)	0-4-0DM	1961
—	—	Thomas Hill (138C)	0-4-0DH	1963
Rowntrees No 3	—	R/Hornsby (441934)	4wDM	1960
—*	D2999	Brush (91)/ Beyer Peacock (7856)	0-4-0DE	1958
—	—	G/Batley (420452)	4wDE	1979

*on loan from BSC Orb Works, Newport
†on 10 year loan from Vintage Carriages Trust, but may be away on hire at times

Stock
2 CCTs converted for passenger use Nos 1867 and 2048; CCT as stores van No 2073. Various goods vehicles; 5-ton Booth rail crane; 1 3-ton Smith steam crane; 1 3-ton Isles steam crane; 7.5-ton steam crane

Owners
1310, 385 the Steam Power Trust
RDB998901 the EM2 Locomotive Society

Timetable Service

Midland Railway — Butterley

Derbyshire

Member: HRA, TT
The Midland Railway — Butterley is a rapidly developing Preservation Scheme with a difference. The massive 57 acre Museum site and 35 acre Country Park enabled the Centre to become 'More Than Just a Railway' as its publicity says. The seven road Matthew Kirtley Museum allows much of the historic collection to be on display and most of the locomotives to be stored and displayed under cover. A miniature railway (3.5 and 5in gauge) and a 1-mile narrow gauge line (2ft gauge) carries passengers through the Country Park; Brittain Pit Farm Park, with its wide variety of livestock; and of course there is a 3.5-mile standard gauge line complete with Midland signals,

three restored signalboxes, Butterley station, the scenic delights of Butterley Reservoir and Golden Valley!

The Victorian Railwaymen's Church, the demonstration signalbox, and all the other many attractions that make up the Midland Railway — Butterley will be open throughout the year. 2006 is the 25th anniversary of the re-opening of the line for passenger trains with many special events planned. The new station building and footbridge at Swanwick Junction will also be completed during the year

Location: Midland Railway, Butterley Station, Nr Ripley, Derbyshire DE5 3QZ
OS reference: SK 403520
General Manager: John Hett
Operating society/organisation: Midland Railway Trust Ltd
Telephone: Ripley (01773) 747674, Visitor Information Line (01773) 570140.
Fax: (01773) 570271
Internet address:
e-mail: mrc@rapidial.co.uk
Web site: midlandrailwaycentre.co.uk
Car park: Butterley station on B6179 1 mile north of Ripley
On site facilities: Museum, award winning country park, Brittain Pit Farm Park, souvenir shops, miniature railway, narrow gauge railway, garden railway, model railways
Refreshment facilities: Butterley station buffet, Johnson Buffet (Swanwick), on-train bars and extensive 'Wine and Dine' trains, 'The Midlander' (details from above address).
'Midday Midlander' Sunday lunch trains will run on selected Sundays — these need to be booked in advance
Length of line: Standard gauge 3.5 miles, narrow gauge 0.8-mile
Public opening: Trains run every Sunday and Bank Holiday Monday from 8 January to 31 December, every Saturday from 21 January to 24 December EXCEPT 18 March, 22 April, 23 September, 11 November,
Every day 8-23 April, 27 May to 4 June, 22 July to 31 August, 22-29 October, 20-24 December, 27 December-1 January 2007.
On other dates The Midland

Locomotives and multiple-units

Name	*No*	*Origin*	*Class*	*Type*	*Built*
Princess Margaret Rose	46203	LMS	8P	4-6-2	1935
Duchess of Sutherland	6233	LMS	8P	4-6-2	1938
—	44027	LMS	4F	0-6-0	1924
—	44932	LMS	5MT	4-6-0	1945
—	45491	LMS	5MT	4-6-0	1943
—	47564	LMS	3F	0-6-0T	1928
—	47327	LMS	3F	0-6-0T	1926
—	47357	LMS	3F	0-6-0T	1926
—	47445	LMS	3F	0-6-0T	1927
—	158A	MR	—	2-4-0	1866
—	73129	BR	5MT	4-6-0	1956
—	80080	BR	4MT	2-6-4T	1954
—	80098	BR	4MT	2-6-4T	1955
—	92214	BR	9F	2-10-0	1959
—	92219	BR	9F	2-10-0	1959
—	D2858	BR	02	0-4-0DM	1959
—	D2138	BR	03	0-6-0DM	1960
—	08590	BR	08	0-6-0DE	1959
—	12077	BR	11	0-6-0DE	1950
—	20001	BR	20	Bo-Bo	1957
—	20205	BR	20	Bo-Bo	1967
—	20227	BR	20	Bo-Bo	1968
—	D7671	BR	25	Bo-Bo	1967
—*	31271	BR	31	A1A-A1A	1961
Boudicea	31418	BR	31	A1A-A1A	1959
—	31421	BR	31	A1A-A1A	1959
—	33018	BR	33	Bo-Bo	1960
—	33201	BR	33	Bo-Bo	1962
—	37190	BR	37	Co-Co	1964
Aureol	40012	BR	40	1Co-Co1	1959
Great Gable	D4	BR	44	1Co-Co1	1959
Royal Tank Regiment	45041	BR	45/1	1Co-Co1	1962
—	45133	BR	45/1	1Co-Co1	1961
—	46045	BR	46	1Co-Co1	1963
—	47401	BR	47	Co-Co	1963
—	D1516	BR	47	Co-Co	1963
Sir Edward Elgar	50007	BR	50	Co-Co	1967
Western Lady	D1048	BR	52	C-C	1962
Electra	27000	BR	EM2	Co+Co	1953
—	50015	BR	114	DMBS	1956
—	50019	BR	114	DMBS	1956
—	51073	BR	119	DMBC	1958
—	51188	BR	101	DMBS	1958
—	53170	BR	101	DMC(L)	1957
—	53253	BR	101	DMC(L)	1957
—	55513	BR	141	DMS	1983
—	55533	BR	141	DMS(L)	1983
—	55966	BR	127	DPU	1959
—	55976	BR	127	DPU	1956
—	56006	BR	114	DTC	1956
—	56015	BR	114	DMBSO	1956
—	59575	M/Cam	111	TRBSL(L)	1957
—	59609	BR	127	TC	1959
—	79018	BR	—	MBS	19??
—	79612	BR	—	DTC	19??
—	29663	M/Cam	—	TC	1931
—	29666	M/Cam	—	TC	1931
—	29670	M/Cam	—	TC	1931
Iris	M79900	BR	—	MBS	1956

*on extended loan to Nene Valley Railway

Railway — Butterley will be open for static display.
Golden Valley Light Railway: Trains will run every weekend and Bank Holiday Mondays April to October, EXCEPT 23 September. Daily 14-23 April, 27 May-4 June, 22 July-31 August. Special steam days — check for details.
Butterley Park Miniature Railway: Trains will run Sundays and Bank Holidays Easter to September.
Journey time: Approximately 1hr
Special events: Railway Experience Day— 25 March; Mother's Day Sunday Lunch — 26 March; Diesel Gala— 8/9 April; Easter Eggstravaganza — 8-23 April; Spring on the Farm — 22/23 April; Vintage Train Weekend — 29 April-1 May; 1940s Weekend — 6/7 May; Diesel and Steam Weekend — 13/14 May; Steam Locomotive Gala— 20/21 May; Day out with Thomas — 27 May-4 June; Modellers Weekend — 10/11 June; Schools Days 13, 15 June; Diesel and Steam Weekend — 17/18 June; Father's Day Sunday Lunch — 18 June; Class 40 Celebration — 24/25 June; Free for Disabled and half price for carers — 2/3 July; Diesel and Steam Weekend — 8/9 July; Road Rally and Static Power Event — 9 July; Anything Goes Weekend — 22/23 July; Day out with Thomas — 26 July-6 August; Diesel and Steam Weekend — 12/13 August; Vintage Train Weekend — 29/20 August; Narrow Gauge Railway Gala and Garden Railway Festival — 19/20 August; Silver Jubilee Weekend (25 locomotives) — 26-28 August; 1950s Weekend — 2/3 September; Diesel and Steam Weekend — 9/10 September; Autumn Diesel Weekend — 16/17 September; Railway Experience Day— 23 September; Diesel and Steam Weekend — 30 September, 1 October; Diesel Multiple-Unit Gala — 7/8 October; Day out with Thomas — 14/15 October; Wizards Weekend — 21/22 October; Magic Half-Term — 23-27 October; Fireworks Nights — 28 October, 4 November; Santa Specials — 18/19, 25/26 November, 2/3, 7/8, 9/10, 14, 16/17, 20-24 December; Festive Trains — 27 December-2 January 2007.
Railway Experience Days need to be booked in advance

Locomotive notes: In service 92214, 47327, 6233, 80098, 73129, 46045, 08590, Class 114, *Iris* and 127 DMU, D4, 33201, 37190, 46045, 47401, 50007, D2138, 40012, 12077, 45133 and D7671. Under restoration: 44027, 45491, 44932, 47445, 80080. Awaiting repairs or stored: 46203, D1517, 92219. Boiler and frames only 47564. Static display: 158A, 27000. Expected to enter service in 2006: 53809

Industrial locomotives

Name	*No*	*Builder*	*Type*	*Built*
Gladys	—	Markham (109)	0-4-0ST	1894
Stanton	24	Barclay (1875)	0-4-0CT	1925
Whitehead	—	Peckett (1163)	0-4-0ST	1908
Victory	—	Peckett (1547)	0-4-0ST	1919
Lytham St Annes	—	Peckett (2111)	0-4-0ST	1949
Brown Bailey	4	N/Wilson (454)	0-4-0ST	1894
Castle Donnington	1	RSH (7817)	0-4-0ST	1954
Neepsend		Sentinel (9370)	4wVBT	1947
Andy	2	Fowler (16038)	0-4-0DM	1923
—	RS9	M/Rail (2024)	0-4-0DM	1921
—	RS12	M/Rail (460)	0-4-0DM	1912
Boots	2	Barclay (2008)	0-4-0F	1935
Castle Donnington	2	Barclay (416)	0-4-0DM	1957
High Marnham	—	Barclay (441)	0-4-0DM	1949
Boots	—	R/Hornsby (384139)	0-4-0DE	1955
—		—	H/Clarke	
(D1152) 0-6-0DM	1959			
Albert Fields	—	H/Clarke (D1114)	0-6-0DM	1958
*Princess Elizabeth**	6201	H/Clarke (D611)	4-6-2DM	1938
*Princess Margaret Rose**	6203	H/Clarke (D612)	4-6-2DM	1938

*21in gauge

Golden Valley Light Railway
2ft gauge unless otherwise shown

—	—	Deutz (10249)	4wDM	1932
Tubby	—	M/Rail (8667)	4wDM	1941
Pioneer	—	M/Rail (8739)	4wDM	1942
—	—	M/Rail (8756)	4wDM	1942
Campbell Brick Works	—	M/Rail (60S364)	4wDM	1968
—	—	Lister (3742)	4wDM	1931
—	—	M/Rail (11246)	4wDM	1963
—	2	O&K (7529)	0-4-0WT	1914
—	—	O&K (5215)	4wDM	1936
Wheal Jayne	19	BEV	4wBE	1985
—	—	Ruston (7002/0567/6)	4wDM	1966
Lyddia	—	Ruston (191646)	4wDM	1938
Berryhill	—	Ruston (222068)	4wDM	1943
Hucknall Colliery	3	Ruston (480678)	4wDM	1961
—	—	Hunslet (7178)	4wDH	1971
—	—*	Hunslet (8970)	4wDM	1979
—	—*	Hunslet (8972)	4wDM	1979
Calverton Colliery	22	H/Clarke (1117)	0-6-0DM	1958
Natalie	—	H/Barclay (LD 9351)	0-4-0DM	1994
—	—	Lister (53726)	4wDM	1963
—	—	SMH (40SD529)	4wDM	1983
—	NG24	B/Drewry (3703)	4wBE	1974
Calverton No 7	7	Hunslet (8911)	4wDM	1980
Ellison	—	SMH (102T20)	4wDH	1979
Pearl 2	—	T. D. A. Civil (1)	0-4-2T	1997

*2ft 2in gauge, to be regauged to 2ft

Locomotive notes: In service: *High Marnham, Boots*, *Castle Donnington No 1, Castle Donnington No 2,* NG24, Ruston 222068, SMH (40SD529 & 102T20), *Calverton Colliery No 22,* Lister, Deutz 10249, *Albert Fields*, M/Rail 60S364, *Princess Margaret Rose*. Under restoration: *Andy*, O&K

Facilities for disabled: Toilets, special coach, access to shop and cafeteria
Membership details: J. Hett, at above address
Membership journal: *The Wyvern* — quarterly
Marketing names: 'More than just a railway'; Golden Valley Light Railway (narrow gauge); Butterley Park Miniature Railway (miniature line)

7529, *Lytham St Annes, Castle Donnington No 1*. Awaiting repairs or stored on display: RS9, Hunslet 7178, M/Rails 5906/11246. Static display: *Gladys*, 4, *Boots No 2*, Sentinel 9370, *Welbeck Colliery, Victory*, RS12, *Stanton* No 24, *Brown Bailey* (as Oswald the talking engine)

Stock
Numerous carriages, wagons and cranes. Museum display includes MR Royal saloon, MR 4-wheeled coach, MR brake third, LD&ECR all third, BR horsebox, LMS travelling Post Office, L&YR family saloon, MR motor carvan, MR bogie brake third, restored freight vehicles, LMS 50-ton steam crane, and much more

Owners
158A, 44027 on loan from the National Railway Museum
47357, 47327, 47445, 47564, 73129 Derby City Council
46203, 6233, 46203, 80080, 80098 the Princess Royal Class Locomotive Trust
D4, 45041 and 46045 the Peak Locomotive Preservation Co Ltd
D7671 Derby Industrial Museum
33201 the Birmingham Railwaymen's Crompton Workgroup
Class 141 unit the Llangollen Railcar Group
51073 the Railcar Enterprises

Railway Centre

Midsomer Norton Station

Somerset

Member: HRA
The Midsomer Norton Station Project has secured a foothold on the northern part of the S&D where previous preservation attempts failed. More recently it has been joined by the North Dorset Railway Trust, which has established a presence on the southern part of the route at Shillingstone. The S&DRHT has the central object of preserving the route and infrastructure wherever the opportunities arise, whether for heritage or conventional railways or, more simply, for public recreation and conservation. In practice, energies are being concentrated at Midsomer Norton, with the longer term aim of extending the running line southwards up the notorious 1 in 53 grade towards Chilcompton, and north towards Radstock. The station site is on a 25-year lease from Bath & North East Somerset Council and the Trust is in negotiation with three private landowners to secure access further south for nearly a mile. Beyond that lie Chilcompton Tunnels and the first obstacle of the landfilled cutting. Midsomer Norton station is planned to become one of the few significant visitor attractions in this former coal-mining community, with the S&D legend attracting national and even international attention
Main station: Midsomer Norton South
OS Reference: ST 664537
Chairman: John Baxter, Chairman; Peter Russell, Secretary; Steve Sainsbury, Treasurer; Tim Deacon, Membership Secretary; Richard Stevens, Vice-President
Headquarters: Somerset & Dorset Railway Heritage Trust, Midsomer Norton Station Project, Silver Street, Midsomer Norton, BA3 2EY
Telephone: 01761 411221
Internet address:
e-mail: info@sdjr.co.uk
Web site: www.sdjr.co.uk
Car park: Limited parking on site — 200-place free car parking — 300m towards town centre (OS ref: ST 666542)
Access by public transport: Nearest rail stations Bath Spa (13 miles), Frome (13 miles), Trowbridge (15 miles). Bus (Firstbus) services 173, 178, 184 and 379 all pass by the station (nearest stops in Silver Street and Charlton Road). 179 stops at the Town Hall. 379 runs Monday to

Industrial locomotives

Name	*No*	*Builder*	*Type*	*Built*
David James Cook	—	E/Electric (D1120)	0-6-0DE	1966
—	—	Sentinel	0-4-0DE	1927

Rolling stock: 2 Mk 1 dining cars (ex-Pullman, to be delivered 2006), 1 BR Mk 3 buffet car, 2 ex-MoD box vans, 2 LMS brake vans, Kilmersdon Colliery coal wagon, ex-LSWR box van, ex SR box van, Mk 1 brake composite, Sturgeon bogie wagon, Lafarge cement internal box van. Planned acquisitions during 2006 are a tank wagon and an additional coach

Friday only. 184 also connects to Frome station and runs Monday to Saturday. Combined rail & bus tickets are available but not valid on the S&D line itself.
Updated information on www.firstgroup.com/ukbus/southwest/somerset/home
On site facilities: Sales/information in main station building during opening times; toilets. Static restaurant coach in sidings (for light refreshments). Museum in stable block due to open in 2006
Length of line: Initially 350m of running line being laid through station, plus sidings in goods yard. Medium term scope for extension southwards for approx 1km towards Chilcompton Tunnels. Goods shed workshop housing diesel shunter open for viewing. Signalbox under construction
Opening times: Site and buildings open every Sunday 10.00-17.00 throughout the year (staffed). Site only open, but normally unstaffed at other times
Special events: Please see local and railway press
Disabled access: Wheelchairs can access station forecourt, down platform and main building (via platform) at present. Museum will include gently ramped access path. Car parking for disabled in station car park, but telephone to ensure space is reserved
Membership details: Tim Deacon, 38 Bay Crescent, Swanage, Dorset BH19 1RB — Rates for 2006 — Life membership £180 (single member) £250 (Family/Corporate). Ordinary Adult £12, Junior or Senior Citizen £8 Family/Household (2 spouses/partners + 2 children under 16) £16; Corporate £20; £150 (retired spouses/partners). Membership leaflets available in station
Membership journal: *The Telegraph* — 3 times per annum (April, August and December)

Museum

Monkwearmouth Station Museum

Tyne & Wear

The Museum is one of Britain's finest neo-classical stations and was built in 1848 to commemorate the election of George Hudson as MP for Sunderland. Restored features include the booking office, unchanged since it was installed in 1866, waiting shelter on the west platform and siding area
Location: North Bridge Street, Sunderland SR5 1AP
Telephone: (0191) 567 7075
OS reference: NZ 396576

Rolling stock
NER brake van 1915, LNER CCT van 1939

On site facilities: Car parking on museum forecourt, shop. Self-service refreshment dispenser
Access by public transport: 10min walk from Sunderland Central station. Served by several bus routes from Sunderland city centre, Newcastle and South Shields
Public opening: Daily 1 January-31 December (except New Year's Day, Christmas Day, Boxing Day [please check for Good Friday and Easer Sunday opening times]). Monday to Saturday 10.00-17.00. Sunday 14.00-17.00. Free admission
Access for disabled: Ramped access, suitable for wheelchair users

Miniature Railway

Moors Valley Railway

Dorset

Location: Moors Valley Country Park, Horton Road, Ashley Heath, Nr Ringwood, Dorset. **General Manager:**
Mr J. A. W. Haylock
Telephone: (01425) 471415
Internet address: *e-mail:* shop@moorsvalleyrailway.co.uk
Web site: www.moorsvalleyrailway.co.uk
Car parking: On site
Access by public transport: Wilts & Dorset bus X34, from

Locomotives

Name	*No*	*Builder*	*Type*	*Built*
Horace	2	Haylock	0-4-2DH	1999
Talos	3	Marsh	0-4-2T	1978
Tinkerbell	4	Marsh	0-4-2T	1968
Snapper	5	Marsh/Haylock	4-6-0	1982
Medea	6	Narogauge Ltd	2-6-2T	1981
Aelfred	7	Narogauge Ltd	2-6-4T	1985
Jason	9	Narogauge Ltd	2-4-4T	1989
Offa	10	Narogauge Ltd	2-6-2	1991
Zeus	11	Narogauge Ltd	2-6-2	1991
Pioneer	12	Narogauge Ltd	4-6-2	1992
Tiny Tim	13*	Narogauge Ltd	0-4-0T+T	1993

Bournemouth/Ringwood to Ashley Heath
On site facilities: Picnic areas, lakeside walks, adventure playground, railway shop and refreshments all set in the beautiful Moors Valley Country Park. Car park and toilets (including disabled)
Depots: Adacent to main station
Length of line:7.25 in gauge; 1 mile long
Period of public operation: Weekends all year; daily all school holidays and Spring Bank Holiday to mid-September. Santa Specials in December

Name	*No*	*Builder*	*Type*	*Built*
Horton	14	Narogauge Ltd	2-4-0	1991
William Rufus	15	Narogauge Ltd	2-4-0+0-4-2	1997
Robert Snooks	16	Mantlow	0-4-4T	1999
Hartfield	17	Colbourn	2-4-4T	1999

*may not be on site for all of 2006

Rolling stock
36 passenger vehicles, selection of wagons

Special events: Railway Open Day — 2 April; Tinkerbell Rally — 29/30 April; Grand Summer Gala — 10/11 June; American Weekend — 1/2 July; Hornby/LGB/Bachmann Weekend — 22/23 July; Santa Specials — 3, 10 December

The Museum of Science and Industry in Manchester

Museum

Manchester

Member: HRA
Based in the buildings of the world's oldest surviving passenger railway station (dating from 1830), the Museum has colourful 'hands-on' galleries that amuse, amaze and entertain. Visitors can find out about our industrial past, and walk through a Victorian sewer complete with sounds and smells
Location: Liverpool Road, Castlefield, Manchester (off Deansgate near Granada TV)
OS reference: SJ 831987
Operating society/organisation: The Museum of Science and Industry in Manchester, Liverpool Road, Castlefield, Manchester M3 4FP
Telephone: (0161) 832 2244
Internet address: *e-mail:* marketing@msim.org.uk
Web site: http://www.msim.org.uk
Car parks: On site, plus parking in the area (Museum car park £5, subject to change)
Access by public transport: Manchester Victoria, Piccadilly, Oxford Road and Deansgate main line stations. GM bus 33. G-Mex Metrolink station
On site facilities: Oldest passenger railway station, listed buildings containing exhibitions about

Locomotives

Name	*No*	*Origin*	*Class*	*Type*	*Built*
Lion	57	L&MR	—	0-4-2	1838
Pender	3††	IoMR	—	2-4-0T	1873
Novelty	Replica of 1829 locomotive using some original parts				1986
—	3157†	PR	—	4-4-0	1911
—	2352§	SAR	GL	4-8-2+2-8-4	1929
Ariadne	1505 (27001)	BR	EM2 (77)	Co-Co	1954
Hector	26048	BR	EM1 (76)	Bo-Bo cab only	1952
*Planet**	—	Replica	—	2-2-0	1992

Industrial locomotives

Name	*No*	*Builder*	*Type*	*Built*
Lord Ashfield	—	Barclay (1964)	0-4-0ST	1929
—	258	E/Electric (1378)	4wBE	1944

*full scale model of 1830-built locomotive
††ex-Isle of Man Railways, 3ft gauge, sectioned (B/Peacock 1255)
†ex-Pakistan Railways, 5ft 6in gauge (V/Foundry 3064)
§ex-South African Railways, 3ft 6in gauge (B/Peacock 6693)

Rolling stock
BR Mk 2 SO E5241, 1966
Reproduction M&BR 1st class carriage c1840 using original fragments
2 full scale working models L&MR 2nd class carriages c1835
1914 L&YR ambulance carriage rebuilt 1923 as Medical Examination Car, LMS No 10825 (under restoration, assembled in 1917 from 1916 made modules)
B782903 4-wheeled covered goods van, BR (Wolverton), 1961
B783709 4-wheeled covered goods van, BR (Wolverton), 1962
3-plank loose coupled goods wagon, GCR (Chatham), c1890

Owners
Lion on loan from the National Museums, Liverpool

science, industry, aviation, space, water supply and sewage disposal, gas and electricity. Xperiment the 'hands-on' science centre and the 'Out of this world' space gallery. World's largest collection of working steam mill engines in the Power Hall, demonstrated every afternoon. The Collections Centre has research facilities and access to reserve collections. Museum shop, restaurant, Learning and Conference Centres
Public opening: Daily except 24-26 December, including Saturdays and Sundays, 10.00-17.00. Entrance in Lower Byrom Street. Admission free to permanent galleries, although prices still apply for special exhibitions. Please ring for details. Groups can book a visit by calling (0161) 833 0027
Special notes: Good wheelchair access, toilets for the disabled, lecture and conference facilities

Novelty on loan from the National Railway Museum, York

Note:
Full scale (working) model — reproduction made to other than original specification
Replica — reproduction made by original company in original way
Reproduction — item made in original way by other than original company

Museum

National Railway Museum

North Yorkshire

Member: HRA, TT, MLSOG
Location: National Railway Museum, Leeman Road, York YO26 4XJ
OS reference: SE 594519
Operating society/organisation: Part of the National Museum of Science and Industry
Telephone: 0870 421 4001
Internet addresses: *e-mail:* nrm@nmsi.ac.uk
Web site: www.nrm.org.uk
Car park: Available on site, charge applies. Coach parking is available — pre-booking required
Access by public transport: The museum is within a few minutes' walking distance of the railway station (and buses to) in York. The York City & District Bus Service operates to the door. A road-train operates betweem the Museum and the city centre
On site facilities: Museum shop, restaurant and toilets. Reference library (free by appointment). Also model railway, miniature railway, train rides (seasonal), baby changing facilities, indoor and outdoor play areas, children's interactive learning centre, conference centre
Public opening: Daily 10.00-18.00. Closed 24-26 December. Admission is free for all, except the museum reserves the right to charge for special events
Facilities for disabled: Most areas of the museum are accessible. Wheelchairs may be borrowed from the entrances and special parking is available at the museum's City entrance
Special notes: The museum has been open since 1975 and has welcomed over 20 million visitors. In 2001 it was awarded the prestigious 'European Museum of the Year' title. In 2004 it saved *Flying Scotsman* for the nation.

As the world's largest railway museum, it offers the visitor three extensive exhibition halls. The Great Hall, the Station Hall and The Works house the world's premier collection of railway related material.

The Great Hall displays are on the theme of railway technology. There is a magnificent display of railway locomotive development round the turntable. Signalling, the modern railway and the Channel Tunnel are also represented. The displays reflect the present and the past and include a full-sized model of the nose cone of a state-of-the -art Transmanche Super Train operating between England and the Continent. A new permanent exhibition now features the only Bullet Train on display outside Japan and tells the story of how this revolutionary high speed train took the world by storm. Regular temporary exhibitions exploring various aspects of railway history/technology. Displays on the operation of the railways, tape/slide presentations can be found on the Balcony Galleries.

The Station Hall illustrates the concept of travel by train — for passengers and freight. Several trains are drawn up at platforms with a number of footplates and carriages open to visitors. The vehicles displayed range from the superb Royal carriages to humble freight wagons.

The Interactive Learning Centre provides visitors with 'hands-on' experience of various aspects of railway operation.

The museum's extensive reference library (including the photographic and drawings collections) continues to be free to all booked enquirers every weekday from 10.00-17.00, please call 01904 686235.

The tables which follow indicate the whereabouts (display, on loan, in store) of the National Railway Collection. It must be emphasised that the appearance of any particular item on public display cannot be guaranteed. If it is vital to discover the exact whereabouts of a specific item, enquirers should contact the museum in York before the trip.

The National Railway Museum is open for evening hire for private viewings and celebrations; menus and details are available on request, please call 01904 686227.

Details of membership of the museum's support group, including a quarterly newsletter are available from: The Secretary, Friends of the National Railway Museum, c/o the above address

Locomotives — Steam

Name	*No*	*Origin*	*Builder*	*Class*	*Type*	*Built*
Agenoria	—	Shutt End Colliery	Foster/Raistrick	—	0-4-0	1829
Coppernob	3	FR	Bury, Curtis & Kennedy	—	0-4-0	1846
Pet	—	LNWR	Crewe	—	0-4-0ST	1865
Aerolite	66	NER	Gateshead	X1(LNER)	2-2-4T	1869
—	1	GNR	Doncaster	—	4-2-2	1870
Bauxite	2	Hebburn Works	B/Hawthorn	—	0-4-0ST	1874
—	1275	NER	Gateshead	—	0-6-0	1874
Boxhill	82	LBSCR	Brighton	A1	0-6-0T	1880
Gladstone	—	LBSCR	Brighton	—	0-4-2	1882
Wren	—	LYR	B/Peacock	—	0-4-0ST	1887
—	1008	LYR	Horwich	—	2-4-2T	1889
Hardwicke	790	LNWR	Crewe	—	2-4-0	1892
—	1621	NER	Gateshead	M	4-4-0	1893
—	993	RR	Sharp Stewart	7A	4-8-0	1896
—	245	LSWR	Nine Elms	M7	0-4-4T	1897
—	673	MR	Derby	—	4-2-2	1899
—	737	SECR	Ashford	D	4-4-0	1901
—	1000	MR	Derby	4	4-4-0	1902
—	87	GER	Stratford	J69	0-6-0T	1904
—	1217	GER	Stratford	J17	0-6-0	1905
—	2818	GWR	Swindon	2800	2-8-0	1905
Lode Star	4003	GWR	Swindon	'Star'	4-6-0	1907
Flying Scotsman	4472	LNER	Doncaster	A3	4-6-2	1923
Cheltenham	925	SR	Eastleigh	V/Schools	4-4-0	1934
Rocket (replica)	—		R. Stephenson	—	0-2-2	1934

Name	No	Origin	Builder	Class	Type	Built
—	5000	LMS	Crewe	5MT	4-6-0	1935
—	607	Chinese Govt Rlys	Vulcan	KF7	4-8-4	1935
Mallard	4468	LNER	Doncaster	A4	4-6-2	1938
Eustace Forth	15	—	RSH (7063)	—	0-4-0ST	1942
—	C1	SR	Brighton	Q1	0-6-0	1942
Winston Churchill	34051	SR	Brighton	BB	4-6-2	1946
Ellerman Lines	35029	BR(SR)	Sectioned	MN	4-6-2	1949
Frank Galbraith	5	Tees-Side Bridge & Engineering Co	Sentinel	—	4wTG	1957
Evening Star	92220	BR	Swindon	9F	2-10-0	1960
Rocket (replica)	—	—	Loco Enterprises	—	0-2-2	1979
Iron Duke (broad gauge replica)	—	GWR	RESCO	—	4-2-2	1985

Locomotives — Electric

Name	No	Origin	Builder	Class	Type	Built
—	1	NSR	Bolton & Sons	—	0-4-0WE	1917
—	809	GPO	Green Bat	—	2w-2E	1931
—	26020	BR	Gorton/Metrovick	76	Bo-Bo Electric	1951
—	RA.36	TML	Hunslet	—	4wBE/WE	1990
Royal Scot	87001	BR	Crewe	87	B0-B0	1973

Locomotives — Diesel

Name	No	Origin	Builder	Class	Type	Built
Rorkes Drift	—	WD	Drewry	_	0-4-0DM	1934
—	—	Yorkshire Water Authority	R/Hornsby (187105)	—	4wDM	1937
—	08911	BR	Horwich	08	0-6-0 DE	1962
—	D8000	BR	E/Electric	20	Bo-Bo	1957
—	5500	BR	Brush	31	A1A-A1A	1957
—	D200	BR	E/Electric	40	1Co-Col	1958
—	03090	BR	—	03	0-6-0DM	1960
—	D2860	BR	YEC	02	0-4-0 DH	1960
Western Fusilier	D1023	BR	Swindon	52	C-C	1963
—*	41001	BR	Crewe	41	Bo-Bo	1972
Prince William	47798	BR	Crewe	47	Co-Co	1965

*stored at MoD Kineton

Locomotives on loan

Livingston Thompson from the Ffestiniog Railway
Penydarren from the Welsh Industrial & Maritime Museum

Rolling Stock Powered Units — Electric

1916 LNWR Motor Open Third Brake No 28249
1925 SR Motor Third Brake No S8143S
1937 SR Motor Third Open Brake No S11179S
1941† LMS Class 502 BMS No 28361
1941† LMS Class 502 DTC No 29896
1975 Birmingham Airport Maglev passenger car
1976 Series 'O' Shinkasen No 2214

Rolling Stock Powered Units — Diesel

1959 BR DMU Class 108 Nos 51562 & 51922

Rolling Stock — Departmental

1890 GNR Locomotive Tender No 1002
1899 GWR Hand Crane No 537
1906 NER Dynamometer Car No 902502
1907 NER Steam Breakdown Crane No CME 13
1907 Match Truck No DE942114
1926 LNER Match Truck No DE320952
1931/2 LNER Petrol-driven platelayers' trolley No 960209
1936 GWR Ballast Wagon No 80659
1938 LMS Mobile test unit No 1, No 45053
1955 GEC 12.5-ton Coles Crane
1969 BR Plasser Tamping & Liner No 73010
1989 Molhouser side discharge muck car ASDR 3105 (Channel Tunnel)

Rolling Stock — Passenger

1834 B&WR 1st & 2nd composite
1834 B&WR 2nd class
1834 B&WR 3rd class
1842 L&BR Queen Adelaide's Saloon
1850 NER Brake End (body only)
1851 ECR 1st class No 1
1860 Cornwall Rly broad gauge coach (body only)

1861 NBR Port Carlisle branch 'dandy car'
1869 LNWR Queen Victoria's Saloon
1885 MR 6-wheel composite brake No 901
1885 WCJS 8-wheel TPO No 186
1887 GNR Brake Van No 848
1897 Lynton & Barnstaple Rly brake composite No 6992
1898 ECJS 3rd class No 12
1899 Privately owned Duke of Sutherland's Saloon No 57A
1900 LNWR (ex-WCJS) Dining Car LMS 76
1902 LNWR King Edward's Saloon No 800
1902 LNWR Queen Alexandra's Saloon No 801
1903 LSWR Tricomposite brake No 3598
1908† ECJS Royal Saloon No 395
1913 Pullman Car Co 1st class parlour car *Topaz*
1914 MR Dining car No 3463
1930 L&MR 1st *Huskinson* (replica)
1930 L&MR 1st *Traveller* (replica)
1930 L&MR 2nd (replica)
1930 L&MR 2nd (replica)
1936 CIWL Night Ferry sleeping car No 3792
1937 LNER Buffet Car No 9135
1937 LMS corridor 3rd class brake No 5987,
1938 GJR TPO (replica)
1941 LMS Royal Saloon 799 (armoured car)
1945 GWR Royal Saloon No 9007
1955 BR Lavatory composite No E43046
1960 Pullman Car Co 1st class Parlour car No 326 *Emerald*
1962 BR Mk II 2nd brake corridor No 35468
1969 BR Mk IIb 2nd open No 5455

Rolling Stock — Freight & Non Passenger Carrying

1815 Little Eaton (Derby Canal) Gangroad Wagon
1815 Peak Forest Canal Tramway Wagon No 174
1816 Grantham Canal Tramway Truck
1828 Dandy Cart
1840 Stratford & Moreton Tramway Wagon
1894 LSWR Brake van No 99
1908 LNWR Open carriage truck No 11275
1912 GNR 8-ton van No E432764
1917 GCR Box Van
1917 LNWR Box Van
1924 LMSR Van
1931 GWR Fruit Van No 112884
1931 Stanton Iron Works 12-ton wagon
1933 LMSR 20-ton Goods Brake Van No 295987
1935 SR Bogie goods brake van No 56297
1935 PLM Train Ferry Van No 475014
1936 LMSR 3 plank open wagon No 472867
1937 GWR Siphon bogie milk van No 2775
1937 LMSR Milk Tank Wagon No 44057
1937 2 x Yorkshire Water Authority side-tipper wagons
1944 LMS Lowmac No M700728
1944 GWR 13-ton open wagon No DW143698
1949 BR Bogie bolster D No B941000
1950 BR 20-ton Weltrol No B900805
1951 ICI Liquid chlorine tank wagon No 47484
1951 BR 8-ton cattle wagon No B893343
1962 BR Speedfreight container No BA 4324B
1966 Milk Marketing Board 6-wheel tank No 42801
1970 BR 2,000gal Road/Rail Milk Tank No ADM707111
1989 TML side-tipping muck cart No R T239

†stored at MoD Kineton

Items on Loan from the NRM
Locomotives

Original type/No/Name	*Location*	*Builder*	*Built*
Wylam Colliery	Science Mus	—	1813
Hetton Colliery 0-4-0	Beamish	G. Stephenson	1822
SDR 0-4-0 *Locomotion*	Darlington	R. Stephenson & Co	1825
L&MR 0-2-2 *Rocket*	Science Mus	R. Stephenson & Co	1829
L&MR 0-2-2 *Novelty*	Museum of Science & Technology (Manchester)	Braithwaite & Ericsson	1829
SDR 0-6-0 No 24 *Derwent*	Darlington Nth Rd Mus	A. Kitching	1845
GJR 2-2-2 *Columbine*	Science Mus	Crewe	1845
Wantage Tramway 0-4-0WT No 5 *Shannon*	Didcot Rly Ctr	G. England	1857
LNWR 0-4-0ST 1439	East Lancs	Crewe	1865
MR 2-4-0 No 158A	Midland Rly Ctr	Derby	1866
South Devon Rly 0-4-0WT *Tiny*	South Devon Rly	Sara	1868
LSWR 2-4-0WT No 30587	Bodmin	B/Peacock	1874
NER 2-4-0 No 910	Darlington Nth Rd Mus	Gateshead	1875
NER 2-4-0 No 1463	Darlington Nth Rd Mus	Gateshead	1885
C&SL No 1	LT Museum	B/Peacock	1890
S&MR 0-4-2WT *Gazelle*	Col Stephens Rly Mus	Dodman	1893
GER 2-4-0 No 490	Bressingham	Stratford	1894
GWR 0-6-0 No 2516	Steam	Swindon	1897
TVR 0-6-2T No 28	Dean Forest	TVR	1897
GNR No 990 *Henry Oakley*	Bressingham	Doncaster	1899
LSWR 4-4-0 No 120	Bluebell Rly	Nine Elms	1899
LT&SR 4-4-2T No 80 *Thundersley*	Bressingham	R. Stephenson	1909
GCR 2-8-0 No 102	Great Central	Gorton	1911
WD No 1377 (2ft Gauge)	LBR	Simplex	1918

Original type/No/Name	*Location*	*Builder*	*Built*
GCR 506 *Butler Henderson*	Barrow Hill	Gorton	1920
NSR No 1	Churnet Valley	Stoke	1922
GWR 4-6-0 No 4073 *Caerphilly Castle*	Steam	Swindon	1923
LMS 0-6-0 No 4027	Midland Rly Ctr	Derby	1924
GWR 2-2-2 *North Star* (replica)	Steam	R. Stephenson	1925
SR 4-6-0 No 777 *Sir Lamiel*	GCR	N/British	1925
SR 4-6-0 No 850 *Lord Nelson*	Eastleigh Works†	Eastleigh	1926
GWR No 6000 *King George V*	Steam	Swindon	1927
GWR 0-6-0PT No 9400	Steam	Swindon	1947
BR 4-6-2 No 70013 *Oliver Cromwell*	Great Central	Crewe	1951
BR Bo-Bo No E3036	Barrow Hill	N/British	1960
BR Co-Co D9000 *King's Own Yorkshire Light Infantry*	Barrow Hill	E/Electric	1961

†private site

Powered Units

NER electric parcels van No 3267, G. Stephenson Mus

GWR diesel railcar No 4, Steam

BR Class 101 vehicle Nos 51192/54352 East Lancs

Departmental Stock

1932 LMS Ballast plough brake van No 197266, Embsay

1949 BR(LMS) Dynamometer car No 3, No 45049, Barrow Hill

Passenger Stock

1846 SDR 1st & 2nd composite No 31, Darlington Nth Rd Mus

1850 NER 4-wheel coach body, Darlington

1910 GCR Open 3rd class No 666, Nottingham

1925 GWR 3rd class dining car No 9653, Severn Valley Rly

1925 LMS 3rd class vestibule No 7828 *(on loan to LMS Carriage Association)*

1934 GWR Buffet Car No 9631, Steam,

1936 LNER 3rd Open, No 13254, NYMR

1941 LMS Royal saloon No 798, Glasgow Museum of Transport

1960 Pullman Car Co 1st class Kitchen car No 311 *Eagle,* Bluebell

1985 GWR 3rd (broad gauge replica), Didcot

Freight & Non Passenger Carrying Stock

1850 South Hetton Colliery Chaldron Wagon No 1155, D Bahn Museum, Nuremberg

1898 CR well trolley bogie crocodile, Bo'ness

1902 NER 20-ton wooden hopper wagon No 4551, Tyne & Wear

1909 GWR Girder Wagon Set (Pollen E) Nos DW84997, 84998, 84999, 85000, Didcot

1912 LBSCR Open wagon No 27884, Yeovil

1912 LSWR Gunpowder van No KDS61209, Yeovil

1914 GWR Shunters' truck No W94988, Steam

1920 LSWR Lowmac, No DE563024, NYMR

1922 LBSCR cattle truck No 7116, Isle of Wight Steam Rly

1928 ICI Nitric acid tank wagon No 14, Yeovil

1941 LNER 20-ton brake van, No 246710, NYMR

1948 BR(SR) 12-ton shock absorbing wagon No 14036, NYMR

1950 BR 12-wheel well wagon, No KDB901601, East Lancs

1955 BR 16-ton mineral wagon No B227009, Middleton

1959 BR Fish van No B87905, Hull

Museum

National Waterways Museum

Glos

Member: HRA
The museum completed a Lottery update of the galleries and site in 2001
Location: Gloucester Docks — signposted 'Historic Docks'
OS Reference: SO 826183
Operating society/organisation: National Waterways Museum, The Waterways Trust, Llanthony Warehouse, Gloucester Docks, Gloucester GL1 2EH
Tel: (01452) 318200
Fax: (01452) 318202
Internet address: *e-mail:* bookingsnwm@thewaterwaystrust.org
Web site: www.nwm.org.uk
Car parks: Pay & display outside museum. Free coach parking
Access by public transport: Main line Gloucester station, 1 mile
On site facilities: Tea room, souvenir and specialist bookshop (canal-related with some railway literature). School room/children's holiday activities. Working

demonstrations vary. Tug driving and blacksmith courses. Trip boats and other museums in docks
Facilities for disabled: Full facilities, lifts, ramps, toilets. All indoor displays, quaysides and tea room accessible. Floating exhibits not accessible
Public opening: Daily, 10.00-17.00, except 25 December. Admission charged. Last admissions 16.00
Special events: Preservation, modellers' & craft events; leisure learning courses (send for further information)
Membership details: 'Friends' support organisation. Membership Secretary, c/o Museum address, Volunteers active in restoration/fundraising. Winter Meetings programme
Membership journal: *Llanthony Log* — quarterly

Industrial locomotives

Name	*No*	*Builder*	*Type*	*Built*
—	1	A/Barclay (2126)	0-4-0F	1942

Ex-Gloucester Corporation, Castle Meads Power Station, Gloucester Docks. Now on static display

Rolling stock
William Balmforth of Rodley crane, c1880. Small collection of GW, Midland, LMS and BR vans with local connections. Sharpness Docks open wagons and Gloucester-built flat wagon, Manchester Ship Canal (ex-GWR) Toad brake van

Timetable Service — Nene Valley Railway — Cambs

Member: HRA, TT
This unique railway's collection includes locomotives and coaches from 10 countries and two continents. It is a regular location for TV and film makers — from films like *Goldeneye* with Pierce Brosnan as 007 to ITV's *London's Burning*. The railway and the pleasant Cambridgeshire countryside have doubled for locations as diverse as Russia and Spain
General Manager: Mr M. A. Warrington
Headquarters: Nene Valley Railway, Wansford Station, Stibbington, Peterborough, Cambs PE8 6LR
Telephone: Stamford (01780) 784444; Talking Timetable (01780) 784404
Main station: Wansford
Other public stations: Orton Mere, Ferry Meadows, Peterborough NVR (15min walk from city centre)
OS reference: TL 903979
Car park: Wansford, Orton Mere, Ferry Meadows, Peterborough NVR
Access by public transport: Buses from Peterborough to Orton Mere and Ferry Meadows
Refreshment facilities: Wansford, bar coach on most trains

Locomotives

Name	*No*	*Origin*	*Class*	*Type*	*Built*
Mayflower	1306	LNER	B1	4-6-0	1948
City of Peterborough	73050	BR	5MT	4-6-0	1954
—	D9504	BR	14	0-6-0DH	1964
—	D9516	BR	14	0-6-0DH	1964
—	D9523	BR	14	0-6-0DH	1964
—*	14029*	BR	14	0-6-0DH	1964
—†	31271	BR	31	A1A-A1A	1961
Atlantic Conveyor	D306	BR	40	1Co-Co1	1960
—	56057	BR	56	Co-Co	1978
—	64.305-6	DB	64	2-6-2T	1936
—	7173	DB	52	2-10-0	1943
—	656	DSB	F	0-6-0T	1949
—	101	SJ	B	4-6-0	1944
—	1178	SJ	S	2-6-2T	1914
—	3.628	Nord	3500	4-6-0	1911
—	5485	PKP	Typ	0-8-0T	19xx
—	51401	BR	117	DMS	1959
—	51347	BR	117	DMBS	1959
—	59508	BR	117	TCL	1959

*on hire to Channel Tunnel Rail Link
†on loan from Midland Railway

Industrial locomotives

Name	*No*	*Builder*	*Type*	*Built*
—	—	Avonside (1945)	0-6-0ST	1926
Toby	—	Cockerill (1626)	0-4-0VBT	1890
Yvonne	—	Cockerill (2945)	0-4-0VBT	1920
Muriel	—	E/Electric (1123)	0-4-0DH	1966
Rhos	—	H/Clarke (1308)	0-6-0ST	1918
Derek Crouch	—	H/Clarke (1539)	0-6-0ST	1924
Thomas	—	H/Clarke (1800)	0-6-0T	1947
Jacks Green	—	Hunslet (1953)	0-6-0ST	1939
—	75006	Hunslet (2855)	0-6-0ST	1943
—	—	R/Hornsby (294268)	4wDM	1951

Souvenir shops: Wansford
Exhibition: Wansford
Depot: Wansford
Length of line: 7.5 miles
Passenger trains: Yarwell Junction-Wansford-Ferry Meadows-Orton Mere-Peterborough NV
Period of public operation: Sundays from mid-February; weekends from Easter to end of October; Wednesdays from May, plus other midweek services in summer. Santa Specials at end of November and throughout December (telephone for details)
Special events: Take place throughout the year including Thomas' Weekend, Gala Weekend, Steamin' Blues and Vintage Rail/Mail Weekend (telephone for details). The shop, café, bookshop, model railway and exhibition are open on operating days and the locomotive yard is open all year for viewing. NVR is also the home of *Thomas* the children's favourite engine
Facilities for disabled: Ramp access to all stations and shops. Full toilets in Wansford station, souvenir shop. Disabled persons and helpers are eligible for concessionary fares. Passengers can be assisted on and off trains
Membership details: Bill Foreman, c/o above address
Membership journal: *Nene Steam* — 3 times/year
Marketing name: Britain's International Steam Railway

Name	*No*	*Builder*	*Type*	*Built*
Doncaster	—	YEC (2654)	0-4-0DE	1957
—	11	Rebuilt Hill	4wD	1963
Stanton No 50	—	YEC (2670)	0-6-0DE	1958
—	DL83	R/Royce (10271)	0-6-0DH	1967

Stock
15 BR Mk 1 coaches; Wagons Lits sleeping car, Italian-built; Wagons Lits dining car, Belgian-built; 6 coaches from Denmark; 1 coach from France; 4 coaches from Belgium; 1 steam rail crane; SR Travelling Post Office; TPO coach M30272M; 20 12-ton Vanfits plus items of freight stock

Timetable Service

North Bay Railway

North Yorkshire

This 20in gauge railway opened in 1931 and is almost a mile long, with all the features of a main line railway including a tunnel, bridges, signals stations and gradient boards reproduced to scale. The steam outline locomotives are based on Sir Nigel Gresley's Class A1 design for the LNER.
Location: Northstead Manor Gardens, Scarborough
Headquarters: Scarborough Borough Council, Town Hall, St Nicholas Street, Scarborough YO11 2HG
Telephone: General enquiries: 01723 383636
Internet address: *e-mail:* tourismbureau@scarborough.gov.uk
Main public station: Peasholme Park
Other public stations: Scalby Mills
Car parks: Nearby pay & display
Access by public transport: The railway is within walking distance of the main line stations and local bus services
Refreshment facilities: Within the gardens
Length of line: 0.875 mile, 1ft 8in gauge
Period of public operation: Daily mid-March-end October

Locomotives

Name	*No*	*Builder*	*Type*	*Built*
Neptune	1931	H/Clarke (D565)	4-6-2DH s/o	1931
Triton	1932	H/Clarke (D573)	4-6-2DH s/o	1932

Stock
10 bogie coaches

Steam Centre

North Ings Farm Museum

Lincolnshire

The museum contains agricultural equipment, tractors and railway items
Contact: Tim Hall or Malcolm Phillips (joint owners)
Headquarters: North Ings Farm Museum, Fen Road, Dorrington, Lincoln LN4 3QB
Telephone: 01526 833100
Internet address: *e-mail:* info@northingsfarmmuseum.co.uk
Web site: www.northingsfarmmuseum.co.uk
Car parks: At the museum entrance
Access by public transport: Nearest main line station Ruskington, 3 miles

Refreshment facilities: Only available by prior arrangement
Length of line: 600yd, 2ft gauge
Period of public operation: Open first Sunday, April to October. 10.00-17.00
Facilities for disabled: Toilet, wheelchairs can be accommodated on the train. Part of the museum is not easily accessible for wheelchairs

Locomotives

Name	*No*	*Builder*	*Type*	*Built*
Swift	—	Marshall	0-4-0VBT	1970
—	—	R/Hornsby (200744)	4wDM	1940
—	—	R/Hornsby (371937)	4wDM	1956
—	—	R/Hornsby (375701)†	4wDM	1954
—	—	R/Hornsby (421433)	4wDM	1959
—	—	M/Rail (7403)	4wDM	1939
—	—	M/Rail (7493)	4wDM	1940
—	—	O&K	4wDM	1932
—	—	Lister Railtrack*	4wDM	—
—	—	H/Hunslet (77120)	4wDM	1969

†dismantled
*constructed from spare parts

Owners
M/Rail (7403) and R/Hornsby (200744) on loan from Narrow Gauge Railway Museum Trust

Museum

North Woolwich Old Station Museum

London

This attractive Victorian terminus building overlooks the Thames. Railway artefacts, documents, drawings, etc, are well displayed in glass cases or on the walls, the stock being stabled in the platform area. Convenient for City Airport and connections for the Docklands Light Railway
Location: North Woolwich Old Station Museum, Pier Road, North Woolwich, London E16 2JJ
OS reference: TQ 433798
Organisation: Newham Museum Service
Telephone: 020 7474 7244
Internet address: *E-mail:* leisure.heritage@newham.gov.uk
Car park: Only in adjoining streets

Locomotives

Name	*No*	*Origin*	*Class*	*Type*	*Built*
—	229	GER	209	0-4-0ST	1876

Industrial locomotives

Name	*No*	*Builder*	*Type*	*Built*
—	—	Hibberd (3294)	4wDM	1948

Stock
1 ex-LNER coach; 2 compartment sections of LTSR coach; NLR Luggage Van; 1 ex-Royal Arsenal Ammunition Van (18in gauge)

Public transport: Train: Silverlink services to North Woolwich. Buses: 101 and 473
Facilities: Museum shop
Public opening: Open Weekends January-November 13.00-17.00. Daily during Newham children's school holidays only 13.00-17.00
Admission: Free
Facilities for disabled: Access to all displays, indoors and out

Timetable Service

North Yorkshire Moors Railway

North Yorkshire

Member: HRA, TT
This 18-mile line runs through the picturesque North York Moors National Park and is host to an extensive collection of main line locomotives
General Manager: Philip Benham
Headquarters: Pickering Station, Pickering, North Yorkshire YO18 7AJ
Telephone: Pickering (01751) 472508 for passenger enquiries, charter and diner bookings
Internet address: *e-mail:* admin@nymrpickering.fsnet.co.uk
Web site: www.northyorkshiremoorsrailway.com
Main station: Pickering
Other public stations: Grosmont, Goathland, Levisham
OS reference: Pickering NZ 797842, Levisham NZ 818909, Goathland NZ 836013, Grosmont NZ 828053
Car parks: Grosmont, Goathland, Levisham, Pickering

Access by public transport: Arriva Northern rail service to Grosmont from Whitby and Middlesbrough. Bus services Leeds-York-Malton-Pickering-Goathland-Whitby; Helmsley-Pickering-Scarborough
Refreshment facilities: Available on most trains and at Grosmont, Goathland and Pickering.Tea bar at Levisham most weekends
Souvenir shops: Pickering, Goathland, Grosmont and Grosmont MPD
Locomotive Depot: Grosmont
Length of line: 18 miles
Passenger trains: Steam-hauled services Grosmont-Pickering. Pullman evening dining service and 'Moorlander' Sunday lunch service run regularly. Saloons are also available for special occasions (eg wedding parties, conferences, etc)
Note: NYMR trains are planned to run to/from Whitby on the following dates:
27 May; 29 May-2 June; Tuesdays and Wednesdays 5-26 June; Tuesday, Wednesdays and Thursdays 24 June to 17 July, 5-7 September, 24-25 October;

Locomotives and multiple-units

Name	*No*	*Origin*	*Class*	*Type*	*Built*
George Stephenson	44767§	LMS	5MT	4-6-0	1947
Eric Treacy	45428*	LMS	5MT	4-6-0	1937
—	53809	S&DJR	7F	2-8-0	1925
—	2392	NER	P3	0-6-0	1923
—	63395*	NER	T2	0-8-0	1918
Sir Nigel Gresley	60007*	LNER	A4	4-6-2	1937
Lord of the Isles	62005§	LNER	K1	2-6-0	1949
—	69023§	LNER	J72	0-6-0T	1951
—	3814*	GWR	2884	2-8-0	1940
—	6619	GWR	5600	0-6-2T	1928
—	825	SR	S15	4-6-0	1927
—	30830††	SR	S15	4-6-0	1927
Repton	30926	SR	V	4-4-0	1934
Eddystone	34028†	SR	WC	4-6-2	1946
Hartland	34101††	SR	WC	4-6-2	1950
The Green Knight	75029	BR	4MT	4-6-0	1954
—	80135	BR	4MT	2-6-4T	1956
Dame Vera Lynn	3672††	MoS	WD	2-10-0	1943
—	2253††	USATC	S160	2-8-0	1943
—	D2207	BR	04	0-6-0DM	1953
—	08556	BR	08	0-6-0DE	1959
—	4018	BR	08	0-6-0DE	1961
Helen Turner	D5032	BR	24	Bo-Bo	1959
—	D5061	BR	24	Bo-Bo	1960
The Diana	D7541	BR	25	Bo-Bo	1965
Sybilla	D7628	BR	25	Bo-Bo	1965
Lion	50027	BR	50	Co-Co	1968
—	51511	BR	101	DMC	1959
—	53204	BR	101	DMBS	1957

Mondays Tuesday, Wednesdays and Thursdays 24 July-28 August; 1, 7/8, 15, 21/22 October;
Special events: Steam & Swing Weekend — 22/23 April; Diesel Gala — 5-7 May; Moors '65, Return to the '60s — 17/18 June; Vintage Vehicle Weekend 8/9 July; Music on the Moors — 27/28 August; Day out with Thomas — 9/10 September; Autumn Steam Gala — 29/30 September/1 October; Wartime Weekend — 13/15 October; Wizard Weekend – 28/29 October
Period of public operation: Daily 1 April-29 October, Santa Specials and other Xmas services in December/January and New Year
Facilities for disabled: The NYMR welcomes disabled visitors and special attention will gladly be provided if advance notice is given
Special notes: Operates through North York Moors National Park

Name	No	Origin	Class	Type	Built
—	59539	M/Cam	101	TSL	1958
Name	*No*	*Origin*	*Class*	*Type*	*Built*
—	60110†	BR	205	DMBS	1957
—	60810†	BR	205	DTS	1957

†unit 205205
*undergoing major overhaul at Grosmont
§undergoing restoration off-site
††awaiting overhaul

Industrial locomotives

Name	*No*	*Builder*	*Type*	*Built*
—	29	Kitson (4263)	0-6-2T	1904
—	5	R/Stephenson (3377)	0-6-2T	1909
Antwerp	—††	Hunslet (3180)	0-6-0ST	1944
Neil D. Barker	12139	E/Electric (1553)	0-6-0DE	1948
—	16	Drewry	0-4-0DM	1941
—	2	R/Hornsby (421419)	4wDM	1958
—	3*	R/Hornsby (441934)	4wDM	1960
Ron Rothwell	1	Vanguard (129V)	0-4-0DM	1963
—	2	Vanguard (131V)	0-4-0DM	1963

*on loan to Middleton Railway
††awaiting overhaul

Stock
5 pre-Grouping, 12 pre-Nationalisation, 32 x BR Mk 1, 4 x Pullman, 5 other BR coaches, 2 x Camping Coach, 1 x BR Mk 3 sleeper, 11 x brake vans, 4 diesel cranes, 2 x 45-ton steam cranes, 88 other vehicles

Owners
825 and 30830 the Essex Locomotive Society
62005, 63395 and 69023 the North Eastern Locomotive Preservation Group
60007 Sir Nigel Gresley Locomotive Preservation Trust
34028 the Southern Locomotives Ltd
Antwerp the National Mining Museum
5 and 29 Lambton Locomotives Trust
D5032 T. J. Thomson & Co
D5061 the Class 24 Society
50027 the Class 50 Support Group
3814, 6619, 34101 and 44767 private
53809 the 13809 Preservation Group

Steam Centre

Northampton & Lamport Railway

Northants

Member: HRA
Part of the Northampton to Market Harborough branch originally opened in 1859 and finally closing in 1981. That year a group was formed with the intention of re-opening the branch. Trains restarted in 1995 with 0.75 mile of running line and sidings. When completed to Lamport the line will be 6 miles long
Headquarters: Pitsford & Brampton Station, Pitsford Road, Chapel Brampton, Northampton NN6 8BA
Location: About 5 miles north of

Locomotives and multiple-units

Name	*No*	*Origin*	*Class*	*Type*	*Built*
—	3862	GWR	2884	2-8-0	1942
—	08357	BR	08	0-6-0DE	1958
—	27056	BR	27	Bo-Bo	1962
—	31289	BR	31	A1A-A1A	1961
—	33008	BR*	33	Bo-Bo	1960
The Royal Artilleryman	45118	BR	45	1Co-Co1	1962
—	47205	BR	47	Co-Co	1965
—	56098	BR	56	Co-Co	1981
—	97651	BR	97	0-6-0DE	1959
—	51359	BR	117	DMBS	1959
—	51400	BR	117	DMS	1959
—	55001	BR	122	DMBS	1958

*expected to arrive following restoration

Northampton, Pitsford Road off A5199 (formerly A50) or A508
Chairman: Dr Colin Wilson
Operating company: Northampton Steam Railway Ltd
Telephone: 01604 820327. Sundays and weekday afternoons, recorded announcements other times
Internet address: *Web site:* www.nlr.org.uk
Access by public transport: None
On site facilities: NLR souvenir shop, buffet coach, toilets, second-hand bookshop
Length of line: 1.3 miles, extension to bridge 14 now open
Public opening: Every Sunday and Bank Holiday Monday from 5 March to 29 October. Santa Specials every Saturday and Sunday from 3-23 December. Plus some Saturdays during special events
Special events: Easter Egg Specials — 15-17 April; Day out with Thomas — 29/30 April-1 May; Teddy Bears' Holiday — 27-29 May; Classic & Sports Car Show — 4 June; MG Owners Club — 2 July; Day out with Thomas — 26-28 August; Fabulous 40s Weekend — 30 September/1 October; Day out with Thomas — 14/15 October; Santa Specials — 3, 9/10, 16/17 December (pre-booking essential); Mince Pie Specials — 1 January 2007
Membership details: Membership Secretary, Pitsford & Brampton Station, Pitsford Road, Chapel Brampton, Northampton NN6 8BA
Membership journal: *Premier Line* — 4 times a year

Industrial locomotives

Name	No	Builder	Type	Built
Colwyn	45	Kitson (5470)	0-6-0ST	1933
Westminster	1378	Peckett (1378)	0-6-0ST	1914
—	2104	Peckett (2104)	0-4-0ST	1948
Vanguard	5374	Chrzanow (5374)	0-6-0T	1959
Northampton	7646	Chrzanow (5387)	0-6-0T	1959
Bunty	146C	Fowler (4210018)/ rebuilt T/Hill	0-4-0DH	1950 1964
—	21	Fowler (4210094)	0-4-0DH	1955
—	1	R/Hornsby (275886)	4wDM	1949
Sir Gyles Isham	764	R/Hornsby (319286)	0-4-0DM	1953

Stock

Coaches: 2 x BR Mk 1 TSO; 1 x BR Mk 1 BSO; 1 x BR Mk 1 CK; 1 x BR Mk 1 RBR; 1 x Mk 2 TSO; 1 x Mk 2 BSO (trolley buffet); 1 x BR Mk 1 NAV; 2 x BR NJV; 2 x SR PMV; 1 x GWR full brake; 1 x LMS CCT
Wagons: A number of various types

Owners

Colwyn the Colwyn Preservation Society
7646 the Northampton Locomotive Co
08357 and 31289 on loan from Fragonset Railways

Steam Centre

Northamptonshire Ironstone Railway Trust

Northants

The museum is a working display as well as a collection of historic memorabilia. Many of the items that are currently being renovated are housed in a shed that accommodates the museum display
Location: Hunsbury Hill Industrial Museum, Hunsbury Hill Country Park, Hunsbury Hill Road, Camp Hill, Northampton
OS reference: SP 735584
Operating organisation: Northamptonshire Ironstone Railway Trust Ltd
Telephone: 01604 702031
Contact: W. Nile, 14 Lyncrest Avenue, Dunston, Northampton (Tel: 01604 757481)
Access by public transport: Northampton Transport bus routes, 24, 25 to Camp Hill from Greyfriars bus station
On site facilities: Light refreshments, shop, toilets.

Multiple-units

Name	No	Origin	Class	Type	Built
—	13004	SR	4DD	DMBS	1949
—	56285	BR	121	DTS	1960
—	70284	BR	4CEP / 411	TS	1956
—	70296	BR	4CEP / 411	TS	1956
—	69304	BR	4BIG / 422	TSRB	1965
—	14352†	BR	415 / 4EPB	DMS	1954
—	15396†	BR	415 / 4EPB	TS	1954
—	14351†	BR	415 / 4EPB	DMS	1954

†unit No 415176

Industrial locomotives

Name	No	Builder	Type	Built
Vigilant†	—	Hunslet (287)	0-4-0ST	1882
Belvedere◊	—	Sentinel (9365)	0-4-0TG	1946
Musketeer◊	—	Sentinel (9369)	0-4-0TG	1946
Hylton	—	Planet (3967)	0-4-0DH	1961
Charles Wake	—	Fowler (422001)	0-4-0DH	1965
Lois	—	Fowler (422033)	0-4-0DH	1965
Muffin	46	R/Hornsby (242868)	4wDM	1946
—	16	Hunslet (2087)	0-4-0DM	1940
AMOCO	56	R/Hornsby	0-4-0DM	1956

Children's play areas and picnic areas
Length of line: 2.25 miles with yard, engine shed and workshops, 2 stations and level crossing
Public opening: Not advised, please contact for details
Times of opening: Not advised, please contact for details
Facilities for the disabled: Passenger coach can accommodate wheelchairs
Special notes: Museum to the Ironstone Industry of Northamptonshire, the museum houses photographs, documents and other items connected with the ironstone industry. The railway is laid on the old trackbed of the quarry system and partly on a new formation with remains of the quarry face and cuttings available for exploration
Membership details: Mr R. Coleman, c/o above address

Name	*No*	*Builder*	*Type*	*Built*
Shire Lodge	53	R/Hornsby	0-4-0DM	1954
Sir Alfred Wood	46	R/Hornsby (319214)	0-6-0DM	1953
—	5	R/Hornsby (338489)	0-4-0DM	1956
—*	87	Peckett (1871)	0-6-0ST	1934
Northampton†	1	Bagnall (2565)	0-4-0ST	1934
*Cherwell***	—	Bagnall (2654)	0-6-0ST	1942
—	—	Grafton	Steam crane	1934

* metre gauge on loan to Irchester Country Park
◊ static display
† being rebuilt
**3ft gauge

Owners
13004, unit No 415176 the Bulleid Preservation Enterprises
70284/70296 Northampton Social Services

Nottingham Transport Heritage Centre

Steam Centre — Notts

Member: HRA
Along with access to nearly 10 miles of the ex-Great Central Railway main line in Nottinghamshire, the Centre is host to a road and rail transport heritage vehicle collection. Ambitious plans are afoot to reconnect its section of main line railway to the existing Great Central Railway based at Loughborough. This will provide visitors with the unique experience of travelling on one of the longest heritage railways in the UK in a realistic re-creation of main line travel of the 1950s and 1960s
Location: On the A60 just south of Ruddington, 3 miles south of Nottingham city centre, off A52, 7 miles north of Loughborough. Signposted
Operating society/organisation: Great Central (Nottingham) Ltd, Nottingham Heritage Centre, Mere Way, Ruddington, Nottingham NG11 6NX
Telephone: (0115) 940 5705

Locomotives and multiple-units

Name	*No*	*Origin*	*Class*	*Type*	*Built*
—	D4115*	BR	08	0-6-0DE	1962
—	13180	BR	08	0-6-0DE	1955
—	D7629	BR	25	Bo-Bo	1965
—	D8048	BR	20	Bo-Bo	1959
—	D9520†	BR	14	0-6-0DH	1964
—	47765	BR	47	Co-Co	1964
—	56097	BR	56	Co-Co	1981
—	51138	BR	116	DMBS	1958
—	51151	BR	116	DMS	1958
—	53645	BR	108	DMBS	1958
—	53926	BR	108	DMBS	1959
—	59389	BR	108	TS	1958
—	—	USATC	S160	2-8-0	—

Gatwick Express units 8301/10, 9108

*expected to depart soon
†off site for further restoration at Nene Valley Railway

Industrial locomotives

Name	*No*	*Builder*	*Type*	*Built*
Victor	2996	Bagnall (2996)	0-6-0ST	1951
—	54	H/Clarke (1682)	0-6-0ST	1937
—	56	RSH (7667)	0-6-0ST	1950

Fax: (0115) 940 5905
Internet address:
Web site: www.nthc.co.uk
Access by public transport: Buses from city centre and Broad Marsh (tel: [0115] 924 0000), via Nottingham Midland station
On site facilities: Car park, shop and café, picnic area and country park walks. 700m-long passenger-carrying miniature railway. Extensive bus museum
Length of line: 7 mile steam train ride
Facilities for disabled: Accessible, and access to toilets
Public opening: Sundays & Bank Holidays Easter to early October, plus Spooky Ghost Trains, Bonfire Night and Santa Specials.
Open 10.45-17.00
(first trains around 11.30)
Special events: 3rd Model Railway Event — 19/20 August. For other events please contact for details
Membership details: Great Central Northern Development Association, c/o above address
Society journal: Quarterly

Name	*No*	*Builder*	*Type*	*Built*
—	63	RSH (7761)	0-6-0ST	1954
Rhiwnant	—	M/Wardle (1317)	0-6-0ST	1895
Dolobran	—	M/Wardle (1762)	0-6-0ST	1910
Abernant	—	M/Wardle (2009)	0-6-0ST	1921
Toby	—	R/Hornsby (235513)	4wDM	1945
—	2 / D2971	R/Hornsby (313394)	0-4-0DM	1954
(Quag)	(1)	R/Hornsby (371971)	0-4-0DM	1954
Staythorpe	D2959	R/Hornsby (449754)	0-4-0DE	1961
Churchill	423	R/Hornsby (459518)	0-4-0DM	1961
—	8	R/Hornsby (494436)	0-4-0DE	1965
—	15100	M/Rail (1930)	4wPM	1919
—	—	M/Rail (2028)	0-4-0DM	1932

Rolling stock: 1 BR Mk 1 FO, 1 BR Mk 2 BSO, 1 BR Mk 2 BFK, 1 BR (ex-WR) cinema coach, 5 ex-Gatwick express coaches, GCR coach (body) CBL No 1663 (oldest surviving GCR coach, built 1903), 4 Barnum coaches, suburban coach, 2 MS&LR 6-wheel coaches, 1 'Internation' concert coach (used as display area and will not run), 1 LNER 45-ton steam breakdown crane, 1 SR GUV, various goods wagons

Owners
Class 108 and 116 DMUs the Nottingham (GC) DMU Group
56097 and 423 the 56097 Locomotive Group
M/Rails 1930, 2028, R/Hornsbys 371971, 449754 the Simplex 2028 Association
R/Hornsby (313394) the Cheshire Locomotive Preservation Group

Steam Centre

Oswestry Railway Centre
(Cambrian Railways Society)

Shropshire

Member: HRA
The Gobowen to Blodwell line is some 8.25 miles long and is currently in an operational 'mothballed' state. The society is negotiating with Network Rail to lease this former Cambrian branch line with a view to restoring a heritage railway service between Gobowen and Llanyblodwell and eventually Llanymynech. The society now operates on four separate sites.

July 2004 saw the purchase of the former Cambrian Institute on Gobowen Road; now open as a social club (19.00-23.00) seven days a week and is available for functions and events.

The Oswestry Railway Centre, Oswald Road, was awarded Phase II status recognition, the Museum being of national importance.

Industrial locomotives

Name	*No*	*Builder*	*Type*	*Built*
—	1	H/Clarke (D843)	0-4-0DM	1954
—	—	H/Clarke (D893)	0-4-0DM	1953
Adam	1	Peckett (1430)	0-4-0ST	1916
—	3	Hunslet (D3526)	0-6-0DM	1954
Oliver Velton	6	Peckett (2131)	0-4-0ST	1951
—	8	Barclay (885)	0-6-0ST	1900
—	322	Planet (3541)	4wDM	1952
Norma	3770	Hunslet (3770)	0-6-0ST	1952
—*	—	Hibberd (3057)	4wDM	1946
—	—	Planet (3716)	0-4-0DM	1955
Telemon	—	Drewry/Vulcan (2568)	0-4-0DM	1955

*mobile compressor

Stock
1 GWR auto-trailer; 1 GWR brake van; 1 LMS brake van; 2 tank wagons; 1 open wagon, 1 box van, 1 tank wagon (No 5), 2 tank wagon 4-wheel chassis (tanks removed) ex-Machynlleth Refuelling Depot, 4-wheel van, 12-ton box van, ex-S&M 10-ton box van.

Owners
Telemon the Cambrian Diesel Group

The Society-owned Grain Transfer Warehouse at Weston, on the outskirts of Oswestry, is now home to the Denbigh and Mold Junction Railway.

August 2004 saw the purchase of the 1.5-mile former Nant Mawr branch line and the start of a two year project to restore this to operational status

Location: Oswestry station yard, Oswald Road, Oswestry, Shropshire SY11 1RE

OS reference: SJ 294297

Operating society/organisation: Cambrian Railways Society Ltd, Oswald Road, Oswestry, Shropshire SY11 1RE

Telephone: (01691) 671749

Internet address: *Web site:* www.cambrian-railways-soc.co.uk

Car park: In Society's depot

CAccess by public transport: By rail — Gobowen station is 2.5 miles north.
By bus — 2min walk from Oswestry bus station.
Please note that there is no Gobowen-Oswestry bus service on Sundays

Length of line: 400yd, opened 7 December 1996, the Light Railway Order having been granted

Public opening: Oswestry Transport Museum is open: Monday-Saturday 09.00-16.00. Sunday 11.00-16.00.
Please contact to confirm when trains are expected to operate.

On site facilities: Refreshment room — the 'Whistle Stop' (open on special days in former Llansantffraid signalbox) and picnic area

Special notes: Railwayana and artefacts. Peckett 2131 and Hunslet 3770 are on display inside the building. Group discount available. Also known as Oswestry Transport Museum

Timetable Service

Paignton & Dartmouth Steam Railway

Devon

The Paignton & Dartmouth Steam Railway is the holiday line with steam trains running for seven miles in Great Western tradition along the spectacular Torbay coast to Churston and through the wooded slopes bordering the Dart estuary to Kingswear. The scenery is superb, with seascapes right across Lyme Bay to Portland Bill on clear days. Approaching Kingswear is the beautiful River Dart, with its fascinating craft, and on the far side, the 'olde worlde' town of Dartmouth and Britannia Royal Naval College, Butterwalk, Bayard's Cove and Dartmouth Castle

Director & General Manager: J. B. S. Cogar

Headquarters: Paignton Queen's Park station, Paignton, Devon

Telephone: Paignton (01803) 555872

Main station: Paignton Queen's Park

Other public stations: Goodrington, Churston, Kingswear (for Dartmouth)

OS reference: SX 889606

Car parks: Paignton municipal car park, Goodrington, Dartmouth (ferry to Kingswear)

Locomotives and multiple-units

Name	*No*	*Origin*	*Class*	*Type*	*Built*
Warrior	4555	GWR	4500	2-6-2T	1924
Trojan	4588	GWR	4575	2-6-2T	1927
Goliath	5239	GWR	5205	2-8-0T	1924
Ajax	6435	GWR	6400	0-6-0PT	1937
Lydham Manor	7827	GWR	7800	4-6-0	1951
Braveheart	75014	BR	4MT	4-6-0	1951
Ardent	D2192	BR	03	0-6-0DM	1962
Volunteer	D3014	BR	08	0-6-0DE	1954
Hercules	D7535	BR	25	Bo-Bo	1965
—	59003*	BR	116	TS	1957
—	59004*	BR	116	TS	1957
—	59488*	P/Steel	117	TCL	1959
—	59494*	P/Steel	117	TCL	1959
—	59503*	P/Steel	117	TCL	1959
—	59507*	P/Steel	117	TCL	1959
—	59513*	P/Steel	117	TCL	1959
—	59517*	P/Steel	117	TCL	1959

*converted to locomotive-hauled vehicles

Stock

15 ex-BR Mk 1 coaches; 1 Pullman observation coach; 2 auto-coaches

Access by public transport: Adjacent to both Paignton main line station and bus station

Refreshment facilities: Paignton and Kingswear

Depot: Churston

Length of line: 7 miles

Passenger trains: Paignton-Kingswear, views of Torbay and Dart estuary, 495yd tunnel

Period of public operation: Easter to October and Santa Specials in December

Facilities for disabled: Limited, special ramp to take wheelchairs onto trains. Disabled toilets at Paignton

Special events: Santa Specials —

please see timetable and press for details. Combined river excursions available
Special note: The railway also operates excursion vessels on the River Dart. Combined river excursions available, Boat trains and Round Robin tickets. Round Robin — single journey to Kingswear, 1hr 30min boat cruise to Totnes and bus back to Paignton

Timetable Service

Peak Rail plc

Derbyshire

Member: HRA
In 1968 the railway between Matlock and Buxton, through the Peak National Park was closed and lifted. This was once part of the Midland Railway's route between Manchester Central and London. In 1975 efforts were started to reopen the line. Services between Matlock and Darley Dale commenced in 1991
Location: *Registered Office:* Matlock Station, Matlock, Derbyshire DE4 3NA
OS reference: Matlock SK 060738
Operating society/organisation: Peak Rail plc, Matlock Station, Matlock, Derbyshire DE4 3NA
Telephone: (01629) 580381
Internet address: *Web site:* www.peakrail.co.uk
Car parks: Matlock station, Darley Dale, Rowsley South station
Length of line: 4 miles — Matlock Riverside-Rowsley South.
A 2ft gauge railway is now operational at Rowsley
On site facilities: Shop at Matlock. Shops and buffets at Darley Dale and Rowsley South. Picnic area and riverside walk
Public opening: Sundays throughout the year, Saturdays April to October. Midweek during summer. Timetable varies
Facilities for disabled: Darley Dale and Rowsley. Matlock Riverside unsuitable for disabled passengers. Specially adapted carriage is fully accessible to wheelchair users (not available on DMU services)
Period of public operation: Not advised, see timetable supplement
Special events: Please contact for details

Locomotives and multiple-units

Name	*No*	*Origin*	*Class*	*Type*	*Built*
—	48624	LMS	8F	2-8-0	1943
—	D2953	BR	01	0-4-0DM	1956
—	D2854	BR	02	0-4-0DH	1960
—	D2866	BR	02	0-4-0DH	1961
—	03027	BR	03	0-6-0DM	1958
—	03099	BR	03	0-6-0DM	1960
—	D2139	BR	03	0-6-0DM	1960
—	D2229	BR	04	0-6-0DM	1955
Alfie	D2272	BR	04	0-6-0DM	1960
—	D2284	BR	04	0-6-0DM	1960
Dorothy	D2337	BR	04	0-6-0DM	1961
—	D2587	BR	05	0-6-0DM	1959
—	07013	BR	07	0-6-0DE	1961
Geoff L. Wright	D3023	BR	08	0-6-0DE	1953
—	12061	BR	11	0-6-0DE	1949
—	D9502	BR	14	0-6-0DH	1964
—	D9525	BR	14	0-6-0DH	1964
—	31270	BR	31	A1A-A1A	1961
—	37151	BR	37	Co-Co	1963
Penyghent	D8	BR	44	1Co-Co1	1959
Renown	50029	BR	50	Co-Co	1968
Repulse	50030	BR	50	Co-Co	1968
—	97654	BR	—	0-6-0DM	1959
—	50627	BR	108	DMBS	1958
—	51566	BR	108	DMSL	1959
—	51567	BR	108	DMSL	1959
—	51933	BR	108	DMBS	1960
—	53933	BR	108	DMBS	1959
—	54484	BR	108	DTC	1960
—	54504	BR	108	DTC	1960
—	59387	BR	108	TS	1958
—	51973 (977806)	BR	108	DMBS	1958

Industrial locomotives

Name	*No*	*Builder*	*Type*	*Built*
The Duke	2746	Bagnall (2746)	0-6-0ST	1944
—	64	Brush (803)	0-6-0DE	1978
Royal Pioneer	150	RSH (7136)	0-6-0ST	1944
Zebedee	—	RSH (7597)	0-6-0ST	1949
Vulcan	—	V/Foundry (3272)	0-4-0ST	1918
—	—	T/Hill	0-6-0DH	
Lucky	48	T/Hill	0-6-0DH	
Claire	—	H/Clarke (D1389)	0-4-0DM	1967
Castlefield	—	H/Clarke (D1388)	0-6-0DH	1970
—	20	R/Hornsby (432479)	0-4-0DM	1959
Rotherham	—	YEC (2480)	0-4-0DM	
Bigga	—	Fowler (4200019)	0-4-0DM	1947
Ken	—	Sentinel (10180)	0-6-0DH	1964

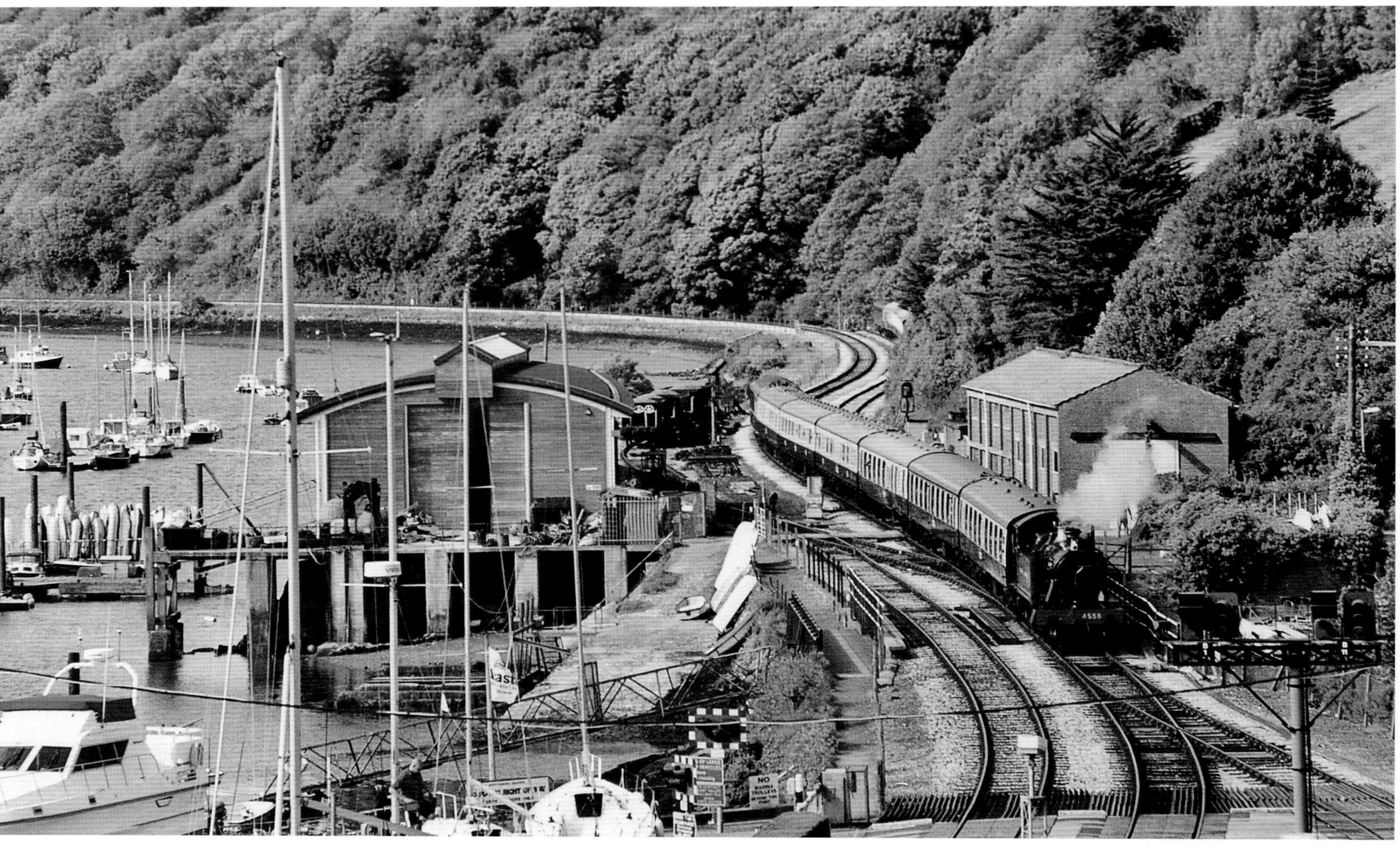

Having a ride on a heritage railway is an easy way of seeing some wonderful scenery. The Paignton & Dartmouth Railway commences at the seaside town of Paignton and finishes alongside the estuary of the River Dart at Kingswear. No 4555 arrives at Kingswear from Paignton. *Phil Barnes*

Name	No	Builder	Type	Built
—	—	Drewry (2552)	0-6-0DM	1953

Rolling stock — coaches: 2 BR Mk 1 RMB, 1 BR Mk 1 SLF, 3 BR Mk 1 TSO, 2 BR Mk 1 SO, 3 BR Mk 1 SK, 1 BR Mk 1 BSK, 2 BR Mk 1 BG, 1 BR Mk 1 GUV, 1 BR Mk 2 SO, 1 BR Mk 2 BSO, 1 BR Mk 2 BFK, 1 LMS TK, 2 LMS BCK, 1BTK, 1 Bullion coach, 3 parcels vans

Rolling stock — wagons: 1 5 plank, 1 LMS 5 plank, 3 match wagons, 1 LNER flat wagon, 1 LMS 5 plank tube, 1 LMS 2 plank tube, 1 BR Grampus 20-ton ballast, 1 LNER flat, 1 LMR water bowser, 1 Plasser & Theurer tamper, 2 LMS fish vans, 2 Austrian ferry wagons, 1 SR parcels van, 1 Shell tank wagon, 1 Esso tank wagon, 2 tank wagons, 2 LNER 2 plank dropsides, 3 BR 12-ton box vans, 1 12-ton van (wooden underframe), 2 BR Pallet vans, 1 Charles Roberts covered van, 1 LNER crane, 2 LMS brake vans, 1 BR brake van, 1 MR brake van, 1 BR Sturgeon rail wagon, 1 BR Lowmac, 1 BR Welltrol, 1 BR Salmon, 2 BR Dogfish ballast hoppers

Owners
03084 the Amber Valley Locomotive Group
50029 and 50030 The Renown Repulse Restoration Group
D8 the North Notts Loco Group
Vulcan the Vulcan Loco Trust
7597 Peak Rail and Peak Railway Association
D3023 the Heritage Shunters Trust
12061 on loan to the Heritage Shunters Trust

Derbyshire Dales Narrow Gauge Railway
Industrial narrow gauge locomotives (2ft gauge)

Name	No	Builder	Type	Built
—	—	M/Rail (22070)	4wDM	1960
—	—	R/Hornsby (264252)	4wDM	1952
—	—	R/Hornsby (393325)	4wDM	1956
—	—	R/Hornsby (487963)	4wDM	1963

Miniature Railway

Perrygrove Railway

Glos

Member: Britain's Great Little Railways (corporate member of HRA)
Headquarters: Perrygrove Railway, Coleford, Gloucestershire GL16 8QB
Contact: Michael Crofts
Telephone/Fax: 01594 834991
Internet addresses: *e-mail:* 1@perrygrove.co.uk
Web site: www.perrygrove.co.uk
OS reference: SO 579094
Main station: Perrygrove
Other public stations: Rookwood, Heywood, Oakiron
Car park: Parking at Perrygrove for 60 cars plus 2 coach bays
Access by public transport: Network Rail: Lydney (7 miles). Dean Forest Railway: Parkend (3 miles). Bus routes from: Cinderford — Duke Travel 732; Gloucester — Stagecoach 31; Lydney — Duke Travel 721; Monmouth — Duke Travel 722; Ross on Wye — Duke Travel 35; Ruardean — Duke Travel 738. Enquiries: 01452 425610
Refreshment facilities: Light

Locomotives

Name	No	Builder	Type	Built
Spirit of Adventure	—	ESR (295)	0-6-0T	1995
Ursula	—*		0-6-0T	
—	—†		0-4-0+0-4-0	
Workhorse	—	Simplex (1064)	0-4-0DM	
Jubilee	—	Hunslet (9337)	0-4-0DH	1994

*based on Heywood locomotive of 1916
†Tasmanian K1 Garrett

Stock
Various carriages and assorted wagons

refreshments in Perrygrove station café
Souvenir shops: Small shop at Perrygrove
Museum: Heywood Collection of minimum gauge railways on display at Perrygrove
Depot: All sheds are at Perrygrove. Tours are encouraged under supervision when staff are available
Length of line: 0.75 miles, 15in (381mm) gauge
Period of public operation: Five days per week in local school holidays plus many other weekends
Special events: Christmas trains operate, advance booking essential.

The railway has an informal enthusiasts' day to coincide with the annual open day at Alan Keef Ltd, light railway engineers. Usually first or second weekend in September
Facilities for disabled: All disabilities catered for. About 75% of the site is accessible to wheelchairs, although some of the woodland paths are rough. There is space for a wheelchair on the train
Membership details: No formal society but volunteers welcome
Membership journal: Diary pages on web site

Steam Centre

Plym Valley Railway

Devon

Member: HRA
A scheme dedicated to the restoration of services over the former GWR Marsh Mills-Plym Bridge line, a distance of 1.5 miles
Location: 5 miles from centre of Plymouth, Devon, north of A38. From Marsh Mills roundabout, take B3416 to Plympton, follow signs
Internet address: *Web site*: www.plymrail.co.uk
OS reference: SX 517564
Operating society/organisation: Plym Valley Railway Co Ltd, Marsh Mills Station, Coypool Road, Marsh Mills, Plymouth, Devon PL7 4NW
Access by public transport: Buses from Plymouth, Nos 20, 20A, 21, 22A, 51 stop close to site
On site facilities: Shop and refreshments at Marsh Mills, Coypool (Sundays only)
Public opening: Sundays from 10.00, and other selected days. Trains are scheduled to operate: 16 April; 14 May; 11, 25 June; 9, 23 July; 13, 27 August; 10, 24 September; 8 October, 12 November, 10, 17 December. 13.00-16.00 at half hourly intervals
Length of line: Half-mile currently in use for passenger rides

Locomotives and multiple-units

Name	*No*	*Origin*	*Class*	*Type*	*Built*
—	75079	BR	4MT	4-6-0	1956
—	13002	BR	08	0-6-0DE	1953
William Cookworthy	37207	BR	37	Co-Co	1963
—	51365	BR	117	DMBS	1960
—	51407	BR	117	DMS	1960

Industrial locomotives

Name	*No*	*Builder*	*Type*	*Built*
Byfield No 2	—	Bagnall (2655)	0-6-0ST	1941
Albert	—	Barclay (2248)	0-4-0ST	1948
—	3	H/Leslie (3597)	0-4-0ST	1926
—	—	T/Hill (125V)	4wDH	1963
—	—	Hibberd (3281)	4wDM	1948

Rolling stock: 3 x BR Mk 1 coaches, 1 LBSCR compartment coach (body only), 2 x BR GUVs, 3 x brake vans, various wagons. Self-propelled Smith & Rodley diesel crane of 1956

Special events: Hot Cross Bun Specials — 16 April; Mince Pie Specials — 10, 17 December
Special notes: Visitors are advised that, at the moment, the railway and two locomotives are still under restoration. 2 working locomotives and DMU. The line was extended beyond the first bridge in 2003. Train rides behind the 13002 on some Sundays (normally 2nd in the month)
Membership details: Tina Newton, Plym Valley Railway, Marsh Mills Station, Coypool Road, Marsh Mills, Plymouth, Devon PL7 4NW
Membership journal: *Plym Valley Railway News* — 3/year
Marketing name: The Woodland Line

Timetable Service

The Poppy Line (North Norfolk Railway)

Norfolk

Member: HRA, TT
Part of the former Midland & Great Northern Joint Railway, other elements of the LNER have crept in in the guise of the 'B12' and a Gresley buffet car. GER 'J15' is now in service. Guest locomotives can be viewed at various times throughout the year. The line runs through beautiful coast, wood and heathland scenery with a nature trail running along its side between Weybourne and Kelling Heath
Managing Director: Hugh Harkett
General Manager: Geoff Gowing
Headquarters: North Norfolk Railway plc, Sheringham Station, Sheringham, Norfolk NR26 8RA
Telephone: Sheringham (01263) 820800
Fax: (01263) 820801
Internet address: *Web site:* www.nnr.co.uk
Main station: Sheringham
Other public stations: Weybourne, Kelling Halt, Holt
OS reference: Sheringham TG 156430, Weybourne TG 118419
Car parks: Sheringham (public), Weybourne, Holt
Access by public transport: By train to Sheringham station ('one' railway)
Refreshment facilities: Sheringham, Weybourne, Holt
Souvenir shops: Sheringham, Weybourne, Holt
Depot: Weybourne
Length of line: 5.25 miles
Passenger trains: Steeply graded (1 in 80), Sheringham-Weybourne-Holt
Period of public operation: Most days from mid-March to end October. Weekends in November and December plus Christmas week
Special events: Diesel Gala — 10/11 June*; Vintage Transport — 9 July; 5th Poppy Line Beer Festival — 14-16 July; Battle of Britain Real Ale and Music Train — 29 July (evening); The Great '40s Weekend — 16/17 September; Summer Steam Gala — 7/8 October; Day out with Thomas — 21-23 October; Santa Specials — 2/3, 9/10, 16/17, 20-24 December; Carol Concert — 15 December (evening); Mince Pie Specials — 26 December-3 January;
*provisional dates
Facilities for disabled: All stations have level access. Wheelchair access to most trains, and to gift shop and buffet at Sheringham. Disabled parking at Holt station
Membership details: Midland & Great Northern Joint Railway Society, Mr D. Bicknell, 55 Monmouth Close, Ipswich, Suffolk IP2 8RS
Tel: 01473 604402
Membership journal: *Joint Line* — quarterly

Locomotives and multiple-units

Name	*No*	*Origin*	*Class*	*Type*	*Built*
—	564	GER	J15	0-6-0	1912
A. J. Hill	69621	GER	N7	0-6-2T	1924
—	65033†	NER	J21	0-6-0	1889
—	8572	LNER	B12	4-6-0	1928
—	68088	LNER	Y7	0-4-0T	1923
92 Squadron	34081	SR	BB	4-6-2	1948
—	90775	MoS	WD	2-10-0	1943
—	D2280	BR	04	0-6-0DM	1960
Camulodunum	D3940	BR	08	0-6-0DE	1960
—	D3935	BR	08	0-6-0DE	1961
—	12131	BR	11	0-6-0DE	1952
—	D5207	BR	25	Bo-Bo	1962
—	5580	BR	31	A1A-A1A	1960
—	31207	BR	31	A1A-A1A	1960
Mirage	D6732	BR	37	Co-Co	1962
—	47367	BR	47	Co-Co	1965
—	51228	M/Cam	101	DTSL	1958
—	54062	M/Cam	101	DMBS	1957
—	79960	W&M	—	Railbus	1958
—	79963*	W&M	—	Railbus	1958
—	LEV1	BR/Leyland	—	Railbus	1978

Guest locomotives for 2006 include No 34081 *92 Squadron*
*on loan to Mangapps Farm Railway
†on long term loan from Beamish

Industrial locomotives

Name	*No*	*Builder*	*Type*	*Built*
Ring Haw	—	Hunslet (1982)	0-6-0ST	1940
—	3809	Hunslet (3809)	0-6-0ST	1954
*Wissington**	—	H/Clarke (1700)	0-6-0ST	1938
—	—	Bagnall (2370)	0-6-0F	1929

*under restoration

Stock
3 ex-LNER coaches, GNR quad set (under restoration), 7 ex-BR coaches, 3 coach King's Cross suburban set; Gresley buffet, 2 CCT wagons, small number of wagons and Southern Railway PMV

Owners
564, 8572, 31207 and 90775 the Midland & Great Northern Railway Society
69621 East Anglian Railway Museum
34081 the Battle of Britain Locomotive Society
5580 A1A Locomotives
47367 The Stratford Class 47 Group
LEV1 on loan from National Railway Museum

Steam Centre

The Railway Age, Crewe

Cheshire

Location: Crewe Heritage Centre, Vernon Way, Crewe
OS reference: SJ 709552
Operating society/organisation: Crewe Heritage Trust Ltd
Telephone: (01270) 212130
Internet address: *Web site:* www.therailwayage.co.uk
Car park: On site, town centre, Forge Street, Oak Street,
Access by public transport: Main line Crewe
Refreshment facilities: Adjacent Safeway superstore
On site facilities: Gift shop, picnic area, children's corner, weekend train rides, standard gauge and miniature railway, exhibition hall, main line viewing area, 3 working signalboxes with 'hands-on' visitor operation
Public opening: Daily 10.00-16.00 (last admission 15.00). Family tickets available. Please contact for details of events
Facilities for disabled: Toilets
Membership details: Heritage Centre Supporters Association, c/o above address
Notes: Steam locomotives passed for use over main line tracks are stabled between duties from time to time

Locomotives and multiple-units

Name	*No*	*Origin*	*Class*	*Type*	*Built*
—	49395	LNWR	G2	0-8-0	1921
—	5224§	GWR	4200	2-8-0T	1924
—	6638	GWR	5600	0-6-2T	1928
—	D2073	BR	03	0-6-0DM	1959
—	31442	BR	31	A1A-A1A	1960
—	D120†	BR	45	1Co-Co1	1961
Ixion	D172†	BR	46	1Co-Co1	1962
—	D1842	BR	47	Co-Co	1965
Robert Burns	87035	BR	87	Bo-Bo	1974
—	18000	BR	—	A1A-A1A	1949
—	55032*	P/Steel	121	DMBS	1960

†on site occasionally, but usually kept at private locations
*may not be on site for all of 2006
§on loan to West Somerset Railway

Industrial locomotives

Name	*No*	*Builder*	*Type*	*Built*
Robert	—	H/Clarke (1752)	0-6-0T	1943

Rolling stock
APT vehicle Nos 48103, 48106, 48404, 48602, 48603, 48606, 49002; 1 BR Mk 1 BSK; various ex-BR coaches and passenger brake vans from time to time for repairs

Owners
49395 the National Railway Museum

Museum

Railworld

Cambs

Member: HRA
Railworld is primarily an exhibition centre and museum, promoting 'Sustainable Transport' and a '21st Century Showcase for Rail'. In addition it has a museum which is mainly about Peterborough's railway history,;its model railway is impressive. There are also 'Age of Steam' exhibits and a database of over 7,000 names of local railworkers since the 1840s (50p extra access charge)
Location: Situated alongside the Town station of the Nene Valley Railway. Walk — 15min walk from train and bus stations. By car — turn off A605 Oundle Road

Locomotives

Name	*No*	*Origin*	*Class*	*Type*	*Built*
—	996	DSB	4MT	4-6-2	1950

Industrial locomotives

Name	*No*	*Builder*	*Type*	*Built*
—	804	Alco (77778)	Bo-Bo	1949
*Nutty**	5	Sentinel (7701)	4wVBT	1929
—†	740	O&K (2343)	0-6-0T	1907

*2ft 6in gauge (off-site at present)
† 2ft gauge and on loan to Leighton Buzzard Railway until August 2007
remainder standard

Other stock: Britain's RTV 31 Hovertrain vehicle, Presflo 2-axle flyash wagon (No B874076 of 12965) and a 2-axle 8,650gal tank wagon (No 55223 of 1966). Birmingham International Airport Maglev car No 01 of 1984 supplied by Metro-Cammell, operational 1984-1995 — the world's first train without wheels in commercial service

(town end) into Council's long stay car park, drive through to Railworld. The Railworld car park is free to visitors. By bike — situated on the 'Green Wheel' cycle route. By boat — alongside river quay
OS reference: TL 189981
Operating society/organisation: Railworld, Oundle Road, Peterborough, Cambridgeshire PE2 9NR
Contact: Rev Richard Paten
Telephone: 01733 344240
Fax: 01733 319362
Internet address: *e-mail:* railword@aol.com
Web site: www.railworld.net
On site facilities: Buffet and small shop, open weekends March to October. Picnic area. Model railway
Public opening: Daily March-October 11.00-16.00. Also Monday to Fridays November-March 11.00-16.00
Special events: National Science Week — 11-20 March; 'Environment Week' (Integrated Transport) — 11-19 June
Access for disabled: Reasonable wheelchair access
Admission charge: Adult £4, Child £2, Concessions £3, Family £10 (2A+4C)
Membership details: John Crane, 21 St Margarets Road, Peterborough PE2 9EA
Membership journal: *Friends of Railworld* — biannually

Timetable Service

Ravenglass & Eskdale Railway

Cumbria

Member: HRA
From the coast through two of Lakeland's loveliest valleys to the foot of England's highest mountain, small steam engines haul trains in the heart of the national park
General Manager: Trevor Stockton
Headquarters: Ravenglass & Eskdale Railway, Ravenglass, Cumbria CA18 1SW
Telephone: (01229) 717171
Fax: (01229) 717011
Internet address: *e-mail:* rer@netcomuk.co.uk
Web site: www.ravenglass-railway.co.uk
Main station: Ravenglass
Other public stations: Muncaster Mill, Irton Road, The Green, Beckfoot, Eskdale (Dalegarth)
OS reference: SD 086964
Car parks: All stations
Access by public transport: Main line services to Ravenglass; bus service from Whitehaven
Refreshment facilities: Ravenglass, Dalegarth. Bar meals at 'Ratty Arms'
Picnic areas: At both termini
Souvenir shops: Ravenglass, Dalegarth
Museum: Ravenglass
Length of line: 7 miles, 15in gauge
Passenger trains: Steam- or diesel-hauled narrow gauge trains Ravenglass-Dalegarth

Locomotives

Name	*No*	*Builder*	*Type*	*Built*
River Irt	—	Heywood	0-8-2	1894
River Esk	—	Davey Paxman (21104)	2-8-2	1923
River Mite	—	Clarkson (4669)	2-8-2	1966
Northern Rock	—	R&ER	2-6-2	1976
Bonnie Dundee	—	K/Stuart (720)*	0-4-2	1901
Shelagh of Eskdale	—	R&ER/Severn-Lamb	4-6-4D	1969 rebuilt 1998
Quarryman	—	Muir-Hill (2)	0-4-0P/Paraffin	1928
Perkins	—	Muir Hill (NG39A)	0-4-4DM	1929
Lady Wakefield	—	R&ER	B-B	1980
Synolda	—	Bassett-Lowke	4-4-2	1912
—	—	Greenbat (2782)	0-4-0BE	1957
Cyril	—	Lister	0-4-0DM	1987
Douglas Ferreira	—	TMA Engineering	Bo-Bo	2005

*rebuilt to 15in gauge 1981

Period of public operation: Daily late March-early November. Limited winter service November-March
Family ticket: All day travel at reduced price
Facilities for disabled: Special coaches for wheelchair passengers. Advance notice preferred. Wheelchair access to toilets, café and museum at Ravenglass; toilets, shop and cafe at Eskdale (Dalegarth)
Special notes: At Ravenglass the R&ER has two camping coaches and the company also operates the 'Ratty Arms' public house formed by conversion of the former BR station buildings. During the high summer, mid-July through August, five steam locomotives are normally in use Monday-Thursday
Membership details: Mr N. Dickinson, 3 Clifton Terrace, Ravenglass, Cumbria CA18 1SE
Membership journal: *The R&ER Magazine* — quarterly
Marketing names: 'la'al Ratty' — Cumbrian dialect for little narrow track, now a watervole stationmaster!

Museum

Ribble Steam Railway

Lancashire

Member: HRA
Preston Docks have had a railway infrastructure since 1850, and when the final tar trains ran in 1995, it looked like that tenancy had come to an end. However, Steamport Southport began negotiations with Preston Borough Council, and during 1999, the group formerly based at the old engine shed in Southport moved to their new home on the dockside at Preston.

Due to the main line traversing the swing bridge in the Marina, the timetable will be dictated by the tide — the only preserved steam line to have such a feature.

Heritage passenger and modern freight operations blend together as restored diesel locomotives handle bulk bitumen trains on behalf of Total Bitumen. This traffic has switched from road transport since the railway reopened

Location: Off Chain Caulway, Riversway, Preston Docks, Preston, Lancs
OS reference: SD 504295
Operating society/organisation: Steamport Southport Ltd, 3 Lincoln Drive, Old Road, Liverpool L10 3LJ
Telephone: 01772 72882
Internet address: *e-mail:* enquiries@ribblesteam.org.uk
Web site: www.ribblesteam.org.uk
Car park: On site
Main station: Chain Caul Road
Other station: Strand Road
Access by public transport: By train — to Preston (www.nationalrail.co.uk).
By bus — Preston Bus 27, 127 Preston to Larches; Stagecoach 75 Preston to Poulton.
Buses stop on Peddars Way between McDonalds and roundabout on Navigation Way.
By road — follow the signs for Riversway Docklands
On site facilities: Buffet, museum and workshop.
Car paring: On site
Length of lines: 1.5 miles (under restoration)
Public opening: Sundays in March and 7-28 October, weekends 1 April-30 September, plus Bank

Locomotives and multiple-units

Name	*No*	*Origin*	*Class*	*Type*	*Built*
—	46441	LMS	2MT	2-6-0	1950
—	1097	LYR	—	0-4-0ST	1910
—	D2148	BR	03	0-6-0DM	1960
—	03189	BR	03	0-6-0DM	1961
—	D9539	BR	14	0-6-0DH	1965
—	601	NSR	600	0-6-0DE	1956
—	625	NSR	600	0-6-0DE	1956

Industrial locomotives

Name	*No*	*Builder*	*Type*	*Built*
—	272	G/Ritchie (272)	0-4-0T	1894
Daphne	—	Peckett (737)	0-4-0ST	1899
The King	—	Borrows (48)	0-4-0WT	1906
Lucy	—	Avonside (1568)	0-6-0ST	1909
Efficient	—	Barclay (1598)	0-4-0ST	1918
MDHB No 26	—	Avonside (1810)	0-6-0ST	1918
—	1883	Avonside (1883)	0-6-0ST	1922
Alexander	—	Barclay (1865)	0-4-0ST	1926
Heysham No.2	—	Barclay (1950)	0-4-0F	1928
Derbyshire	—	Barclay (1969)	0-4-0ST	1929
Gasbag	—	Sentinel (8024)	4wVBT	1929
Hornet	—	Peckett (1935)	0-4-0ST	1937
Linda	—	H/Leslie (3931)	0-6-0ST	1938
Kinsley	—	Hunslet (1954)	0-6-0ST	1939
North Western Gas Board	—	Peckett (1999)	0-4-0ST	1941
Walkden	—	Hunslet (3155)	0-6-0ST	1944
St Monans	—	Sentinel (9373)	4wVBT	1947
Agecroft No.2	—	RSH (7485)	0-4-0ST	1948
No. 6	—	Barclay (2261)	0-4-0ST	1949
Respite	—	Hunslet.(3696)	0-6-0ST	1950
Shropshire	—	Hunslet (3793)	0-6-0ST	1953
Glasshoughton No.4		Hunslet (3855)	0-6-0ST	1954
Hotto	—	Howard (965)		1930
Mighty Atom	—	H/Clarke (D628)	0-4-0DM	1943
Sparky	—	H/Clarke (D629)	0-4-0DM	1945
Persil	—	Fowler (4160001)	0-4-0DM	1950
Margaret	—	H/Clarke (D1031)	0-4-0DM	1956
BICC	—	NBL (27653)	0-4-0DH	1957
D2595	—	Hunslet (7179)	0-6-0DM	1959
D2870	—	YEC (2667)	0-4-0DH	1960
Mardale	—	YEC (2748)	0-6-0DE	1959
Simon	—	Sentinel (10020)	4wDH	1959
Energy	—	Sentinel (10165)	4wDH	1965
Stanlow	—	T/Hill (160V)	0-4-0DH	1966
Enterprise	—	Sentinel (10282)	4wDH	1968
Progress	—	Sentinel (10283)	4wDH	1968
'YellowBat'	—	E/Electric (EE788)	4wBE	1930
Greenbat	—	G/Batley (2000)	4wBE	1945

Owners
625 Middlepeak Railways

Holidays.
Open from 10.30. Trains hourly 11.00-16.00.
Return trip c40min
Unlimited travel on day of admission
Special events: Mother's Day — 26 March, Father's Day — 18 June; Riversway Festival — 24/25 June; Diesel Day — 7 October; Santa Specials — 2/3, 9/10, 16/17, 23 December. Additional events are anticipated, please see web site for details
Membership details:
RSR Memberships, 4 Powell Drive, Billinge WN5 7RX
Membership journal: *The Ribble Pilot* — 3 copies a year
Special note: The railway is not open or accessible at any other times than those advertised. Access will be refused outside these times

Timetable Service

Romney, Hythe & Dymchurch Railway

Kent

Member: HRA
This line was built in 1926/27 as a one-third size miniature main line, and is by far the longest and most fully equipped 15in gauge railway in the world. It carries not only daytrippers and holidaymakers but also children to and from the local school at New Romney.
Headquarters: Romney, Hythe & Dymchurch Railway, New Romney Station, Kent TN28 8PL
Telephone: (01797) 362353/363256
Fax: 01797 363591
Internet addresses: *e-mail:* info@rhdr.org.uk
Web site: http://www.rhdr.org.uk
OS reference: TR 074249
Main station: New Romney
Other public stations: Hythe, Dymchurch, St Marys Bay, Romney Sands, Dungeness
Car parks: Hythe, Dymchurch, New Romney, Dungeness
Access by public transport: Folkestone Central station (South Eastern Trains) and then bus to Hythe (4 miles) or Rye station (Southern) and then bus to New Romney (8 miles)
Refreshment facilities: Cafeterias at New Romney and Dungeness, picnic areas at Dymchurch, New Romney and Dungeness. Also licensed observation coach on certain trains
Souvenir shops: Hythe and New Romney (plus Dymchurch and Dungeness in main season)
Model Railway Exhibition: New Romney, with displays of old, and not so old, toys; plus two large operating model railways
Depot: New Romney
Length of line: 13.5 miles, 15in gauge

Locomotives

Name	*No*	*Builder*	*Type*	*Built*
Green Goddess	1	Davey Paxman	4-6-2	1925
Northern Chief	2	Davey Paxman	4-6-2	1925
Southern Maid	3	Davey Paxman	4-6-2	1926
The Bug	4	Krauss (8378)	0-4-0TT	1926
Hercules	5	Davey Paxman	4-8-2	1926
Samson	6	Davey Paxman	4-8-2	1926
Typhoon	7	Davey Paxman	4-6-2	1926
Hurricane	8	Davey Paxman	4-6-2	1926
Winston Churchill	9	YEC (2294)	4-6-2	1931
Doctor Syn	10	YEC (2295)	4-6-2	1931
Black Prince	11	Krupp (1664)	4-6-2	1937
John Southland	12	TMA Birmingham	Bo-Bo	1983
Captain Howey	14	TMA Birmingham	Bo-Bo	1989
—	PW1	M/Rail (7059)	4wDM	1938
—	PW2	RH&DR	4wPM	1965
Redgauntlet	PW3	Jacot/RH&DR	4wPM	1963
*Trembly**	—	Lister (37658)	4wDM	1952

*on loan fitted with a *Toby* body for Thomas the Tank events

Stock
40 saloon bogie coaches; 12 open bogie coaches; 5 luggage/brake saloons; 1 parlour car; 1 mess coach; 40 assorted wagons

Passenger trains: Train frequency depends on the time of year: maximum frequency is 30 minutes
Period of public operation: Trains run daily from 1 April to 1 October. Also weekends and school holidays in February, March and October. Out of season the school train departs New Romney at 15.00 with limited public accommodation (Monday-Friday, term times only)
Special events: Mother's Day — 26 March; Steam & Diesel Gala Weekend — 13/14 May; Bug Club Day — 10 June; Father's Day — 18 June; RNLI Dungeness Open Day — 27 August; Day of Syn Festival — 27/28 August; Day out with Thomas — 2/3 September (special fares apply); Double-header Day — 7 October; Halloween Week Special Event — 21-29 October. Mince Pie Specials — 30/31 December, 1 January 2007. Santa Specials in December (pre-booking essential). Dungeness Fisherman — 24 June and 9 September (Saturday evenings)
Jazz Trains — 6 July (Thursday evening in conjunction with Hythe Festival
Special notes: Senior citizen concessions any day except Bank Holiday, and advertised special events. Family tickets available. Special trains can be run at most times by prior arrangement. Parties can be catered for at New Romney and Dungeness cafés and Jazz trains. Evening dining train service

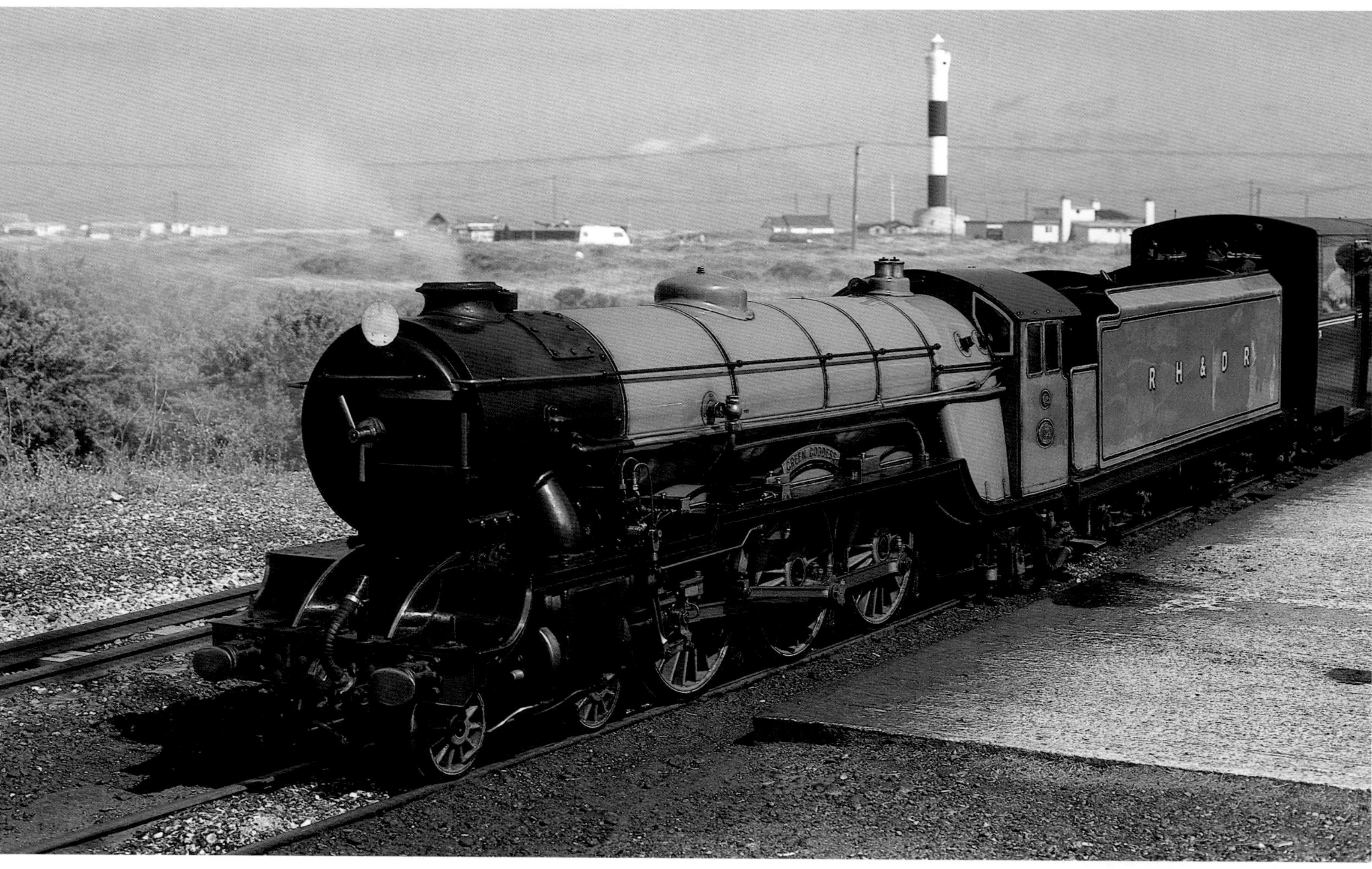

With a lighthouse in view and an LNER-style Pacific in the foreground this can only be Dungeness on the Romney, Hythe & Dymchurch Railway. No 1 *Green Goddess* awaits the right away with a service train destined for Hythe.
Alan Barnes

on selected Saturdays in the summer
Facilities for disabled: Ramps and level crossings at all stations for easy access. Special wheelchair coach available on any train by prior arrangement. Stair lift between café and Model Railway Exhibition. Disabled toilets at Hythe, Dymchurch, New Romney and Dungeness
Membership details: RH&DR Association, 26 Norman Close, Battle, East Sussex TN33 0BD
Membership journal: *The Marshlander* — quarterly

Diesel Centre — Rother Valley Railway — East Sussex

Member: HRA
The original section of what was to become known as the Kent & East Sussex Railway was thought to be lost to preservation for ever following decisions of Transport Minister, Barbara Castle, in the late 1960s. However, more enlightened attitudes in recent years mean that work is now in hand to reinstate the missing link between Robertsbridge and the K&ESR at Bodiam
Location/headquarters: Robertsbridge Station, Robertsbridge, East Sussex TN32 4DG
Telephone: 01580 881833
Internet addresses: *Web site:* www.rothervalleyrailway.co.uk
Operating society/organisation: Rother Valley Railway Ltd, 3-4 Bower Terrace, Maidstone, Kent ME16 8RY, and the Rother Valley Railway Supporters Association, 375 New Hythe Lane, Larkfield, Aylesford, Kent ME20 6RY
OS reference: TQ 734235
Access by public transport: SouthEastern Trains on Charing Cross and Tunbridge Wells to Hastings service call at Robertsbridge station. Arriva bus services 4 and 5 on Maidstone-Hastings service call at High Street, Robertsbridge
Car parks: Robertsbridge station and Station Road, Robertsbridge
On site facilities: Visitor centre housed in former VSOE lounge with souvenir shop and buffet. Rolling stock under restoration, picnic area
Facilities for disabled: Access to the visitor centre, buffet, shop and all public areas
Length of line: Standard gauge — c400yd at present. When restored, length to Bodiam will be 3.5 miles, with end-on connection to K&ESR
Public opening: Every Sunday and Bank Holiday Monday (except Christmas and Boxing Day). 10.30-17.00 (dusk if earlier)
Special events: Annual model railway exhibition. Subject to Ministry approval brake van rides will commence this year
Membership secretary: Peter Coombs, 375 New Hythe Lane, Larkfield, Aylesford, Kent ME20 6RY. (Tel: 01622 717491)
Society journal: *The Phoenix* — quarterly

Industrial locomotives

Name	*No*	*Builder*	*Type*	*Built*
Titan	43	Vulcan/Drewry	0-4-0DM	1955
—	7	Sentinel	0-4-0DH	1959
—	D77	Vulcan/Drewry	0-4-0DM	1947
—	97701	Matisa	0-4-0DE	1975

Rolling stock
Ex-SR brake van, ex-SR Maunsell brake third, ex-SR Maunsell open third, ex-SR corridor Comp (converted to General Manager's saloon), ex-BR Mk 1 TSO, ex-SR GBL, BY, and PMV vans, Trout hopper wagon, 2 tank wagons, open wagon, Lowmacs, Permaquip Panec track machine and a Thos Smith 5-ton rail crane

Miniature Railway — Royal Victoria Railway — Hampshire

Location: Royal Victoria Country Park
Headquarters: Royal Victoria Railway, Royal Victoria Country Park, Netley, Southampton SO31 5GA
Contact: Peter Bowers
Telephone: 023 8045 6246
Internet address: *Web site:* www.royalvictoriarailway.co.uk
OS reference: xx
Main station: Netley
Car parking: On site £1.20
Access by public transport: By rail: SouthWest Trains to Netley, follow signs to Royal Victoria Country Park.
By road: Exit M27 at Jct 8 and follow brown tourist signs to Royal Victoria Country Park, approx 3 miles
On site facilities: Small souvenir shop. Museum on site for Royal Victoria Hospital
Depots: At main station, engine and carriage sheds and turntable, possibly largest for 10.25in gauge

railway
Length of line: 1 mile, 10.25in gauge
Period of public operation: All local school holidays except 3 days before Xmas and closed Christmas Day. Weekends all year
Special events: Please check website
Facilities for disabled: Most areas accessible

Locomotives

Name	No	Builder	Type	Built
—*	—	Kitson		
*Royal Scot**	6100	B/Lowke	4-6-0	
—*	—	B/Lowke	4-4-2	
Western Thunderer		D. Curwen	C-C	1964
—†	—	C. Lane	4wPM-4	1955
—	—	Triang	4wPM-4	
—	—	Triang	4wPM-4	

*historic locomotive
†3-car Sante Fe set

Rolling stock
2 Triang Pullman coaches, 4 Triang toastrack coaches, 2 4-car articulated units (2 covered, 2 open carriages), various goods vehicles

Note: If wishing to view the historic locomotives please contact before making journey

Timetable Service

Rudyard Lake Railway

Staffordshire

Member Applicant for HRA, Britain's Great Little Railways. The railway is the third on this site and provides a 3 mile scenic return trip alongside the lake that gave Rudyard Kipling his name. Trains are normally steam hauled and a two train service operates on busy days. The fleet of goods wagons is extensive and impressive and so goods trains also often feature. A further one mile extension is being planned
Contacts: Mike & Eileen Hanson, Directors
Headquarters: Rudyard Station, Rudyard, Nr Leek, Staffordshire ST13 8RS
Telephone: 01995 672280
Fax: 01995 672280
Internet address:
e-mai: : info@rlsr.org
Web site: www.rlsr.org
Main station: Rudyard
OS reference SJ 955579
Other stations: The Dam (SJ 953584), Hunthouse Wood (SJ 946598)
Car parking: On site, free at Rudyard
Access by public transport; Nearest mainline rail at Stoke on Trent, Macclesfield, Congleton. Bus services to Leek
Souvenier shop: On trains
Refreshment facilities: Café at Dam Head, alight at Dam station
Length of Line: 1.5 miles, 10.25 inch gauge
Operation: 11.00-16.00, every Sunday & Bank Holiday 12 March to 29 October 2006.
Every Saturday 29 April to 30 September.
All School Holidays — every Tuesday, Wednesday and Thursday February to October
Special Events:
Easter Egg Specials — 14-17 April; Lollipop Specials — 29/30 April-1, 27-29 May, 26-28 August; Steam Gala — 16/17 September; Halloween Special — 28/29 October; Santa Specials — 10, 16/17 December
Disabled Facilities: Access to all stations but wheelchairs not allowed on trains. Disabled toilets at the Dam Head.
Membership details: Eileen Hanson at above address or via e-mail

Locomotives

Name	No	Builder	Type	Built
Modred	2	T. Stanhope	4w	1969
Rudyard Lady	5	L. Smith	4-4w	1989
Waverley		D. Curwen	4-4-2	1952
Excalibur	6	Exmoor SR	2-4-2T	1993
Merlin	7	Exmoor SR	2-4-2T	1998
Pendragon	9	Exmoor SR (297)	2-4-2T	1994
King Arthur	8	Exmoor SR	0-6-2T	2005

Rolling Stock
8 coaches
2 4w vans, 3 4w open, 1 4w tank, 1 4w crane, 1 4w brake van, 3 bogie ballast

Owner
Waverley — the Waverley Group

Special Notes
Driver training courses run throughout the year

Timetable Service

Ruislip Lido Railway

London

Member: HRA
The 12in gauge line is operated by enthusiast volunteers as an attraction within Ruislip Lido, a country park which is maintained by the London Borough of Hillingdon
Location: Ruislip Lido, Reservoir Road, Ruislip, Middlesex
Operating society/organisation: Ruislip Lido Railway Society Ltd, Secretary, Mr S. W. Simmons, 9 Wiltshire Lane, Eastcote, Pinner, Middx HA5 2LH
Telephone: 020 8866 9654
Car park: Available at Lido
Access by public transport: Ruislip Underground station (Metropolitan and Piccadilly lines) then by bus H13 or 331 nearby (daily). Lido is off the A4180 road
Refreshment facilities: New family pub/restaurant (Brewers Fayre) on site. Picnic areas also available
Length of line: 1.25-mile single journey, 2.5 miles return including new extension now open which terminates near the main entrance to car park
Public opening: The line is open at weekends from 11 February to 19 November. Daily from 1 July to 3 September and daily during Hillingdon school holidays. Also Sunday Santa Specials on 26 November, 3, 10, 17 December
24-hour recorded train information service (01895) 622595. Full service leaflet on request to 020 8866 9654. Party bookings 020 8866 9654
Journey time: Single 20min, return 40min
Facilities for disabled: Wheelchair passengers can travel on all trains
Membership details: Membership Secretary, 6 Bronte Crescent, Hemel Hempstead, Herts HP2 7NT
Membership journal: *Woody Bay News* — 3 issues per year

Locomotives

Name	*No*	*Builder*	*Type*	*Built*
Robert	3	Severn-Lamb	B-2 DH	1973
Lady of the Lakes	5	Ravenglass & Eskdale Railway	B-B DM	1985
Mad Bess	6	RLRS	2-4-0ST+T	1998
Graham Alexander	7	Severn-Lamb	B-B DM	1990
Bayhurst	8	Severn-Lamb	B-B DM	2003
John Rennie	9	Severn-Lamb	B-B DM	2005

Locomotive notes: All locomotives are normally available for service. Limited steam-hauled service

Stock
6 open coaches; 9 closed coaches; miscellaneous service stock

Steam Centre

Rutland Railway Museum

Rutland

Member: HRA
This museum is dedicated to portraying the railway in industry, particularly iron ore mining, and has a wide range of industrial locomotives and rolling stock. Indeed, its collection of quarry freight rolling stock is probably the most comprehensive in the country and regular demonstrations are a feature of the 'steam days'.
Location: Cottesmore Iron Ore Mines Siding, Ashwell Road, Cottesmore, near Oakham, Rutland — museum situated midway between villages of Cottesmore and Ashwell, approximately 4 miles north of Oakham (locally signposted)
OS reference: SK 886137

Locomotives and multiple-units

Name	*No*	*Origin*	*Class*	*Type*	*Built*
NCB No 7	(D9518)	BR	14	0-6-0DH	1964

Industrial locomotives

Name	*No*	*Builder*	*Type*	*Built*
Dora	—	Avonside (1973)	0-4-0ST	1927
Firefly	—	Barclay (776)	0-4-0ST	1896
BSC No 2	—	Barclay (1931)	0-4-0ST	1927
Drake	—	Barclay (2086)	0-4-0ST	1940
Sir Thomas Royden	—	Barclay (2088)	0-4-0ST	1940
Uppingham	—	Peckett (1257)	0-4-0ST	1912
Elizabeth	—	Peckett (1759)	0-4-0ST	1928
Singapore	—	H/Leslie (3865)	0-4-0ST	1936
—	24	Hunslet (2411)	0-6-0ST	1941
Coal Products No 6	—	Hunslet (2868)/ (Rebuilt Hunslet 3883)	0-6-0ST	1943 / 1963
—	65	Hunslet (3889)	0-6-0ST	1964
—	8	Peckett (2110)	0-4-0ST	1950
—	7	Sentinel (9376)	4wVBT	1947

Operating society/organisation: Rutland Railway Museum, Cottesmore Iron Ore Mines Siding, Ashwell Road, Cottesmore, Nr Oakham, Rutland LE15 7BX
Telephone: Oakham (01572) 813203
Car park: Free car park on site
Access by public transport: Nearest main line station, Oakham. Bus service, Paul James, Nottingham-Melton Mowbray-Ashwell-Oakham, Corby/Peterborough-Oakham-Ashwell (service 19).
On site facilities: Free train rides, demonstration freight trains, toilets, museum, picnic sites, demonstration line with lineside walk and viewing areas, static displays of over 30 steam and diesel locomotives; over 50 wagons, vans and coaches (believed to be the largest collection of preserved quarry freight stock in the UK).
Museum shop and refreshments available on open days
Length of line: Three-quarter-mile
Passenger trains: Regular shuttle service operates on open days (approximately every 15min)
Public opening: Open weekends or by arrangement, some weekdays (please telephone prior to visit). Open 11.00-17.00. (Leaflets available, SAE please).

School and private parties by special arrangement
Special events: Not advised, please contact for details
Facilities for disabled: Site relatively flat. Members willing to assist
Special notes: The open-air museum houses an extensive collection of industrial locomotives and rolling stock typifying past activity in local ironstone quarries, nationwide mines and factories. A demonstration line approximately three quarters of a mile long has been relaid on the former MR Cottesmore mineral branch (originally built to tap local ironstone quarries), on which restored locomotives and stock are run

Name	*No*	*Origin*	*Class*	*Type*	*Built*
—	—	Sentinel (9596)		4wVBT	1955
—	—	Barclay (352)		0-4-0DM	1941
—	1	Barclay (415)		0-4-0DH	1957
—	20-90-01	Barclay (499)		0-4-0DH	1965
—	8	Bagnall (3209)/ RSH (8364)		0-4-0DH	1962
—	—	Brush (804)		0-6-0DE	1978
—	BSC 1	E/Electric (D1049)		0-6-0DH	1965
—	—	E/Electric (D1231)		0-6-0DH	1967
—	4	Fowler (4240012)		0-6-0DH	1961
—	—	Fowler (4240015)		0-6-0DH	1962
Phoenix	—	Hibberd (3887)		4wDM	1958
—	21	H/Clarke (D707)		0-6-0DM	1950
—	No 1	Hunslet (6688)		0-4-0DH	1968
—	3	N/British (27656)		0-4-0DH	1957
Betty	8411/04	R/Royce (10201)		0-4-0DH	1964
—	D21	R/Royce (10270)		0-6-0DH	1967
—	—	R/Hornsby (305302)		4wDM	1951
—	—	R/Hornsby (306092)		4wDM	1950
—	—	R/Hornsby (347747)		0-6-0DM	1957
—	110	R/Hornsby (411319)		4wDM	1958
—	3	R/Hornsby (421436)		0-4-0DE	1958
—	20-90-02	R/Hornsby (504565)		0-4-0DH	1965
Hays	—	R/Hornsby (544997)		0-4-0DE	1969
—	—	T/Hill (120c) (Rebuild of Sentinel 9619/1957)		4wDH	1962
—	RoF No 1	T/Hill (132c) (Rebuild of Fowler 22982/1942)		0-4-0DH	1963
—	CEGB 24	T/Hill (188c) (Rebuild of Sentinel 9597/1955)		4wDH	1967
—	10	T/Hill (234v)		4wDH	1971
—	—	YEC (2641)		0-6-0DE	1957
—	20	YEC (2688)		0-6-0DE	1959
—	No 28	YEC (2791)		0-6-0DE	1962
—	1382	YEC (2872)		0-6-0DE	1962

Locomotive notes: In service *Dora, Singapore,* 7, 1, 20-90-01, 8 (Bagnal 3209), No 1 (HE6688), 21, CEGB 24, RoF No1 and BSC 1

Stock
1 coaches; 4 brake vans; 14 covered goods vans; 57 wagons (includes rakes of wagons as used in local ironstone and industrial railways); 3 rail cranes

Owners
110 the National Army Museum

Free admission at weekends for general viewing, charges on Steam and Diesel Open Days (11.00-17.00). Special rates for Santa Specials
Membership details: Membership Secretary, c/o above address

Museum

Science Museum

London

Built on land acquired with the profits from the Great Exhibition of 1851, the Science Museum was one of the first to include industrial archaeology. The railway exhibits are drawn from the collection based at the National Railway Museum. They form part of a major gallery, 'Making the Modern World', which opened in June 2000 on the site of the former Land Transport gallery

Locomotive

Name	No	Origin	Class	Type	Built
Rocket	—	Liverpool & Manchester Railway	—	0-2-2	1829
Columbine	—	Grand Junction Railway	—	2-2-2	1845
Puffing Billy	—	Wylam Colliery	—	0-4-0	1814

Locomotive note: Restored to static display condition

Location: South Kensington
OS reference: TQ 268793
Operating society/organisation: Science Museum, Exhibition Road, South Kensington, London SW7 2DD
Telephone: 020 7942 4000
Internet address: *Web site:* www.sciencemuseum.org.uk
Access by public transport: South Kensington Underground station
Catering facilities: Cafés on ground floor, hot meals, tea, coffee, sandwiches, etc. Picnic area in basement
On site facilities: Bookshop, toilets on most floors
Public opening: Daily 10.00-18.00. Closed 24-26 December
Special events: All organised by the National Railway Museum, York, which is part of the Science Museum. Telephone (01904) 621261 for details
Facilities for disabled: Toilets on most floors, ramp and lifts to all floors. Parties should contact before arrival if extra assistance is required
Special notes: Static exhibits only in 'Making the Modern World'

Timetable Service

Seaton & District Electric Tramway

Devon

Member: HRA, South West Tourism
A unique 2ft 9in gauge electric tramway, operating on the trackbed of the former Southern Railway branch line between Seaton, Colyford and Colyton in east Devon. Panoramic views of the beautiful Axe Valley and estuary together with a host of wading birds and other wildlife

Trams

No	Prototype based on	Type	Built
2	London Metropolitan Tramways	A	1964
4	Blackpool	'Boat'	1961
6	Bournemouth (later Llandudno & Colwyn Bay)	'open-top'	1954
7	Bournemouth (later Llandudno & Colwyn Bay)	'open-top'	1954
8	†—	—	1968
12	London Metropolitan Tramways	'Feltham'	1966
14*	London Metropolitan Tramways	A	1904
16*	Bournemouth		1921
17	Manx Electric Tramway	'toastrack'	1988
19*	Exeter Corporation	—	1906
9	new build	double-deck	2001
10	new build	double-deck	2001
11	new build	double-deck	2001

†a larger version of the ex-Bournemouth design of cars 6 and 7
*rebuilds of actual prototypes
9, 10, 11 are based on elements of designs from Plymouth and Blackburn

Location: Harbour Road Car Park, Seaton; Swan Hill Road, Colyford (next to White Hart Inn); Station Road, Kingsdon, Colyton
OS reference: SY 252904
Operating society/organisation: Modern Electric Tramways Ltd t/a Seaton Tramway, Car Depot, Harbour Road, Seaton, Devon EX12 2NQ
Telephone: 01297 20375
Fax: 01297 625626
Internet address:
e-mail: info@tram.co.uk
Web site: www.tram.co.uk
Access by public transport: Nearest railway station: Axminster. Buses: Axe Valley Mini Travel service 885 from Axminster, service 899 from Lyme Regis and Sidmouth. First Southern National service X53 from Weymouth and Exeter, service 20 from Taunton and Honiton. Bus enquiries 0870 608 2608 or

www.devon.gov.uk/devonbus
On site facilities: Gift shops at Seaton and Colyton. Restaurant and picnic area at Colyton
Length of line: 3 miles, 2ft 9in gauge
Period of public operation and departure times (2006):
Daily 20-24 February, 10.00-16.00. Saturdays & Sundays 18 February-26 March, 10.00-16.00. Daily 1 April-22 July, 10.00-17.00. Daily 23 July-2 September, 10.00-20.40. Daily 4 September-28 October, 10.00-16.00. Saturday & Sunday 30 October-24 December, 10.00-16.00. Halloween Tram of Terror — 28/29 October. Santa Specials — 10, 17, 21/22 December, enquire for details.
Private hire all year round for groups of 20+
Special events: Vintage Vehicle Rally — 10 June; Gala Day — 11 June; Seaton Carnival Late Night Service —23 September; Colyton Carnival Late Night Service — 9 September; End of Season Gala — 21/22 October
Fares for 2006: Seaton to Colyton return fares — Adult £7.00, OAP £6.30, Child £4.90. Single fares and rover tickets also available. Discounts for local residents, families and parties of 12 or more
Facilities for disabled: Tramcar No 17 carries up to 12 wheelchairs. Please note that it has open sides and is therefore exposed to the weather. It is sometimes possible to accommodate individuals at short notice, but groups should book in advance. Disabled toilets at Seaton and Colyton
Special notes: Tram driving lessons available through the season except 24 July-3 September. Bird watching trips available January to May and September to December. Enquire for details. Service operated by open-top double-deck bogie cars (enclosed saloon cars during inclement weather)

Timetable Service

Severn Valley Railway

Worcestershire

Member: HRA, TT
The railway hosts more main line engines than any other preserved line in the country, enjoying the back-up of a large volunteer and professional workforce and extensive engineering workshops and equipment. Railway travel like it used to be
General Manager: Alun Rees
Headquarters: Severn Valley Railway Co Ltd, Railway Station, Bewdley, Worcs DY12 1BG
Telephone: Bewdley (01299) 403816; 24hr timetable — (01299) 401001
Internet address: *Web site:* http://www.svr.co.uk
Main stations: Bridgnorth, Bewdley, Kidderminster Town
Other public stations: Arley, Highley, Hampton Loade, Northwood Halt, Country Park Halt
OS reference: Bridgnorth SO 715926, Bewdley SO 793753
Car parks: At all main stations
Access by public transport: First Bus service 192 to Kidderminster and Bewdley and 125 & 297 to Bridgnorth. Rail service to Kidderminster (main line) with immediate connections to SVR station. Through tickets available from all manned main line stations
Refreshment facilities: At most stations, but not on all operating days and on most trains. Fully

Locomotives and multiple-units

Name	*No*	*Origin*	*Class*	*Type*	*Built*
The Great Marquess	61994†	LNER	K4	2-6-0	1938
Union of South Africa	60009	LNER	A4	4-6-2	1937
Gordon	AD600	LMR	WD	2-10-0	1943
—	43106	LMS	4MT	2-6-0	1951
—	46443	LMS	2MT	2-6-0	1950
RAF Biggin Hill	45110	LMS	5MT	4-6-0	1935
—	47383	LMS	3F	0-6-0T	1926
—	48773	LMS	8F	2-8-0	1940
—	42968	LMS	5P4F	2-6-0	1933
—	813	GWR	—	0-6-0ST	1901
—	2857	GWR	2800	2-8-0	1918
—	5164	GWR	5101	2-6-2T	1930
—	4150	GWR	5101	2-6-2T	1947
—	5764	GWR	5700	0-6-0PT	1929
—	7714	GWR	5700	0-6-0PT	1930
—	4566	GWR	4500	2-6-2T	1924
Bradley Manor	7802	GWR	'Manor'	4-6-0	1939
Erlestoke Manor	7812	GWR	'Manor'	4-6-0	1939
Hinton Manor	7819	GWR	'Manor'	4-6-0	1939
*Hagley Hall**	4930	GWR	'Hall'	4-6-0	1929
Taw Valley	34027	SR	WC	4-6-2	1946
—	1501	GWR	1500	0-6-0PT	1949
—**	7325	GWR	4300	2-6-0	1932
—	75069	BR	4MT	4-6-0	1955
—§§	80079	BR	4MT	2-6-4T	1954
—	D3022	BR	08	0-6-0DE	1952
—	08133	BR	08	0-6-0DE	1955
—	D3586	BR	08	0-6-0DE	1953
—	D3937	BR	08	0-6-0DE	1960
—	12099	LMS	11	0-6-0DE	1952
—	D5410	BR	27	Bo-Bo	1962
—	D7029	BR	35	B-B	1963
Greyhound	D821	BR	42	B-B	1960
Hood	D431	BR	50	Co-Co	1968

licensed bars at Bridgnorth and Kidderminster Town
Souvenir shops: Bridgnorth, Kidderminster Town
Depots: Bridgnorth (locomotives), Bewdley and Kidderminster (stock)
Model railways: At Kidderminster and Hampton Loade
Length of line: 16.5 miles
Passenger trains: Steam-hauled trains running frequently from Kidderminster Town to Bewdley and Bridgnorth. Diesel-hauled service on limited occasions as advertised
Period of public operation: Every weekend, Santa Steam Specials weekends in December. Daily service 6 May to 1 October, plus February, Easter and October local school holidays. Open for limited viewing at other times
Special events: Day out with Thomas — 6/7, 13/14 May; 1940s Weekends — 24/25 June, 1/2 July; Severn Valley in Bloom — 29/30 July; Day out with Thomas — 2/3, 9/10 September; Autumn Steam Gala — 23-25 September; Diesel Gala — 13-15 October; Classic Vehicle Day — 8 October; Santa Steam Specials —2/3, 9/10, 16/17, 23/24 December. Festive Season service — 26 December-2 January 2007
Facilities for disabled: Facilities available, special vehicle available to carry wheelchairs by prior arrangement. Disabled people's toilets and ramp access to refreshment facilities at Kidderminster and Bridgnorth. Enlarged versions of all leaflets are available for the visually impaired from staffed booking offices
Special notes: A number of special enthusiasts' weekends and special events are held when extra trains are operated. In addition, supplementary trains with diesel haulage are run as advertised. 'Severn Valley Limited' and 'Severn Valley Venturer' Restaurant Car service operates on Sundays, some Wednesdays and as required on other occasions. Advance booking required. Charter trains with or without dining facilities can be arranged
Membership details: Mrs Kate Kirk, c/o above address
Membership journal: *Severn Valley Railway News* — quarterly
Share details: Mrs W. Broadhurst, c/o above address

Name	*No*	*Origin*	*Class*	*Type*	*Built*
Ark Royal	50035	BR	50	Co-Co	1968
Exeter	D444	BR	50	Co-Co	1968
Defiance	D449	BR	50	Co-Co	1967
Western Ranger	D1013	BR	52	C-C	1962
Western Courier	D1062	BR	52	C-C	1963
—§	E6005	BR	73	Bo-Bo	1962
—§	E6006	BR	73	Bo-Bo	1962
—	51935	BR	108	DMBS	1960
—	51941	BR	108	DMBS	1960
—	52064	BR	108	DMC	1960
—	56208	BR	108	DTCL	1958
—	59250	BR	108	TBS	1958

*on display at the McArthur Glen complex, Swindon
**on display at Steam: Museum of the Great Western Railway, Swindon
†at private site for overhaul
§on loan from the Dean Forest Diesel Association
§§on loan to Locomotion

Industrial locomotives

Name	*No*	*Builder*	*Type*	*Built*
Warwickshire	—	M/Wardle (2047)	0-6-0ST	1926
The Lady Armaghdale	—	Hunslet (686)	0-6-0T	1898
—	—	Ruston (319290)	0-4-0DM	1953
—	—	R/Hornsby (414304)	0-4-0DM	1957
—	—	R/Hornsby (408297)	0-4-0DM	1957

Stock

27 ex-GWR coaches; 13 ex-LMS coaches; 24 ex-BR Mk 1 coaches; 9 ex-LNER coaches; numerous examples of ex-GWR, LMS and other freight vehicles and two 30-ton steam cranes

Owners

813 the GWR 813 Fund
1501 the 15xx Fund
2857 the 2857 Fund
42968 the Stanier Mogul Fund
4150 the 4150 Locomotive Fund
4566 the 4566 Fund
5164 the 51xx Fund
5764, 7714 the Pannier Tank Fund
34027, 60009 and 61994 are privately owned
7325 the Great Western (SVR) Association
7802 and 7812 the Erlestoke Manor Fund
7819 the Severn Valley Rolling Stock Trust
43106 the Ivatt 4 Fund
46443 the SVR 46443 Fund
47383 the Manchester Rail Travel Society
48773 the Stanier 8F Locomotive Society
D431, 50035 and D444 the 50 Fund
D449 Operation Defiance
D821 and D7029 the Diesel Traction Group
75069 the 75069 Fund
80079 the Passenger Tank Fund
AD600 the Royal Corps of Transport Museum Trustees
D821 and D7029 the Diesel Traction Group
D1013 and D1062 the Western Locomotive Association
D3022 the Class 08 Society
D5410 Sandwell Metropolitan Council
4930 and 45110 the SVR(H) plc

Museum

The Silk Mill — Derby's Museum of Industry and History

Derbyshire

Member: TT
As would be expected of a railway town, the museum has an extensive collection of railway material including locomotives and rolling stock (most on display at the Midland Railway Centre). The railway gallery tells the stories of railway industries in Derby, especially as they relate to the Midland Railway and its successors. Replica Midland Railway signalbox and model railway (under construction). The story is brought up to date by the Railway Research Gallery which looks at the role of the Railway Technical Centre and includes a replica of an InterCity 225 driving cab. The museum is now also home to the Midland Railway Study Centre. Appointments can be made on (01322) 255308 or through www.midlandrailwaystudycentre.org.uk
Location: Silk Mill Lane, Derby
Operating society/organisation: Derby Industrial Museum, Silk Mill Lane, off Full Street, Derby DE1 3AF
Telephone: (01332) 255308
Fax: (01332) 255108
Car park: Local car parks around city
Access by public transport: Bus station quarter mile, railway station three-quarter mile
On site facilities: Shop, baby changing facilities
Opening times: Admission free. Mondays 11.00-17.00, Tuesdays to Saturdays 10.00-17.00, Bank Holidays 13.00-16.00 Sundays 13.00-16.00
Facilities for disabled: Parking by arrangement. Level access to building, lifts and ramps to all gallery areas, toilets, sign language and subtitles in Rolls-Royce gallery

Timetable service

Sittingbourne & Kemsley Light Railway

Kent

Member: HRA
The Sittingbourne & Kemsley Light Railway is part of the 2ft 6in gauge railway built to convey paper and other materials between mills at Sittingbourne and Kemsley and the Dock at Ridham on the banks of the Swale. The first section of the line opened in 1877 with horse-drawn haulage, while steam haulage was introduced in 1906. Two of the engines then in use remain on the line today.The railway now operates on the old paper mills trackbed as a tourist attraction. Passenger trains are normally steam-hauled and are formed of a varied selection of open and covered coaches. For the first half mile of the journey the narrow gauge railway twists and turns through Milton Regis on a unique early reinforced concrete viaduct which was one of the first reinforced concrete viaducts.

2006 is the start of the second centenary of steam operation
Operating Director: Noel Young
Registered charity: 105 7079

Locomotives

Name	*No*	*Builder*	*Type*	*Built*
Alpha	—	Bagnall (2472)	0-6-2T	1932
Triumph	—	Bagnall (2511)	0-6-2T	1934
Superb	—	Bagnall (2624)	0-6-2T	1940
Unique	—	Bagnall (2216)	2-4-0F	1924
Premier	—	K/Stuart (886)	0-4-2ST	1905
Leader	—	K/Stuart (926)	0-4-2ST	1905
Melior	—	K/Stuart (4219)	0-4-2ST	1924
Chevellier No 1	—*	M/Wardle (1877)	0-6-2ST	1915
Edward Lloyd	—	R/Hornsby (435403)	4wDM	1961
Victor	—	Hunslet (4182)	4wDM	1953
Barton Hall	—	Hunslet (6651)	4wDM	1965

*visiting

Industrial standard gauge locomotives

Name	*No*	*Builder*	*Type*	*Built*
Bear	—	Peckett (614)	0-4-0ST	1896
—	1	Barclay (1876)	0-4-0F	1925

Locomotive notes: In service: *Triumph, Melior, Victor*. Under repair: *Superb, Leader* (both due back in service during 2006)
Static display: *Premier, Alpha, Unique* and standard gauge exhibits

Stock
10 bogie coaches (including 4 ex-Chattenden & Upnor Railway); 2 open coaches; 39 various wagons

Headquarters: Sittingbourne & Kemsley Light Railway Ltd, PO Box 300, Sittingbourne, Kent ME10 2DZ
Telephone: 0871 222 1568 (talking timetable) or 01622 755313 (advance bookings — evenings)
Internet address:
e-mail: info@sklr.net
Web site: www.sklr.net
Main station: Sittingbourne Viaduct
Other public stations: Milton Regis Halt, Kemsley Down
Car park: Sittingbourne Viaduct (opposite McDonalds and Homebase)
Party, credit card & advance bookings and Footplate Experience courses: Tony Nokes, 111 Hillary Road, Penenden Heath, Maidstone, Kent ME14 2JX. Tel: 0871 222 1569
Access by public transport: Sittingbourne Viaduct — Sittingbourne (South Eastern) station;
Milton Regis Halt — Mill Way, Sittingbourne (access from Asda car park); (Kemsley Down access by rail or on foot from Saxon Shore Way only)
Access by road: M2, A249 then A2 to Sittingbourne (follow brown tourist signs)
OS reference:
Sittingbourne TQ 905642,
Milton Regis Halt TQ 909648
Kemsley Down TQ 920661
On site facilities at Kemsley Down: Refreshment facilities; Souvenir shop; Small Exhibits Museum; Museum Walk; Wildlife garden; children's play/picnic area; model and miniature railways
Depot: Kemsley Down (access by rail or on foot from Saxon Shore Way only)
Length of line: 2 miles, 2ft 6in gauge
Passenger trains: Hourly from 11.00, or 13.00 to 16.00 (refer to timetable: www.sklr.net or 0871 222 1568
Journey time: 15min each way
Period of public operation: April to end September. Sundays and Bank Holidays. Wednesday during most school holidays during season
Special events: Extended openings and timetables for special events including: Story Time (Jack the Station Cat and Edward Bear — 30 April/1 May; Steam and Beer Festival — 1/2 July (Festival fares apply); Model Railway Day — 13 August; Gala Weekend — 23/24 September. Santa Specials — 2/3, 9/10, 16/17, 26 December
Special notes: There is no public access to Kemsley Down other than by the railway or on foot from Saxon Shore Way on operating dates. When the line is closed all stock is stored in security compounds within the paper mill premises. Family fares and senior citizens tickets available. Special rates for parties. Footplate experience courses available
Membership details: John Sparrow, 20 Park Road, Sheerness, Kent ME12 1UY.
Marketing name: Sittingbourne's Steam Railway

Museum — Snibston Discovery Park — Leicestershire

Members: TT
Location: Snibston Discovery Park, Ashby Road, Coalville, Leicestershire LE67 3LN
Telephone: (01530) 278444
Fax: (01530) 813301
Operating group: Leicestershire County Council, Commercial & Support Services, Community Services Dept.
Tel: 01530 278444
Internet address: *e-mail:* snibston@leics.gov.uk
Web site: www.snibston.com
Museum contact: Mr N. Pell, Assistant Keeper, Transport & Mining (museum collection enquiries). Tel: 01530 278452
Public opening: April-September — daily 10.00-17.00. October-March — Monday to Friday 10.00-15.00, weekends (10.00-17.00)
Car & coach parking: On site, free
Access by public transport:

Multiple-unit

Name	*No*	*Origin*	*Class*	*Type*	*Built*
—	70576	BR	4CEP/411	TBC	1956

Industrial locomotives (standard gauge)

Name	*No*	*Builder*	*Type*	*Built*
Mars II†	—	RSH (7493)	0-4-0ST	1948
—	2§	Barclay (1815)	0-4-0F	1924
—*	—§	Brush (314)	0-4-0ST	1906
Clair	—	H/Clarke (D1388)	0-6-0DH	1970
Cadley Hill No 1†	—	Hunslet (3851)	0-6-0ST	1962
Pitt the Colliery Engine	16	Hunslet (6289)	0-6-0DM	1966
—	—	R/Hornsby (393304)	4wDM	1955

§on display in museum galleries

Industrial locomotives (2ft 6in gauge)

Name	No	Builder	Type	Built
—	—	E/Electric (2416)	4wBE	1957
—	—	H/Clarke (DM1812)	0-6-0DM	1960
—	—	Hunslet (7385)	4wDMF	1976
—	63/000/449	Hunslet (8973)	4wDH	1979

Locomotive notes: 2006 locomotive for passenger trains will be Hunslet 6289, *Pitt the Colliery Engine* and Hudswell Clarke (1388) *Clair*
†locomotive is stored, but may be brought out for display on special events

Arriva Fox from Loughborough and Nottingham (route 99); from Leicester (route 117); from Swadlincote (route 118), Mon-Sat; route 217/8 Sun & Bank Holiday Mondays; Hinckley (route 159); routes 118 and 254 also run from Leicester. Connections at Ashby with Burton upon Trent. Further information, tel: 0870 608 2608
On site facilities: Shop, toilets, car park, café. Conference facilities. Family tickets, picnic areas, science play area, Sheepy Magna wheelwrights workshop. Special event days, nature reserve, golf driving range, colliery building tours

*originally Powlesland & Mason No 6 taken over by GWR in 1924 and numbered 921
Plus 2ft 6in gauge English Electric battery-operated electric man-riding locomotives — ex-NCB

Rolling stock: 1920 Midland Railway brake van, other goods vehicles

Disabled facilities: Fully available on site apart from small section of colliery tour. Access to passenger trains
Railways on site: Approx two thirds of a mile of standard gauge track with passenger trains on selected days. Please telephone for further information.
Narrow gauge railway about 350yd in length (non operational).
Volunteers to help maintain and run the railway are welcome to join our 'Friends of Coaltracks' support group; please contact Mr N. Pell at above address if interested

Museum

Somerset & Dorset Railway Trust

Somerset

Member: HRA
Situated at Washford on the West Somerset Railway, the Trust Museum houses Somerset & Dorset memorabilia and artefacts to stir memories of cross-country travel in the era of steam. The sidings and restoration shed give the visitor a chance to see locomotives, wagons and carriages close up. Midford signalbox display
Headquarters: Washford Station, Minehead Road, Washford, Somerset TA21 0PP
Telephone: 01984 640869
Internet address: *Web site:* http://www.sdrt.org
Car park: Small car park by main road
Access by public transport: West Somerset Railway trains on operating days, March to end October. Nearest main line station: Taunton. First Bus service 28 (Taunton-Minehead) passes the station
On site facilities: Souvenir counter at the station. No refreshments on station but adjacent inn offers food and children are welcome
Public opening: 10.30-16.30 throughout June, July, August and September, plus Bank Holiday weekends and Gala Days
Membership details: Ian Briggs, S&DJR Trust, 24 Preston Close, Stanton-under-Bardon, Markfield, Leics LE67 9TX
Membership journal: *Pines Express* (4 issues/year, plus 2 newsletters/year)

Locomotive

Name	*No*	*Origin*	*Class*	*Type*	*Built*
—	88	S&DJR	7F	2-8-0	1925

Industrial locomotives

Name	*No*	*Builder*	*Type*	*Built*
Isabel	—	H/Leslie (3437)	0-6-0ST	1919
Kilmersdon	—	Peckett (1788)	0-4-0ST	1929

Stock
3 Somerset & Dorset 6-wheeled coaches undergoing restoration. Large wagon collection. Display of narrow gauge equipment from Sedgemoor peat railways

Timetable Service

South Devon Railway

Devon

Member: HRA, TT
A typical West Country branch line meandering up the Dart Valley to Buckfastleigh which is home to the railway's workshops, a butterfly and otter farm and several other attractions. The line is accessible from Totnes (main line) via a footbridge (4min walk)
General Manager: R. Elliott
Headquarters: South Devon Railway, Buckfastleigh Station,

Buckfastleigh, Devon TQ11 0DZ
Telephone: 0845 345 1470
Internet addresses: *e-mail:* southdevonrailway.org
Web site: www.southdevonrailway.org
Main station: Buckfastleigh
Other public stations: Staverton, Totnes (Littlehempston)
OS reference: Buckfastleigh SX 747663, Staverton SX 785638
Car park: Buckfastleigh (free), Staverton (free). Totnes — use main line pay & display or council car parks
Access by public transport: Bus, X38/9 Exeter-Plymouth; 88 Newton Abbot-Buckfastleigh; X80 Plymouth-Torquay. Main line trains to Totnes
Refreshment facilities: Buckfastleigh, Totnes (café at Totnes Rare Breeds Centre adjacent to and only accessible via SDR station)
Souvenir shop: On the train and Buckfastleigh station
Museum: Buckfastleigh
Depot: Buckfastleigh
Vintage bus: Operates to Buckfast Abbey and Buckfastleigh town most days (free service)
Miniature railway: Operates most Sundays and gala days at Buckfastleigh (7.25in gauge, half mile)
Model railway: Extensive 00 gauge model railway at Buckfastleigh. Admission included in train fare
Length of line: 7 miles
Passenger trains: Buckfastleigh-Totnes alongside the River Dart
Period of public operation: Daily April to October
Facilities for disabled: Good
Membership details: South Devon Railway Association, c/o above address
Membership journal: *Bulliver* — quarterly

Locomotives and multiple-units

Name	*No*	*Origin*	*Class*	*Type*	*Built*
—	1420	GWR	1400	0-4-2T	1933
—	1369	GWR	1366	0-6-0PT	1934
—	3205	GWR	2251	0-6-0	1946
—	3802*	GWR	2884	2-8-0	1939
—	3803	GWR	2884	2-8-0	1939
Dumbleton Hall	4920	GWR	'Hall'	4-6-0	1929
—	5526	GWR	4500	2-6-2T	1929
—	5542†	GWR	4575	2-6-2T	1928
—	5786	GWR	5700	0-6-0PT	1930
—	D2246	BR	04	0-6-0DM	1956
—	D3666	BR	09	0-6-0DE	1959
—	8110	BR	20	Bo-Bo	1962
—	20118	BR	20	Bo-Bo	1962
—	25901	BR	25	Bo-Bo	1966
—	33002	BR	33	Bo-Bo	1960
Loch Trieg	37037	BR	37	Co-Co	1962
Superb	50002	BR	50	Co-Co	1967
—	51592	BR	127	DMBS	1959
—	51604	BR	127	DMBS	1959
—	55000	BR	121	DMBS	1959
—	59659	BR	115	TS	1960
—	59719	BR	115	TCL	1960
—	59740	BR	115	TS	1960
Broad gauge — 7ft 0.25in					
Tiny	—	SDR	—	0-4-0VBT	1868

*expected to arrive during 2006
†on loan for 2006

Industrial locomotives

Name	*No*	*Builder*	*Type*	*Built*
Ashley	1	Peckett (2031)	0-4-0ST	1942
Lady Angela	1690	Peckett (1690)	0-4-0ST	1926
Sapper	WD132	Hunslet (3163)	0-6-0ST	1943
Glendower	—	Hunslet (3810)	0-6-0ST	1954
Carnarvon	47	Kitson (5474)	0-6-0ST	1935
—	—	Fowler (421014)	0-4-0DM	1958
Name	*No*	*Builder*	*Type*	*Built*
Errol Lonsdale	68011	Hunslet (3796)	0-6-0ST	1953
4ft 6in gauge				
Lee Moor No 2	—	Peckett (784)	0-4-0ST	1899

Stock

13 ex-BR Mk 1 coaches; 12 ex-GWR coaches; 3 ex-GWR auto trailers; 25 wagons. Lee Moor Tramway china clay wagon (4ft 6in gauge)

Owners

Tiny, 7ft 0.25in gauge, part of the National Collection
3802 the GW 3802 Ltd
3803 the South Devon Railway Trust
Glendower is privately owned
Errol Lonsdale the South Devon Railway Trust
1420 the South Devon Railway Association
5526 the 5526 Ltd
D2246 and 50002 the Devon Diesel Society
D8110, 20118, 25901 and 33002 the South Devon Diesel Traction Group
5786 the Worcester Locomotive Society
Sapper & 4920 the South Devon Railway Trust
1369 the South Devon Railway Association
5542 the 5542 Ltd

Timetable Service

South Tynedale Railway

Cumbria

Member: HRA
A narrow gauge line passing through the attractive scenery of the South Tyne valley, in the North Pennine area of outstanding natural beauty
Location: Approximately 0.75-mile north of Alston town centre, on A686 Hexham road
OS reference: NY 717467
Operating society: South Tynedale Railway Preservation Society, The Railway Station, Alston, Cumbria CA9 3JB
Telephone: Alston (01434) 382828 (timetable information); (01434) 381696 (other enquiries)
Internet address: *Web site:* www.strps.org.uk
Car park: Alston station
Access by public transport: Bus services vary seasonally. Routes include Haltwhistle-Alston, Carlisle-Alston and Newcastle-Hexham-Alston-Penrith. Please check with local Tourist Information Centres or, for public transport information in Cumbria, phone 0870 608 2608
On site facilities: Book and souvenir shop, picnic area, toilets (including disabled persons), parking, lineside footpath
Catering facilities: Most weekend trains serve coffee, tea, soft drinks and snacks. (Tea room at Alston is not operated by Society.) Confectionery, ice cream and soft drinks on sale in the railway shop at Alston
Length of line: 2.25 miles, 2ft gauge from Alston to Kirkhaugh
Public opening: Trains will run: 1-18, 22/23, 29/30 April; 1, 6/7, 13/14, 20/21, 27-31 May; 1-4, 6, 8, 10/11, 13/14, 17/18, 20, 22, 24/25, 27, 29 June; daily in July EXCEPT 3, 7, 10, 14; daily in August; 1-3, 5, 7, 9/10, 12, 14, 16/17, 19, 21, 23/24, 26, 28, 30 September; 1, 7/8, 14/15, 21/22, 28/29 October; 2/3, 9/10, 16/17, 21 December

Locomotives

Name	No	Builder	Type	Built
Barber	—	T/Green (441)	0-6-2ST	1908
Naworth	4	H/Clarke (DM819)	0-6-0DM	1952
Thomas Edmondson	6	Henschel (16047)	0-4-0T	1918
—	9	Hunslet (4109)	0-4-0DM	1952
Naklo	10	Chrzanow (3459)	0-6-0WTT	1957
Green Dragon	—	Fowler (13355)	0-4-2T	1914
Cumbria	11	Hunslet (6646)	0-4-0DM	1967
—	13	Hunslet (5222)	0-4-0DM	1958
Helen Kathryn	14	Henschel (28035)	0-4-0T	1948
—	—	Hunslet (4110)	0-4-0DM	1952
—	—	H/Clarke (DM1167)	0-6-0DM	1960
—	15	H/Clarke (DM1366)	0-6-0DM	1965
—	—	EE/Baguley (2519/3500)	4wBE	1958
—	17	B/Drewry (3704)	4wBE	1973
		rebuilt A/Barclay (6526)		1987
Carlisle	16	Hunslet (1859)	0-4-2T	1937
Permanent Way	DB965062			
Trolley		Wickham (7597)	4wDM	1957

Owners
4, 6, 9, 10 & 16 the South Tynedale Railway Preservation Society
11, 13, 14, 15, DM4110, DM1167, 2519/3500, DB965082 and Baguley/Drewry are privately owned

Stock
5 bogie coaches; 1 brake vans; 3 bogie open wagons; 8 4-wheel open wagons; 1 4-wheel box van; 3 4-wheel flat wagons; 1 4-wheel fuel tank wagon; 2 bogie well wagons, 4 4-wheel skip wagons; 5 bogie flat wagons; 6 bogie hopper wagons; 1 4-wheel hopper wagon; 1 4-wheel weedkiller wagon; 1 bogie compressor wagon; 2 4-wheel chassis

Owner
Barber is on loan from Leeds Industrial Museum

Steam haulage scheduled for: 14-17, 29/30 April; 1, 17-29 May; 3/4, 10/11, 17/18, 24/25 June; 1/2, 8/9, July, daily 15 July-3 September; 9/10, 16/17, 23/24, 30 September; 1, 28/29 October; 2/3, 9/10, 16/17, 21 December
Special events: Teddy Bears' Picnic — 24/25 June: Halloween Specials — 28/29 October; Santa Specials — 2/3, 9/10, 16/17, 21 December.
Facilities for disabled: A carriage with access for wheelchair users is available. Advance booking is recommended, tel: 01434 381696. Wheelchair accessible toilet at Alston
Special notes: The line has been constructed on the trackbed of the former BR Haltwhistle-Alston branch
Membership details: Membership Secretary, c/o above address
Membership journal: *Tynedalesman* — quarterly
Marketing name: England's Highest Narrow Gauge Railway

Above: An overview of the station area at Buckfastleigh on the South Devon Railway. GWR 1420 is providing the attraction for the public. *Phil Barnes*

Below: On the occasion of the 20th Anniversary of the closure by British Railways of the Tunbridge Wells to Eridge line Class 33 No 33065 stands at Tunbridge Wells West with the 16.00 to Birchenden on what is now the Spa Valley Railway. *Phil Barnes*

Steam Centre

Southall Railway Centre

London

Due to circumstances the GWRPG were forced to end their activities within the former steam/DMU depot in 1997 and adopt new activities. With the vacation of part of the former depot by *Flying Scotsman* (now on display at the National Railway Museum) the Group were able to move into the former Wheel Drop Shop and ancillary building including open areas and sidings.

The Group now has to make the site suitable for public access which may take some time. In the meantime prospective visitors and potential members are advised to check the web site for updates

Operating society/organisation: GWR Preservation Group Ltd, 16 Grange Close, Heston, Middx TW5 0HW
Contact: Bob Gorringe, Chairman
Tel: 020 8574 1529
Fax: 020 8571 6538
Internet address: *Web site:* www.gwrpg.co.uk
Location: Southall, former steam/ DMU depot
Car parking: Currently on site
Access by public transport: Southall station, access via Park Avenue or Armstrong Way
On site facilities: Light refreshments and shop are scheduled

Locomotives

Name	*No*	*Origin*	*Class*	*Type*	*Built*
—	2885*	GWR	2885	2-8-0	1938
—	4110†	GWR	4100	2-6-2T	1936
—	9682§	GWR	5700	0-6-0PT	1949

*cosmetically restored and on display at Moor Street station, Birmingham
†under restoration at Tyseley Locomotive Works
§on hire to Chinnor & Princes Risborough Railway

Industrial locomotives

Name	*No*	*Builder*	*Type*	*Built*
William Murdoch	—*	Peckett (2100)	0-4-0ST	1949
Birkenhead	—*	RSH (7386)	0-4-0ST	1948
—	1	AEC	0-4-0	1939
—	AD251	R/Hornsby (390772)	0-4-0DM	1956
—	AD911	B/Drewry	4wDM	—

*anticipated return to Southall from East Anglian Railway Museum for 2006

Rolling stock

2 BR Mk 1 TSOs, 1 BR Mk 1 BSK1 GWR Toad brake van, 1 GWR 'Mink' tool van, 1 GWR Gane A, 1 GWR Rectank, 1 LNER CCT, 1 BR parcels van, 1 BR stores van, 1 BR generator van, 1 BR box van, 1 BP tank wagon, 1 LMS Staff coach, 1 LMS brake van

Owners

William Murdoch GWRPG are custodians for Portsmouth City Museum

Period of public opening: Weekends once opening date fixed
Membership details: Andrew Hunter c/o above address
Membership journal: *Southall Semaphore* — quarterly

Timetable Service

Spa Valley Railway

Kent

Member: HRA
This railway originally formed part of a system of cross-country lines in East Sussex running through the Wealden countryside
Location: The main station at Tunbridge Wells West is located in the western end of the town close to the A26 road and the popular 'Pantiles' area
OS reference: Tunbridge Wells West station TQ 577384
Operating society/organisation: Tunbridge Wells & Eridge RPS, Tunbridge Wells West Station, Nevill Terrace, Tunbridge Wells, Kent TN2 5QY
Telephone: 01892 537715
Internet address: *Web site:* www.spavalleyrailway.co.uk
Car parking: Tunbridge Wells West — several car parks nearby in town centre. Note: Sainsbury's car park, adjacent to station, is limited to 2 hours for their customers only. High Rocks — large free car park. There is *no* parking at Groombridge
Access by public transport: National Rail services to Tunbridge Wells, then 15min walk, or short bus ride. Nearest bus stop served by many local bus services is at Sainsbury's, Tunbridge Wells, then

approx 100yd walk
Refreshment facilities: Static buffet car at Tunbridge Wells West. Also bar car *Kate* on some trains
Souvenir shop: Tunbridge Wells West (within engine shed)
Depot: Tunbridge Wells West shed is an original LBSCR design dating from 1891 and consists of four roads which house various items of rolling stock and motive power
Length of line: 4 miles Tunbridge Wells-Birchden Jct. Plus future extension planned Birchden Jct to Eridge, 1 mile
Passenger trains: Weekends and Bank Holidays from 5 April to 29 October plus some weekdays in April, July and August. Santa Specials in December.
Special events: Day out with Thomas — 25/26 March, 1/2 April; Easter Specials — 14-17 April; St George's Day — 23 April; Morris Day — 1 May; Steam Gala — 6/7 May; Father's Day — 18 June; Wings Wheels & Steam — 9 July; Diesel Gala — 5/6 August; Gala Weekend — 16/17 September; Day out with Thomas — 7/8, 14/15 October; Santa Specials — 2-24 December
Facilities for disabled: Separate disabled persons' toilet at Tunbridge Wells West station. Level or ramp access to all station platforms. Ramps available for wheelchair access to trains
Membership details: c/o Tunbridge Wells West Station
Membership journal: *Spa Valley Starter* and *Eridge Express*

Locomotives and multiple-units

Name	*No*	*Origin*	*Class*	*Type*	*Built*
Sutton	32650*	LBSCR	A1X	0-6-0T	1876
—	47493	LMS	3F	0-6-0T	1927
—	68077	LNER	J94	0-6-0ST	1947
—	09004	BR	09	0-6-0DE	1959
Colonel Tomline	D3489	BR	10	0-6-0DE	1958
—	15224	BR	12	0-6-0DE	1949
R J Mitchell	33063	BR	33/0	Bo-Bo	1962
Sealion	33065	BR	33/0	Bo-Bo	1962
—	E6047	BR	73	Bo-Bo	1966
—	51669†	BR	115	DMBS	1960
—	51849	BR	115	DMBS	1960
—	54408	BR	101	DTS(L)	1958
—	60142	BR	207	DMBS	1962
—	60616§	BR	207	TC	1962
—	60916	BR	207	DTS	1962

*undergoing overhaul
†converted to locomotive hauled stock
§undergoing restoration off-site, expected to arrive during 2006

Industrial locomotives

Name	*No*	*Builder*	*Type*	*Built*
*Scottie**	—	R/Hornsby (412427)	4wDM	1957
*Samson**	57	RSH (7668)	0-6-0T	1950
*North Downs**	13	RSH (7846)	0-6-0T	1955
Princess Margaret	—	Barclay (376)	0-4-0DM	1947
Lady Ingrid	—	Barclay (2315)	0-4-0ST	1951
Southerham	—	Drewry/Vulcan (2591)	0-4-0DM	1959
*Topham**	—	Bagnall (2193)	0-6-0ST	1922
Fonmon	—	Peckett (1636)	0-6-0ST	1924
*Spartan**	—	Chrzanow (3135)	0-6-0T	1954
*Hotspur**	—	Chrzanow (2944)	0-6-0T	1952

*undergoing overhaul

Stock
5 BR Mk 1 coaches; 1 BR Mk 2 coaches; buffet car from Class 420 EMU; 2 ex-London Transport T stock coaches; 1 LCDR coach body; 3 brake vans; 3 cranes; various freight wagons

Owners
Sutton by the London Borough of Sutton
33063 and 33065 the South East Locomotive Group
68077 on long term loan from Keighley & Worth Valley Railway

Museum

STEAM — Museum of the Great Western Railway

Wiltshire

Member: HRA
STEAM — Museum of the Great Western Railway tells the remarkable story of the men and women who built, operated and travelled on the Great Western Railway. Situated on the old Swindon Railway Works site, the museum is housed in a 72,000sq ft Victorian machine shop. As well as locomotives, carriages and wagons the story is told by imaginative displays and plenty of 'hands-on' exhibits — build a bridge and shunt the wagons! Have a go at putting a locomotive together and take a ride on the train-driving simulator
Keeper: Felicity Ball

Location: Kemble Drive, Swindon, Wiltshire SN2 2TA
OS reference: tba
Operating society/organisation: Swindon Borough Council
Telephone: Swindon (01793) 466646
Internet address: *Web site:* www.swindon.gov.uk/steam

Car park: Shared with the Great Western Designer Outlet Centre
Access by public transport: Swindon main line station 1 mile (20min walk)
On site facilities: Shop
Facilities for disabled: Fully accessible
Period of public opening: Daily 10.00-17.00. Closed Christmas Day, Boxing Day and New Year's Day.
Membership details: The Friends of Swindon Railway Museum, c/o STEAM
Membership journal: *North Star* — quarterly

Locomotives

Name	*No*	*Origin*	*Class*	*Type*	*Built*
—	2516	GWR	2301	0-6-0	1897
—	4248	GWR	4200	2-8-0T	1916
Caerphilly Castle	4073	GWR	'Castle'	4-6-0	1923
King George V	6000	GWR	'King'	4-6-0	1927
—	9400	GWR	9400	0-6-0PT	1947
*North Star**	—	GWR	—	2-2-2	1837
—	4	GWR	Diesel railcar	Bo-Bo	1934
Hagley Hall†	4930	GWR	'Hall'	4-6-0	1929
—	7325	GWR	4300	2-6-0	1932
Glorious	50033	BR	50	Co-Co	1968

*broad gauge (7ft 0.25in) replica
†on display in McArthur Glen's 'Designer Outlet' shopping centre located in the old works

Owners
4930 and 7325 on loan from Severn Valley Railway
All other locomotives are part of the National Railway Museum Collection

Steam Centre — Stephenson Railway Museum & North Tyneside Railway — Tyne & Wear

Member: HRA
A display in buildings which began life as the Tyne & Wear Metro Test Centre now features locomotives and exhibitions which illustrate railway development from waggonways to the present day
Location: Middle Engine Lane, West Chirton
OS reference: NZ 396576
Internet address: *NTSRA web site:* ntsra.org.uk
Operating society/organisation: The Stephenson Railway Museum and the North Tyneside Railway are managed as a partnership between North Tyneside Council, Tyne & Wear Museums and the North Tyneside Railway Association (NTSRA). Each can be contacted c/o Stephenson Railway Museum, Middle Engine Lane, West Chirton, North Shields, Tyne & Wear NE29 8DX
Car park: On site, free
Length of line: North Tyneside Railway, 2 miles, Stephenson Railway Museum to Percy Main Village
Access by public transport: Bus services 300 from Newcastle (Haymarket bus station); 337/339 from Wallsend (Metro station interchange). Ring 0870 608 2608 for times and fares. Tyne & Wear Metro to Percy Main (then short walk to NTR station) when North Tyneside Railway is in operation
Public opening: May to September: Museum — daily (except Fridays), admission free; railway — Sundays and Bank Holiday Mondays, also Saturdays during local school holidays. Closed October to April. Write, phone (0191 200 7146) or visit the NTSRA web site for details, including early/late season

Locomotive and multiple-unit

Name	*No*	*Origin*	*Class*	*Type*	*Built*
—	D2078	BR	03	0-6-0DM	1959
—	3267	NER	—	DMLV	1904

Industrial locomotives

Name	*No*	*Builder*	*Type*	*Built*
Billy	—	Killingworth or RS & Co (1)	0-4-0	c1826
—	A No 5	Kitson (2509)	0-6-0PT	1883
Ashington No 5 / Jackie Milburn	5	Peckett (1970)	0-6-0ST	1939
Ted Garrett, JP, DL, MP	1	RSH (7683)	0-6-0T	1951
—	E4	Siemens-Schuckert (457)	Bo-BoWE	1909
Thomas Burt MP 1837-1902	401	Bagnall (2994)	0-6-0ST	1950
—	10	Consett Iron Co	0-6-0DM	1958

Stock
1 LNER Gresley BFK; 3 BR Mk 1 non-gangwayed coaches, 2 BR Mk 2 coaches, 1 LNER Gresley BGP

Owner
NER van National Railway Museum

variations and special events
Special notes: Stephenson Railway Museum and North Tyneside Railway share facilities in buildings. North Tyneside Steam Railway Association operates and maintains exhibits from the Museum Collection
Facilities for disabled: Access for wheelchairs to Museum building at Middle Engine Lane. Access to stations; also wheelchair ramp onto train

Timetable Service

Swanage Railway — 'The Purbeck Line'

Dorset

Member: HRA
Overlooked by the historic ruins of Corfe Castle, this railway is slowly extending towards Wareham and a connection to the main line network
Location: Swanage station
Operations Manager: Mike Stanghaft
Passenger Services Manager: David Green
Operating society/organisation: Swanage Railway Co Ltd, Station House, Swanage, Dorset BH19 1HB
Telephone: Swanage (01929) 425800. Talking Timetable — (01929) 425800
Fax: (01929) 426680
Internet addresses: *e-mail:* general@swanrail.freeserve.co.uk
Web site: www.swanagerailway.co.uk
Other public stations: Herston Halt, Harman's Cross, Corfe Castle and Norden
OS reference: SZ 026789
Car park: Norden park & ride signposted off A351 Wareham-Swanage road on the approach to Corfe Castle. Limited parking available at Swanage station
Access by public transport: Regular bus services operated by Wilts & Dorset from Bournemouth, Poole and Wareham to Swanage and Norden park & ride
On site facilities: Souvenir shop at Swanage. Buffet car on most trains. Picnic areas at Swanage, Harman's Cross and Norden. Exhibition and cinema coach at Corfe. 5in gauge railway at Swanage on some weekends. Travel Agency at Swanage station
Length of line: 6 miles, Swanage-Herston Halt-Harman's Cross-Corfe Castle-Norden
Public opening: Swanage station open every day except Christmas

Locomotives and multiple-units

Name	*No*	*Origin*	*Class*	*Type*	*Built*
—	6695	GWR	5600	0-6-2T	1928
—	30053*	LSWR	M7	0-4-4T	1905
Sidmouth	34010	SR	WC	4-6-2	1945
Eddystone	34028†	SR	WC	4-6-2	1946
Manston	34070	SR	BB	4-6-2	1947
257 Squadron	34072	SR	BB	4-6-2	1948
—	80078	BR	4MT	2-6-4T	1954
—	80104	BR	4MT	2-6-4T	1955
—	08436	BR	08	0-6-0DE	1957
—	D3591	BR	08	0-6-0DE	1958
—	20188	BR	20	Bo-Bo	1967
Stan Symes	D6515	BR	33	Bo-Bo	1960
—	33034	BR	33	Bo-Bo	1960
Vampire	33108	BR	33	Bo-Bo	1960
—	51341*	P/Steel	117	DMBS	1959
—	51346	P/Steel	117	DMBS	1959
—	51353*	P/Steel	117	DMBS	1959
—	51356*	P/Steel	117	DMBS	1959
—	51388	P/Steel	117	DMS	1959
—	51392*	P/Steel	117	DMS	1959
—	51395*	P/Steel	117	DMS	1959
—	51398*	P/Steel	117	DMS	1959
—	59486*	P/Steel	117	TCL	1960
—	59492*	P/Steel	117	TCL	1960
—	59516	P/Steel	117	TCL	1960
—	59521*	P/Steel	117	TCL	1960

*undergoing overhaul off-site
†on loan to North Yorkshire Moors Railway

Industrial locomotives

Name	*No*	*Builder*	*Type*	*Built*
May	2	Fowler (4210132)	0-4-0DM	1957
Beryl	—	Planet (2054)	4wPM	1937
Progress	—	Peckett (1611)	0-4-0ST	1923
*Secondus**	—	Bellis & Seekings	0-6-0WT	1874

*2ft 8in gauge, on display in Corfe Castle goods shed

Locomotive notes: 30053, 80078 and 80104 will be away periodically on short-term loan

Stock
3 ex-LSWR coach bodies; 4 ex-SR vans; 9 ex-SR coaches; 17 ex-BR Mk 1 coaches; 1 ex-BR Mk 1 Pullman; 15 various types of wagons; 1 ex-BR Mk 3 Sleeping coach; 1 ex-SR 15-ton diesel-electric crane; 1 ex-BR Corridor 2nd converted to disabled persons' coach. Brake vans from SR, LMS, LSWR including 3 'Queen Marys', GWR

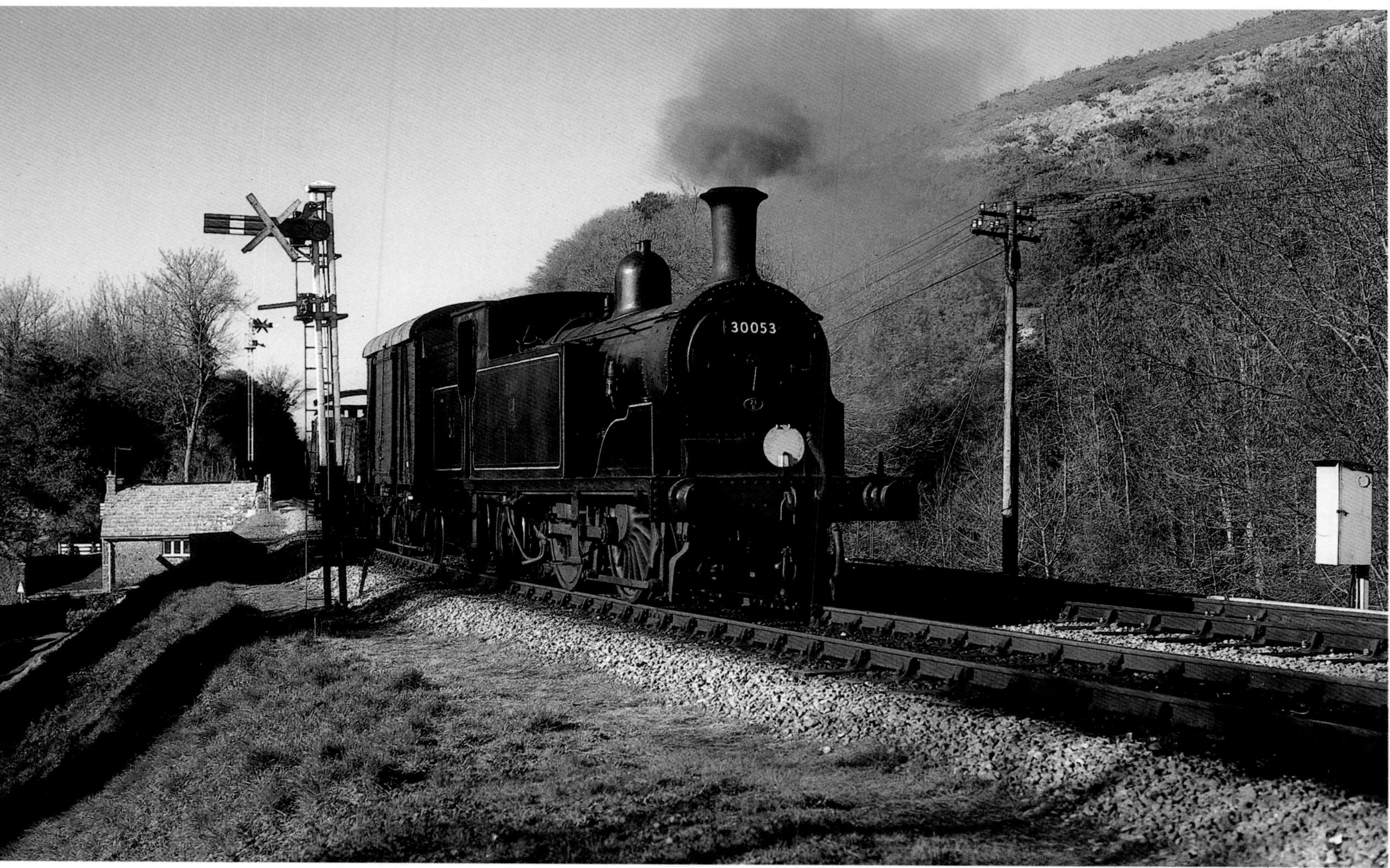

Former London & South Western Railway Class M7 No 30053 is seen leaving Corfe Castle on the Swanage Railway. During 2005 work was completed here enabling trains to pass for the first time in preservation. *Alan Barnes*

Day. Trains operate weekends all year round from early February to end of December. Daily from 1 April until end October (except 3, 7, 10, 14, 17, 21, 31 October). Also 26 December 2006 to 1 January 2007
Special events: Branchline Weekend — 1/2 April; Easter Specials — 14-17 April; Swanage Beer Festival — 19-21 May; Swanage Railway Fete — 29 May; Swanage Carnival Firework Specials — 29 July and 5 August; Steam Gala & Vintage Transport Rally — 9/10 September; Day out with Thomas — 21-29 October; 1960s Weekend — 25/26 November; Santa Specials — 2/3, 9/10, 16/17, 22-24 December. See press for details of local special events
Facilities for disabled: Access to shop and toilets; disabled facilities on most trains
Membership details: Sue Payne, c/o Southern Steam Trust at above address
Membership journal: *Swanage Railway News* — quarterly
Marketing name: The Purbeck Line

Owners
6695 the Great Western Railway Preservation Group
34010, 34028, 34070, 34072, 80078 and 80104 the Southern Locomotives Ltd
30053 the Drummond Locomotive Society
D6515 and 33034 the 71A Locomotive Group
33108 the Class 33/1 Preservation Co Ltd

Steam Centre

Swindon & Cricklade Railway

Wiltshire

Member: HRA, TT
This is the only preserved section of the former Midland & South Western Junction Railway, the society having had to re-lay track and associated works. There is the station and the engine shed complex at Hayes Knoll
Location: Tadpole Lane, Blunsdon (approximately midway between Blunsdon St Andrew and Purton)
Chairman: J. Larkin
Operating society/organisation: Swindon & Cricklade Railway, Blunsdon Station, Blunsdon, Swindon, Wiltshire SN25 2DA
Telephone: 01793 771615
Internet address: *Web site:* www.swindon-cricklade-railway.org
Station: Blunsdon
OS reference: SU 110897
Length of line: 1 mile
Car park: Tadpole Lane, Blunsdon
Refreshment facilities: Blunsdon station in former Norwegian State Railways coach. Buffet car at Hayes Knoll on open days. Picnic area
Toilet: Blunsdon station amenities building
Souvenir shop: Blunsdon station. Various sales stands on Open Days around station area. Museum currently being enlarged to reopen in 2006
Depot: Hayes Knoll

Locomotives and multiple-units

Name	*No*	*Origin*	*Class*	*Type*	*Built*
Foremarke Hall†	7903	GWR	'Hall'	4-6-0	1949
—	4277	GWR	4200	2-8-0T	1920
—*	5637	GWR	5600	0-6-2T	1924
—	2022	BR	03	0-6-0DM	1958
—	03152	BR	03	0-6-0DM	1960
—	13261	BR	08	0-6-0DE	1956
—	51074	GRCW	119	DMBC	1959
—	51104	GRCW	119	DMS	1958
—	59514	P/Steel	117	TCL	1959
—	60127	BR	207	DMBS	1962
—	60901	BR	207	DTS	1962

*on loan to East Somerset Railway
†on loan to Gloucestershire Warwickshire Railway

Industrial locomotives

Name	*No*	*Builder*	*Type*	*Built*
Swordfish	—	Barclay (2138)	0-6-0ST	1941
Salmon	—	Barclay (2139)	0-6-0ST	1942
—	—	Barclay (2352)	0-4-0ST	1954
Richard Trevithick	—	Barclay (2354)	0-4-0ST	1954
Woodbine	—	Fowler (21442)	0-4-0DM	1936
—	—	Fowler (4210137)	0-4-0DM	1958
—	—	Fowler (4220031)	0-4-0DH	1964
—*	70	H/Clarke (1464)	0-6-0T	1921
Slough Estates No 3	—	H/Clarke (1544)	0-6-0ST	1924
—	—	H/Clarke (1857)	0-6-0T	1952
Gunby	—	Hunslet (2413)	0-6-0ST	1941

*on loan to Avon Valley Railway

Stock
7 BR Mk 1 coaches; 2 GWR coaches; Selection of goods rolling stock; Wickham railcar. Self-propelled Plasser & Theurer track machine (98504 of 1985)

Public opening: Site open: 10.00-16.00 Saturdays, Sundays and Bank Holidays throughout the year.
Passenger trains: A steam train planned to operate from 11.00-16.00 every Sunday from Easter to 29 October and on the dates listed below unless stated otherwise. A train service will also operate from 11.00-16.00 every Saturday from Easter to 28 October and Sunday when special events are not planned and on Wednesdays during local school holidays
Special events:
Mother's Day — 26 March; Easter Egg Specials (diesel) — 14/15 April; Easter Egg Specials (steam) — 16/17 April; Ivor the Talking Engine — 29/30 April, 1 May§; Murder Mystery Evening* — 20 May; Children's Treasure Hunt — 28/29 May; Teddy Bears' picnic — 25 June; Murder Mystery Evening* — 22 July; Vintage Transport Weekend — 12/13 August; Ivor the Talking Engine — 26-28 August§; Wartime Weekend — 9/10 September (10.30-17.00); Brunel 200 Weekend — 16/17 September; Halloween — 27 October (18.30-20.45) 28 October (18.00-20.45); Santa Specials — 25/26 November, 2/3, 9/10, 16/17, 23/24 December.
*Ticket only events
§On 29 April and 26 August it is planned that Ivor will be static at Hayes Knoll and available for footplate visits (service will be diesel)
Service operate:
School holiday (diesel), 11.00-16.00 — 5, 12 April, 31 May, 26 July, 9, 16, 30 August, 25 October;
Saturday service (diesel), 11.00-16.00 — Saturdays from 22 April to 28 October;
Sunday service (steam), 11.00-16.00 — Sundays from 23 April to 29 October;
Sunday service (diesel), 11.00-16.00 — Sundays to 9 April, 5-19 November
Facilities for disabled: Access to trains, locomotive shed, shop, toilets and refreshments
Membership details: Membership Secretary, c/o above address
Membership journal: S&CR magazine, quarterly

Owners
7903 the Foremarke Hall Locomotive Group
5637 the 5637 Locomotive Group
Slough Estates the Slough & Windsor Railway Society
51074, 51104 and 59514 the Gloucester Railcar Trust

Timetable Service

Tanfield Railway

County Durham

Member: HRA
The oldest railway in the world, featuring 1725 route, 1725 Causey embankment, 1727 Causey arch, 1766 Gibraltar bridge and 1854 Marley Hill engine shed. Also collection of local engines, Victorian carriages and vintage workshop
Location: Off the A6076 Sunniside to Stanley road
OS reference: NZ 207573
Operating society/organisation: The Tanfield Railway, Marley Hill Engine Shed, Sunniside, Gateshead NE16 5ET
Telephone: (0191) 388 7545
Internet address: *Web site:* www.tanfield-railway.co.uk
Main stations: Andrews House, Sunniside, Causey, East Tanfield
Car park: Marley Hill, Causey picnic area, East Tanfield
Access by public transport: X30 (weekdays) stops outside main entrance; 705, 706, 770 Sundays to Sunniside only, near to Sunniside station
Catering facilities: Light

Locomotive

Name	*No*	*Origin*	*Class*	*Type*	*Built*
—	M2*	TGR	M	4-6-2	1951

*3ft 6in gauge, Tasmanian Government Railways (RSH 7630)

Industrial locomotives

Name	*No*	*Builder*	*Type*	*Built*
—	9	AEG (1565)	4w-4wE	1913
Gamma	—	Bagnall (2779)	0-6-0ST	1945
—	—	Baguley (3565)	2w-2DHR	1962
Horden	—	Barclay (1015)	0-6-0ST	1904
—	6	Barclay (1193)	0-4-2ST	1910
—	17	Barclay (1338)	0-6-0T	1913
—	32	Barclay (1659)	0-4-0ST	1920
Beryl	—	S/Crossley (7697)	0-6-0DM	1953
—	3	E. Borrows (37)	0-4-0WT	1898
—	6	Fowler (4240010)	0-6-0DH	1960
Enterprise	—	R&W Hawthorn (2009)	0-4-0ST	1884
Cyclops	112	H/Leslie (2711)	0-4-0ST	1907
—	2*	H/Leslie (2859)	0-4-0ST	1911
Stagshaw	—	H/Leslie (3513)	0-6-0ST	1923
—	3	H/Leslie (3575)	0-6-0ST	1923
—	13	H/Leslie (3732)	0-4-0ST	1928
—	3	H/Leslie (3746)	0-6-0F	1929
Renishaw Ironworks No 6	—	H/Clarke (1366)	0-6-0ST	1919
Irwell	—	H/Clarke (1672)	0-4-0ST	1937
—	38	H/Clarke (1823)	0-6-0T	1949
—	501	Hunslet (6612)	0-6-0DH	1965

refreshments available on operating days
On site facilities: Shop and toilets
Length of line: 3 miles
Public opening: Trains run every Sunday and Bank Holiday Monday from January to November. Also Wednesdays and Thursdays in summer. Santa trains in December before Christmas. Marley Hill engine shed open daily for viewing
Special events:
Not advised, please contact for details
Family tickets: Available
Facilities for disabled: Access to East Tanfield and Andrews House stations and Marley Hill engine shed. Toilets at Causey car park and Andrews House station
Membership details:
Miss E. Martin, 33 Stocksfield Avenue, Fenham, Newcastle upon Tyne NE5 2DX
Membership journal: *Tanfield Railway News* — 4 times/year
Special notes: Families can alight at Causey station for 2 miles of walks through the picturesque Causey Woods; picnic facilities and toilet available in car park

Name	*No*	*Builder*	*Type*	*Built*
—	—	Planet (3716)	0-4-0DM	1955
—	4	Sentinel (9559)	0-4-0T	1953
Twizell†	3	Stephenson (2730)	0-6-0T	1891
—	L2	R/Hornsby (312989)	0-4-0DE	1952
—	35	R/Hornsby (418600)	0-4-0DE	1958
—	158	RSH (6980)	0-4-0DM	1940
Hendon	—	RSH (7007)	0-4-0CT	1940
—	62	RSH (7035)	0-6-0ST	1940
—	3	RSH (7078)	4w-4wE	1940
—	49	RSH (7098)	0-6-0ST	1943
Progress	—	RSH (7298)	0-6-0ST	1946
Cochrane	—	RSH (7409)	0-4-0ST	1948
Bromborough No 2	—	RSH (7746)	0-6-0DM	1954
—	44	RSH (7760)	0-6-0ST	1953
—	38	RSH (7763)	0-6-0ST	1954
—	21	RSH (7796)	0-4-0ST	1954
—	47	RSH (7800)	0-6-0ST	1954
—	1	RSH (7901)	0-4-0DM	1958
—	16	RSH (7944)	0-6-0ST	1957
FGF	—	Barclay (D592)	0-4-0DH	1969
—	—	Barclay (D615)	0-4-0DH	1977
—	2	A/Whitworth (D22)	0-4-0DE	1933

*on loan to Locomotion
†on long-term loan from Beamish

2ft gauge

Name	*No*	*Builder*	*Type*	*Built*
Escucha	11	B/Hawthorn (748)	0-4-0ST	1883
—	—	Clayton (133141)	4wBE	1984
—	—	Hunslet (7332	4wDM	1973
—	—	L/Blackstone (53162)	4wDM	1962
—	—	L/Blackstone (54781)	4wDM	1962
—	—	R/Hornsby (323587)	4wDM	1952
—	—	R/Hornsby (244487)	4wDM	1946
—	25	RSH (8201)	4wBE	1960
—	—	W/Rogers	4wBE	—

Stock
19 4-wheel carriages; 3 6-wheel carriages; 1 6-wheel van; 14 hopper wagons; 9 contractors bogies; 3 brake vans; 3 steam cranes; 8 covered wagons; 4 open wagons; 4 black wagons; 3 flat wagons

Steam Centre

Telford Horsehay Steam Trust

Shropshire

Member: HRA
Telford Steam Railway is based at Horsehay & Dawley station and goods yard in Telford on the Great Western branch from Wellington to Craven Arms via Ironbridge. The site at Horsehay has a longer history, being at the site of one of the Coalbrookdale companies' first blast furnaces. The line saw its last passenger train in 1962 but the route from Lightmoor to Horsehay was kept open for freight traffic until 1979. The TSR acquired the former goods yard at Horsehay & Dawley in 1983. The railway is now extending northwards to Lawley Common, and southwards to Doseley. Excavation of Lawley Common cutting is continuing
Location: Horsehay, Telford, Shropshire
OS reference: SJ 675073
Operating society/organisation: Telford Horsehay Steam Trust, The Old Loco Shed, Horsehay, Telford, Shropshire TF4 2LT
Sales line: 07765 858348
Internet address: *Web site:* www.telfordsteamrailway.co.uk
On site facilities: Extensive model railway display, tea room, picnic area, children's play equipment, narrow gauge steam tramway, miniature railway operated by Phoenix Model Engineers (separate charge); ticket gives unlimited travel (except miniature railway)
Public opening: Every Sunday and

Bank Holiday from Easter until last Sunday in September including Bank Holidays 11.00-16.30. Last Sunday in month steam-hauled and also steam on Bank Holidays and all Sundays in August, but steam tram every Sunday. Also pre-Christmas weekends in December when Thomas the Tank pays a visit
Facilities for disabled: Limited, see below, or Accessibility on web site.
Mk 1 coaches are not really suitable for wheelchair access, DMUs when in service on diesel days have ramped brake van access. Small chairs can be accommodated in GWR brake van, platforms have easy access and shop, although steep ramp at Horsehay & Dawley. Tea room and model railway have level access

Locomotives and diesel multiple-units

Name	*No*	*Origin*	*Class*	*Type*	*Built*
—	5619	GWR	5600	0-6-2T	1925
—	50531	BRCW	104	DMC	1957
—	50479	BRCW	104	DMBS	1957
—	50556	BRCW	104	DMC	1957
—	59228	BRCW	104	TBSL	1958
—	RB004	Leyland		Railbus	1984

Industrial locomotives

Name	*No*	*Builder*	*Type*	*Built*
Ironbridge No 3	—	Peckett (1990)	0-4-0ST	1940
Beatty	—	H/Leslie (3240)	0-4-0ST	1917
—	MP1	Barclay (1944)	0-4-0F	1944
Tom	27414	N/British (27414)	0-4-0DH	1954
—	D2959	R/Hornsby (382824)	4wDM	1955
Folly	—	R/Hornsby (183062)	4wDM	1937
—	—	R/Hornsby (525947)	0-4-0DH	1968
Joanna	—	T/Hill (177C)	0-4-0DM	1967
	rebuild of Sentinel (9401) 0-4-0ST of 1950			
—	—	YEC (2630)	0-6-0DE	1956
—	—	YEC (2687)	0-4-0DE	1968
Thomas	—*	Kierstead	4wVBT	1979

*2ft gauge

Stock
2 ex-BR Mk 1 coaches; 1 ex-BR Mk 3 sleeper; 1 ex-GWR auto-trailer; 1 ex-GWR Toad brake van; 1 ex-GWR 3-ton hand crane; 1 Wickham trolley; Permaquip PW transporter vehicle No 68800; Various wagons

Museum

Tiverton Museum of Mid Devon Life

Devon

The Museum, dominated by No 1442, affectionately known as the 'Tivvy Bumper', houses a large collection of railway relics
Location: Tiverton, Devon
OS reference: SS 955124
Operating society/organisation: Tiverton & Mid Devon Museum Trust, Becks Square, Tiverton, Devon EX16 6PH
Telephone: (01884) 256295
Car park: Adjoining access by public transport: rail to Tiverton Parkway, then by bus, or bus from Exeter
On site facilities: Museum, shop and toilets
Public opening: February to Christmas: Monday to Friday — 10.30-16.30; Saturdays — 10.00-13.00; closed Sundays
Special notes: Disabled access to view locomotive. The locomotive gallery will re-open in April 2006 following re-display

Locomotives

Name	*No*	*Origin*	*Class*	*Type*	*Built*
(Tivvy Bumper)	1442	GWR	1400	0-4-2T	1935

Steam Centre

Tyseley Locomotive Works

Birmingham

Member: HRA
Location: 670 Warwick Road (A41), Tyseley, Birmingham B11 2HL
OS reference: SP 105841
Operating organisation: Vintage Trains
Supporting society: Vintage Trains Society
Telephone: (0121) 707 4696
Fax: (0121) 764 4645
Internet address: *Web site:* www.vintagetrains.co.uk/brm.htm
Car park: Site
Access by public transport: Travel

West Midlands route No 37 from city centre. Main line rail service to Tyseley station (Central Trains and Chiltern Railways)
On site facilities: The Museum is on the site of a former GWR/BR steam shed and has been equipped with specialised railway engineering machinery. It carries out many contract repairs to steam locomotives and rolling stock. Souvenir shop, restaurant, passenger demonstration line and station, schools' education service
Refreshment facilities: Available in visitor centre
Length of line: Third of a mile
Public opening: Weekends and Bank Holidays only 10.00-16.00.
Special events: 'Shakespeare Express' runs from July to September 2006. Running from Birmingham Snow Hill to Stratford-upon-Avon twice daily
Special notes: Tyseley is a centre for 'Steam on the Main Line' railtours over a large area of the national rail network. Full education service providing guided tours, worksheets and live presentation
Membership details: Membership is available to the public, providing free entry to site events and four copies of *Steam in Trust* magazine
Facilities for disabled: Disabled access to 'Shakespeare Express' available, but must be notified in advance
Note: All attractions and facilities are advertised subject to availability

Locomotives

Name	*No*	*Origin*	*Class*	*Type*	*Built*
Kinlet Hall	4936	GWR	'Hall'	4-6-0	1929
Pitchford Hall	4953	GWR	'Hall'	4-6-0	1929
Rood Ashton Hall	4965	GWR	'Hall'	4-6-0	1929
Earl of Mount Edgcumbe	5043	GWR	'Castle	4-6-0	1936
Defiant†	5080	GWR	'Castle'	4-6-0	1939
Clun Castle	7029	GWR	'Castle'	4-6-0	1950
—	4110	GWR	5101	2-6-2T	1937
—	4121	GWR	5101	2-6-2T	1937
—	7752	GWR	5700	0-6-0PT	1930
—	7760	GWR	5700	0-6-0PT	1930
—	9600	GWR	5700	0-6-0PT	1945
Kolhapur§	5593	LMS	'Jubilee'	4-6-0	1934
Leander	5690	LMS	'Jubilee'	4-6-0	1936
Duches of Hamilton	46229	LMS	'Duchess'	4-6-2	1939
—	670	LNWR*	Bloomer	2-2-2	1986
—	13029	BR	08	0-6-0DE	1953
—	20059	BR	20	Bo-Bo	1961
—	20177	BR	20	Bo-Bo	1966
—	31301	BR	31	A1A-A1A	1962
—	31461	BR	31	A1A-A1A	1959
—	37264	BR	37	Co-Co	1965
—	47525	BR	47	Co-Co	1967
Royal Oak	50017	BR	55	Co-Co	1968
Rodney	50021	BR	55	Co-Co	1968
Gordon Highlander	55016	BR	55	Co-Co	1961
Les Ross	86259	BR	86	Bo-Bo	1965

*replica built at Tyseley Locomotive Works
†on loan to Buckinghamshire Railway Centre
§on loan to Barrow Hill Roundhouse

Industrial locomotives

Name	*No*	*Builder*	*Type*	*Built*
Cadbury No 1	—	Avonside (1977)	0-4-0T	1925
—	1	Peckett (2004)	0-4-0ST	1942
—	—	Baguley (800)	0-4-0PE	1920

Note: Not all locomotives are on site, and some are undergoing restoration. Contract restoration work includes Nos (GWR) 3850 and 7029, LMS 46229 (for streamlining), and GWR steam railmotor and industrial RSH 7289/1945; locomotives away on loan include 5593 and *Henry* (Barrow Hill), 5080 (Buckinghamshire)

Stock

17 BR Mk 2 coaches, 3 BR Mk 1 coaches, 3 BR Mk 1 Pullman Cars, goods and departmental vehicles, steam and diesel cranes

Museum

Vintage Carriages Trust Museum

West Yorkshire

Member: HRA, TT, AIM, ABTEM
A fascinating collection of elderly railway carriages and small locomotives, interestingly presented. Sit in a fully restored, prize winning 1876-built Manchester, Sheffield & Lincolnshire Railway carriage or relive the dark days of wartime travel in one of the three Metropolitan Railway carriages. Listen to the 'Travellers' Tales' and view the collection of railway posters and other items. Video presentation. The carriages and locomotives have appeared in over 50 cinema and television productions including *Booze Cruise 3* (2005), *North & South* (2004), *Inside Out* (2003), *He Knew He*

Was Right (2003), *The Forsyte Saga* (2002), *Calendar* (2003), *Hound of the Baskervilles* (2002), *No Man's Land* (2002), *Turner – The Man Who Painted Britain* (2002), *A for Acid* (2001), *The Hours* (2001), *The Way We Live Now* (2001), *The Cazalets* (2000), *Possession* (2000), *The Railway Children* (1970 and 1968 versions)
Location: Vintage Carriages Trust Museum, Ingrow Station Yard, Halifax Road, Keighley, West Yorkshire BD22 8NJ. On the A629 road
Operations Manager: Michael Cope, Hon Secretary, VCT
Operating society/organisation: Vintage Carriages Trust (a Registered Charity No 510776)
Telephone: Keighley (01535) 680425
Fax: (01535) 610796
Internet address: *e-mail:* admin@vintagecarriagestrust.org
Web site: www.vintagecarriagestrust.org

The web site includes a database on over 4,300 preserved carriages, with over 3,700 photos. Also on CD-Rom
Car Park: Yes. Also coach parking at Ingrow station
Access by public transport: Northern Rail through trains from Carlisle, Settle, Morecambe, Lancaster to Keighley (one mile). Fast and frequent Metro Train services from Bradford Forster Square, Leeds, Shipley, and Skipton to Keighley. Then either KWVR train to Ingrow West (adjacent) or buses 500, 502, 663, 664, 665, 696, 697 and 720 from Keighley bus station.
Buses: First Calderline bus 502 from Hebden Bridge. Calderline bus 502 from Halifax (Sundays only). Keighley & District buses 696 and 697 from Bradford via Thornton and Denholme.
Tel: (0113) 245 7676 for bus and Metro Train information or log onto VCT web site for internet links to timetables and route map

Stock

Railway	*BR or previous owner Number*	*Type*	*Date built*	*Seats*	*Weight*	*Length*
MS&LR	176	4-wheel 1st/2nd/3rd/ luggage	1876	34	12T	28ft 0in
GNR	589	6-wheel 3rd brake	1888	40	14T	34ft 11in
MR	358	6-wheel 1st/3rd/ luggage	1886	32	15T	34ft 0in
Met	427	BS	1910	84	30T	54ft 0in
Met	465	S	1919	108	30T	54ft 0in
Met	509	F	1923	84	30T	54ft 0in
SR (SECR)	S3554S	BSK	1924	42	33T	65ft 3in
BR (SR)	S1469S	TSO	1951	64	32T	67ft 1in
GN	2856	Non vestibule composite, lav brake	1898	34	22T	45ft 0in

Industrial locomotives

Name	*No*	*Builder*	*Type*	*Built*
*Bellerophon**	—	Haydock Foundry (C)	0-6-0WT	1874
Sir Berkeley†	—	M/Wardle (1210)	0-6-0ST	1891
Lord Mayor	—	H/Clarke (402)	0-4-0ST	1893

*on loan to the Foxfield Railway for 10 years
†on 10 year loan to Middleton Railway

On site facilities: Transport relics shop specialising in out of print magazines, lamps and hardware. Hot and cold drinks, ice cream and chocolate available. Toilets with full disabled access. A determined effort has been made to provide a museum which will interest the casual visitor who is not knowledgeable about railways
Public opening: Daily 11.00-16.30, openings outside these times can be arranged for groups.
Closed 25 and 26 December
Facilities for disabled: The museum building is level with easy access for wheelchair users. A stairlift has been provided to allow wheelchair users to view carriage interiors, and enter guards' brake areas, though naturally wheelchairs are too wide to enter individual passenger compartments. Toilets with full access for wheelchair users. Braille leaflet, guidebook and audio tape for loan during visit. Wheelchair available for loan.

Winner of the 1998 Adapt Museum Award for best practice in access for disabled and older people. Runners up for the 1998 Yorkshire Electricity/Yorkshire & Humberside Museums Council Access Awards. Highly commended in the 1999 White Rose Tourist For All Awards
Special notes: Visitors are welcome to either browse in the shop or visit the museum
Membership details: Membership Secretary, c/o above address
Marketing names: Vintage Carriages Trust or VCT

Timetable Service

Volks Electric Railway

East Sussex

In 1883 Magnus Volk opened an electric powered railway along the seafront at Brighton. It was the first 'proper' electric railway in Britain. Today it holds the deserved position of being the oldest remaining operating electric railway in the world

Manager: Stuart Strong

Headquarters: Quality of Life & Green Spaces, Brighton & Hove City Council, Kings House, Grand Avenue, Hove BN3 2LS

Office/Works: 285 Madeira Drive, Brighton BN2 1EN

Telephone:
01273 292718 (railway)

Internet address: *Web site:* www.brighton-hove.gov.uk or the Volks Electric Railway Association website: www.volkselectricrailway.co.uk

Motor cars

Nos	*Type*	*Seats*	*Body*	*Built*
3, 4	Semi-opens	40	—	1892
5	Winter car		—	1930
6, 7, 8	Semi-opens	40	—	1901
9	Open	40	—	1910
10	Open	40	—	1926

Main stations: Aquarium, Black Rock (5min walk from Marina)

Other public stations: Peter Pan's Playground

Car parks: Along the Promenade and town centre car parks

Access by public transport:
Main line trains to Brighton
Bus services: No 7 from station tTo Marina (every 7min) then short walk to Black Rock station; Nos 12 and 13 from Churchill Square, Nos 14 and 27 from main line station (also 77 on Sundays and weekdays during local school holidays)

Depot: Peter Pan's Playground

Length of line: Approx 1 mile, 2ft 8.5in gauge

Period of public operations:
Weekdays (11.00-17.00)
Weekends (11.00-18.00)

Facilities for disabled: Disabled toilets in Black Rock station building and 50yd from Aquarium. Disabled access to stations and trains

Museum

Weardale Railway

Co Durham

Member: HRA

The line was originally built by the Stockton & Darlington Railway in 1847 to transport limestone to the ironworks of Teesside, and by 1895 had been extended to its final terminus of Wearhead. Although the passenger service was withdrawn in 1953, the line was retained for freight use transporting bulk cement from the Blue Circle works at Eastgate. This use also ceased in 1993, so the line was mothballed and threatened with lifting. 1993 saw the formation of the Weardale Railway with services re-commencing in 2004. Services ceased a few months later with the line going into administration. At the time of going to press an offer was in-hand to restart passenger services. Please see local or railway press for details

Director: Steve Raine

Sales & Marketing: : Tim Hall

Headquarters: Weardale Railways Ltd, Stanhope Station, Stanhope, Nr Bishop Auckland, Co Durham DL13 2YS

Telephone: 01388 526203

Fax: 01388 529286

Internet addresses: *e-mail:* info@weardale-railway.co.uk
Web site: www.weardale-railway.co.uk

Main stations: Wolsingham and Stanhope

Other public stations: Frosterley,. Eastgate (beyond Stanhope) will eventually be the terminus

Car park: Limited parking at each station

Access by public transport: Buses from Bishop Auckland and Crook daily. Main line station at Bishop Auckland

Locomotives and multiple-units

Name	*No*	*Origin*	*Class*	*Type*	*Built*
—	20189*	BR	20	Bo-Bo	1967
—	37414	BR	37	Co-Co	1965
—	55503	BR	141	DMS	1984
—	55510	BR	141	DMS	1984
—	55523	BR	141	DMSL	1984
—	55530	BR	141	DMSL	1984

*undergoing overhaul off-site

Industrial locomotives

Name	*No*	*Builder*	*Type*	*Built*
Met	—	H/Leslie (2800)	0-4-0ST	1909
Mardy Monster	—	Peckett (2150)	0-6-0ST	1954

Refreshment facilities: Stanhope (the Signal Box Café) in station building with light refreshments
Souvenir shop: Stanhope (Lamp Room Gift Shop)
Depot: Wolsingham (no public access)
Length of line: 5 miles. 7.5 miles when Eastgate opens in June 2005. 18.5 miles when fully opened
Period of public operation: Daily late March to end October (provisional only, please contact for confirmation
Special events: Several planned and *may* include Santa Specials, Days out with Thomas, Teddy Bears Picnic, and Transport Festival during last weekend in June
Membership details: Mr Frank Holmes, Membership Secretary, Weardale Railway Trust, at above address. Tel: 01388 526262
Membership journal: *Between the Lines* — quarterly

Timetable Service

Wells & Walsingham Light Railway

Norfolk

Member: HRA, TT
One man's railway, the life and love of retired naval commander, Roy Francis, this delightful line which is totally uncommercialised runs along the old Wells branch to Walsingham where the old station has been transformed into a Russian Orthodox Church by the addition of an onion-shaped dome to its roof. A must if you find yourself nearby
Location: On A149, Stiffkey Road, Wells next the Sea, Norfolk
General Manager: Lt-Cdr R. W. Francis
Operating organisation: Wells & Walsingham Light Railway, Wells next the Sea, Norfolk NR23 1RB
Enquires: 01328 711630
Car park: Yes
Access by public transport: Eastern Counties buses
On site facilities: Souvenir shop, toilets and tea shop
Length of line: 4 miles, 10.25in gauge
Public opening: Daily Good Friday to the end of October
Special notes: Journey may be commenced at either end. Believed to be the world's longest 10.25in gauge line. Built on the old Wells & Fakenham Railway trackbed. Old Swainsthorpe signalbox on site at Wells. Motive power is provided by a Garratt and a tram locomotive.
Life passes in the form of a gilt edged enamel medallion now available, please enquire for details
Facilities for disabled: Disabled can be seated in normal carriages and wheelchairs carried in luggage van. Occupied wheelchairs cannot be carried due to limitations of track gauge
Membership details: Membership Secretary, Wells & Walsingham Light Railway Support Group, c/o above address
Membership journal: Newsletter — quarterly

Timetable Service

Wensleydale Railway

North Yorkshire

The Wensleydale Railway Association was formed in 1990 with a view to restoring the route from Northallerton to Garsdale. In 2000 agreement was reached to transfer the remaining 22 miles of line from Northallerton to Redmire to Wensleydale Railway plc. In 2003 services started between Leeming Bar and Leyburn, extending in 2004 to Redmire. Medium term plans are to extend eastwards to Northallerton and in the west from Redmire and then on towards Aysgarth. The ultimate aim is to restore the entire route from Northallerton to Garsdale
Membership: HRA
Contact address:
Wensleydale Railway plc, Leeming

Locomotives and multiple-units

Name	*No*	*Origin*	*Class*	*Type*	*Built*
—	31166	BR	31	A1A-A1A	1960
—	31188	BR	31	A1A-A1A	1960
—	37003	BR	37	Co-Co	1960
—	37198	BR	37	Co-Co	1964
—	37275	BR	37	Co-Co	1965
—	51210	BR	101	DMBS	1958
—	51247	BR	101	DMBS	1958
—	53746	BR	101	DMC	1957
—	59500	BR	117	TSL	1959
—	59505	BR	117	TSL	1959
—	59509	BR	117	TSL	1959
—	51813	BRCW	110	DMBC	1961
—	51842	BRCW	110	DMCL	1961
—	59701	BRCW	110	TSL	1961

Industrial locomotives

Name	*No*	*Builder*	*Type*	*Built*
—	—	R/Hornsby (476141)	4wDM	1963

Bar Station, Leases Road, Leeming Bar, Northallerton DL7 9AR
Ticketline: 08454 505474
Fax: 01677 776240
Internet addresses: *e-mail:* admin@wensleydalerailway.com
Web site: www.wensleydalerailway.com
Main stations: Leeming Bar and Leyburn
Other stations: Bedale, Finghall and Redmire
Car Parking: On site
Access by public transport: Yes
Refreshment facilities: Leeming Bar
Souvenir shops: Leeming Bar and Leyburn
Depots: Leeming Bar
Length of line: 22 miles; 18 additional miles to rebuild)

Owners
Class 31s by Colne Valley Diesels
Class 37s the Class 37 Loco Group and Bedale Locomotives
Class 101 and 117 by Wensleydale Railway plc
Class 110 by Allan Schofield
R/Hornsby by the Wensleydale Railway Association

Passenger trains: See above
Period of public operation: Daily Easter to Autumn, Santa Special Events and winter weekends Phone ticketline for current brochure 08454 505474 or see web site
Facilities for disabled: Under improvement, but ramp to facilitate access to trains and access to both platforms are wheelchair friendly
Membership details: Wensleydale Railway Association: Secretary, Ruth Annison, Dyke House, Askrigg, Leyburn, N Yorks DL8 3HG
Membership journal: *Relay* – 4 per year.
Special notes: Very helpful tourist information centre at Leyburn – tel 01969 623069 – will deal with a wide range of enquiries including Wensleydale Railway matters

West Lancashire Light Railway

Steam Centre — Lancashire

Member: HRA
The WLLR is located in the village of Hesketh Bank, midway between Preston and Southport. Built by enthusiasts in 1967 in an endeavour to conserve some of the mainly industrial equipment that was fast disappearing. The railway serves as a working museum for a variety of historic locomotives and other railway equipment from industrial sites from Britain and overseas
Location: Alty's Brickworks, Station Road, Hesketh Bank, Nr Preston, Lancashire PR4 6SP
OS reference: SD 448229
Operating society/organisation: The West Lancashire Light Railway Association, Secretary, 8 Croft Avenue, Orrell, Wigan, Lancs WN5 8TW
Telephone: (01772) 815881 Railway (24hr) or (01695) 622654 Secretary (evenings)
Internet address: *e-mail:* sec@westlancs.org
Web site: www.westlancs.org
Car parks: On site
Access by public transport: Main line rail to Preston or Southport. Bus routes 100 and 102, between Preston and Southport
On site facilities: Gift shop, light refreshments, picnic tables, 2ft

Industrial locomotives

Name	*No*	*Builder*	*Type*	*Built*
Clwyd	1	R/Hornsby (264251)	4wDM	1951
Tawd	2	R/Hornsby (222074)	4wDM	1943
Irish Mail	3	Hunslet (823)	0-4-0ST	1903
Bradfield	4	Hibberd (1777)	4wPM	1931
—	5	R/Hornsby (200478)	4wDM	1940
—	7	M/Rail (8992)	4wDM	1946
Pathfinder	8	H/Hunslet (4480)	4wDM	1953
Joffre	9	K/Stuart (2405)	0-6-0T	1915
—	10	Hibberd (2555)	4wDM	1946
—	11	M/Rail (5906)	4wDM	1934
—	16	R/Hornsby (202036)	4wDM	1941
—	19	Lister (10805)	4wPM	1939
—	20	Baguley (3002)	4wPM	1937
—	21	H/Hunslet (1963)	4wDM	1939
—	25	R/Hornsby (297054)	4wDM	1950
—	26	M/Rail (11223)	4wDM	1963
Mill Reef	27	M/Rail (7371)	4wDM	1939
—	30	M/Rail (11258)	4wDM	1964
Montalban	34	O&K (6641)	0-4-0WT	1913
Utrillas	35	O&K (2378)	0-4-0WT	1907
—	36	R/Hornsby (339105)	4wDM	1953
—	38	Hudswell (D750)	0-4-0DM	1949
—	39	Hibberd (3916)	4wDM	1959
—	40	R/Hornsby (381705)	4wDM	1959
—	41	Lister (29890)	4wPM	1946
—	43	Greenbat (1840)	4wBE	1942
Welsh Pony	44	Wingrove (640)	4wWE	1926
—	45	Chrzanow (3506)	0-6-0T+WT	1957
Stanhope	46	K/Stuart (2395)	0-4-2ST	1917
—	47	Henschel (14676)	0-8-0T	1917
—	48	Fowler (15513)	0-4-2T	1920

gauge line
Public opening: Trains commence 2 April and then operate every Sunday to 29 October, plus Bank Holiday Mondays. Opening times 12.30-17.30
Special events: Friendly Engines Day — 2 April; Easter — Good Friday (14 April) Easter Monday (17 April); Teddy Bears' Day — 14 May; Gala Weekend — 12/13 August, Autumn Gala (Fun Trains) — 8 October; Santa Specials — 16/17, 23/24 December
Membership details: The Hon Secretary, WLLR, Station Road, Hesketh Bank, Nr Preston, Lancashire PR4 6SP

Stock
Toastrack coach built 1986 by WLLR
Semi-open coach built 1993 by WLLR
Brake van built 1987 by WLLR
Large collection of goods rolling stock

Timetable Service

West Somerset Railway

Somerset

Member: HRA, TT
Running for 20 miles, the WSR is Britain's longest standard gauge heritage line and superbly captures the secondary main line atmosphere of the great age of steam. There are many points of railway interest. Williton signalbox is the only working example built by the Bristol & Exeter Railway and Blue Anchor box still controls a traditionally operated level crossing. Destinations served include the historic port of Watchet and medieval Dunster with its castle
Managing Director: Mark L. Smith
Headquarters: West Somerset Railway, The Railway Station, Minehead, Somerset TA24 5BG
Telephone:
Minehead (01643) 704996
Internet address: *e-mail:*
info@west-somerset-railway.co.uk
Web site:
www.west-somerset-railway.co.uk
WAP-phone:
www.wapdrive.com/wsrwap/
Main station: Minehead
Other public stations: Dunster, Blue Anchor, Washford, Watchet, Williton, Doniford Halt, Stogumber, Crowcombe, Bishops Lydeard
OS reference: Minehead SS 975463, Williton ST 085416, Bishops Lydeard ST 164290

Locomotives and multiple-units

Name	*No*	*Origin*	*Class*	*Type*	*Built*
—	88	S&DJR	7F	2-8-0	1925
—	3850	GWR	2884	2-8-0	1942
—	4160	GWR	5101	2-6-2T	1948
—	4561	GWR	4500	2-6-2T	1924
—	9351	GWR	9351	2-6-0	2004
—	5542†	GWR	4575	2-6-2T	1928
—	6412	GWR	6400	0-6-0PT	1934
Dinmore Manor	7820	GWR	'Manor'	4-6-0	1950
Odney Manor	7828	GWR	'Manor'	4-6-0	1950
Braunton	34046	SR	WC	4-6-2	1946
—	80136	BR	4MT	2-6-4T	1956
—	D2119	BR	03	0-6-0DM	1959
—	D2133	BR	03	0-6-0DM	1959
—	D2271	BR	04	0-6-0DM	1952
—	D3462	BR	08	0-6-0DE	1957
—	D9526	BR	14	0-6-0DH	1964
—	25173	BR	25	Bo-Bo	1963
—	D6566	BR	33	Bo-Bo	1961
—	D6575	BR	33	Bo-Bo	1961
—	D7017	BR	35	B-B	1962
—	D7018	BR	35	B-B	1962
Western Campaigner	D1010	BR	52	C-C	1962
—	50413	P/Royal	103	DMBS	1957
—	51663	BR	115	DMBS	1960
—	51852	BR	115	DMBS	1960
—	51859	BR	115	DMBS	1960
—	51880	BR	115	DMBS	1960
—	51887	BR	115	DMBS	1960
—	56169	P/Royal	103	DTCL	1957
—	59506	BR	117	TC	1960
—	59678	BR	115	TC	1960

Note: 9351 rebuilt from '5151' class 2-6-2T No 5193
†on South Devon Railway during 2006

Car parks: Free parking at Bishops Lydeard, Dunster and Williton. Pay & display at Minehead and Watchet. No parking at Doniford Halt
Access by public transport: Nearest main line station, Taunton. First Bus (01823) 272033
Refreshment facilities: Minehead, Bishops Lydeard (limited opening). Dining Trains from Bishops Lydeard (01823 433856). Please contact for dates, reservations essential.
Buffet car on most steam trains
Souvenir shops: Large shops at Bishops Lydeard and Minehead. Sales counters at other stations except Doniford Halt. 'Readers Halt' secondhand stall at Minehead
Museum: Somerset & Dorset Railway Museum Trust, Washford (contact 01984 640869 for opening times). GWR Museum at Blue Anchor (open Sundays & Bank

Industrial locomotives

Name	*No*	*Builder*	*Type*	*Built*
Isabel	—	H/Leslie (3437)	0-6-0ST	1919
Kilmersdon	—	Peckett (1788)	0-4-0ST	1929
—	24	Ruston (210479)	4wDM	1941
—	—	Ruston (183062)	4wDM	1937
—	16	Sentinel (10175)	0-6-0DH	1964
—	501	Brush/Bagnall (3066)	0-4-0DE	1954
—	512	Brush/Bagnall (3102)	0-4-0DE	1954

Stock
21 ex-BR Mk 1 coaches; 2 ex-BR Restaurant cars; 1 ex-BR Sleeping car; 3 ex-S&DJR 6-wheel coaches, 7 ex-GWR camping coaches; 1 ex-GWR Sleeping coach; 1 ex-GWR 5-ton hand crane; more than 40 freight vehicles

Owners
88, *Isabel, Kilmersdon* the Somerset & Dorset Museum Trust
D1010, D7017, D7018 and D9526 the Diesel and Electric Preservation Group
D2119, D3462 and D7523 Dr John F. Kennedy
5542 the 5542 Ltd
3850 and 7820 the Dinmore Manor Locomotive Ltd
4160 the 4160 Ltd
7828, 9351 and D2271 the WSR plc

The road bridge to the north of Bishops Lydeard station on the West Somerset Railway provides a good vantage spot for photographers as can be seen here. No 9351 prepares to head towards Minehead. *ACB*

Holidays WSR operating season). Gauge Museum at Bishops Lydeard (open daily). Diesel Heritage Visitor Centre open Saturdays May-September
Depots: Bishops Lydeard, Williton, Washford, Minehead
Length of line: 20 miles
Passenger trains: Steam and diesel trains to Bishops Lydeard
Period of public operation: 4/5, 11/12, 18/19, 23-25, 26, 28-31, March; daily April (EXCEPT 3/4, 7, 10, 24, 28); daily May (EXCEPT 8, 12, 15, 19, 22); daily in June, July, August and September; daily October (EXCEPT 2, 9, 13, 16, 20, 30); 1/2 November; 27 December-2 January 2007
Main special events: Spring Steam Gala — 18/19, 23-26 March; Days out with Thomas — 8/9 July; Steam Fayre & Vintage Rally at Bishops Lydeard — 5/6 August; CAMRA Real Ale Festival at Minehead — 17/18 September; Grand Trains Extravaganza — 21/22 October; Dunster by Candlelight — 2/3 December (advance booking essential); Carol Trains — 11/12 December (advance booking essential); Santa Specials — 2/3, 9/10, 16/17, 22-24 December (advance booking essential); Winter Steam Festival — 29 December
Other special events: Fish & Chip Specials — 6 May, 24 June, 12, 26 August; Murder Mystery Night Specials — 17 June, 8 July, 2 September, 1, 22 October, 16 December; Jazz Evenings — 2 July; Cream & Steam— 2, 9, 16, 23 June, 7, 14, 21 July, 11, 18, 25 August, 1, 8 September; Father's Day Specials — 18 June; Advance booking essential for most of the above, please ask for Catering Specials leaflet
Facilities for disabled: Trains have limited accommodation for passengers in wheelchairs. There is level or ramped access to all stations except Doniford, and RADAR key access toilets at Bishops Lydeard and Minehead. Advance booking essential for groups
Membership details: West Somerset Railway Association, The Railway Station, Bishops Lydeard, Taunton TA4 3BX.
Tel: 01823 433856
Membership journal: *WSR Journal* — quarterly

Museum

Winchcombe Railway Museum

Glos

One mile from Winchcombe station on the Gloucestershire Warwickshire railway, the diverse collection includes signalling equipment, lineside fixtures, horse-drawn road vehicles, tickets, lamps, etc. Indoor and outdoor displays set in half an acre of traditional Victorian Cotswold garden. Visitors are encouraged to touch and operate exhibits
Location: 23 Gloucester Street, Winchcombe, Gloucestershire
OS reference: SP 023283
Operating society/organisation: Winchcombe Railway Museum Association, 23 Gloucester Street, Winchcombe, Gloucestershire
Telephone: Winchcombe (01242) 609305
Car park: On street at entrance
Access by public transport: Bus service from Cheltenham operated by Castleways Ltd
On site facilities: Relics and souvenir shop
Public opening: Easter to end October 2006.
Wednesdays, Thursdays, Fridays, weekends and Bank Holiday Mondays — 13.30-17.00; daily throughout August — 13.30-17.00
Facilities for disabled: Access to all parts except toilets
Special notes: Many visitor-operated exhibits, picnic area, pet animals

Steam Centre

Windmill Farm Railway

Lancashire

The line was set up in 1997 by Austin Moss as a place to store and operate the historic engines and rolling stock he had collected. Of particular interest is the collection of ex-Fairbourne Railway locomotives and rolling stock; these include *Katie* and *Whippet Quick*.
Location: Situated within the grounds of Windmill Animal Farm
Headquarters: Windmill Animal Farm, Red Cat Lane, Burscough, L40 1UQ
Contact: Austin Moss
Telephone: Farm 01704 892282; Austin Moss 07971 221343;
Internet address: *Web site:* www.windmillfarmrailway.co.uk
Main station: At Farm
Other station: Lakeview, 1/2 mile away
Car parking: On site
Access by public transport: None
On site facilities: Farm café, shop
Depots: At farm site
Length of line: 1/2 mile each way (1 mile return) 15in gauge

Period of public operation: 14 February to Christmas 10.00-17.00. Weekends March to December. Daily Easter to end of September plus school holidays. Santa weekends in December, Daily June to September plus school holidays
Trains every 1/2 hour from 11.00 until 16.30
Special events: None planned but see web site
Facilities for disabled: Accessibility for wheelchairs around farm facilities etc, prior warning on railway
Membership details: No membership as such, just volunteer. Contact Austin Moss for details
Fare: £1.00 adults, 75p children plus farm entry fee.

Industrial locomotives

Name	*No*	*Builder*	*Type*	*Built*
Blue Pacific	4	Guinness	4-6-0VB	1935
Whippet Quick	–	Lister	4w-4DM	1935
Gwril	–	Lister	4wPM	1943
Princess Anne	—	Barlow	4-6w-2DE	1948
Duke of Edinburgh	—	Barlow	4-6-2	1950
Prince Charles	—	Barlow	4-6-2	1950
Katie	—	Guest	2-4-2	1953
Siân	—	Guest	2-4-2	1963
Connie	_	Severn-Lamb	2-8-0DH	1974
Neptune / (St Nicholas)	_	Severn-Lamb	2-8-0GH	1978
–	14	Walker	2w-2PM	1985
City Of London Jubilee	2870	Volante	4-6-0DH	1987
'The Bar Stool'	—	Moss	2w-2PM	1989
St Christopher	—	Exmoor	2-6-2T	2001

Railway Centre | Yeovil Railway Centre | Somerset

Member: HRA
The Yeovil Railway Centre is operated by the South West Main Line Steam Co and is adjacent to the former London & South Western Railway main line at Yeovil Junction. It features the original British Railways turntable
Location: Adjacent to the main line at Yeovil Junction on the London (Waterloo)-Salisbury-Exeter line
Chaiman: Richard Abbott
Contact address: South Western Main Line Steam Co (Yeovil Railway Centre), Yeovil Junction Station, Stoford, Nr Yeovil, Somerset BA22 9UU
Telephone: 01935 410420
Fax: 01935 478373
Internet address: *Web site:* www.yeovilrailway.free servers.com
Car park: On site. Follow signs to Yeovil Junction from Yeovil town centre or from A35 Dorchester-Yeovil road
Access by public transport: SouthWest Trains to Yeovil Junction or bus from Yeovil Bus station
On site facilities: Exhibition of relics and photographs in the newly acquired transfer shed (dating from 1864) and shop. Light refreshments when brake van rides are operating
Length of line: 500 metres
Opening times: Shop open Sunday mornings throughout the year (except Christmas/New Year). Train Days are planned for 1st and 3rd Sundays April to September inclusive. 11.00-16.30 when brake van rides, shunting and turntable demonstrations feature. Also open on days when main line steam is being serviced (telephone or see web site for details), for Santa Specials in December and special events
Special events: Model Railways — 21 May; Arts & Crafts — 3/4 June; Real Ale — 16 (evening)/17 June; Military Weekend — 29/30 July; Traction Display — 17 September; Arts & Crafts — 30 September/1 October; Santa Specials — 10, 17, 23/24 December
Disabled access: To site, but no wheelchair access (at present) to brake van rides
Membership details: Quentin McConnell, High Croft, Yeovil Junction, Stoford, Somerset BA22 9UU
Membership journal: *The Turntable*, quarterly

Locomotive

Name	*No*	*Origin*	*Class*	*Type*	*Built*
Fearless	50050	BR	50	Co-Co	1967

Industrial locomotive

Name	*No*	*Builder*	*Type*	*Built*
Pectin	—	Peckett (1579)	0-4-0ST	1921
—	—	Fowler (22900)	0-4-0DM	1941
—	—	Fowler (22900)	0-4-0DM	1947
Yeo	—	R/Hornsby (4000007)	4wDM	1961

Locomotive notes: Main line locomotives occasionally present for servicing during railtours

Rolling stock: Selection of freight wagons

Scotland

Steam Centre | Alford Valley Railway | Aberdeenshire

The Alford Valley Railway operates from the restored station yard which once marked the terminus of the branch line linking the villages of upper Donside with Kintore Junction, thence to Aberdeen
Location: On A944, 25 miles west of Aberdeen, adjacent to Grampian Transport Museum
Headquarters: Alford Valley Railway Co Ltd, Alford Station, Alford, Aberdeenshire
Internet adress: *Web site:* www.alford.org.uk/avr.htm
Main station: Alford
Car park: On site
Length of line: 3km, 2ft gauge
Museum: Grampian Transport Museum adjacent
Depot: Alford station
Period of public operation: Railway operates: April, May September — weekends only (13.00-17.00); June, July and August — daily 13.00-17.00. Trains depart at 30min intervals. Seasonal tickets available.
Alford Heritage Centre is open daily (10.00-17.00)
Special events: Easter Fayre, Santa Specials — please contact for details
Membership details: Membership Secretary, AVR Association, Creagmwor, Main Street, Alford, Aberdeenshire AB33 8AD

Industrial locomotives

Name	*No*	*Builder*	*Type*	*Built*
Hamewith	—	Lister (3198)	4wDM	c1930
—	—	A/Keef (63)	4wDM	2001
—	—	M/Rail (22129)	4wDM	1962
—	—	M/Rail (2221)	4wDM	1964
James Gordon	—	Keef (63)	0-4-0T (SO)	2001
Aberdeen Corporation Gas Works	3*	A/Barclay (1889)	0-4-0ST	1926

*standard gauge

Rolling stock

Two 24-seat coaches, 50-seat coach, 24-seat ex-Aberdeen tramcar, various wagons

Museum | Almond Valley Heritage Trust | West Lothian

Member: HRA
Part of a wide-ranging heritage centre containing a museum of Scotland's shale oil industry with award winning children's exhibits, working watermill, farmsteading with traditional livestock. indoor play areas, countryside walks and farmhouse kitchen tea room.
Operating society/organisation: Almond Valley Heritage Centre, Millfield, Livingston Village, West Lothian EH54 7AR
OS reference: NT 034667
Telephone: 01506 414957
Fax: 01506 497771
Internet address: *e-mail:* info@almondvalley.co.uk

Industrial locomotives

Name	*No*	*Builder*	*Type*	*Built*
05/576	—	Barclay (557)	4wDH	1970
Oil Company No 2	—	Baldwin (20587)	4wWE	1902
—	20	Brook Victor (612)	4wBE	1972
—	38	Brook Victor (698)	4wBE	1972
—	42	Brook Victor (700)	4wBE	1972
—	—	Brook Victor (1143)	4wBE	1972
3585	13	Greenwood (1698)	4wBE	1940
ND3059	Yard No B10	Hunslet (2270)	0-4-0DM	1940
—	7330	Hunslet (7330)	4wDM	1973
—	—	Simplex (40SPF522)	4wDM	1981
—	—	B/Drewry (3752)	4wDM	1980

Note

Barclay 557 and Hunslet 2270 operate passenger services

Web site: www.almondvalley.co.uk
Access by public transport: Main line trains to Livingston North (1 mile)
On site facilities: Children's exhibits, indoor play areas, tea room
Public opening: Daily (except 25/26 December, 1/2 January) 10.00-17.00.
Trains operate weekends from March-September, daily July and August and certain public holidays
Length of line: 500m 2ft 6in gauge line from Livingston Mill to Almondhaugh stations, with plans to extend
Facilities for disabled: Full disabled access to site, but not to coaches

Timetable Service

Bo'ness & Kinneil Railway

West Lothian

Member: HRA, TT, Registered Museum
Historic railway buildings, including the station and train shed, have been relocated from sites all over Scotland. In two purpose-built exhibition halls, the Scottish Railway Exhibition tells the story of the development of the railways in Scotland, and their impact on the people. The rich geology of the area, with its 300 million year old fossils, is explained during a conducted tour of the caverns of the former Birkhill Fireclay Mine
Operating society/location: Scottish Railway Preservation Society, Bo'ness Station, Union Street, Bo'ness, West Lothian, EH51 9AQ
Access by public transport: Nearest ScotRail station — Linlithgow. Bus services from Linlithgow, Falkirk, Stirling
OS reference: NT 003817
Telephone: Train services & Events 01506 825855
Talking timetable: 01506 822298
Fax: 01506 828766
Internet address: *e-mail:* enquiries@srps.org.uk
Web site: www.srps.org.uk
Main station: Bo'ness
Other station: Birkhill
Car parks: At Bo'ness and Birkhill (free)
Refreshment facilities: Extensive (unlicensed) buffet at Bo'ness. Picnic tables at both stations
Souvenir shop: Bo'ness
Depot: Bo'ness
Length of line: 3.5 miles
Period of public operation: Weekends 1 April-29 October, Tuesdays and Thursdays 29 May-29 June, daily 1 July-27 August (Mondays diesel-hauled)

Locomotives

Name	*No*	*Origin*	*Class*	*Type*	*Built*
—	419	CR	439	0-4-4T	1908
Morayshire	246	LNER	D49	4-4-0	1928
Glen Douglas	256	NBR	D34	4-4-0	1913
—	42	NBR	Y9	0-4-0ST	1887
Maude	673	NBR	J36	0-6-0	1891
—	80105	BR	4MT	2-6-4T	1955
—	D2774	BR	—	0-4-0DH	1960
—	08443 (D3558)	BR	08	0-6-0DE	1958
—	14901 (D9524)	BR	14	0-6-0DH	1964
—	D8020	BR	20	Bo-Bo	1959
—	25235 (D7585)	BR	25	Bo-Bo	1965
—	25309 (D7659)	BR	25	Bo-Bo	1966
—	26004 (D5303)	BR	26	B0-Bo	1958
—	26024 (D5323)	BR	26	Bo-Bo	1959
—	27001 (D5347)	BR	27	Bo-Bo	1961
—	D5351	BR	27	Bo-Bo	1961
—	37025	BR	37	Co-Co	1961
—	47643	BR	47	Co-Co	1968
—	51017*	BR	126	DMS	1959
—	51043	BR	126	DMS	1959
—	59404	BR	126	TC	1959
—	79443	BR	126	TRBF	1956

*at Midland Railway — Butterley for restoration

Industrial locomotives

Name	*No*	*Builder*	*Type*	*Built*
Clydesmill	3	Barclay (1937)	0-4-0ST	1928
—	3	Barclay (2046)	0-4-0ST	1937
—	24	Barclay (2335)	0-6-0T	1953
Texaco	—†	Fowler (4210140)	0-4-0DM	1958
(Lord King)	—	H/Leslie (3640)	0-4-0ST	1926
—	19	Hunslet (3818)	0-6-0ST	1954
DS3	—	R/Hornsby (275883)	4wDM	1949
DS4	P6687	R/Hornsby (312984)	0-4-0DE	1951
(Ranald)	—	Sentinel (9627)	4wVBT	1957
—	970214	Wickham (6050)	2w-2PMR	c1951
—	—	Matisa (48626)	—	—
—	5	Hunslet (3837)	0-6-0ST	1955
—	(7)	Bagnall (2777)	0-6-0ST	1945
Borrowstounness	—*	Barclay (840)	0-4-0T	1899
—	—*	M/Rail (110U082)	4wDH	1970
—	—	Wickham (10482)	2w-2PMR	1970
—	(17)	Hunslet (2880)	0-6-0ST	1943
—	970213	Wickham (6049)	2w-2PMR	c1951
—	17†	Barclay (2296)	0-4-0ST	1952

Special events: Easter Egg Specials — 14-17 April; Diesel Gala — 29/30 April; Steam & Diesel Day — 1 May; Day out with Thomas — 20/21 May; Transport Through The Ages — 17/18 June; Day out with Thomas — 11-13 August; Diesel Gala — 2/3 September; Day out with Thomas — 16/17 September; Steam 'n' Scream — 28/29 October; Santa Specials — 2/3, 9/10, 16/17, 23/24 December; Black Bun Specials — 30/31 December

Facilities for disabled: Disabled access to platform and a specially adapted carriage for wheelchair users. Toilets at Bo'ness station. No facilities for wheelchairs at Birkhill Fireclay Mine

Special notes: The Heritage Railway Association Award 2005 was given to the volunteers of the SRPS for establishing the Living Museum of Scotland's Railways over the past 25 years.

Birkhill Fireclay Mine and Scottish Railway Exhibition open same days as trains operate (except December)

Name	*No*	*Builder*	*Type*	*Built*
Lady Victoria	3	Barclay (1458)	0-6-0ST	1916
The Wemyss Coal Co Ltd	20	Barclay (2068)	0-6-0T	1939
—	(6)	Barclay (2127)	0-4-0CT	1942
No 1	—	Barclay (343)	0-6-0DM	1941
City of Aberdeen	—	B/Hawthorn (912)	0-4-0ST	1887
F82 (Fairfield)	—	E/Electric (1131) (244)	4wBE	1940
Kelton Fell	13	Neilson (2203)	0-4-0ST	1876
Lord Roberts	1§	N/Reid (5710)	0-6-0T	1902
(Tiger)	—	N/British (27415)	0-4-0DH	1954
Kilbagie	DS2	R/Hornsby (262998)	4wDM	1949
—	—	R/Hornsby (321733)	4wDM	1952
DS6	(1)	R/Hornsby (421439)	0-4-0DE	1958
St Mirren	(3)	R/Hornsby (423658)	0-4-0DE	1958
—	D88/003	R/Hornsby (506500)	4wDM	1965
(Denis)	—	Sentinel (9631)	4wVBT	1958
—	—	Arrols (Glasgow)	2w-2DM	c1966

*3ft 0in gauge
†at present off site at Scottish Vintage Bus Museum, Lathalmond, Fife
§official licensed 'Thomas' replica locomotive

Stock

A large selection of coaching stock, many built by Scottish pre-Grouping companies, ex-BR Class 126 DMU, and an appropriate collection of early freight vehicles

Owner

80105 and (*Denis*) owned by Locomotive Owners Group (Scotland)
246 and 24 owned by Royal Museum of Scotland
256 the Glasgow Museum of Transport
27001 the Class 27 Preservation Group
26004 and 26024 the 6LDA Group
37025 the Scottish Class 37 Group

Timetable Service

Caledonian Railway (Brechin)

Angus

Member: HRA

This Scottish country steam railway is a classic branch line starting at the Strathmore line junction station of Bridge of Dun, last stomping ground of the Gresley 'A4' Pacific locomotives, and climbs some steep gradients through scenic farmland with assorted wildlife and flora. The summit is reached at the Edzell & Forfar junction just short of Brechin station, itself one of the most impressive of Britain's preserved railways.

The National Trust for Scotland property House of Dun, built by William Adam in 1730, is approximately 1 mile from Bridge of Dun station, which is also close

Locomotives

Name	*No*	*Origin*	*Class*	*Type*	*Built*
Brechin City	D3059	BR	08	0-6-0DE	1954
*—	12052	BR	11	0-6-0DE	1949
*—	12093	BR	11	0-6-0DE	1951
—	25072	BR	25	Bo-Bo	1963
—	25083	BR	25	Bo-Bo	1963
—	D5314	BR	26	Bo-Bo	1959
—	26035	BR	26	Bo-Bo	1959
—	27024	BR	27	Bo-Bo	1962
Loch Joy	37097	BR	37	Co-Co	1962

*on loan from Scottish Industrial Railway Centre

Industrial locomotives

Name	*No*	*Builder*	*Type*	*Built*
—†	—	Barclay (1863)	0-4-0ST	1926
Harlaxton†	—	Barclay (2107)	0-6-0T	1941
BAC No 1	—	Peckett (1376)	0-4-0ST	1915
Menelaus	—	Peckett (1889)	0-6-0ST	1935

to the Montrose Basin, a tidal wildlife centre. Brechin itself has many attractions including the cathedral and round tower and the new Pictavia centre.

The railway is run entirely by volunteer members of the Brechin Railway Preservation Society

Headquarters: Caledonian Railway (Brechin) Ltd, The Station, 2 Park Road, Brechin, Angus DD9 7AF
Telephone: 01356 622992 (or 07740 363958)
Internet address: *e-mail:* calrail@engineer.com
Web site: www.caledonianrailway.co.uk
Main stations: Brechin and Bridge of Dun
OS reference: NO 603603
Car park: Brechin, Bridge of Dun
Access by car: Via A90 Dundee/Aberdeen to Brechin bypass. Brown tourist signs to stations. Free parking
Access by public transport: By ScotRail, GNER and Virgin services to Montrose (5 miles). By bus from Montrose, Strathtay Scottish — Dundee (01382) 228054/227201
Refreshment facilities: Light refreshments at Brechin on operating days
Picnic area: Bridge of Dun
Souvenir shop: Brechin
Museum: Brechin
Length of line: 4 miles 22 chains
Depot: Brechin
Passenger trains: Industrial steam and heritage diesel-hauled trains between Brechin and Bridge of Dun
Period of public operation: Steam trains run every Sunday end May to early September plus other dates as shown below. Brechin station is open daily for static viewing Tuesday-Friday 11.00-16.00, Bridge of Dun site open daily all week
Special events: Easter Specials — 15/16 April; Father's Day — 18 June; Day out with Thomas — 1/2, 8/9 July;Day out with Thomas — 26/27 August; Santa Specials — 9/10, 16/17, 23/24 December. Murder Mystery Evenings — please contact for details
Facilities for disabled: Ramp access to both stations. Vehicular access to Brechin platforms by prior arrangement. Coach converted to take wheelchairs and attendants, prior notice required for access and car parking
Family tickets: Available
Disclaimer: The Caledonian Railway (Brechin) Ltd reserves the right to amend, cancel or add to these events. And whilst every effort will be made to maintain the above services, the company does not guarantee that trains will depart or arrive at the time stated and reserves the right to suspend or alter any train without notice and will not accept any liability for loss, inconvenience or delay thereby caused
Membership details: M. Jackson, c/o above address
Membership journal: Quarterly
Marketing name: The Friendly Line

Name	*No*	*Builder*	*Type*	*Built*
FC Tingey†	—	Peckett (2084)	0-6-0ST	1948
—	5	Peckett (2153)	0-6-0ST	1954
Diana	1	Hunslet (2879)	0-6-0ST	1943
—	6	Bagnall (2749)	0-6-0ST	1944
—	16	Bagnall (2759)	0-6-0ST	1944
—	—	Hibberd (5198)	4wDM	1955
—	144-6	R/Hornsby (421700)	4wDM	1959
Dewar Highlander†	—	R/Hornsby (458957)	4wDM	1961

†expected to be operational during 2006, others in store/under restoration

Coaching Stock
In service 6 x BR Mk 1, 3 x BR Mk 2s
Stored 4 x BR Mk 1s, plus 1 x BR Mk 1 in use as volunteer accommodation
BR Mk 3a restaurant car in use as a buffet

Engineer's Stock
c50 wagons including: 1 ex-BR diesel-electric 12-ton crane, 2 Dogfish, 1 Mermaid, 4 warflats, 3 rectanks, 1 Ferry van, 2 Lowmacs, 2 minfit, 1 21-ton minfit, 2 LNER vans, 2 LMS vans, 2 demountable tank wagons, 1 ex-BR bolster

Departmental Stock
1 CR origin electrification coach, 1 ex-BR BCK, various vans

Owners
No 1 and *Menelaus* the Angus Railway Steam Engineers
D5314 the Class Twenty Six Preservation Group
D3059, 26035 and 27024 the Caledonian Diesel Group

In addition to the above the following is under restoration adjacent to Bridge of Dun station

Locomotives

Name	*No*	*Origin*	*Class*	*Type*	*Built*
—	46464	LMS	2MT	2-6-0	1950

Museum

Glasgow Museum of Transport

Glasgow

Member: HRA, TT
Glasgow's Museum of Transport celebrated its 40th Anniversary in 2005. The museum uses its collections of vehicles and models to tell the story of transport by land and sea, with a unique Glasgow flavour.

The magnificent railway collection represents one of the best efforts by a municipal authority to preserve a representative collection of items appropriate to the 'locomotive builders of the Empire'

Access by public transport: Strathclyde PTE Underground. Kelvinhall: Strathclyde Buses 6, 6A, 8, 8A, 9, 9A, 16, 42, 42A, 57, 57A, 62, 62A, 62B, 64; Kelvin Scottish Buses 5, 5A; Clydeside Scottish Buses 17

Operating society/organisation: Glasgow City Council, Dept of Cultural & Leisure Services

Location: Museum of Transport, Kelvin Hall, 1 Bunhouse Road, Glasgow G3 8DP

Telephone: (0141) 287 2623 or (0141) 287 2721

Fax: (0141) 287 2692

Internet address: *Web site:* www.glasgowmuseums.com

Car park: Opposite Museum entrance

On site facilities: Toilets, cafeteria, shop and public telephone, cloaking facility

Public opening: Monday-Thursday 10.00-17.00; Friday and Sunday 11.00-17.00. Closed 1/2 January and 25/26 December only. Please check before travelling

Facilities for disabled: Both single-sex and uni-sex disabled facilities now available. A passenger lift to allow disabled access at the front entrance is now in operation

Locomotives

Name	*No*	*Origin*	*Class*	*Type*	*Built*
—	123	CR	123	4-2-2	1886
—	9	G&SWR	5	0-6-0T	1917
—	103	HR	—	4-6-0	1894
Gordon Highlander	49	GNSR	F	4-4-0	1920

Industrial locomotives

Name	*No*	*Builder*	*Type*	*Built*
—	1	Barclay (1571)	0-6-0F	1917
—	—	Chaplin (2368)	0-4-0TG	1888
—	—	BEV (583)	B	1927

Stock

Glasgow District Subway car 39T; Glasgow Corporation Underground cars 1 and 4; LMS King George VI's saloon 498 of 1941

Timetable Service

Keith & Dufftown Railway

Banffshire

Member: HRA
The Keith & Dufftown Railway is an 11 mile line linking the World's Malt Whisky Capital, Dufftown, to the market town of Keith. Re-opened to Keith in 2001, the line passes through some of Scotland's most picturesque scenery. The line links the two towns famous round the world for names such as Chivas Regal and Glenfiddich

Operating society/organisation: Keith & Dufftown Railway Association, Dufftown Station, Dufftown, Banffshire AB55 4BA

Contact: Maureen H. Webster (Chairman)

Telephone: (01340) 821181

Internet address: *e-mail:* kdra@dial.pipex.com
or

Locomotives and multiple-units

Name	*No*	*Origin*	*Class*	*Type*	*Built*
—	73119	BR	73	Bo-Bo	1966
—	51568	BR	108	DMC(L)	1959
—	56491	BR	108	DTC(L)	1959
—	53628	BR	108	DMBS	1958
—	52053	BR	108	DMC(L)	1960
—	55500*	BR	140	DMS	1981
—	55501*	BR	140	DMS	1981
—	Car 87§	M/Cam	5BEL	TPS	1932
—	Car 91§	M/Cam	5BEL	DMPBS	1932

§ex-'Brighton Belle' Pullman cars, converted to locomotive-hauled
*unit No 140001

Industrial locomotives

Name	*No*	*Builder*	*Type*	*Built*
Spirit o' Fife	—	E/Electric (D1193)	0-6-0DH	1967
Wee Mac	—	Clayton	4wDH	1979

info@keith-dufftown.org.uk
Web site:
www.keith-dufftown.org.uk
Main station: Dufftown
Other public stations: Drummuir (access by rail only), Keith Town (not the ScotRail station)
Length of line: 11 miles, with 42 bridges and the twin span 60ft high Fiddich Viaduct
Car park: Dufftown, Keith
Access by public transport: ScotRail station at Keith (short walk to Keith Town)
Refreshments: Dufftown
Souvenirs: Dufftown
On site facilities: Visitor information point is now located at Keith Town station. Information on local accommodation providers, visitor attractions and souvenirs. Woodland walks from Drummuir station and access to the Walled Garden at Drummuir Castle
Period of public operation: Easter until end May and throughout September on Fridays and Saturdays. On Fridays, Saturdays and Sundays during June, July and August
Special events: Spring and autumn Whisky Festivals, please contact for dates. Santa Specials — in December (please enquire about dates)
Membership details: Membership Secretary, c/o above address
Membership journal: *The Keith & Dufftown Express* — quarterly

Rolling stock
3 Canadian 'Speeder' vehicles
A selection of freight vehicles for maintenance purposes

Miniature Railway

Kerr's Miniature Railway

Angus

Location: Along the sea front to the west of town
Headquarters: West Links Park, Arbroath, Angus.
Contact: General Manager: Mathew B. Kerr
Telephone: (01241) 879249
Fax: xx;
Internet address: *e-mail:* kmr@kerr12.f9.co.uk
Web site: www.geocities.com/kmr_scotland
Access by public transport: ScotRail Arbroath station 1.5 miles; Strathtay Buses route A92
On site facilities: None, but park has toilets, snack bar, etc
Length of line: 10.25 in gauge; 400yd (alongside ScotRail line)
Period of public operation: Easter-end of September — weekends (14.00-17.00). All of July and first half of August — daily 14.00-17.00, but trains usually run from noon onwards. All times weather permitting

Locomotives

Name	*No*	*Builder*	*Type*	*Built*
Ivor	—	Coleby-Simkins	0-6-0	1972
King George	2005	Bullock	4-6-0	1935
Auld Reekie	9872	Jennings	4-4-2	1936
—	25081	Eastwood	Bo-Bo	1981
—	D7594	Eastwood	Bo-Bo	1994
Firefly	3007	Bullock	0-6-0	1936

Steam Centre

Leadhills & Wanlockhead Railway

Lanarkshire

Member: HRA
Situated in the Lowther Hills between Abington and Sanquhar, the society was formed in 1983 to construct and operate a 2ft gauge tourist railway between the villages of Leadhills and Wanlockhead. The track now extends to the old county boundary between Lanarkshire and Dumfriesshire. The highest adhesion worked railway in Great Britain at 1,498ft above sea level. Signalbox built using terracotta

Industrial locomotives

Name	*No*	*Builder*	*Type*	*Built*
Charlotte	—	O&K	0-4-0T	1913
Elvan	2	M/Rail (9792)	4wDM	1955
Luce	4	R/Hornsby (7002/0467/2)	4wDM	1966
Little Clyde	5	R/Hornsby (7002/0467/6)	4wDM	1966
Clyde	6	Hunslet (6347)	4wDH	1975
Nith	8	H/Clarke (DM1002)	0-4-0DMF	1956
Mennock	10	H/Barclay (LD 9348)	0-4-0DM	1994
—	—	Decauvill (917)	0-4-0T	1917
—	—	Clayton (18190)	4wDM	1978
—	—	Moyse	4wDM	1941

bricks from the demolished viaduct at Risping Cleuch, with a variety of pre-Grouping signalling & telegraph equipment (eg North British Railway lever frame and Caledonian Railway lattice post signal

Rolling stock
2 air-braked passenger coaches and guard's van built at Leadhills. 1 air-braked coach chassis built by Talyllyn Railway, with the L&WR completing the bodywork. Assorted permanent way wagons and former industrial stock

Operating society/organisation: Leadhills & Wanlockhead Railway c/o A. Ireland, 23 Pinnacle Hill Park, Kelso, Borders TD5 8HA
Telephone: 01573 223691
Internet address: *Web site:* www.leadhillsrailway.co.uk
Main station: Leadhills
Access by public transport: ScotRail trains stop at Sanquhar on Nith Valley Line (approx 10 miles) every 1hr 30min-2 hours. Bus service (Western Scottish Stagecoach) to Leadhills (please check for times). Nearest motorway — M74 — J14 from south/J15 from north. From A76 take B797 to Leadhills
Length of line: 1 mile
Journey time: Approx 30min round trip
On site facilities: Shop, ticket office, toilets, small museum and picnic tables. Extensive country walks. Also on 'Southern Upland Way'. Scottish Lead Mining Museum at Wanlockhead (1 mile). Guided tour of signalbox and engine shed. Disabled access to shop
Period of public operation: Saturdays and Sundays 11.00-17.00 Easter to end September; Sundays 11.00-17.00 in October. Plus Good Friday, Easter Monday and Bank Holidays. Group discount 50%
Special events: Steam Fair weekend (usually late July)
Membership details: c/o above address
Society journal: Quarterly

Timetable Service

Mull Rail

Isle of Mull

Member: HRA, TT
Scotland's original and only island passenger railway. The terminal at Craignure is reached by ferry from Oban. The railway timetable links in with most ferry sailings. The journey is one of great beauty running alongside the Sound of Mull with extensive views of Ben Nevis, the Glencoe Hills, the island of Lismore and the mass of Ben Cruachan
Commercial Manager: Graham E. Ellis
Operations Manager: D. Moseley
Operating society/organisation: Mull & West Highland (NG) Railway Co Ltd, Old Pier Station, Craignure, Isle of Mull PA65 6AY
Telephone/Fax: (01680) 812494
Internet address: *e-mail:* mullrail@deeemm.co.uk
Web site: www.mullrail.co.uk
OS reference: NM 725369
Car park: At Craignure, free
Access by public transport: Caledonian MacBrayne ferry from Oban (40min sail)
On site facilities: Gift shop, car park (free)
Family ticket: Available (2 adults & 2 children under 16)

Locomotives

Name	*No*	*Builder*	*Type*	*Built*
Lady of the Isles	—	Marsh	2-6-4T	1981
Waverley†	—	Curwen	4-4-2	1952
—	—	Alcock	4w-4PM	1973
Glen Auldyn	—	Davies	B0-B0 DH	1986
*Victoria**	—	Vere	2-6-2T	1993
Frances	—	Vere	B0-B0 DH	1999

†currently at Rudyard Lake Railway
*largest tank engine built for 10.25in gauge

Rolling stock
12 coaches (two with wheelchair accommodation); 3 bogie wagons; 1 4-wheel wagon

Owner
Waverley — The Waverley Group

Length of line: 1.25 miles/10.25in gauge
Public opening: Daily Easter week to mid-October
Facilities for disabled: No steps on railway, two compartments for wheelchairs
Membership details: Friends of Mull Rail, David Crombie, 1 Mulberry Drive, Dunfermline, Fife KY11 8BZ. Tel: (01383) 728652
Membership journal: *Crankpin Journal* — annual
Special notes: First island passenger railway in Scotland, runs to Torosay Castle and 12 acres of gardens, superb panoramic views of mountains and sea. Group discount available for 20+ pre-booked passengers. Special trains can be chartered within and outside timetable hours. Joint Torosay Castle/Mull Rail tickets available

Timetable Sailings

Paddle Steamer Preservation Society

Coastal & Inshore Waters

Member: TT, Heritage Afloat
Paddle steamers: *Waverley* & *Kingswear Castle*. Pleasure cruise ship: *Balmoral*
The Paddle Steamer *Waverley*, the last sea-going paddle steamer in the world, was built for the London & North Eastern Railway in 1946, and replaced a vessel of the same name which was sunk off Dunkirk during May 1940. Sold to the PSPS — a Registered Charity — in 1974, *Waverley* sails on day trips and afternoon cruises from ports and piers in most coastal areas and river estuaries of the United Kingdom, from Easter until October each year. Also in the 'fleet' is the traditional motor cruiser *Balmoral*. The river paddle steamer *Kingswear Castle* sails from Chatham Historic Dockyard on the River Medway
Commercial Director: Kathleen O'Neil
Operations Director: Ian McMillan
Headquarters:
Waverley and *Balmoral:* Waverley Excursions Ltd, Waverley Terminal, Anderston Quay, Glasgow G3 8HA
Kingswear Castle: The Historic Dockyard, Chatham, Kent ME4 4TQ
On ship facilities: Self-service restaurants, bars, toilets (disabled toilets on *Waverley* and *Balmoral*), souvenirs
Membership details: Paddle Steamer Preservation Society, PO Box 365, Worcester WR3 7WH
Membership journal: *Paddlewheels* — quarterly.
Details of the full programme of cruises operated by and *Waverley* and *Balmoral* can be obtained from the National Booking Office, Waverley Excursions Ltd, Waverley Terminal, Anderston Quay, Glasgow G3 8HA
Tel: 0845 130 4647.
Book online at: www.waverleyexcursions.co.uk
Further info for *Kingswear Castle: Tel:* 01634 827648
e-mail: kc@pskc.freeserve.co.uk
Online booking for *Kingswear Castle:* www.pskc.freeserve.co.uk

Museum

Prestongrange Industrial Heritage Museum

East Lothian

Location: On the B1348 between Musselburgh and Prestonpans.
OS reference: NT 734737
Operating society/organisation: East Lothian Museum Service, Library & Museum Headquarters, Dunbar Road, Haddington, East Lothian EH41 3PJ
Telephone: (0131) 653 2904 (Prestongrange Visitor Centre), (01368) 861954 (Museum Service)
Internet address: *e-mail:* elms@eastlothian.gov.uk
Car park: On site
On site facilities: Once part of the Scottish Mining Museum, Prestongrange is being developed as a museum which tells the story of people and industries in East Lothian — local coal deposits encouraged the growth of numerous other industries such as pottery, pipe making, soap, glycerine and brewing
Visitor centre: Changing exhibitions of local industries. Displays of local art and crafts — one-off events, demonstrations, workshops. Cornish beam engine, installed 1874 to pump water from the mine. Colliery locomotives restored by Prestongrange Railway Society are housed in the Pit Head Baths
Toilets: Visitor centre
Refreshment facilities: Available at visitor centre
Public opening: April to October, 11.00-16.00, last tour at 15.00
Length of line: 400m (standard gauge). No public rides
Facilities for disabled: Access and toilet at visitor centre. Access to powerhouse exhibition, and footpaths along the site
Special events: Events held throughout the season

Industrial locomotives

Name	*No*	*Builder*	*Type*	*Built*
—	6	A/Barclay (2043)	0-4-0ST	1937
—	17	A/Barclay (2219)	0-4-0ST	1946
Prestongrange	7	G/Ritchie (536)	0-4-2ST	1914
Tomatin	1	M/Rail (9925)	4wDM	1963
—	—*	Hunslet (4440)	4wDM	1952
—	32	R/Hornsby (458960)	4wDM	1962
George Edwards	33	R/Hornsby (221647)	4wDM	1943
—	—	E/Electric (D908)	4wDM	1964

*2ft gauge

Rolling stock
Steam crane, Whittaker No 30, c1890

Special note: The locomotives are stored under cover with no public access at the time of writing. Visitors wishing to see the exhibits MUST make arrangements before visiting.

Contact: For Prestongrange Railway Society — Colin Boyd, 3 Stuart Wynd, Craigmount View, Edinburgh EH2 8XU

Diesel Centre — Royal Deeside Railway — Aberdeenshire

Member: HRA
An ambitious project to reopen part of the former Aberdeen to Ballater branch known as The Royal Deeside Line due to patronage by all monarchs from Queen Victoria to the present Queen Elizabeth II. The Milton of Crathes to Banochry section runs through the historic Leys Estate, lands gifted to the Burnett family by King Robert the Bruce in 1323. The current laird, James Burnett of Leys is an enthusiastic supporter of the railways revival, which will offer fine views of the River Dee and the mountains to the southwest. Milton of Crathes is a popular craft village and restaurant. The adjacent Crathes Castle is one of the National Trust for Scotland properties. The society is putting great effort into acquiring authentic rolling stock for future use on the line, such as the GNSR coaches and 'Sputnik' BEMU. Steam in the form of *Bon Accord* is due to be on site from early 2007. The railway is being rebuilt by volunteer members of the Royal Deeside RPS
Headquarters: Milton of Crathes Craft village
Operating society/organisation: Mr D. Mitchee, Chairman, The Royal Deeside Railway Preservation Society, 3 Alder Drive, Portlethen, Aberdeenshire AB12 4WA
Telephone: 01224 582654
Internet address: *Web site:* www.deeside-railway.co.uk
OS reference: NO 914962
Car Parking: Free, on site
Access by public transport: By bus — Stagecoach Bluebird from Aberdeen rail/bus interchange
By road to Crathes via A93 (14 miles from Aberdeen)
On site facilities: 2 static display coaches with light refreshments available (seasonal weekend opening)
Length of line: 0.25 mile, 2.75 miles when complete
Public opening: Weekends April-September 13.00-17.00
Special events: Occasional events with transport theme, Santa's Grotto in December. Deeside Steam & Vintage Club annual rally held at Milton, second weekend in August (phone for details)
Membership details: Cindy Blackmore, Membership Secretary, 57 Leslie Road, Aberdeen AB24 4HU
Membership journal: *The Queen's Messenger* (quarterly)
Note: Some locomotives and rolling stock undergoing restoration off-site with no public access, please contact for details
Affiliated society:
The Bon Accord Locomotive Society, c/o Mr M. D. Duncan, 19 David Street, Stonehaven, Kincardineshire AB39 2AJ

Locomotives and multiple-units

Name	*No*	*Origin*	*Class*	*Type*	*Built*
—	D2134	BR	03	0-6-0DH	1960
—	D9551	BR	14	0-6-0DM	1965
—	79998*	BR	—	DMBS	1956
—	79999*	BR	—	DTCL	1956

D2134 rebuilt with hydraulic drive
*battery-powered multiple-unit

Industrial locomotives

Name	*No*	*Builder*	*Type*	*Built*
Bon Accord	—*	Barclay (807)	0-4-0ST	1897

*off site for restoration

Rolling stock
2 BR Mk 2 coaches, GNSR full brake, GNSR 5-comp lav composite (body only), GNSR 5-comp lav Third (body only), GNSR 5-comp Third (body only), GNSR 4-comp First (body only), GNSR former steam railmotor (body only), LNWR Picnic Saloon (body only), LMS CCT, BR 25-ton brake van, ex-LMS wagon underframe, 75ton rail-mounted crane (on loan from Strathspey Railway)

Owners
Bon Accord — the Grampian Transport Museum, on long term loan to Bon Accord Locomotive Society

Steam Centre

Scottish Industrial Railway Centre

Ayrshire

Member: HRA, TT, AIM

The Scottish Industrial Railway Centre is based on part of the former Dalmellington Iron Co railway system which was one of the best known industrial railway networks in Britain. Steam worked up until 1978 when the collieries it served in the scenic Doon Valley closed. It is the aim of the centre to preserve part of the railway.

The Centre is operated by the Ayrshire Railway Preservation Group, who also own the former Glasgow & South Western Railway station at Waterside, half a mile from the Centre.

During the winter of 2002/3 the ARPG moved its operations from the former colliery at Minnivey to the Dunaskin Ironworks site at Waterside, and is now based in the former NCB locomotive shed and wagon works there. As part of

Locomotives

Name	*No*	*Origin*	*Class*	*Type*	*Built*
*—	MP228 (12052)	BR	11	0-6-0DE	1949
*—	MP229 (12093)	BR	11	0-6-0DE	1951

*on loan to Caledonian Railway

Industrial locomotives

Name	*No*	*Builder*	*Type*	*Built*
—	16	A/Barclay (1116)	0-4-0ST	1910
—	8	A/Barclay (1296)	0-6-0T	1912
—	19	A/Barclay (1614)	0-4-0ST	1918
—	8	A/Barclay (1952)	0-4-0F	1928
**Harlaxton*	—	A/Barclay (2107)	0-6-0ST	1941
—	10	A/Barclay (2244)	0-4-0ST	1947
NCB No 23	—	A/Barclay (2260)	0-4-0ST	1949
—	25	A/Barclay (2358)	0-6-0ST	1954
—	1	A/Barclay (2368)	0-4-0ST	1955
—	—	A/Barclay (347)	0-4-0DM	1941
—	118	A/Barclay (366)	0-4-0DM	1943
—	7	A/Barclay (399)	0-4-0DM	1956
Lily of the Valley	—	Fowler (22888)	0-4-0DM	1943
—	—	Fowler (4200028)	0-4-0DM	1948
Tees Storage	—	N/British (27644)	0-4-0DH	1959
—	—	R/Hornsby (224352)	4wDM	1943

Doon Valley Heritage, an industrial heritage centre has now been established at the old Dunaskin Ironworks, based on the iron, coal and brickmaking industries
Location: 10 miles southeast of Ayr on the A713 to Castle Douglas
Contact address: Scottish Industrial Railway Centre, Dunaskin Ironworks, Waterside, Panta, Ayrshire KA6 7JF
OS reference: NS 438085
Operating society/organisation: Ayrshire Railway Preservation Group
Telephone: ARPG information line (01292) 269260. ARPG Secretary (01292) 313579 (evening & weekends)
Internet address: *e-mail:* agcthoms@aol.com
Web site: www.arpg.org.uk
Length of line: Approx 0.3 mile
Access by public transport: Nearest rail station, Ayr (10 miles). Half hourly Stagecoach bus service from Ayr. Tel: (01292) 613500
On site facilities: Steam-hauled brake van rides (over third mile). Small museum of railway relics and photographs, and souvenir shop
Public opening: To be announced in spring 2006
Special events: Steam days (with at least one engine in steam) will be held on: Sundays 2, 9, 16, 23, 30 July; 6, 13, 20, 27 August; 3 September. Opening times 11.00-16.30. Additional dates to be announced spring 2006
Membership details: Mr Charles Robinson, 3 Links Crescent, Troon, Ayrshire KA10 6SS
Special notes: For further information and details of special events, please contact the information line (01292) 269620, or the secretary Gordon Thomson (01292) 313579, or write to 8 Burnside Place, Troon, Ayrshire KA10 6LZ

Name	*No*	*Builder*	*Type*	*Built*
Blinkin Bess	—	R/Hornsby (284839)	4wDM	1950
Johnnie Walker	—	R/Hornsby (417890)	4wDM	1959
—	—	R/Hornsby (421697)	0-4-0DM	1959
—	107	Hunslet (3132)	0-4-0DM	1944
—	—	Sentinel (10012)	4wDM	1959
—	—	Donnelli (163)	4wDMR	1979
3ft gauge (stored off-site)				
—	—	R/Hornsby (256273)	4wDM	1949
—	—	Hunslet (8816)	4wDH	1981
2ft 6in gauge (stored off-site)				
—	2	R/Hornsby (183749)	4wDM	1937
—	3	R/Hornsby (210959)	4wDM	1941
—	1	R/Hornsby (211681)	4wDM	1942

Note: Not all standard gauge locomotives are on public display
*on loan to Caledonian Railway

Stock
1 BR Mk 1 TSO, 1 BR Mk 1 BSK, 2 Wickham trolleys; 1 steam crane; various other items

Above: Built by Andrew Barclay in 1926, Caledonian railway-based this 0-4-0ST receives attention at Dunaskin shed at the Scottish Industrial Railway Centre in July 2005. *SIRC*

Timetable Service

Strathspey Railway

Inverness-shire

Member: HRA, TT
Scotland's steam railway in the Highlands connects the busy tourist resort at Aviemore to the more traditional highland village of Boat of Garten, famed as one of the few nesting places of the osprey (viewing site 3 miles from station). The golf course here was designed by James Braid, who also designed Gleneagles. Beyond Boat of Garten the scenery changes as the 'strath' opens out giving fine views of the Spey enroute to Broomhill. This station appears as 'Glenbogle' in the TV series 'Monarch of the Glen'. Broomhill is approximately 3.5 miles from Grantown on Spey, the railway's ultimate goal
Superintendent of the Line: Laurence Grant
Enquiries: Aviemore Station, Dalfaber Road, Aviemore, Inverness-shire PH22 1PY (SAE for copy of timetable brochure)
Telephone: 01479 810725.
Internet address: *e-mail:* strathtrains@strathspeyrailway.co.uk
Web site: www.strathspeyrailway.co.uk
Main station: Aviemore. The railway occupies one platform at the main line Aviemore station
Other public stations: Boat of Garten and Broomhill
OS reference: Aviemore NH 898131, Boat of Garten NH 943789
Car parks: Aviemore (Strathspey Railway side of station (off Dalfaber Road) for railway customers only, Boat of Garten and Broomhill
Access by public transport: ScotRail services and express bus to Aviemore. Local service to Boat of Garten
Refreshment facilities: On-train buffet car or facilities on many trains. Picnic tables at Boat of Garten (for use of ticket purchasers). No refreshment facilities on 'Branch Line Days' services
Souvenir shop: Boat of Garten and Aviemore
Depot: Aviemore (not open to public), sidings at Aviemore and

Locomotives and multiple-units

Name	No	Origin	Class	Type	Built
—†	5025	LMS	5MT	4-6-0	1934
E. V. Cooper, Engineer†	46512	LMS	2MT	2-6-0	1952
—†	828	CR	812	0-6-0	1899
—	D2774	BR	—	0-4-0DH	1960
—	08490	BR	08	0-6-0DE	1959
—†	D5302	BR	26	Bo-Bo	1958
—†	26025	BR	26	Bo-Bo	1958
—*	D5394	BR	27	Bo-Bo	1963
—	31327	BR	31	A1A-A1A	1962
—	51367	BR	117	DMBS	1959
—	51402	BR	117	DMS	1959
—†	51990	BR	107	DMBS	1961
—	52008	BR	107	DMBS	1960
—	52030	BR	107	DMC	1960
—	54047	BR	114	DTC	1959

Industrial locomotives

Name	No	Builder	Type	Built
—	48†	Hunslet (2864)	0-6-0ST	1943
Cairngorm	9†	RSH (7097)	0-6-0ST	1943
—	60†	Hunslet (3686)	0-6-0ST	1948
Niddrie	6	Barclay (1833)	0-6-0ST	1924
Forth	10*	Barclay (1890)	0-4-0ST	1926
Balmenach	2	Barclay (2020)	0-4-0ST	1936
—	17	Barclay (2017)	0-6-0T	1935
Inveresk	16	R/Hornsby (260756)	0-4-0DM	1950
Inverdon	15§	Simplex (5763)	4wDM	1957
—	14	North British (27549)	0-4-0DH	1956
Queen Anne	20†	R/Hornsby (265618)	4wDM	1948

*not on site
†stored and/or not on public display
§likely to leave during 2006

Locomotive notes: In service: 17, 08490, 51367, 51402, 52008 and 54047. Under restoration: 9, 828, 46512, D5394

Stock
20 ex-BR coaches; 4 ex-LMS coaches; 2 ex-LMS sleeping cars; 1 ex-LNER sleeping car; 1 ex-HR coach; 1 ex-NBR coach; numerous examples of rolling stock

Owners
6, 17 and 46512 the Highland Locomotive Co Ltd
828 the Scottish Locomotive Preservation Trust Fund
5025 the Watkinson Trust
D5302 and 26025 the Highland Diesel Locomotive Co Ltd
51367 and 51402 the Blue Square Heritage Group
51990, 52008, 52030 and 54047 My Little Sprinter Ltd

Designed by the LMS but not built until after nationalisation No 46512 is seen at Aviemore on the Strathspey Railway. *Alan Barnes*

Boat of Garten are not open to the public, those at Broomhill are visible from the road
Length of line: 10 miles
Journey time: Aviemore-Boat of Garten 15min; Aviemore-Broomhill 45min (outward) 35min, (inward). Round trip takes approximately 90min
Passenger trains: Steam-hauled services. Aviemore-Boat of Garten/ Broomhill. Most Saturdays, unless a special event is taking place, services are run with a 'branch line' set
Period of public operation: 1/2, 5/6, 8/9, 12-17, 19/20, 22/23, 26/27, 29/30 April; 1, 3/4, 6/7, 10/11, 13/14, 17/18, 20/21, 24/25, 27-29, 31 May; daily June to September; 1, 4/5, 7/8, 11/12, 14/15, 18/19, 21/22, 25/26, 28/29 October; 27, 31 December; 1/2 January 2007
Special events: Two Train Days — 29/30 April, 27/28 May, 23, 30 July, 6, 13 August; Santa Specials — 10, 16/17, 23/24 December
Facilities for disabled: Access possible at Aviemore, Boat of Garten and Broomhill. Please contact in advance for directions and if a party involved
Special notes: First and third class travel available on most trains. Family fares available for third class travel. Special rates/arrangements for parties. Luncheon on the train — Sundays 2 April until 29 October, also on Fridays 2 June until 29 September. Evening diner, the 'Strathspey Highlander', every Wednesday and Friday 2 June until 15 September. Bicycles and dogs carried at a 'flat fee' of £1 — groups must give prior notice (bicycles must not be ridden on platforms or pedestrian pathways)
Membership details: Strathspey Railway Association at above address
Membership journal: *Strathspey Express* — quarterly

Museum

Summerlee Heritage Park

Lanarkshire

Due to major Heritage Lottery Fund support redevelopment, Summerlee's main exhibition hall and tramway will be closed during 2006 and 2007 seasons. Other parts of the site may also be closed from time to time, for safety reasons. If planning a visit, please call the office for full details
Manager: Neil Ballantyne
Operating society/organisation: Summerlee Heritage Park, Heritage Way, Coatbridge ML5 1QD (operated by North Lanarkshire Council)
Telephone: (01236) 431261
Fax: (01236) 440429
Public opening: Daily 10.00-17.00, except 25/26 December and 1/2 January.
Closes 16.30 Nov-March
Access by public transport: STP electric service from Glasgow Queen Street Low Level to Coatbridge Sunnyside (Airdrie/Drumgelloch line). Or from Glasgow Central via Motherwell to Coatbridge Central. Trains also run from Cumbernauld to Coatbridge Central, but not on Sundays
Car park: Opposite site
Facilities for disabled: Toilets, wheelchair available

Locomotives

Name	*No*	*Origin*	*Class*	*Type*	*Built*
Springbok	4112	SAR	GMAM	4-8-2+2-8-4	1956
(3ft 6in gauge/built by North British Loco Co)					
Unit 936103	977844	BR	303	DTS	1960
(303103)	977845	BR	303	DTS	1960
	977846	BR	303	MBS	1960

Industrial locomotives

Name	*No*	*Builder*	*Type*	*Built*
—	—	Barclay (472)	0-4-0DH	1966
—	—	H/Clarke (895)	0-6-0T	1909
—	—	G/Hogg	0-4-0T	1898
Robin	—	Sentinel (9628)	4wTG	1957

Stock

2 rail-mounted steam cranes.
Also on site are two former Glasgow trams one, the Coplawhill Motor School training car, has just entered service at Summerlee; the second, a 'Coronation' class car, will shortly commence a full restoration to operational standards

Wales

Timetable Service | Bala Lake Railway (Rheilffordd Llyn Tegid) | Gwynedd

Member: HRA, TT
This delightful narrow gauge railway follows the route of the former Bala-Dolgellau Railway, along the shore of Wales' largest natural lake. The railway's headquarters are to be found in the fine old station building at Llanuwchllyn at the south-western end of the line. Do not be deterred by the fact that the railway runs down the opposite shore of the lake to the main road — it is well worth the detour
General Manager: Roger Hine
Headquarters: Rheilffordd Llyn Tegid (Bala Lake Railway) Llanuwchllyn, Bala, Gwynedd LL23 7DD
Telephone: Llanuwchllyn (01678) 540666
Internet address: *Web site:* www.bala-lake-railway.co.uk
Main station: Llanuwchllyn
Other public stations: Llangower, Bala. Request halts at Pentrepiod and Bryn Hynod
OS reference: Llanuwchllyn SH 880300, Bala SH 929350
Car parks: Llanuwchllyn, Llangower and Bala town centre
Access by public transport: Arriva service No 94 to both Bala and Llanuwchllyn (from Wrexham or Barmouth)
Road access: Off the A494 Bala-Dolgellau road
Refreshment facilities: Llanuwchllyn. Large picnic site with toilet facilities by lake at Llangower
Souvenir shop: Llanuwchllyn
Depot: Llanuwchllyn
Length of line: 4.5 miles, 1ft 11.625in gauge
Passenger trains: Llanuwchllyn-Bala. Journey takes 25min in each direction
Period of public operation: 8 April-1 October (except some Mondays and Fridays)
Facilities for disabled: Facilities available on most trains
Special notes: Small parties (10/12) may just turn up, but a day's notice required for larger groups
Family tickets: Available for all round trip journeys
Membership details: Membership Secretary, c/o Llanuwchllyn station
Membership journal: *Llanuwchllyn Express*

Industrial locomotives

Name	*No*	*Builder*	*Type*	*Built*
George B	—	Hunslet (680)	0-4-0ST	1898
Holy War	3	Hunslet (779)	0-4-0ST	1902
Alice	3	Hunslet (802)	0-4-0ST	1902
Maid Marian	5	Hunslet (822)	0-4-0ST	1903
Triassic	1270	Peckett (1270)	0-6-0ST	1911
Meirionnydd	11	Severn-Lamb (7322)	Bo-Bo	1973
Chilmark	12	R/Hornsby (194771)	4wDM	1939
Bob Davies	—	YEC (L125)	4wDM	1983
Cernyw	—	R/Hornsby (200748)	4wDM	1940
Lady Madcap	—	R/Hornsby (283512)	4wDM	1949

Locomotive notes: *Holy War* and *Alice* are in regular use, remainder are on static display
Triassic is being overhauled, *George B* is being re-assembled, *Maid Marian* is awaiting delivery of a new boiler

Steam Centre | Barry Steam Railway | Vale of Glamorgan

Member: HRA
Steam and diesel-hauled rides over 3 miles of branch line
Location: Barry Island Station, Barry Island, South Wales
General Manager: Janet Small
Operating society: Vale of

Locomotives and multiple-units

Name	*No*	*Origin*	*Class*	*Type*	*Built*
—	2861	GWR	2800	2-8-0	1918
—	4115	GWR	4101	2-6-2T	1936
—	5227	GWR	5205	2-8-0T	1924
—	5539	GWR	4575	2-6-2T	1928
—	6686	GWR	5600	0-6-2T	1928

Glamorgan Railway Co
Car park: Large public car park near site
OS reference: ST 115667
Access by public transport: Frequent train services from Cardiff to Barry Island for cross platform interchange (Arriva Valley Lines)
On site facilities: Museum, shop, light refreshments
Public opening: Easter to mid-September (weekends and Bank Holidays), December (tel: 01466 748816 for more details)
Special events: Events include Easter Bunny — 14/15 April; Day out with Thomas — 22/23, 29/30 April, 1 May, 22/23, 29/30 July; Transport Festival — 10/11 June; Rail Ale — 24/25 June; '60s Weekend — 12/13 August; Diesel Gala — 28 August; Waterfront Festival — 2/3 September; Ghost Trains — 29/31 October; Bonfire Night Shuttle — 5 November; Santa Specials — 3, 9/10, 16/17, 22/23 December
Length of line: 3 miles
Further information: The Chairman, Vale of Glamorgan Railway Co, Barry Island Station, South Wales CF62 5TH
Membership details: Membership Secretary c/o above address

Name	*No*	*Origin*	*Class*	*Type*	*Built*
—	44901	LMS	5MT	4-6-0	1945
—	48518†	LMS	8F	2-8-0	1944
—	80150	BR	4MT	2-6-4T	1956
—	92245	BR	9F	2-10-0	1958
—	08481	BR	08	0-6-0DE	1958
—	D9521	BR	14	0-6-0DH	1964
—	20228	BR	20	Bo-Bo	1966
—	D1725	BR	47	Co-Co	1964
—	51339	P/Steel	117	DMBS	1959
—	51382	P/Steel	117	DMS	1959
—	51655	BR	115	DMBS	1959
—	51677	BR	115	DMBS	1959
—	51919	BR	108	DMBS	1956
—	52048	BR	108	DMCL	1960
—	54279	BR	108	DTC	1959
—	59664	BR	115	TC	1959

Locomotive notes: In store, not on public view, except 5538 on site.
†some of the locomotives listed above are expected to be used as a source of parts for 're-creation' projects

Industrial locomotives

Name	*No*	*Builder*	*Type*	*Built*
Pamela	—	Hunslet (3840)	0-6-0ST	1956
Ugly	62	RSH (7673)	0-6-0ST	1950
—	7705	RSH (7705)	0-4-0ST	1952
Bill Caddick	—	H/Clarke (1168)	0-6-0DM	1959
—	—	Unilok (2183)		1964

Stock
BR Mk 1 coaches, TVR coach No 153, operational steam crane, various freight vehicles

Owners
D9521 the D9521 Locomotive Group
08481, 47768 and DMU vehicles the Barry Railcar Project
20228 Traditional Traction

Timetable Service

Brecon Mountain Railway

Merthyr Tydfil

A narrow gauge passenger-carrying railway close to Merthyr Tydfil built on part of the trackbed of the former Brecon & Merthyr Railway. Gradually being extended northwards, the railway has some interesting narrow gauge steam locomotives imported from East Germany and South Africa
General Manager: A. J. Hills
Headquarters: Brecon Mountain Railway, Pant Station, Dowlais, Merthyr Tydfil CF48 2UP
Telephone: Merthyr Tydfil (01685) 722988
Fax: (01685) 384854

Locomotives

Name	*No*	*Builder*	*Type*	*Built*
—	2	Baldwin (61269)	4-6-2	1930
—	—	Baldwin (15511)	2-6-0	1898
Sybil	—	Hunslet (827)	0-4-0ST	1903
Graf Schwerin-Löwitz	—	Arn Jung (1261)	0-6-2WT	1908
Pendyffryn	—	de Winton	0-4-0VBT	1894
Redstone	—	Redstone	0-4-0VBT	1905
—	146*	Henschel	2-8-2	1959
—	—	Brecon MR (001)	0-6-0DH	1987

*former South African Railways locomotive

Stock
Two balcony end 39-seat coaches; 2 balcony end 40-seat coaches; 1 19-seat Caboose; 4 flat cars, crane and tamper, miscellaneous rail-carrying and ballast wagons; Wickham petrol trolley

Main station: Pant
Car park: Pant station
OS reference: SO 063120
Access by public transport: Bus to Pant Cemetery — half hour frequency from Merthyr bus station. Main line rail service to Merthyr from Cardiff Central
Depot: Pant
Length of line: 5 miles (3.5 miles open for passenger traffic), 1ft 11.75in gauge
Journey time: Return trip approx 65min
Period of public operation: Daily 25 March-29 October.
EXCEPT for: 27, 31 March; 3, 7, 10, 24, 28 April; 8, 12, 15, 19, 22, 26 May; 18, 22, 25, 29 September; 2, 6, 9, 13, 16, 20 October
Refreshment facilities: Cafés at Pant and Pontsticill
Special events: Santa Specials — December
Facilities for disabled: Facilities for disabled include ramps, toilets and carriage designed to carry wheelchairs
Special notes: There is no road access to Pontsticill

Museum

Conwy Valley Railway Museum

Betws-y-coed (Conwy CB)

Conveniently situated alongside Betws-y-coed railway station, the Museum presents some well-displayed distractions to pass the time including model train layouts to delight both adult and child
Location: Adjacent to Betws-y-coed station
OS reference: SH 796565
General Manager: Mr C. M. Cartwright
Operating society/organisation: Conwy Valley Railway Museum, The Old Goods Yard, Betws-y-coed, Conwy LL24 0AL
Telephone: 01690 710568
Fax: 01690 710132
Car park: On site
Access by public transport: Betws-y-coed main line station
On site facilities: Refreshments in buffet car. Bookshop and model/gift shop in museum foyer, operating train layouts, miniature railway (1.25-miles, 7.25in gauge) steam-hauled. Picnic area.
15in Tramway (operates daily) with 1989-built single-deck bogie tram
Public opening:
Daily 10.00-17.30
Facilities for disabled: Access to café, museum and toilets from car park. Toilets are adapted for disabled

Locomotives

Name	*No*	*Builder*	*Type*	*Built*
Britannia	70000	TMA Engineering (1ft 3in gauge)	4-6-2	1988
*Old Rube**	—	Milner Eng	2-8-0	1983
*Siân**	—	Humphries	0-4-2T	1989
*Shoshone**	—	Simkins/Milner	2-8-0	1975
*Union Pacific**	—	R. Greatrex	Bo-Bo	1991
*Douglas**	—†	P. Frank	2-4-0T	2004
*Dragonfly**	—†	P. Frank	2-4-0T	2004
*Gwyda Castle**	—	P. Zwicky-Ross/P. Frank	Bo-Bo	2004
—	—§	—	4-6-2	1935

*7.25in gauge
†based on Isle of Man Railway locomotives
§6in gauge Canadian Pacific locomotive, a prize winner at the Model Engineer Exhibition

Stock
Standard gauge: 1 GWR fitter's van; 1 LMS 6-wheel van; 1 LNER CCT van; 1 BR Mk 1 coach; 2 SR luggage vans; 1 Pullman coach; 15in bogie tramcar
7.25in gauge: 5 articulated sit-in coaches; 1 twin-set articulated sit-in coaches; 2 sets 3 articulated sit-in open coaches; 4 wagons plus 'self-drive' 0-4-0 'Toby Tram' and 2-4-0 *Billy*. 1 bogie ballast wagon (P. Frank)
15in gauge: 1 wagon

Railway Centre/Museum

Corris Railway and Museum

Gwynedd

Member: HRA
In the heart of Wales' 'narrow gauge country', the Corris Railway provides a 50min round trip on the restored section of Mid Wales' first public narrow gauge railway. The Museum, situated in the remaining buildings of Corris station, displays relics, photographs and models of the railway
Location: In Corris village off A487 trunk road. Turn opposite Braichgoch Hotel, five miles north of Machynlleth and 11 miles south of Dolgellau
OS reference: SH 755078
Operating society: The Corris Railway Society, Corris Station Yard, Gwynedd (postal address: Corris, Machynlleth, Powys SY20 9SH)
Telephone: 01654 761303
Internet address:
e-mail: enquiries@corris.co.uk
Web site: www.corris.co.uk
Car park: Adjacent
Access by public transport: Central Trains services to Machynlleth. Bus Gwynedd services 2 (Aberystwyth-Dolgellau-Machynlleth), 30 (Machynlleth-Tywyn) and 34 (Machynlleth-Aberllefenni); Dyfi Valley service 530 (Tywyn-Machynlleth-Abergynolwyn)
Catering facilities: Snacks, teas and light refreshments
On site facilities: Souvenir shop, toilets and children's playground; close to Corris Craft Centre and King Arthur's Labyrinth; two miles from Centre for Alternative Technology
Passenger trains: Corris to Maespoeth
Length of line: Three-quarter-mile, 2ft 3in gauge track. Planning permission for a further two miles of track has been granted
Public opening:
(Full details on web site.)
Railway — passenger trains (usually steam-hauled) operate at weekends, Bank Holidays and daily on specified weeks in season leaving Corris hourly 11.00-16.00. Santa Specials 16/17 December.
Museum — Weekends and Bank Holidays from Easter to October, daily from 15 July-31 August (10.30-17.00)
Special trains and Museum openings can be booked by prior arrangement. Please check web site or write for further details
Special events: Race the Train Fun Run — 20 May (provisional); Mini Steam Gala and Teddy Bears' Picnic, Corris — 1/2 July; Model Railway Exhibition, Machynlleth — 26-28 August
Facilities for disabled: Disabled access carriage on all trains. Access to display area of Museum and shop
Membership details: Membership Secretary, c/o above address

Locomotives

Name	*No*	*Builder*	*Type*	*Built*
Alan Meaden	5	M/Rail (22258)	4wDM	1965
—	6	R/Hornsby (51849)	4wDM	1966
—	7	Winson/Watkins	0-4-2ST	2005
—	8	Hunslet (7274)	4wDM	1973

Locomotive notes: 5, 6 and 7 operational. 7 based on Corris No 4 now Talyllyn No 4 *Edward Thomas*. 8 undergoing restoration

Stock
3 carriages (4th under construction) , 4 brake vans, 18 works wagons and 5 historic wagons

Owner
8 on loan from the National Mining Museum

Timetable Service

Fairbourne Railway

Gwynedd

Member: Britain's Great Little Railways
Since 1986 this railway has been regauged from 15in to 12.25in and has been transformed by the introduction of new locomotives and rolling stock, a tunnel through the sand dunes, signalboxes, new workshops, a café overlooking the Mawddach estuary. During the main season a two-train service is in operation. A free indoor nature attraction and small museum are open at Fairbourne terminus
Headquarters: North Wales Coast Light Railway Co Ltd, Fairbourne & Barmouth Steam Railway, Beach Road, Fairbourne, Gwynedd LL38 2EX
Telephone: (01341) 250362
Fax: (01341) 250240
Internet address: *e-mail:* fairbourne.railway@btinternet.com
Web site: http://www.fairbournerailway.com
Main station: Gorsaf Newydd (Fairbourne)
Other public stations: Gorsafawddachaidraigodanheddogleddollonpenrhynareurdraethceredigion, Penrhyn Point (Barmouth Ferry Station)
OS reference: SH 616128

Car parks: Gorsaf Newydd
Access by public transport: Fairbourne railway station. Bus Gwynedd service (No 28)
Refreshment facilities: Penrhyn Point café, tea shop on platform at Gorsaf Newydd (Fairbourne)
Souvenir shop: Gorsaf Newydd (Fairbourne)
Depot: Fairbourne
Length of line: 2.5 miles, 12.25in gauge
Passenger trains: A 2.5-mile journey connecting with ferry at Penrhyn Point to Barmouth. 20min single journey. Through tickets to Barmouth (including ferry) available
Period of public operation: Daily service (except Fridays) 15 April-24 September; daily service (inc Friday) 16 July-31 August. 7/8, 14/15, 21-26, 28/29 October. Note: the line will not be open on Fridays in 2006 except between 15 July and 31 August. It will also be introducing an Intermediate Service, with 5 trains per day, as compared to the Normal (3 trains) and Peak (8 trains) and this will be operated at various times throughout the season.
Special events: Open Day — 16 April; Friendly Fairbourne Engines — 28-31 May; Car Rally & Craft Fair — 10/11 July; Friendly Fairbourne Engines — 23-25 July; 'Ride a Lifeboat' along the line— 28 July; Friendly Fairbourne Engines — 20-22 August; Santa Specials — 9/10 December
Membership details: Fairbourne Railway Supporters' Association, c/o 2 Leicester Road, Fleckney, Leics LE8 8BF
Special notes: During inclement weather the service may be restricted or cancelled. Extra trains and special parties by arrangement with the manager

Locomotives

Name	*No*	*Builder*	*Type*	*Built*
Beddgelert	—	Curwen	0-6-4ST	1979
Yeo	—	Curwen	2-6-2T	1978
Sherpa	—	Milner	0-4-0STT	1978
*Russell**	—	Milner	2-6-4T	1985
Lilian Walter†	—	FLW	A1-1AD	1985
Gwril	—	FLW	4wBE	1987
T. J. Thurston	—	Thurston	4-6-2	

FLW — Fairbourne Locomotive Works
*built as replica Leek & Manifold *Elaine*, rebuilt to present form 1985 at FLW
†originally built by G&S Engineering in 1961 as 15in gauge *Sylvia*. Rebuilt at Fairbourne in 1985

Stock
18 coaches; 15 freight

Timetable Service

Ffestiniog Railway

Gwynedd

Member: HRA
In many ways, evocative of the early Swiss mountain railways as it climbs high above Porthmadog with some breathtaking views, the railway still operates an interesting variety of locomotives including some unusual Victorian survivors. Passengers have replaced slate as the principal traffic over this former quarry line
General Manager: Paul Lewin
Headquarters: Ffestiniog Railway Co, Harbour Station, Porthmadog, Gwynedd, LL49 9NF
Telephone: Porthmadog (01766) 516000
Fax: 01766 516006
Internet address: *Web site:* http://www.festrail.co.uk
Main stations: Porthmadog Harbour, Blaenau Ffestiniog
Other public stations: Boston Lodge, Minffordd, Penrhyn, Plas

Locomotives

Name	*No*	*Builder*	*Type*	*Built*
Princess	1	G/England (199/200)	0-4-0STT	1863
Prince	2	G/England	0-4-0STT	1863
Palmerston	4	G/England	0-4-0STT	1863
Welsh Pony	5	G/England (234)	0-4-0STT	1867
Earl of Merioneth	—	FR	0-4-4-0T	1979
Merddin Emrys	10	FR	0-4-4-0T	1879
David Lloyd George	12	FR	0-4-4-0T	1992
Taliesin	—	FR	0-4-4T	1999
Moelwyn	—	Baldwin (49604)	2-4-0DM	1918
*Lilla**	—	Hunslet (554)	0-4-0ST	1891
Blanche	—	Hunslet (589)	2-4-0STT	1893
Linda	—	Hunslet (590)	2-4-0STT	1893
*Britomart**	—	Hunslet (707)	0-4-0ST	1899
Mountaineer	—	Alco (57156)	2-6-2T	1917
Livingston Thompson†	3	FR	0-4-4-0T	1886
Harlech Castle	—	B/Drewry (3767)	0-6-0-DH	1983
Ashover	—	Hibberd (3307)	4wDM	1948
Conway Castle	—	Hibberd (3831)	4wDM	1958
Moel Hebog	—	Hunslet (4113)	0-4-0DM	1955
Mary Ann	—	M/Rail (596)	4wDM	1917
Criccieth Castle	—	FR	0-6-0DH	1995
The Colonel	—	M/Rail (8788)	4wDM	1943

Halt, Tan-y-Bwlch, Dduallt, Tanygrisiau
OS reference: SH 571384
Car parks: Porthmadog, Tan-y-Bwlch, Tanygrisiau, Blaenau Ffestiniog
Access by public transport: Minffordd and Blaenau Ffestiniog main line stations. Porthmadog, Minffordd and Blaenau Ffestiniog served by local buses
Refreshment facilities: Licensed restaurant at Porthmadog, café at Tan-y-Bwlch, refreshments also on most trains
Souvenir shops: Porthmadog, Tan-y-Bwlch, Blaenau Ffestiniog
Museum: Interesting artefacts in Spooner's Bar, Porthmadog
Depot: Boston Lodge
Length of line: 13.5 miles, 1ft 11.5in gauge
Passenger trains: Porthmadog-Blaenau Ffestiniog

Name	*No*	*Builder*	*Type*	*Built*
Diana	—	M/Rail (21579)	4wDM	1957
Stefcomatic	—	Matisa (48589)	2-2-0DH	1956
Vale of Ffestiniog	—	Funkey	Bo-Bo	1968
Moel-y-Gest	—	Hunslet (6659)	0-4-0DM	1965

*privately owned
†on loan to National Railway Museum

Stock
33 bogie coaches; 7 4-wheel coaches; 4 brake vans, plus numerous service vehicles

Period of public operation: Daily 1 April to 29 October, limited winter service
Special events: 1940s themed weekend (in conjunction with Welsh Highland Railway [Porthmadog]) — 19 April-1 May. Other events being planned, please visit our web site for details
Facilities for disabled: Porthmadog and Blaenau Ffestiniog easily accessible for wheelchairs. Limited facilities on trains for disabled in wheelchairs by prior arrangement
Membership details: Ffestiniog Railway Society (see above address)
Membership journal: *Ffestiniog Railway Magazine* — quarterly

Timetable Service

Great Orme Tramway

Conwy

Member: HRA
A cable-hauled street tramway to the summit of the Great Orme is operated as two sections involving a change halfway. Opened in July 1902, it includes gradients as steep as 1 in 3.9
Location: Great Orme Tramway, Victoria Station, Church Walks, Llandudno
OS reference: SH 7781
Operating society/organisation: Conwy County Borough Council, Property Services, Library Buildings, Mostyn Street, Llandudno LL30 1JP
Telephone: (01492) 879306
Internet address: *e-mail*: tramwayenquiries@conwy.gov.uk
Web site: www.greatormetramway.com
Car park: Approximately 100yd from Lower Terminal or adjacent to Summit Terminal
Access by public transport: Good
On site facilities: Shop
Exhibits for viewing: There are exhibits displayed at the Halfway station and a small exhibition (free)
Period of public operation: March to end of October (daily) 10.00-18.00 (17.00 October). Can be subject to change
Special notes: The only remaining cable-hauled street tramway in Britain. 1 mile long rising to 650ft (3ft 6in gauge)
Stock: 4 tramcars each seating 48, built 1902/3
Family tickets: Available, along with joint tickets for Great Orme Mine — Bronze Age Heritage Centre
Facilities for disabled: The tramway has limited disabled access and is unsuitable for the wheelchair-bound, although wheelchairs can be folded away in the tramcars

Timetable Service

Gwili Railway (Rheilffordd Gwili)

Carmarthenshire

Member: HRA, TT
Runs alongside the River Gwili on part of the former Carmarthen-Aberystwyth line. Attractions include a fully restored signalbox and historic station building. Extension to Danycoed opened in April 2001. A 7.25in gauge miniature railway and a riverside picnic site at Llwyfan Cerrig.
Headquarters: Gwili Railway Co Ltd, Bronwydd Arms Station, Bronwydd Arms, Carmarthen, SA33 6HT
Telephone: Carmarthen (01267)

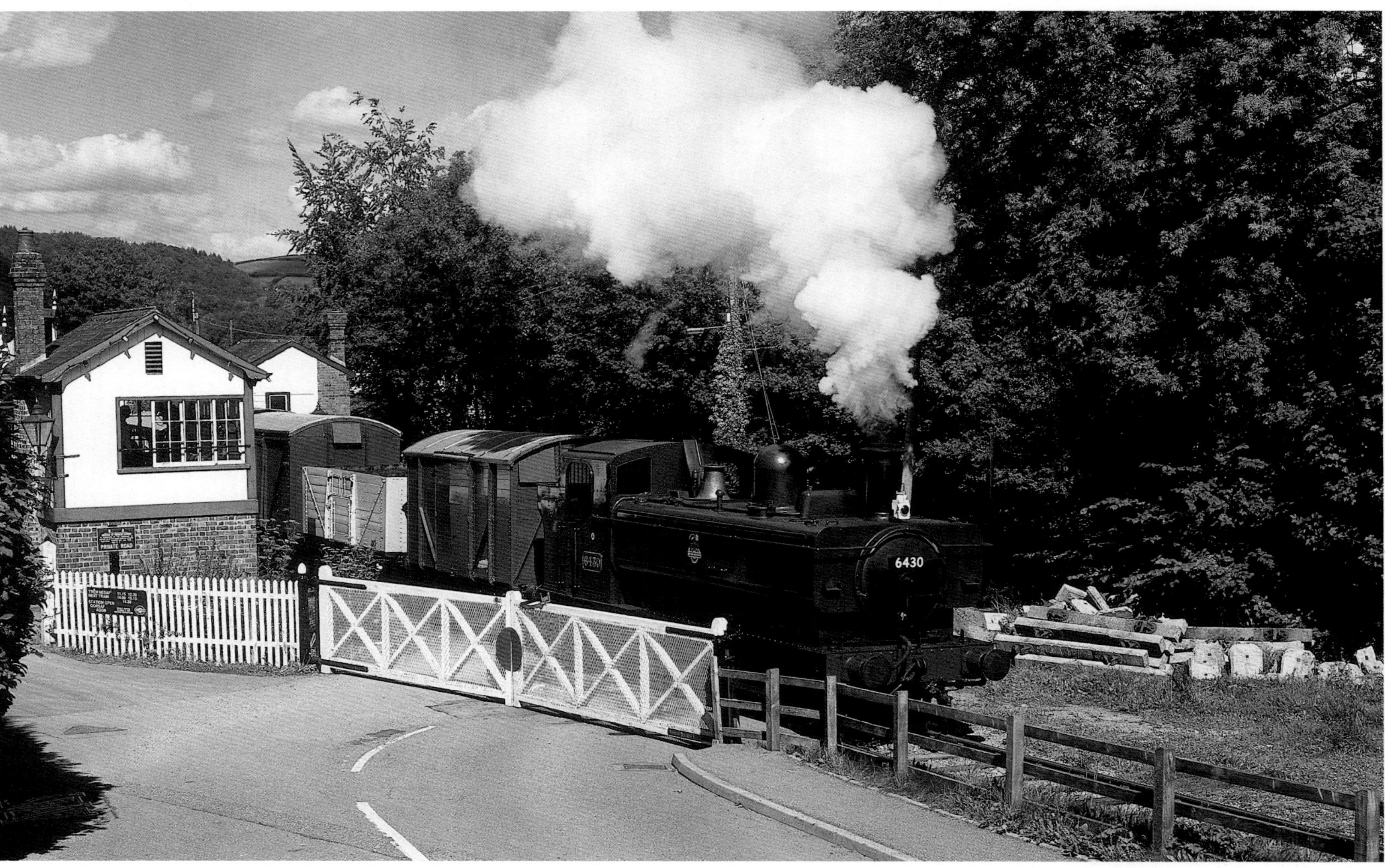

One aspect of the railway scene that has almost vanished is that of the traditional gated level crossing. Here at Bronwydd Arms on the Gwili Railway No 6430, on loan from the Llangollen Railway, is seen in action. *Alan Barnes*

230666
Internet address: *e-mail:* company@gwilirailway.co.uk
Web site: www.gwili-railway.co.uk
OS reference: Bronwydd Arms SN 417239
Llwyfan Cerrig SN 405258,
Main station: Bronwydd Arms
Other public station: Llwyfan Cerrig, Danycoed
Car park: Bronwydd Arms (free) (not 14-18 April, 27-29 October when Park & Ride from Carmarthen must be used)
Access by public transport: Carmarthen railway station, then First Cymru services (Info Line: 0870 608 2306)
Refreshment facilities: Bronwydd Arms
Souvenir shop: Bronwydd Arms
Depot: Bronwydd Arms, stock also kept at Llwyfan Cerrig
Length of line: 2.5 miles
Passenger trains: Bronwydd Arms-Llwyfan Cerrig-Danycoed, approximately 1 hour service
Period of public operation: 14-18 April; 7, 14, 21, 28-31 May; 1-4, 7, 11, 14, 18, 21, 25, 28 June; 2, 5, 9, 12, 16, 18 July; daily – 13 July to 31 August (EXCEPT 27 July, 5, 12, 19 August); 3, 10, 17, 24 September; 27-29 October; 9/10, 16/17, 20-24 December
Public opening: Trains leave Bronwydd Arms at 11.15, 12.30, 14.00, 15.15 and 16.30 on most operating days. A more frequent service operates in December
Facilities for disabled: Access to stations and trains
Special events: Day out with Thomas — 14-18 April, 27-29 October; Santa Specials — 9/10, 16/17, 20-24 December, details: Booking Hotline 01656 663925
Special notes: Family tickets available except for Day out with Thomas and Santa Special events. Trains may be hired for special events, tour parties, birthdays, etc

Locomotives

Name	*No*	*Origin*	*Class*	*Type*	*Built*
—**	D2178	BR	03	0-6-0DM	1962

Industrial locomotives

Name	*No*	*Builder*	*Type*	*Built*
Trecatty	—	R/Hornsby (421702)	0-6-0DM	1959
Olwen	—	RSH (7058)	0-4-0ST	1942
Welsh Guardsman	71516	RSH (7170)	0-6-0ST	1944
Nellie	02101	YEC(2779)	0-4-0DE	1960
Victory	—	A/Barclay (2201)	0-4-0ST	1945
Sir John†	—	Avonside (1680)	0-6-0ST	1914
*Swansea Jack**	—	R/Hornsby (393302)	4wDM	1955
*Haulwen†**	—	V/Foundry (5272)	0-6-0ST	1945

Stock
8 ex-BR Mk 1 coaches; 1 ex-BR griddle car; 1 ex-BR Mk 3 sleeper; 1 ex-TVR coach (built 1891); 1 Booth diesel-hydraulic crane; 1 ex-GWR 'Mink' van; 2 ex-GWR Fruit D; 1 ex-GWR Crocodile; 1 GWR Bloater; 2 ex-GWR Loriot D; 3 GWR Toad brake vans; 2 GWR bogie bolster wagons; 1 SECR parcels van; 2 SR parcels vans; 1 SR bogie parcel van; 1 LMS 20-ton brake van; 1 LNER open wagon; 2 LNER vans; 2 Army vans; 6 BR open wagons; 2 BP tank wagons; 3 open wagons

Owners
*The Railway Club of Wales
** Caerphilly Railway Society
†Vale of Neath Railway Society
†*National Museum of Wales Industrial & Maritime Museum in care of Caerphilly Railway Society

Timetable Service | Llanberis Lake Railway (Rheilffordd Llyn Padarn) | Gwynedd

Member: HRA
A narrow gauge passenger-carrying railway starting at the historic Dinorwic Quarry workshops (now part of the National Museum of Wales) and running along the shores of the Llanberis lake using the trackbed of the former slate railway line to Port Dinorwic. Excellent views of Snowdonia and good picnic spots along the line
General Manager: David Jones
Headquarters: Llanberis Lake Railway, Gilfach Ddu, Llanberis, Gwynedd LL55 4TY

Industrial locomotives

Name	*No*	*Builder*	*Type*	*Built*
Elidir	1	Hunslet (493)	0-4-0ST	1889
Thomas Bach/Wild Aster	2	Hunslet (849)	0-4-0ST	1904
Dolbadarn	3	Hunslet (1430)	0-4-0ST	1922
Topsy	7	R/Hornsby (441427)	4wDM	1961
Twll Coed	8	R/Hornsby (268878)	4wDM	1956
—	—	R/Hornsby (425796)	4wDM	1958
Garrett	11	R/Hornsby (198286)	4wDM	1939
—	18	M/Rail (7927)	4wDM	1941
Llanelli	19	R/Hornsby (451901)	4wDM	1961
*Una**	—	Hunslet (873)	0-4-0ST	1905

*not part of the railway's motive power stock. Housed at the adjacent slate museum and can sometimes be seen working demonstration freight trains

Stock
13 bogie coaches; 20 wagons

Telephone: Llanberis (01286) 870549
Internet address: *e-mail:* info@lake-railway.co.uk
Web site: www.lake-railway.co.uk
Main station: Padarn Park station/Gilfach Ddu
Other public stations: Cei Llydan and Llanberis (village)
OS reference: SH 586603
Car park: Padarn Park station/Gilfach Ddu
Refreshment facilities: Padarn Park station/Gilfach Ddu
Souvenir shop: Padarn Park station/Gilfach Ddu
Length of line: 2.5 miles, 1ft 11.5in gauge
Journey time: approx 60min
Passenger trains: Gilfach Ddu-Llanberis-Penllyn-Gilfach Ddu
The half mile extension from Gilfach Ddu to Llanberis village is now open
Journey time: Return trip approx 60min
Period of public operation: Tuesdays in February and early March, and daily February half term week. Mondays to Thursdays in March and October. Sundays to Fridays, April to September. Also Saturdays June, July and August. Family tickets available, under 3s free
Facilities for disabled: Level approaches throughout shop, café and to train. Special toilet facilities provided. Specially adapted carriage for wheelchair users
Marketing names: Rheilffordd Llyn Padarn Cyfyngedig (Padarn Lake Railway Ltd); Llanberis Lake Railway

Timetable Service

Llangollen Railway

Denbighshire

Member: HRA, TT
The line, which is presently 7.5 miles long, is the only operational preserved standard gauge heritage line in North Wales. Situated in the Dee Valley, it follows the course of the River Dee for much of its route, and affords good views of the dramatic Welsh countryside between Llangollen and Carrog, the latter station having been reached in 1996. In that year the railway was the winner of the Ian Allan 'Independent Railway of the Year' award. The section from Glyndyfrdwy to Carrog was the venue for BBC 2's re-enactment of the Rainhill Trials using the replica locomotives *Rocket*, *Sans Pareil* and *Novelty* in 2002, whilst 2003 saw the renovation of the Berwyn Viaduct and reinstatement of the cantilevered platform extension. An extension of 2.5 miles westward from Carrog to the small town of Corwen is planned and will require construction of a new terminus. There are many pleasant walks through the scenic splendour of the Dee Valley beginning and ending at the railway's stations
Location: Llangollen station, Abbey Road, A542 from Ruthin, A539 from Ruabon, A5 from Shrewsbury/Betws-y-coed
Chairman: Gordon Heddon
Operating company: Llangollen Railway plc
Supporting organisation/ leaseholder: Llangollen Railway

Locomotives and multiple-units

Name	*No*	*Origin*	*Class*	*Type*	*Built*
—	2859	GWR	2800	2-8-0	1918
—	3802*	GWR	2800	2-8-0	1938
—	5199	GWR	5101	2-6-2T	1934
—	5532	GWR	4575	2-6-2T	1928
—	5538	GWR	4575	2-6-2T	1928
—	6430	GWR	6400	0-6-0PT	1937
—	7754	GWR	5700	0-6-0PT	1930
Foxcote Manor	7822	GWR	'Manor'	4-6-0	1950
—	47298	LMS	3F	0-6-0T	1924
Magpie	44806	LMS	5MT	4-6-0	1944
—	80072	BR	4MT	2-6-4T	1954
—	03162	BR	03	0-6-0DM	1960
—	13265	BR	08	0-6-0DE	1956
—	D8142	BR	20	Bo-Bo	1966
Chirk Castle	25313	BR	25	Bo-Bo	1966
—	37240	BR	37	Co-Co	1964
Mirlees Pioneer	37901	BR	37	Co-Co	1963
—	46010	BR	46	1Co-Co1	1961
Oribi	D1566	BR	47	Co-Co	1962
—	50416	Wickham	109	MBS	1958
—	50447	BRCW	104	DMBS	1957
—	50454	BRCW	104	DMBS	1957
—	50528	BRCW	104	DMC	1957
—	51118†	Gloucester	100	MBS	1957
—	51618	BR	127	DMBS	1959
—	51907	BR	108	DMBS	1960
—	54490	BR	108	DTC	1960
—	55513†	BR	141	DMS	1984
—	55533†	BR	141	DMSL	1984
—	56097†	Gloucester	100	DTCL	1957
—	56171	Wickham	109	DTC	1958
—	56456	Cravens	105	DMBS	1958
—	56171	Wickham	109	DMBS	1957
—	50416	Wickham	109	DMBS	1957

†at Midland Railway Centre for restoration
*expected to return to South Devon Railway during 2006

Trust Ltd, The Station, Abbey Road, Llangollen, Denbighshire LL20 8SN (both organisations)
Telephone:
General enquiries: 01978 860979 (office hours).
Talking Timetable: 01978 860951 (24hr).
Santa booking: 01978 860979 (1 October to 24 December).
Fax: 01978 869247
Internet address: *Web site:* http://www.llangollen-railway.co.uk/
Main station: Llangollen
Other stations: Berwyn, Deeside Halt (by request), Glyndyfrdwy, Carrog
OS reference: SJ 214422
Car park: Llangollen (Market St) and Mill St (Lower Dee Mill), Carrog — station car park on B5437 off A5 west of Llangollen
Access by public transport:
Nearest station: Ruabon (5 miles) on Shrewsbury-Chester line, then by bus
Bus services: Bryn Melyn bus services Wrexham-Llangollen via Ruabon station half-hourly Monday-Saturday, also Arriva service 94 Wrexham to Barmouth service (6 a day).
For up-to-date bus information please call Wrexham Bus Enquiries: 01978 266166
Refreshment facilities: Llangollen, Berwyn (most weekends), Glyndyfrdwy (most weekends) and Carrog (closed Christmas to end of January, not Mondays except for special events)
Souvenir shop: Llangollen
Length of line: 7.5 miles
Passenger trains: Llangollen-Carrog
Period of public operation:
Weekends March to 5 November. 10-21, 25-27 April. Daily services from 1 May to 6 October. 10-12, 21-October to 5 November. Plus school holidays including half-term (see timetable for details). Party rates are available for more than 10 passengers
Special events: Spring Steam Gala — 8/9 April; Railcar Gala — 10-12 June; Day out with Thomas — 17-20 August; Autumn Steam Gala — 9/10 September; Autumn Diesel Gala — 6-8 October; Day out with Thomas — 21-29 October; Santa Specials — 2/3, 9/10, 16/17, 23/24 December; Mince Pie Specials — 26 December to 1 January 2007
Driver experiences: The railway offers a varied programme of footplate and railway experience courses from early spring through to late autumn, ranging from the basic Summer Evening Ramble to the more advanced all-day railway experience. A brochure is available from Llangollen station
Facilities for disabled: Special passenger coach for wheelchairs.
Membership details: Mr Graham Hoyland, Llangollen Railway Trust Ltd, c/o above address
Membership journal: *Steam at Llangollen*
Special note: For safety reasons visitors to the railway are not permitted access to locomotives and rolling stock unless accompanied by a qualified member of Llangollen Railway

Industrial locomotives

Name	*No*	*Builder*	*Type*	*Built*
Eliseg	—	Fowler (22753)	0-4-0DM	1939
Jennifer	—	H/Clarke (1731)	0-6-0T	1942
Jessie	—	Hunslet (1873)	0-6-0ST	1937
Darfield No 1	—	Hunslet (3783)	0-6-0ST	1953
Austin No 1†	—	Kitson (5459)	0-6-0ST	1932
—	391•	YEC (2630)	0-6-0DE	1959
—	398•	YEC (2769)	0-6-0DE	1959
—	D2892	YEC/BTH (2782)	0-4-0DE	1960
—	D2899	YEC (2854)	0-6-0DE	1961
John Brunner	—	E/Electric (1901)	0-6-0DE	1951

†expected to be away on hire for 2006
•on five year loan from Wilmott Bros, Ilkeston

Stock: *coaches, 45 in total including* — Service sets of Mk 1 stock, 4 BR suburban coaches; 1 LNER Thompson lounge car; 2 GWR autocoaches; 1 GN brake, etc, some under restoration

Stock: *wagons, approx 50 including* — 2 Bolster wagons; 3 GWR Toad brake vans; 1 BR(E) brake van; 4 BR ballast wagons; 1 BR Presflow wagon; 1 GWR 'Fruit D'; 2 GWR Tube wagons; 1 Esso tank wagon; 1 Shell tank wagon plus various other items of freight stock

Stock: *maintenance* — Cowans 50-ton breakdown crane, ARD96718 ex-Laira; 1 Matisa track recording machine; 1 Trackmaster light shunting vehicle; O&K road-railer

Llangollen Railway is also home to the 6880 *Betton Grange* project, which is making substantial progress towards the creation of the 81st 'Grange' class locomotive.

Owners
2859 and 5532 the Llangollen Railway GW Locomotive Group
3802 the GW 3802 Ltd
5199 the 5199 Project
7754, 13265, *Jennifer* and *Austin No 1* the Llangollen Railway Trust Ltd
7822 the Foxcote Manor Society
80072 the 80072 Steam Locomotive Co Ltd
03162 the Wirral Borough Council
All DMUs the Llangollen Railcar group
All main line diesel fleet (except 37901) plus *John Brunner* the Llangollen Diesel Group

Museum

Penrhyn Castle Industrial Railway Museum

Conwy

Member: HRA
A collection of historic industrial steam locomotives, both standard and narrow gauge, displayed in Penrhyn Castle, a well-known National Trust property in the area regularly open to visitors
Location: Llandegai, near Bangor. One mile east of Bangor on the A5
OS reference: SH 603720
Operating society/organisation: National Trust, Penrhyn Castle, Industrial Railway Museum, Llandegai, Nr Bangor LL57 4HN
Telephone: Bangor (01248) 353084
Internet address: *Web site:* www.nationaltrust.org
Car park: Within castle grounds
Access by public transport: By rail: Bangor (3 miles). Bus: Arriva Cymru 5, 6, 7 and 67, 5X
On site facilities: The castle is open to the public, and contains a gift shop. Light refreshments are available
Public opening: Daily 25 March-29 October. July/August — 10.00-17.00. Other months —11.00-17.00. Last admission 30min before closing

Industrial locomotives

Name	No	Builder	Type	Built
Kettering Furnaces No 3	—	B/Hawthorn (859)	0-4-0ST	1885*
Watkin	—	de Winton	0-4-0VBT	1893*
Fire Queen	—	Horlock	0-4-0	1848†
Hawarden	—	H/Clarke (526)	0-4-0ST	1899
Vesta	—	H/Clarke (1223)	0-6-0T	1916
Charles	—	Hunslet (283)	0-4-0ST	1882§
Hugh Napier	—	Hunslet (855)	0-4-0ST	1904§
—	1	Neilson (1561)	0-4-0WT	1870
Haydock	—	Stephenson (2309)	0-6-0T	1879
Acorn	—	R/Hornsby (327904)	0-4-0DM	1948

*3ft gauge
†4ft gauge
§1ft 10.75in gauge

Stock
10 narrow gauge rolling stock exhibits from the Padarn/Penrhyn system. The small relics section includes a comprehensive display of railway signs and model locomotives in the upper stable block

Facilities for disabled: Access to castle and museum
Special notes: For those interested in stately homes the castle is well worth a visit. The entrance fee covers both the castle and the railway exhibits housed in the castle courtyard.

Ruston Hornsby locomotive *Acorn* can be seen operating on some occasions during opening times. For exhibits not on display please ask a member of museum staff for assistance

Steam Centre

Pontypool & Blaenavon Railway

Torfaen

Member: HRA
The historic Blaenavon site, complete with its railway installations and locomotives, can easily be included in a visit to Big Pit Mining Museum
Location: Just off the B4248 between Blaenavon and Brynmawr. Signposted as you approach Blaenavon
OS reference: SO 237093
Operating society/organisation: Pontypool & Blaenavon Railway Co (1983) Ltd, Council Offices, 101 High Street, Blaenavon NP4 9PT
Telephone/Fax: (01495) 792263
Internet address: *e-mail:* railwayoffice@aol.com

Locomotives

Name	No	Origin	Class	Type	Built
—	2874	GWR	2800	2-8-0	1918
—	3855	GWR	2884	2-8-0	1942
—	4253	GWR	4200	2-8-0T	1917
—	5668	GWR	5600	0-6-2T	1926
Bickmarsh Hall	5967	GWR	'Hall'	4-6-0	1937
—	9629	GWR	5700	0-6-0PT	1946
—	51351	P/Steel	117	DMBS	1959
—	51397	P/Steel	117	DMS	1959
—	51942	BR	108	DMCL	1960
—	52044	BR	108	DMCL	1960
—	54270	BR	108	DTCL	1960
—	53632	BR	108	DMCL	1960
—	59520	P/Steel	117	TC	1959
—	60117	BR	205	DMBS	1957
—	60828	BR	205	DTC	1957

Web site: www.pontypool-and-blaenavon.co.uk
Car park: Adjacent to railway terminus
On site facilities: Light refreshments and souvenir shop on train
Public opening: Weedends and bank holidays (except Good Friday) 15 April to 1 October, daily 19-28 August.
Trains run every half hour from Furnace Sidings station from 11.30-16.30.
Santa trains run every half hour 11.00-15.30.
Note: All services will be either DMU or diesel-locomotive hauled
Special events: Easter Bunny Specials — 16/17 April; Teddy Bears' Picnic — 30 April/1 May; Lucky Dip Specials — 28/29 May; Father's Day Specials — 18 June; Railwayana Display — 29/30 July; DMU and DEMU week — 21-26 August; Transport Rally — 27/28 August; Santa Specials — 2/3, 9/10, 16/17, 23 December.
Please visit web site for up-to-date information.
Special notes: The railway incorporates the former mineral/LNWR passenger lines running through Big Pit. Both north and southward extensions are being considered. Service currently operates between Furnace Sidings platform and Whistle Inn platform. The railway runs near to the Garn Lakes — ideal for picnics after a train ride
Membership details: c/o above address, or call at 'The Railway Shop', Broad Street, Blaenavon

Industrial locomotives

Name	*No*	*Builder*	*Type*	*Built*
Harry	—	Barclay (1823)	0-4-0ST	1926
Tom Parry	—	Barclay (2015)	0-4-0ST	1935
—	8	RSH (7139)	0-6-0ST	1944
Llanwern	104	E/Electric (D1249)	0-6-0DH	1968
—	106	E/Electric (D1226)	0-6-0DH	1971
—	RT1	Fowler (22497)	0-6-0DM	1938
Ebbw	170	Hunslet (7063)	0-8-0DH	1971
—	14	H/Clarke (D615)	0-6-0DH	1938
—	1387	H/Clarke (D1387)	0-4-0DH	1968
Panteg No 1	—	Sentinel (10083)	0-6-0DH	1961

Stock
10 ex-BR Mk 1 coaches, 5 ex-GWR coaches, 2 ex-LSWR coaches, 23 other vans, china clay, coke and tank wagons

Timetable Service

Rheilffordd Eryri — Welsh Highland Railway (Caernarfon)

Gwynedd

Member: HRA
The Welsh Highland Railway Construction Ltd has been incorporated to reconstruct much of the original WHR line. The new northern terminus is at Caernarfon, with reopening to Porthmadog anticipated by 2009
General Manager: Paul Lewin
Headquarters: Ffestiniog Railway Co, Harbour Station, Porthmadog LL49 9NF
Telephone: Porthmadog (01766) 516000
Fax: 01766 516006
Internet address: *Web site:* http://www.festrail.co.uk
Main station: Caernarfon
Other public station: Bontnewydd, Dinas, Waunfawr, Plas y Nant, Snowfon Ranger, Rhyd Ddu
OS reference: SH 481625
Car parks: Caernarfon
Access by public transport: Caernarfon is served by local buses. The station at Bangor is served by Virgin and Arriva Trains (Wales). There is a regular bus service between Bangor and Caernarfon
Depot: Dinas
Length of line: 12 miles, 1ft 11.5in gauge
Passenger trains: Caernarfon-Rhyd Ddu

Locomotives

Name	*No*	*Builder*	*Type*	*Built*
—	K1	B/Peacock (5292)	0-4-0+0-4-0	1909
—†	87	Cockerill (3267)	2-6-2+2-6-2	1937
—**	133	S. F. Belge	2-8-2	1953
—**	134	S. F. Belge	2-8-2	1953
*Millennium/ Mileniwm**	138	B/Peacock	2-6-2+2-6-2	1958
—*	140	B/Peacock	2-6-2+2-6-2	1958
—*	143	B/Peacock	2-6-2+2-6-2	1958
Castell Caernarfon	—	Funkey	Bo-Bo	1968
Upnor Castle	—	Hibberd (3687)	4wDM	1954

*former South African Railways NGG16 class locomotives
**former South African Railways NG15 class locomotives
†not on site
The above locomotives may not be on site. Ffestiniog Railway Co locomotives may operate some services

Stock
12 bogie coaches, 1 brake van (goods), numerous service vehicles

Future extensions: Rhyd Ddu-Porthmadog
Period of public operation: Daily 8 April-1 October, limited winter service
Facilities for disabled: Limited facilities on trains for disabled in wheelchairs by prior arrangement
Refreshments: A refreshment trolley is available on most trains. Snowdonia Parc Hotel is situated at Waunfawr station serving a large selection of snacks, meals and real ale
Souvenir shop: There is a new enlarged gift shop at Caernarfon
Special event: 'Real Ale' Beer Festival — 12-14 May; Super Power — 9/10 September
Membership details: Welsh Highland Railway Society (see above address)
Membership journal: *Snowdon Ranger* — quarterly

Steam Centre | Rhyl Miniature Railway | Denbighshire

Member: Britain's Great Little Railways
The miniature railway operating around the Marine Lake at Rhyl is among the oldest 15in gauge railways anywhere in the world. Its origins go back to 1911, and on peak days you can ride on the same train that visitors in 1920 would have found
Operating society/organisation: Rhyl Steam Preservation Trust
Location: Marine Lake, Wellington Road, Rhyl, Denbighshire
Internet address: *Web site:* www.rhylminiaturerailway.co.uk
Trust secretary: Simon Townsend
Postal address: 10 Cilnant, Mold, Flintshire CH7 1GG.
Telephone: 01352 759109
OS reference: SN 072124

Locomotives

Name	*No*	*Builder*	*Type*	*Built*
Joan	101	Barnes	4-4-2	1920
—	44	Cagney	4-4-0	c1910
Clara	—	Guest & Saunders LE	0-4-2DM (SO)	1961
—	—	Lister	4wDM	1938

Rolling stock: 5 bogie 'cars de luxe' built in the 1910s and a similar vehicle built in 2001, 2 Cagney bogie coaches built c1904. Ballast wagon

Length: Approx 1 mile (1ft 3in gauge)
On site facilities: Car park
Access by public transport: Approx 1 mile from Rhyl main line station, buses to Towyn and Abergele pass by
Period of public operation: Operation (steam) Bank Holiday Sundays and Mondays, every Sunday from mid-June to early September, every Thursday and Saturday during school holidays; all weather permitting from 13.00 or earlier
Membership details: Friends of Rhyl Miniature Railway, details from 01745 339477, newsletters twice a year

Timetable Service | Snowdon Mountain Railway | Gwynedd

Member: HRA
The only public rack and pinion railway in the British Isles, opened in 1896, this bustling line climbs the slopes of Snowdon to the café at the top
General Manager: Alan Kendall
Engineering Manager: Sam Reeves
Commercial Manager: Vince Hughes
Marketing Co-ordinator: Jonathan Tyler
Headquarters: Snowdon Mountain Railway, Llanberis LL55 4TY
Telephone: 0870 458 0033 (advance bookings available via

Locomotives

Name	*No*	*Builder*	*Type*	*Built*
Enid	2	SLM (924)	0-4-2T	1895
Wyddfa	3	SLM (925)	0-4-2T	1895
Snowdon	4	SLM (988)	0-4-2T	1896
Moel Siabod	5†	SLM (989)	0-4-2T	1896
Padarn	6	SLM (2838)	0-4-2T	1922
Ralph	7*	SLM (2869)	0-4-2T	1923
Eryri	8*	SLM (2870)	0-4-2T	1923
Ninian	9	Hunslet (9249)	0-4-0DH	1986
Yeti	10	Hunslet (9250)	0-4-0DH	1986
Peris	11	Hunslet (9305)	0-4-0DH	1991
George	12	Hunslet (9312)	0-4-0DH	1992

All steam locomotives were built by Swiss Locomotive Works, Winterthur
All diesel locomotives were built by Hunslet Engine Co, Leeds
†currently out of service
*currently stored out of service (boilerless)

telephone)
Fax: (01286) 872518
Internet address: *e-mail:* info@snowdonrailway.co.uk
Web site: www.snowdonrailway.co.uk
Main station: Llanberis
Other public stations: Summit, also Clogwyn/Rocky Valley when Summit is inaccessible
OS reference: SH 582597
Car park: Llanberis
Access by public transport: Bangor railway station then by bus, either direct, or alternatively via Caernarfon. Snowdon Sherpa Services to/from Beddgelert and Betws-y-coed stop outside the station
Refreshment facilities: Llanberis, Summit
Souvenir shops: Llanberis, Summit

Stock
8 closed bogie coaches; 1 bogie works car; 1 4-wheel open wagon; a 3-car diesel-electric railcar set built 1995 by HPE Tredegar (fleet Nos 21, 22, 23 [Works Nos 1074/5/6])

Depot: Llanberis
Length of line: 7.5km, 800mm gauge
Passenger trains: Llanberis-Summit. Journey time approx 60min. Departures from Llanberis at 30min intervals during peak periods. Round trip approx 2hr 30min
Period of public operation: Daily 15 March-1 November
Facilities for disabled: Those requiring wheelchair access should please telephone in advance to discuss their particular requirements. Disabled parking is available and there are suitable toilet facilities in both Llanberis station and the Summit. Only officially registered support dogs can travel on the trains
Special notes: All trains subject to weather. Prior to mid-May and in severe weather conditions trains cannot proceed all the way to the summit, so terminate at Clogwyn or Rocky Valley. Advantageous group booking rates are available. Please contact the Marketing Co-ordinator. 'Early Bird' half price fare available on 09.00 departure. Any train may be steam- or diesel-hauled

Timetable Service

Swansea Vale Railway

Swansea

Member: HRA
The Swansea Vale Railway operates over a 1.5 mile section of the former Midland Railway route between Swansea and Brecon, on what was one of the oldest tramroads in South Wales. Passenger services ceased completely in 1950, and by 1968 the last section of the line between Six Pit and the Docks had been closed
Charity No: 1012356
Location/headquarters: Swansea Vale Railway, Upper Bank, Pentrechwyth, Swansea SA1 7DB
Telephone: 01792 461000
Internet address: *e-mail:* swanseavalerailway@thersgb.co.uk
Web site: www.swanseavalerailway.co.uk
Main stations: Nantyffin, Nantyffin Road, Llansamlet, Swansea.
Llansamlet is situated 2 miles north of the City of Swansea, opposite Comet store
Other stations: Cwm Halt and Upper Bank Junction (awaiting development)
OS reference: Nantyffin — SN 683969,

Locomotives and multiple-units

Name	*No*	*Origin*	*Class*	*Type*	*Built*
—	03141	BR	03	0-6-0DM	1960
—	51134	BR	116	DMBS	1958
—	51135	BR	116	DMBS	1958
—	51147	BR	116	DMS	1958
—	51148	BR	116	DMS	1958
—	55026	P/Steel	121	DMBS	1960
—	59445	BR	116	TS	1959
—	59490	P/Steel	117	TCL	1960

Industrial locomotives

Name	*No*	*Builder*	*Type*	*Built*
Llantarnam Abbey	—	Barclay (2074)	0-6-0ST	1939
Mond	1	Peckett (1345)	0-4-0ST	1914
—	2	N/British (27914)	0-4-0DM	1961
—	—	R/Hornsby (312433)	4wDM	1951

Stock: *coaches:* 1 BR Mk 2 BSK
Stock: *wagons:* 1 GWR brake van 'Toad', 1 BR brake van, 3 4-wheel tar tanks (ex-NCB), 3 LMS 12-ton mineral wagons, 1 BR 'Gane A' bogie bolster, 1 GWR 'Mink' 10-ton van, 3 GWR 10-ton vans, 1 10-ton open, 2 GWR 'Tunney' wagons, 1 LNER low-fit, GWR Pooley van, BR 13-ton single bolster wagon
Stock: *cranes:* Smith-Rodley 4-wheel steam crane, Cowans & Sheldon LMS rail-mounted hand crane

Owners
DMUs the Llanelli & District Railway Society
Llantarnam Abbey and *Mond* the Llantarnam Abbey Locomotive Association
Smith-Rodley crane — privately owned
03141 the Dean Forest Diesel Association

Upper Bank Junction — SN 668953
Length of line: 2 miles
Car parks: Free car parks at Six Pit Junction and Upper Bank Works at owner's risk
Access by public transport: By train — Llansamlet (approx 20min walk). By bus — ring Traveline Cymru (0870 608 2608), ask for Nantyffin station (opposite new Comet store), Llansamlet. To visit workshops ask for Upper Bank, Pentrechwyth
Refreshment facilities: On train on operating days only (snacks and hot & cold drinks)
Souvenir shop: On train on operating days only and at Railway Shop, High Street Arcade, Swansea (Tel: 07973536246 [mobile])
Depot: Upper Bank Works
Facilities for disabled: Nantyffin has a wheelchair ramp
Period of public operation: Open all year for viewing. April-October 11.00-17.00; October-April 11.00-16.00
Operating days: Not advised, please contact for details. Party bookings at any time by arrangement
Special events: Not advised please contact for details
Membership details: Andrew Cooper, 2 Caergynydd Road, Waunarlwydd, Swansea SA5 4RQ Tel: 01792 873505
Membership journal: *Vale News*
Steam & Diesel hire: For special parties, school or society outings and educational visits
Driver training experience courses: On steam or diesel multiple-unit

Timetable Service

Talyllyn Railway

Gwynedd

Member: HRA, TT
The very first railway in the country to be rescued and operated by enthusiasts, the line climbs from Tywyn through the wooded Welsh hills past Dolgoch Falls to Nant Gwernol. The trains are hauled by a variety of veteran tank engines, all immaculately maintained by the railway's own workshops at Tywyn Pendre
Managing Director: David Mitchell
Traffic manager: David Leech
Headquarters: Talyllyn Railway Co, Wharf Station, Tywyn, Gwynedd LL36 9EY
Telephone: Tywyn (01654) 710472
Fax: (01654) 711755
Internet address: *Web sites:* www.talyllyn.co.uk www.ngrm.org.uk
Main station: Tywyn Wharf
Other public stations: Tywyn Pendre, Rhydyronen, Brynglas, Dolgoch Falls, Abergynolwyn, Nant Gwernol
OS reference: SH 586005 (Tywyn Wharf)
Car parks: Tywyn Wharf, Dolgoch, Abergynolwyn
Access by public transport: Tywyn main line station. Bus Gwynedd services to Tywyn
Refreshment facilities: Tywyn Wharf, Abergynolwyn hot and cold snacks available. Picnic areas at Dolgoch Falls and Abergynolwyn.

Locomotives

Name	*No*	*Builder*	*Type*	*Built*
Talyllyn	1	F/Jennings (42)	0-4-2ST	1865
Dolgoch	2	F/Jennings (63)	0-4-0WT	1866
Sir Haydn	3	Hughes (323)	0-4-2ST	1878
Edward Thomas	4	K/Stuart (4047)	0-4-2ST	1921
Midlander	5	R/Hornsby (200792)	4wDM	1940
Douglas/Duncan	6	Barclay (1431)	0-4-0WT	1918
*Tom Rolt**	7	Barclay (2263)	0-4-2T	1949
Merseysider	8	R/Hornsby (476108)	4wDH	1964
Alf	9	Hunslet (4136)	0-4-0DM	1950
Bryneglwys	10	Simplex (101T023)	0-4-0DM	c1985

Locomotive notes: In service — Nos 1, 2, 3, 4, 6 and 7
*virtually a new locomotive rebuilt from the original at Pendre Works

Stock
13 4-wheel coaches/vans; 10 bogie coaches; 45 wagons

Narrow Gauge Museum, Tywyn

Name	*No*	*Builder*	*Type*	*Built*
Dot	—	B/Peacock (2817)	0-4-0ST	1887
Rough Pup	—	Hunslet (541)	0-4-0ST	1891
—	2	K/Stuart (721)	0-4-0WT	1902
Jubilee 1897	—	M/Wardle (1382)	0-4-0ST	1897
George Henry	—	de Winton	0-4-0T	1877
—	13	Spence	0-4-0T	1895
*Nutty**	—	Sentinel (7701)	0-4-0VB	1929

Various wagons and miscellaneous equipment
*not currently on site

Railway adventure children's playground at Abergynolwyn station
Souvenir shops: Tywyn Wharf, Abergynolwyn
Museum: Tywyn Wharf
Depot: Tywyn Pendre
Length of line: 7.25 miles, 2ft 3in gauge
Passenger trains: Tywyn-Nant Gwernol
Period of public operation:

The contrast in size between Welsh narrow gauge locomotives is ably demonstrated by these two views. *Sir Haydn* on the Talyllyn Railway (*above*) and *Prince of Wales* (*below*) on the Vale of Rheidol. The latter is only 6in narrower than a Great Western Railway 'King' class 4-6-0 although only running on 1ft 11.75in gauge track. Although neither are the smallest or largest as a visit to Bala Lake or Rheilffford Eryri will show. *Both ACB*

Sundays in March. Daily 26 March to 4 November, 26 December-1 January 2007
Journey times: Tywyn-Nant Gwernol — single 55min, return 2hr 15min
Special events: Tom Rolt Vintage Rally — 28/29 May; Children's *Duncan* Day* — 1 June; Victorian Train— 15*, 29* June, 13* July; Talyllyn Have-a-Go Gala — 16-18 June; Victorian Week — 30 July-5 August; Race the Train (limited service) — 19 August; Land Rover Rally — 27 August; *Duncan's* Special Children's Day — 24* August; Victorian Train — 7*, 21* September; Carol Train (7pm) — 16 December; Santa Specials — 16, 22-24 December.
*Thursdays
Talyllyn Vintage Train: The TR is probably alone in still being able to run its complete original passenger train dating from the 1860s, and invites you to enjoy this unique experience, travelling in original coaches behind an original locomotive. The train will depart at 11.00 on Saturdays 16, 30 June, 14 July and 8, 22 September, featuring photographic opportunities and guided tour. Advance booking is advised. Small supplement payable
Family tickets: Available
Facilities for disabled: No problem for casual visitors, advance notice preferred for groups. Access to shop, museum and cafeteria possible at Tywyn and Abergynolwyn. Disabled toilet facilities at Tywyn and Abergynolwyn. Limited capacity for wheelchairs on trains
Special notes: Parties and private charter trains by arrangement. Children under 5 years of age free. Narrow gauge 'Wanderer' four- and eight-day tickets accepted
Membership details: L. & J. Garvey (TRPS), 35 Dene Hollow, Kings Heath, Birmingham B13 0EG
Membership journal: *Talyllyn News* — quarterly
Marketing names: One of the Great Little Trains. The first preserved railway in the world

Timetable Service

Teifi Valley Railway

Ceredigion

Member: HRA
The line at Henllan was part of an extensive network of railways that spread through the valleys of west Wales in the mid-19th century. Originally laid in broad gauge, before being relaid to standard gauge. After the closure of commercial operations, the narrow gauge line was laid by enthusiasts
Operating society/organisation: Teifi Valley Railway, Henllan Station, Nr Newcastle Emlyn SA44 5TD
Manager: Ivor McFadzean
Telephone: (01559) 371077
Internet address: *Web site:* www.teifivalleyrailway.co.uk
Main station: Henllan
Other public stations: Forest Halt, Pontprenshitw, Llandyfriog
Car park: Henllan (on B4334)
OS reference: SN 358407
Access by public transport: BR station — Carmarthen (14 miles). Bus service 461 to Henllan or 460
Refreshments: Henllan
Souvenirs: Henllan
Length of line: 2 miles (2ft gauge)
On site facilities: Children's play areas, woodland waterfall, nature trails, crazy golf and crazy quoits, picnic area, plus quarter-mile 7.25in gauge miniature railway. Display of narrow gauge freight wagons
Depot: Henllan (not open to public)
Facilities for disabled: All facilities including portable steps and wide door for wheelchairs in two coaches
Period of public operation: Daily 25-31 March, April (except 21/22, 28/29), 1-4, 7-11, 14-18, 21-31 May, daily in June (except 10, 17, 24), daily in July (except 8, 15), daily in August, daily in September (except 8/9, 15/16, 22/23, 29/30), daily in October except 7/8, 14/15)
Special events: Steam Gala in July; Halloween (evening trains), Santa Specials in December. Please contact for further details
Special notes: Pay once only and ride all day
Membership details: Teifi Valley Railway Society, c/o Henllan station
Membership journal: *Right Away* — quarterly

Industrial locomotives (2ft gauge)

Name	*No*	*Builder*	*Type*	*Built*
Alan George	—	Hunslet (606)	0-4-0ST	1894
Sgt Murphy	—	K/Stuart (3117)	0-6-2T	1918
Sholto	—	Hunslet (2433)	4wDM	1941
Simon	—	M/Rail (7126)	4wDM	1936
Sammy	—	M/Rail (605)	4wDM	1959

Industrial locomotive (standard gauge)

Name	*No*	*Builder*	*Type*	*Built*
*Swansea Vale No 1**	—	Sentinel (9622)	4wVBTG	1958

Owners
*The Railway Club of Wales

Timetable Service

Vale of Rheidol Railway

Ceredigion

Member: GLTW

This narrow gauge railway offers a 23-mile round trip from Aberystwyth to Devil's Bridge providing spectacular views which cannot be enjoyed by road. At Devil's Bridge there are walks to the Mynach Falls and Devil's Punch Bowl. Many artists have been inspired by the magnificence of Devil's Bridge and the Rheidol Valley

General Manager: N. Thompson

Headquarters: Vale of Rheidol Railway, The Locomotive Shed, Park Avenue, Aberystwyth SY23 1PG

Telephone: (01970) 625819

Fax: (01970) 623769

Internet address: *Web site:* www.rheidolrailway.co.uk

Main station: Aberystwyth (adjacent to main line station)

Other public stations: Devil's Bridge, Rhiwfron, Rheidol Falls, Aberffrwd, Nantyronen, Capel Bangor, Glanrafon, Llanbadarn

OS reference: SN 587812

Car parks: Aberystwyth, Devil's Bridge

Access by public transport: Aberystwyth main line station, and bus services to Aberystwyth

Refreshment facilities: Aberystwyth (not railway owned), Devil's Bridge (not railway operated)

Souvenir shop: Aberystwyth

Depot: Aberystwyth (not open to the public)

Length of line: 11.75 miles, 1ft 11.75in gauge

Journey time: Single 1hr, return 3hr

Passenger trains: Aberystwyth-Devil's Bridge

Period of public operation: Daily 14 April to 28 October, with some exceptions in April, May, June, September and October

Locomotives

Name	*No*	*Origin*	*Ex-BR Class*	*Type*	*Built*
Owain Glyndwr	7	GWR	98	2-6-2T	1923
Llywelyn	8	GWR	98	2-6-2T	1923
Prince of Wales	9	GWR	98	2-6-2T	1924
—	10	Brecon MR (002)	98/1	0-6-0DH	1987

Stock

16 bogie coaches; 1 4-wheel guard's van; 14 wagons for maintenance use; 1 inspection trolley

The following locomotives are stored on the railway pending restoration and future display

Name	*No*	*Builder*	*Type*	*Built*
—	4	Decauville (1027)	0-4-0T	1926
Kathleen	—	de Winton	0-4-0VBT	1877
—	6	Fowler (10249)	0-6-0T+T	1905
—	21	Fowler (11938)	0-4-2T	1909
—	23	Fowler (15515)	0-6-2T	1920
Margaret	—	Hunslet (605)	0-4-0ST	1894
—	31	Mafei (4766)	0-8-0T	1916
—	—	H/Clarke (D564)	4wDM	1930
—	—*	R/Proctor (50823)	4wPM	1918
—	—	K/Stuart (3114)	0-4-0ST	1918

*metre gauge

Also Henschel bogie tender (11854/25 of 1917)

Steam Centre

Welsh Highland Railway — Porthmadog

Gwynedd

Member: HRA, GLToW

The Welsh Highland Railway Ltd operates services at the south-western end of the old Welsh Highland line and has its base in the bustling holiday town of Porthmadog. The company is developing an exciting project to enhance visitor facilities at the Gelert's Farm site. Extension to Pont Croesor is now under way.

The WHR is very much a family

Locomotives

Name	*No*	*Builder*	*Type*	*Built*
Moel Tryfan	—	Bagnall (3023)	0-4-2T	1953
Gelert	—	Bagnall (3050)	0-4-2T	1953
—	—	Baldwin (44699)	4-6-0T	1917
Russell	—	Hunslet (901)	2-6-2T	1906
Karen	—	Peckett (2024)	0-4-2T	1942
Glaslyn	1	R/Hornsby (297030)	4wDM	1952
Kinnerley	2	R/Hornsby (354068)	4wDM	1953
Cnicht	36	M/Rail (8703)	4wDM	1941
Katherine	9	M/Rail (605363)	4wDM	1968
—	4	M/Rail (605333)	4wDM	1963

orientated attraction and adults have the opportunity to purchase a footplate pass
Location: Tremadog Road, Porthmadog, immediately adjacent to main line railway station and opposite the Queen's Hotel
OS reference: SH 571393
Operating society/organisation: Welsh Highland Railway Ltd, Gelert's Farm Works, Madoc Street West, Porthmadog LL49 9DY
Telephone:
Porthmadog: 01766 513402
24hr information line: 0870 321 2402
Internet address: *Web site:* www.whr.co.uk
Car park: Free — overflow car park opposite the railway; this is council owned, with the usual charges, and includes accommodation for coaches
Catering facilities: 'Russells' supplying a range of adult/children's meals and light refreshments
Access by public transport: Central Trains to Porthmadog station. Bus Gwynedd service 1 and 3 to Porthmadog
On site facilities: Souvenir and railway book/video shop, disabled toilet facilities, information boards, footplate passes and extended shed tours. Steam Driver Experience courses available
Length of line: Three-quarter-mile, 1ft 11.5in gauge, Pen-y-Mount to Tremadog.
Passenger trains: Porthmadog-Pen-y-Mount. Return journey approx 40min incorporating works tours. Steam-hauled Bank Holidays, every weekend and daily from early July to end of August (all other trains are diesel hauled)
Family tickets: Available, 2 adults + 2 children
Tickets: Your ticket enables you to travel all day. Rover tickets available covering both WHR (Porthmadog) and WHR (Caernarfon) together with the Ffestiniog Railway
Period of public operation: Daily 8 April to 1 October, and 7/8, 14/15, 21-29 October
Trains leave Porthmadog 10.45, 11.45, 13.30, 14.30, 15.30, 16.30 (the 16.30 does not run February, March, september and October). Some special events have a different srvice pattern
Special events: LYd2 Day — 14 April; Easter Bunnies — 16/17 April; Spring Gala — 29/30 April/1 May; LYd2 Weekend — 20/21 May; Jack the Station Cat book signing — 28/29 May; Teddy Bears' Picnic — 2/4 June; LYd2 Weekend — 17/18 June; Treasure Hunt — 8/9 July; 100 Not Out — 29/30 July; Jack the Station Cat book signing — 27/28 August; Super Power — 9/10 September; Teddy Bears' Picnic — 23/24 September; Dirty Chappies II — 28/29 October
Facilities for disabled: Toilets, plus ramp to facilitate access to shed for guided tour. Disabled passengers can be accommodated without prior notice
Membership details: Membership Secretaries, R. & P. Hughes, 2 Clos Sulien, Llanbadarn, Aberystwyth, Ceredigion SY23 3GF. Instant membership available at the shop
Membership journal: *The Journal* — quarterly

Name	*No*	*Builder*	*Type*	*Built*
—	5	Hunslet (6285)	4wDM	1968
—	3	R/Hornsby (370555)	4wDM	1953
Jonathon	6	M/Rail (11102)	4wDM	1959
—	7	Hunslet (7535)	4wDM	1977
—	10	R/Hornsby (481552)	4wDM	1962
—	11	Hunslet (3510)	4wDM	1947
*Beddgelert**	NG120	S. F. Belge	2-8-2	1950
Snowdonia/Eryri†	—	Buch (23389)	0-6-0DM	1977
—†	—	Buch (2405)	0-6-0DH	1980
—	—	Barclay (554)	4wDH	1970
—	—	Barclay (555)	4wDH	1970
—	—	M/Rail (22237)	4wDM	1965
Kathy	—	H/Barclay (LD 9350)	0-4-0DM	1994
Emma	—	H/Barclay (LD 9346)	0-4-0DM	1994

*ex-South African Railways Class NG15
†ex-Polish State Railways class LYD2

Locomotive notes: *Gelert* will operate 20054 steam service. Ex World War 1 Baldwin locomotive currently on display will be reconstructed as the famous WHR No 590

Stock
Passengers will have the opportunity to travel in the historic 'Gladstone' coach; other replica Welsh Highland coaches in the course of construction. Rebuilt 1923 Hudson 'Toastrack' coach will be in service

Timetable Service

Welshpool & Llanfair Light Railway

Mid Wales

Member: HRA
There is a decidedly foreign atmosphere to the trains over this line. The steam locomotive collection embraces examples from three continents, and the coaches are turn-of-the-century balcony saloons from Austria or 1950s bogies from Hungary. The line follows a steeply graded route (maximum 1 in 24) through very attractive rolling countryside, and is rather a gem in an area too often missed by the traveller heading for further shores
General Manager: Terry Turner
Headquarters: Welshpool & Llanfair Light Railway Preservation Co Ltd, The Station, Llanfair Caereinion SY21 0SF
Telephone: Llanfair Caereinion (01938) 810441
Fax: (01938) 810861
Internet address: *Web site:* www.wllr.org.uk
Main station: Welshpool (Raven Square)
Other public stations: Castle Caereinion, Sylfaen, Llanfair Caereinion
OS reference: SJ 107069
Car parks: Llanfair Caereinion, Welshpool (both free)
Access by public transport: Main line station at Welshpool, one mile from Raven Square. Arriva buses from Shrewsbury, Oswestry and Newtown to Welshpool
Refreshment facilities: Light refreshments at Llanfair Caereinion. Picnic areas at Welshpool and Llanfair
Souvenir shops: Welshpool, Llanfair Caereinion

Locomotives

Name	*No*	*Builder*	*Type*	*Built*
The Earl	1	B/Peacock (3496)	0-6-0T	1902
The Countess	2	B/Peacock (3497)	0-6-0T	1902
Monarch	6	Bagnall (3024)	0-4-4-0T	1953
Chattenden	7	Drewry (2263)	0-6-0DM	1949
Dougal	8	Barclay (2207)	0-4-0T	1946
Sir Drefaldwyn	10	S. F. Belge (2855)	0-8-0T	1944
Ferret	11	Hunslet (2251)	0-4-0DM	1940
Joan	12	K/Stuart (4404)	0-6-2T	1927
SLR No 85	14	Hunslet (3815)	2-6-2T	1954
Orion	15	Tubize (2369)	2-6-2T	1948
Scooby	16	Hunslet (2400)	0-4-0DM	1941
TSC No 175	17	Diema	0-6-0DM	1978
CFI 764.423	18	Resita (1128)	0-8-0T	1954

Locomotive notes: Locomotives expected in service 20065 — *The Earl, The Countess, Orion,* SLR No 85. Some locomotives may not be accessible by the public

Stock
1 replica of original W&LLR Pickering carriage; 6 ex-Zillertalbahn coaches; 4 ex-Sierra Leone coaches, 2 Hungarian State Railway coaches, 6 W&LLR wagons; 8 ex-Admiralty wagons; 2 ex-Bowater wagons; 1Wickham trolley

Depot: Llanfair Caereinion
Length of line: 8 miles, 2ft 6in gauge
Passenger trains: Welshpool-Llanfair Caereinion
Period of public operation: Weekends Easter to October. Daily in school holidays, plus some other days in July and September
Special events: Vintage Weekend — 24/25 June; Steam Gala — 2/3 September; Santa trains — 9/10, 16/17 December
Facilities for disabled: Specially adapted coaches for wheelchairs. Please phone in advance. Easy access to shops. Disabled toilet facility at Welshpool and Llanfair
Membership details: David Barker, 458 Oxford Road, Gomersal, Cleckheaton, West Yorks BD19 4LB
Membership journal: *The Journal* — quarterly
Marketing name: Llanfair Railway
Special notes: Open balcony coaches — travel right next to the engine at the front of the train. Or see the line rolling away behind the back end!

Channel Islands & Isle of Man

Steam Centre

Alderney Railway

Channel Islands

In 1997 the Alderney Railway was 150 years old, having opened on 14 July 1847. Queen Victoria was the only passenger until 1980
Location: Alderney, Channel Islands
Operating society/organisation: Alderney Railway Society, PO Box 75, Alderney, Channel Islands
Telephone: (01481) 822978
Internet address: *Web site:* www.alderneyrailway.com
Car park: Yes
Access by public transport: Aurigny Air Services from Southampton
Location: Station at Braye Road (tickets & souvenirs)
Public opening: Weekends and Bank Holidays, Easter to end of September
Special events: Alderney Week August. Easter Egg Specials on Easter Sunday. Santa Specials, Saturday before Christmas
On site facilities: Miniature railway (7.25in gauge), quarter-mile circuit operates at Mannez in connection with standard gauge line
Length of line: 2 miles
Facilities for disabled: No, but train crew will always help wherever possible
President: Frank Eggleston
Chairman: Anthony le Blanc (tel: 01481 822978)
Notes: Engine shed at Quarry. Wickham 'train' operates in low season; *Elizabeth* and tube cars in high season and Easter

Industrial locomotives

Name	*No*	*Builder*	*Type*	*Built*
Elizabeth	—	Vulcan (D2271)	0-4-0DM	1949
Molly 2	—	R/Hornsby	0-4-0DM	1958

Stock
4 Wickham cars
2 Goods wagons
2 ex-London Underground 1956 Stock tube cars (locomotive-hauled)
2 Wickham flats

Steam Centre

Great Laxey Mine Railway

Isle of Man

The railway was opened on 25 September 2004 and is a reconstruction of the surface section of the former Great Laxey Mine tramway which was used to haul wagon loads of ore from inside the mine and onto the former ore washing and dressing floors at Laxey. The railway runs beneath the main Laxey to Ramsey road —

Locomotives

Name	*No*	*Builder*	*Type*	*Built*
Ant	—	—	0-4-0WT	2004
Bee	—	—	0-4-0WT	2004

Rolling stock
2004-built passenger vehicle, 6 replica ore wagons dating from 2000

the longest railway tunnel on the Island
Contact: Andrew Scarffe
Operating company: Laxey & Lonan Heritage Trust, West Lynne, Mateland Drive, Laxey, Isle of Man IM4 7N4
Telephone: 01624 861706 (there is no direct telephone on the railway)
Car park: Available in nearby Laxey
Main station: Valley Gardens, Laxey
Access by public transport: A few minutes' walk from Laxey station on the Manx Electric Railway and bus stop of the route 3 Douglas to Ramsey service
On site facilities: No refreshment facilities on site, but café and public house nearby
Length of line: 0.25-mile, 1ft 7in gauge
Public opening: Saturdays and bank holidays Easter until end of September, 11.00-16.30
Facilities for disabled: Unable to carry wheelchair-bound passengers, though Valley Gardens are accessible
Membership details: From above address

Steam Centre | Groudle Glen Railway | Isle of Man

Location: Groudle Glen Railway, Isle of Man
Officer in charge: Tony Beard
Operating company: Groudle Glen Railway Ltd (managed by the Isle of Man Steam Railway Supporters' Association) of 29 Hawarden Avenue, Douglas, Isle of Man IM1 4BP
Telephone: (01624) 622138 (evenings); (01624) 670453 (weekends)
Car park: Yes
Access by public transport: Manx Electric Railway (Groudle Hotel)
On site facilities: Sales shop
Length of line: 0.75-mile, 2ft gauge
Public opening: Easter Sunday and Monday, Sundays May to September (11.00-16.30); Tuesday evening services August (19.00-21.00); Wednesday evening services July/August (19.00-21.00); Santa Trains — December (11.00-15.30)
Facilities for disabled: Due to the line's location, those who are disabled will have some difficulty. It is suggested that they telephone for advice
Further information and membership details: From above address
Membership journal: *Manx Steam Railway News* — quarterly

Locomotives

Name	*No*	*Builder*	*Type*	*Built*
Dolphin	1	H/Hunslet (4394)	4wDM	1952
Walrus	2	H/Hunslet (4395)	4wDM	1952
Sea Lion	—	Bagnall (1484)	2-4-0T	1896
Annie	—	Booth/GGR	0-4-2T	1998
Polar Bear	—	BEV (556801)	2-B-2	2004

Timetable Service | Isle of Man Railway | Isle of Man

Member: HRA
The 3ft gauge Isle of Man Railway is a survivor of a system which previously also operated from Douglas to Peel and Ramsey. Almost continuous operation since 1873 makes it one of the oldest operating railways in the British Isles. The majority of the track was completely renewed between 2002 and 2004 including the provision of platforms at intermediate stations and the installation of automatic level crossings along the line. It runs for over 15 miles between Douglas and Port Erin through the

Locomotives

Name	*No*	*Builder*	*Type*	*Built*
Loch	4	B/Peacock (1416)	2-4-0T	1874
Fenella	8	B/Peacock (3610)	2-4-0T	1894
G. H. Wood	10	B/Peacock (4662)	2-4-0T	1905
Maitland	11	B/Peacock (4663)	2-4-0T	1905
Hutchinson	12	B/Peacock (5126)	2-4-0T	1908
Kissack	13	B/Peacock (5382)	2-4-0T	1908
Caledonia	15	Dubs & Co (2178)	0-6-0T	1885
Viking	17	Schottler (2175)	0-4-0DH	1958
Ailsa	18	Hunslet (22021)	4wDM	1994

Locomotive note: All operational, all other rolling stock stored off the line

On display in museum at Port Erin

Name	*No*	*Builder*	*Type*	*Built*
Peveril	6	B/Peacock (1524)	2-4-0T	1875

island's rolling southern countryside.

The line is owned and operated by the Isle of Man Government

Director of Public Transport: David R. Howard
Head of Railways: M. P. Ogden
Railway Engineer: G. F. Lawson
Headquarters: Isle of Man Transport, Transport Headquarters, Banks Circus, Douglas, Isle of Man IM1 5PT
Telephone: Douglas (01624) 662525
Fax: (01624) 663637
Main station: Douglas
Other public stations: Port Soderick, Santon, Ballasalla, Castletown, Colby, Port St Mary and Port Erin

Name	*No*	*Builder*	*Type*	*Built*
Mannin	16	B/Peacock (6296)	2-4-0T	1926

Rolling stock
16 coaches, 20 runners, 1 van, 2 open wagons, 1 well wagon, 1 track tamping machine

Car parks: Douglas, Ballasalla, Castletown, Port St Mary and Port Erin
Access by public transport: Isle of Man Transport bus to main centres
Refreshment facilities: Port Erin and Douglas
Souvenir shops: None
Museum: Port Erin
Depot: Douglas
Length of line: 15.5 miles, 3ft gauge

Passenger trains: Douglas-Port Erin
Period of public operation: Daily April-October 2006
Facilities for disabled: Level access throughout Douglas and Port Erin stations including refreshment area. Carriages able to carry wheelchairs, ramps provided. Advance notice helpful

Timetable Service

Manx Electric Railway

Isle of Man

Member: HRA
The 3ft gauge Manx Electric Railway is a unique survivor of Victorian high technology. A mixture of railway and tramway practice, it was built in 1893 and was a pioneer in the use of electric traction. It illustrates an example of a true electric interurban line. Two of the original cars are still in service making them the oldest tramcars still in operation on their original route in the British Isles. After leaving Douglas, the railway passes the Groudle Glen Railway before reaching the charming village of Laxey, for the Snaefell Mountain Railway. The line continues over some of the most breathtaking coastal scenery in the island before reaching its terminus at Ramsey nearly 18 miles from Douglas.

The line is owned and operated by the Isle of Man Government

Director of Public Transport: David R. Howard
Head of Railways: M. P. Ogden
Railway Engineer: G. F. Lawson
Headquarters: Isle of Man Transport, Transport Headquarters, Banks Circus, Douglas, Isle of Man IM1 5PT
Telephone: Douglas (01624) 662525

Motor cars

Nos	*Type*	*Seats*	*Body*	*Built*
1, 2	Unvestibuled saloon	34	Milnes	1893
5, 6, 7, 9	Vestibuled saloon	32	Milnes	1894
16	Cross-bench open	56	Milnes	1898
19-22*	Winter saloon	48	Milnes	1899
26	Cross-bench open	56	Milnes	1898
32, 33	Cross-bench open	56	UEC	1906
34	Engineer's Car	—	IoMT	2004

*22 rebodied 1991, McArd/MER

Trailers

36, 37	Cross-bench open	44	Milnes	1894
40, 41, 44	Cross-bench open	44	EE Co	1930
42, 43	Cross-bench open	44	Milnes	1903
45-48	Cross-bench open	44	Milnes	1899
49-51, 53, 54	Cross-bench open	44	Milnes	1893
56*	Cross-bench open	44	ERTCW	1904
57, 58	Saloon	32	ERTCW	1904
59	Special Saloon	18	Milnes	1895
60	Cross-bench open	44	Milnes	1896
61, 62	Cross-bench open	44	UEC	1906

*rebuilt as disabled access trailer in 1993

Note: Other rolling stock stored off the line

Fax: (01624) 663637
Main stations: Douglas (Derby Castle), Laxey and Ramsey
Other public stations: Groudle, Dhoon Glen, Ballaglass and numerous wayside stops
Car parks: Douglas, Laxey, Ramsey (nearby)

Access by public transport: Isle of Man Transport buses to main centres. Douglas Corporation Horse Tramway to Derby Castle in summer
Depots: Douglas and Ramsey
Refreshment facilities: Laxey in summer

Length of line: 17.5 miles, 3ft gauge
Passenger service: Douglas-Ramsey
Period of public operation: Daily in summer. Due to extensive engineering works dates will not be available until April
Special notes: Folded wheelchairs can be carried. Please notify in advance. One trailer with disabled access used on advance request

Timetable Service

Snaefell Mountain Railway

Isle of Man

Member: HRA
The 3ft 6in gauge Snaefell Mountain Railway is unique. It is the only electric mountain railway in the British Isles. Almost all the rolling stock is original and dates back to 1895. The railway begins its journey at the picturesque village of Laxey where its station is shared with the Manx Electric Railway. The climb to the summit of Snaefell (2,036ft) is a steep one and the cars travel unassisted up gradients as severe as 1 in 12. From the summit, the views on a clear day extend to Wales, Scotland, England and Ireland.

The line is owned and operated by the Isle of Man Government
Director of Public Transport: David R. Howard
Head of Railways: M. P. Ogden

Trams

Nos	*Type*	*Seats*	*Body*	*Built*
1-4, 6	Vestibuled saloon	48	Milnes	1895
5 (rebuild)	Vestibuled saloon	48	MER/ Kinnin	1971

Railway Engineer: G. F. Lawson
Headquarters: Isle of Man Transport, Transport Headquarters, Banks Circus, Douglas, Isle of Man IM1 5PT
Telephone: Douglas (01624) 662525
Fax: (01624) 663637
Main station: Laxey
Other public stations: Bungalow, Summit
Car parks: Laxey, Bungalow (nearby)
Access by public transport: Manx Electric Railway or Isle of Man Transport bus to Laxey
Depot: Laxey
Refreshment facilities: Laxey, Summit
Souvenirs shops: None
Length of line: 4.5 miles, 3ft 6in gauge
Passenger service: Laxey-Snaefell summit
Period of public operation: Daily in summer. Due to extensive engineering works dates will not be available until April

Northern Ireland

Timetable Service

Downpatrick & County Down Railway

County Down

Member: HRA
The railway museum is the only preserved Irish standard gauge (5ft 3in) railway operating in Ireland. It is a representative of the former Belfast & County Down railway terminus in Downpatrick, which closed in 1950, two years after being taken into state ownership
Location: The Railway Station, Market Street, Downpatrick, Co Down BT30 6LZ
OS reference: J483444
Operating society/organisation: Downpatrick & County Down Railway Society
Telephone: 077 9080 2049
Internet address: *Web site:* www.downrail.co.uk
Car park: Free parking adjacent to station
Access by public transport: A regular service is operated by Ulsterbus from Belfast Europa bus centre (next to Great Victoria Street railway station).
Tel: (028) 9032 0011
Refreshment facilities: Buffet carriage open on operating days
On site facilities: Souvenir shop, toilets
Length of line: 4 miles open to public traffic. Current terminus: King Magnus's Halt. Track was extended southwards to Balldugan and north to a new station at Inch Abbey
Public opening: Special events (see below) and weekends 17 June-10 September
Journey time: 45min return journey from Downpatrick town to Downpatrick Loop Platform and King Magnus's Halt and Inch Abbey

Diesel locomotives and multiple-unit

Name	*No*	*Origin*	*Class*	*Type*	*Built*
W. F. Gillespie OBE	E421	CIE	421	C	1962
—	E432	CIE	421	C	1962
—	G611	CIE	611	B	1962
—	G613	CIE	611	B	1962
—	G617	CIE	611	B	1962
—	RB3	BRE-Leyland	—	4wDM	1981

Name	*No*	*Origin*	*Class*	*Manufacturer*	*Type*	*Built*
—	712	CIE	–	Wickham (8919)	4wDH	1962

Steam locomotives

Name	*No*	*Builder*	*Type*	*Built*
—	1	O&K (12475)	0-4-0T	1934
—	3	O&K (12662)	0-4-0T	1935

Rolling stock
2 CIE Brake open standards (Nos 1918 & 1944); CIE Travelling Post Office (No 2978); 1 CIE Brake open standard generating steam van (No 3223); CIE Buffet open standard (No 2419); NIR '70' class railcar brake open standard intermediate (No 728); B&CDR 'Royal Saloon' (No 153); B&CDR 1st/2nd composite (No 152); B&CDR 3rd open (ex-railmotor); B&CDR 6-wheeled 2nd (No 154); B&CDR 6-wheeled brake 3rd (No 39); GS&WR 3rd open (No 836); GSWR 6-wheeled brake first (No 69); Ulster Railway Family Saloon (No 33); GNR 6-wheeled third, M&GW full brake c1900; 4 LMS (NCC) parcels vans; 2 LMS (NCC) open wagon; LMS (NCC) brake van; CIE closed van; 2 GNR closed vans; GNR brake van; GSWR ballast hopper; GSWR ballast plough; LMS (NCC) steam crane; 2 private oil company tankers, CIE track inspection vehicle No 712; selection of carriage and wagon underframes for internal use

Owners
712, G611 and G617 the Irish Traction Group
G613 and M&GW full brake privately owned
RB3 is owned by Translink
E421 and E432 the Downpatrick & County Down Railway Society

Special events: St Patrick's Day Specials — 17 March; Easter Egg Specials — 16/17 April; May Day Specials — 1, 29 May; Hallowe'en Ghost Trains — 28/29 October; Santa Specials — 2/3, 9/10, 16/17 December
Facilities for disabled: Toilets, shop, platform and trains accessible for disabled

Membership details: The Membership Secretary, Downpatrick & County Down Railway Society, The Railway Station, Downpatrick, Co Down BT30 6LZ

Timetable Service

Giant's Causeway & Bushmills Railway

Co Antrim

The GC&BR was opened in 2002 using the stock of the former Shane's Castle Railway on the last two miles of the site of the Portrush to Giant's Causeway electric tramway closed in 1949. The line runs between Bushmills and the Giant's Causeway with its charming views along the River Bush, and spectacular vistas across the sea to Donegal

Location: The railway links the distillery (open to visitors) in the village of Bushmills to the entrance of the Giant's Causeway. Follow the signs to either Bushmills or the Giant's Causeway and the railway is clearly signposted. Car parking is dedicated to railway passengers at both Bushmills and the Giant's Causeway

Operating organisation: Giant's Causeway & Bushmills Railway, Giant's Causeway Station, Runkerry Road, Bushmills, Co Antrim, Northern Ireland BT57 8SZ

Telephone: (028) 2073 2594 (information line)

Telephone/Fax: (028) 2073 2844

Internet address: *e-mail:* infogcbr@btconnect.com

Web site: www.giantscausewayrailway.org

OS reference: 943437 (Irish Grid)

Access by public transport: Nearest Translink railway stations are Portrush (5 miles), Coleraine (7 miles). Various bus routes (including an open topped vehicle on fine days in the summer) operate from either or both, depending on the route. For timetables either contact Translink enquiries on (028) 9066 6630 or www.translink.co.uk

Length of line: 2 miles, 3ft gauge

On site facilities: Souvenir shop, toilets and picnic tables at Giant's Causeway station. Free parking at both stations for railway passengers

Passenger trains: Bushmills-Giant's Causeway

Public opening: Usually St Patrick's Day (17 March) and daily at Easter. Daily during July and August.

Note: Trains will operate at other times for advance party bookings in excess of 20 persons

Industrial locomotives

Name	*No*	*Builder*	*Type*	*Built*
Tyrone	1	Peckett (2264)	0-4-0T	1904
Rory	2	Simplex (102T016)	4wDH	1976
Shane	3	Barclay(2281)	0-4-0T	1949

Steam Centre

Railway Preservation Society of Ireland

County Antrim

Members: HRA, TT

The RPSI was formed in 1964, making it one of the older preservation societies in these islands. It has always specialised in main line steam operations, and runs an intensive summer programme of trips out of both Belfast and Dublin. The main maintenance base is situated at Whitehead, 15 miles north of Belfast on the NIR route to Larne Harbour. Here not only are the traffic locomotives shedded but the locomotive shed is also used for heavy maintenance; currently the society is completing the full rebuilding of its sixth boiler 'in-

Locomotives

Name	*No*	*Origin*	*Class*	*Type*	*Built*
Merlin	85*	GNR(I)	V	4-4-0	1932
Uranus	131**	GNR(I)	Q	4-4-0	1901
Slieve Gullion	171†	GNR(I)	S	4-4-0	1913
—	4	LMS (NCC)	WT	2-6-4T	1947
—	184†	GS&WR	J15	0-6-0	1880
—	186§	GS&WR	J15	0-6-0	1879
—	461†	D&SER	K2	2-6-0	1922
Lough Erne	27	SL&NCR	Z	0-6-4T	1949
Eagle	101	NIR	DL	Bo-Bo	1969
Falcon	101	NIR	DL	Bo-Bo	1969

Industrial locomotives

Name	*No*	*Builder*	*Type*	*Built*
Guinness	3	H/Clarke (1152)	0-4-0ST	1919
R. H. Smyth	3	Avonside (2021)	0-6-0ST	1928
—	23	Planet (3509)	0-4-0DM	1951

house'. A large engineering workshop has just been constructed for the Locomotive Department, with the 100-year-old overhead crane which was originally in the Belfast & County Down Railway Locomotive Erecting Shop at Queen's Quay in Belfast. This workshop which will undertake all heavy engineering for the Society is currently being fitted out. A large carriage shed is also on site where traffic vehicles are maintained and coaches are fully rebuilt. There are also heavy lifting facilities on site, and access may occasionally be limited for safety reasons when these are in use. Annual operations commence with 'Easter Bunny' trains out of Belfast, usually on Easter Monday. In May the 'International Railtour' is the main event, a three day steam extravaganza. During June there are main line trips out of both Belfast and Dublin, including a Midsummer Barbecue train and a Musical Special. July and August see the 'Portrush Flyers' from Belfast to Portrush and back, around 180 miles of main line steam, as well as the 'Sea Breeze' excursions from Dublin to Rosslare and back, covering 205 miles. During June, July and August there are steam train rides on site at Whitehead on Sunday afternoons, and at the end of July there will be an Open Day in conjunction with the Whitehead Community Association when not only will there be train rides but also at least two locomotives will be in steam and there will be access to the workshop areas. The season usually ends with further excursions in September to Rosslare and Whitehead, and Halloween shuttles between Belfast and Whitehead. November sees the operation of a Santa Special to Derry out of Belfast, before the Santa Specials out of both capital cities

Name	*No*	*Builder*	*Type*	*Built*
—	1	R/Hornsby	0-4-0DM	1954

*on loan from Ulster Folk & Transport Museum
**frames and boiler only
†awaiting restoration
§returned to traffic in 2004

Stock
The Society also owns some 20 operational coaches, normally divided between Whitehead and Dublin. Further coaches are awaiting restoration and a small number of freight wagons are also preserved, as well as a steam crane. A serious fire due to vandalism a couple of years ago destroyed several vehicles, and any rebuilding is likely to be some years in the future at best. The Society has purchased a variety of Mk 2 coaches which are undergoing major overhaul and six of which returned to traffic in 2004 with two more to follow in 2006. The Society's secondary maintenance base is at Mullingar, Co Westmeath, but there is **no** access to the public.

Location: Whitehead Excursion Station, Co Antrim, Northern Ireland
Operating society: Railway Preservation Society of Ireland, Castleview Road, Whitehead, Carrickfergus, Co Antrim BT38 9NA
Telephone/fax:
From UK (028) 2826 0803.
From Eire (01) 280 9147
Internet address: *e-mail:* rpsitrains@hotmail.com
Web site:
http://www.rpsi-online.org
Car park: Public car parking is readily available adjacent to the Society premises, with a further large car park less than 5min walk away on the sea front. Both car parks are normally free
Access by public transport: Northern Ireland Railways or Ulsterbus to Whitehead
On site facilities: Souvenir shop (operating days only)
Public opening: Visitors welcome most weekends. Site not open during the week (except public holidays) or when main line trains are operating from Whitehead or Belfast. Special opening for parties, or in the evening, may be arranged by telephoning in advance
Special notes: The RPSI is noted for its main line excursions and traditional rolling stock. For details: RPSI Railtours, Box 171 Larne BT40 1UU (9x4 SAE please).
Facilities for disabled: Please note that wheelchair facilities can be provided on trains, with advance notice if possible. A dedicated coach for carrying wheelchairs operates out of Whitehead on Belfast-based trains. Wheelchair access around the workshops at Whitehead is possible, but difficult, and advance warning is requested of any visitors who may need special facilities
Membership details: Membership Secretary, 148 Church Road, Newtownabbey, Co Antrim BT36 6HJ
Future developments: Completion of a new heavy engineering workshop is planned, as well as a projected extension to the Carriage Shed and additional stores and maintenance areas, and there are further developments in the pipeline which will hopefully improve access. Additional locomotive and coach restoration is proposed.

A complete set of Mark 2 coaches is in the process of being put into traffic to meet current legislation in Northern Ireland

Museum

Ulster Folk & Transport Museum

County Down

Member: HRA
Forty-five acres are devoted to the Transport Galleries. Permanent exhibitions include the earliest forms of transport, horse-drawn vehicles, bicycles, motor cars and the Museum's *Titanic* exhibition.

The Irish Railway Collection is displayed in an award-winning purpose-built gallery — the largest Transport Museum gallery in Ireland.

The collection features *Maedb* — the largest locomotive run in Ireland. The display includes narrow gauge and standard gauge rolling stock, locomotives, carriages, goods wagons, railcars and railbuses along with memorabilia

Location: Ulster Folk & Transport Museum, Cultra, Holywood
Operating organisation: Ulster Folk & Transport Museum, Cultra, Holywood BT18 0EU
Telephone: (028) 9042 8428
Fax: (028) 9042 8728
Internet address: *Web site:* www.magni.org.uk
Access: By car or bus the museum is about 7 miles from Belfast city centre on the A2 Belfast-Bangor road. You can also reach the museum by train
Car park: Extensive free parking
On site facilities: Shops, toilets, tea room
Opening times: All year round; opening times vary with season, check with the Museum for details

Locomotives (5ft 3in)

Name	*No*	*Origin*	*Class*	*Type*	*Built*
—	93	GNR(I)	JT	2-4-2T	1895
—	30	BCDR	I	4-4-2T	1901
Dunluce Castle	74	LMS(NCC)	U2	4-4-0	1924
Maedb	800	GSR	B1A	4-6-0	1939
—	1	R/Stephenson (2738)	—	0-6-0ST	1891
*Merlin**	85	GNR(I)	V	4-4-0	1932
—	1	GNR(I)	—	Railbus	1932

*on loan to Railway Preservation Society of Ireland at Whitehead

Locomotives (narrow gauge)

Name	*No*	*Origin*	*Class*	*Type*	*Built*
Blanche	2	CDRJC	5A	2-6-4T	1912
Kathleen	2	CLR	—	4-4-0T	1887
Phoenix	11	CVR	—	4wD	1928
—	20	Industrial	—	0-4-0	1905
—	2	Industrial	—	0-4-0	1907

Stock
1 Dublin, Wicklow & Wexford Railway coach; 1 Dundalk, Newry & Greenore Railway coach; 1 Midland & Great Western Railway director's saloon (ex-private vehicle); 1 Electric tramcar of Bessbrook-Newry Tramway; 2 trams from Giant's Causeway Tramway, Great Northern Railway Ireland Fintona tram, Great Northern Railway Ireland Hill of Howth electric tramcar, 1 Cavan-Leitrim Railway coach; 2 County Donegal Railway railcars; 1 County Donegal Railway director's coach; 1 County Donegal Railway trailer coach (bodywork ex-Dublin & Lucan Railway coach); 1 Giant's Causeway (P&BVR) saloon trailer; 1 Castlederg & Victoria Bridge Tramway 1st/3rd coach; 1 County Donegal Railway 7-ton open wagon, 3 Belfast trams, 1 Belfast trolleybus, 1 Belfast double-deck bus. Extensive collection of cars, motorcycles, bicycles, commercial vehicles, horse-drawn vehicles, fire-fighting equipment and industrial railway vehicles

Republic of Ireland

Cavan & Leitrim Railway

Steam Centre — County Leitrim

Restoration work commenced in June 1993 and to date some half-mile of line has been rebuilt, water tower and engine shed refurbished and new workshops and carriage shed constructed. The ultimate objective is to rebuild a further 5.75 miles of line to Mohill

Location/headquarters: The Narrow Gauge Station, Dromod, Co Leitrim, adjacent to the Irish Rail station

General Manager: Michael Kennedy

Telephone/Fax: 00353-71-9638599 (from UK)

Internet address:
e-mail: dromod@eircom.net
Web site: www.irish-railway.com

Main station: Dromod

Car park: Dromod terminus

Access by public transport: Rail service to Dromod (Irish Rail) on the Dublin-Sligo line. Bus Eireann and Ulsterbus routes also call at Dromod

Refreshment facilities: Tea room open by arrangement. Full meals available at nearby bars

Souvenir shop: Dromod

Length of line: Half-mile (3ft gauge)

Museum: Large collection of locomotives, rolling stock, road vehicles and aircraft, many still awaiting restoration

Period of public operation: Daily, year round

Special events:
Vintage Rally — 30 April;
Ghost Trains — 31 October;
Santa Trains — 3, 10, 17 December

Contact address: The Cavan & Leitrim Railway Co Ltd, Station Road, Dromod, Co Leitrim, Republic of Ireland

Locomotives

3ft gauge

Name	*No*	*Builder*	*Type*	*Built*
Dromod	1	K/Stuart (3024)	0-4-2ST	1916
*Nancy**	1	Avonside (3024)	0-6-0T	1908
Dinmor	F511	Fowler (3900011)	4wDM	1947
—	LM11	Ruhrthaler (1082)	4wDM	1936
—	9	M/Rail (115U093)	4wDH	1970
—	LM350	Simplex (60SL748)	4wDM	1980
—	LM91	R/Hornsby (371962)	4wDM	1952
—	LM131	R/Hornsby (379086)	4wDM	1955
—	LM87	R/Hornsby (329696)	4wDM	1952
—	LM131	R/Hornsby (382809)	4wDM	1955
—	LM260	Deutz (57841)	0-4-0DM	1965
—	LM180	Deutz (57122)	0-4-0DM	1960
—	LM186	Deutz (57132)	0-4-0DM	1960
—	—	Hunslet (6075)	4wDM	1961

**Nancy* under restoration at Alan Keef Ltd, Ross on Wye

5ft 3in gauge

Name	*No*	*Builder*	*Type*	*Built*
—	SZA 979	Scammel lorry	2-2wDM	1959

2ft gauge

Name	*No*	*Builder*	*Type*	*Built*
—	D5	H/Hunslet (2659)	4wDM	1942
—	1	H/Hunslet (7340)	4wDM	1940
—	2	H/Hunslet (7341)	4wDM	1940
—	3	H/Hunslet (7341)	4wDM	1943
—	LM198	R/Hornsby (398076)	4wDM	1954

1ft 10in gauge (Ex Guinness locomotives)

Name	*No*	*Builder*	*Type*	*Built*
—	22	Spence	0-4-0T	1912
—	31	Planet (3446)	4wDM	1950
—	36	Planet (3447)	4wDM	1950
—	26	Planet (3255)	4wDM	1948

Railcars

Name	*No*	*Builder*	*Type*	*Built*
—	*5	Drewry Car (1945)	4wDMR	1927
—	C11	Bord na Móna	4wDMR	–
—	C42	Wickham (7129)	4wPMR	1955
—	C47	Bord na Móna	4wPMR	1958
—	C56	Wickham (7681)	4wPMR	1957

—	W6/11-4	Wickham (9673)	2-2-0PM	1964

*built as 5ft 3in gauge inspection car for Great Southern Railway, regauged in 1994
C42 used as unpowered p-way trolley

Rolling stock
Tralee & Dingle coaches 47C (6T), 45C (7T), 48C (8T) and 44C (10T) all built 1890 ; Great Northern Railway (Ireland) AU345 built 1955 as motor bus. Alan Keef-built No 13, (built 1997)
GNR Gardiner Bus No 389, built Dundalk 1951

Museum

County Donegal Railway Restoration Society

County Donegal

Member: HRA
Old Station House opened as a permanent Railway Museum & Heritage Centre from Easter 1995. There are numerous outside exhibits ranging from *Drumboe* to a garden railway. Inside attractions include a video-viewing room, railway pictures and railway memorabilia
Location/Headquarters: Old Station House, Tírconaill Street, Donegal Town, Co Donegal, Ireland
Telephone: (00353-7497 [from UK]) (07497 [from Ireland]) 22655
Fax: (00353-7497 [from UK]) (07497 [from Ireland]) 23843
Internet address: *e-mail:* rrailway@gofree.indigo.ie
Web site: http://cdrrs.future.easyspace.com/
Contacts: Anne Temple
Public opening: October-May Monday-Friday 09.00-16.00 (closed weekends). June-September Monday-Saturday 09.00-17.00, Sunday 14.00-17.00
Membership details: From above address
Membership journal: *The Phoenix*

Special notes: Outline planning permission has been received for a 3/4-mile long line from the station to Gorrelks crossing

Locomotives

Name	*No*	*Origin*	*Class*	*Type*	*Built*
*Drumboe**	5	CDR	5	2-6-4T	1907

*on loan from the Foyle Valley Railway

Stock
1 CDR brake/third coach No 28
1 CDR railcar No 14
1 CDR trailer No 5
1 CDR combined goods/cattle and horse van (247 of 1893)
1 goods van

Viewing of all rolling stock is by arrangement only

Steam Centre

Cumann Traenach na Gaeltacht Láir

County Donegal

This stretch of track has been laid on the formation of the Fintown-Glenties line. The railway runs along the shore of Lough Finn and it is planned to have a dual ride, out by rail and return by boat. The rolling stock presently used consists of an ex-mining Simplex locomotive with three turn of the century (19th/20th) passenger tramcars from Charleroi (Belgium)
Location/headquarters: Fintown Railway Station, Fintown, Co

Locomotives

Name	*No*	*Builder*	*Type*	*Built*
—	LM77	R/Hornsby (329680)	4wDM	1952
—	—	M/Rail (102T007)	4wDM	1974

Railcar

Name	*No*	*Origin*	*Class*	*Type*	*Built*
—	18	CDRJC	—	Diesel railcar	1940

Rolling stock
3 Belgian tramcars

Donegal, Eire
Manager: Anne-Marie Bonner
Main station: Fintown Station
Car park: Located at station area
Access by public transport: Local buses
Refreshment facilities: Local café at top of station lane
Souvenir shop: Located at station area
Length of line: 2.5 miles (3ft gauge)
Museum: Not in operation but a collection of antiquated farm machinery is being restored
Period of public operation: June — Monday/Friday 13.00-16.00, Sunday 13.00-17.00; July-September Monday/Friday 11.00-17.00, weekends 1.00-18.00. Departures from Fintown every half hour
Special events: Halloween Ghost Train, Santa Specials in December
On site facilities: Toilet, it is also hoped to have a playground in operation
Membership details: Bernadette McGee, (Membership Secretary), c/o above address
Membership journal: *An Mhuc Dhubh* — annually

Steam Centre

Irish Steam Preservation Society

County Laois

Member: HRA, NTET
Location: Stradbally Hall, eight miles from Athy, six miles from Portlaoise (on N80 road).
Telephone: 00353 502 25444 (from UK)
Internet address: *Web site:* www.irishsteam.ie
Access by public transport: Irish Rail train to Athy or Portlaoise. Kavanagh's Bus Portlaoise-Stradbally-Athy-Carlow (Monday-Saturday), also Bus Eireann Waterford-Kilkenny-Stradbally-Portlaoise-Athlone (one daily service including Sunday)
On site facilities: 3ft gauge railway
Catering facilities: None on site but town centre quarter-mile away
Length of line: 1km
Public opening: Easter Sunday and Stradbally Point-to-Point Races* — 16 April; Easter Monday — 17 April; May Bank Holiday weekend Sunday & Monday —30 April-1 May; Stradbally Point-to-Point Races* — 7 May; June Bank Holiday weekend Sunday & Monday — 4/5 June; 40th National Steam Rally* and August Bank Holiday weekend Sunday & Monday — 6/7 August; October Bank Holiday weekend Sunday & Monday — 29/30 October.
Trains run as required 1430-17.00 on all dates except 1/2 August when 12.00-18.30
*On these dates admission charge in addition to train fare.
Any additional operating dates which may be arranged will be shown on the web site
Special notes: This is the longest established heritage railway in Ireland. Please contact Rally Secretary, ISPS, Bunnacrannagh, Timahoe Road, Stradbally, Co Laois for further details or telephone above number or visit web site. All trains will be operated by a veteran diesel locomotive, pending repairs to the steam locomotive

Industrial locomotives

Name	*No*	*Builder*	*Type*	*Built*
—	2	Barclay (2264)	0-4-0WT	1949
—	—	Hunslet (2281)	4wDM	1941
Nippy	—	Planet (2014)	4wDM	1936
—	4	R/Hornsby (326052)	4wDM	1952

Stock
1 passenger coach; 2 ballast wagons; 1 brake van

Museum

Irish Traction Group

County Tipperary

Member: HRA
The Irish Traction Group was formed in 1989 with the objective of preserving at least one of each class of diesel locomotive to have operated on the Irish railway system. The ultimate aim of the Group is to restore its collection of locomotives to full main line

Locomotives/Railcar

Name	*No*	*Origin*	*Class*	*Manufacturer*	*Type*	*Built*
—	1	NIR	DH	E/Electric (D1266)	6wDH	1969
—	A3R	CIE	001/A	M/Vickers (889)	Co-Co	1955
—	A39	CIE	001/A	M/Vickers (925)	Co-Co	1956
—	B103	CIE	101/B	BRCW (DEL22)	A1A-A1A	1956
—	226	CIE	201/C	M/Vickers (972)	Bo-Bo	1957
—	C231	CIE	201/C	M/Vickers (977)	Bo-Bo	1957
—	G601	CIE	601/G	Deutz (56119)	4wDH	1956

standard
Location: The former goods store adjacent to Carrick-on-Suir railway station
Operating society/organisation: Irish Traction Group, 31 Hayfield Road, Bredbury, Stockport, Cheshire SK6 1DE, England
Telephone: 07713 159869 (Mon-Sat 09.00-18.00 only)
Car park: Available in station goods yard
Access by public transport: Infrequent train service. Services operated by Bus Eireann from Dublin, Limerick and Waterford
Facilities: Toilets on IE station. Site is located quarter-mile from town centre
Special events: Operation of railtours over IE/NIR systems
Opening times: Premises not open to the public, although most locomotives are stabled outside

Name	*No*	*Origin*	*Class*	*Manufacturer*	*Type*	*Built*
—	G611	CIE	611/G	Deutz (57225)	4wDH	1962
—	G616	CIE	611/G	Deutz (57227)	4wDH	1962
—	G617	CIE	611/G	Deutz (57229)	4wDH	1962
—	712	CIE	–	Wickham (8919)	4wDH	1962

Timetable service

Tralee & Blennerville Steam Railway

County Kerry

The Tralee & Blennerville Steam Railway is Europe's most westerly line and as part of the former Tralee & Dingle Light Railway (1891-1953) it has folklore and tradition stretching back over 100 years. The railway links the town of Tralee with Blennerville on the coast
Location: Tralee (Ballyard) station is situated near the Aqua Dome, Blennerville station is adjacent to the windmill, 1 mile to the west of town on the main road to Dingle (N86)
Headquarters: Tralee & Blennerville Steam Railway, Tralee, Co Kerry, Republic of Ireland
General Manager: Nora Teahon
Telephone: 35366 7121064 (from UK)
Internet address: *e-mail:* blenmill@eircom.net
Web site: www.tdlr.org.uk

Locomotives
3ft gauge

Name	*No*	*Builder*	*Type*	*Built*
—	5*	Hunslet (555)	2-6-2T	1892
—	LM92L	R/Hornsby (371967)	4wDM	1954

*an original Tralee & Dingle Railway locomotive

Rolling stock
A selection of passenger coaches and works wagons

Car park:
At Tralee (Ballyard) station.
Blennerville Windmill car park
Access by public transport:
By rail service to Tralee (Irish Rail).
By air to Kerry airport (10 miles) (car hire available).
By Bus Eireann to Tralee
Refreshment facilities: Restaurant at Blennerville in windmill complex
Length of line: 3km (3ft gauge)
Period of public operation: Daily June to September (subject to confirmation)
Passenger service: Trains operate from Blennerville 10.30-16.30 (17.30 in July and August); from Tralee at 11.00-17.00
Facilities for disabled: Toilets and wheelchair access, museum and catering facilities available at Blennerville windmill

Timetable Service

Waterford & Suir Valley Railway

Co Waterford

This heritage narrow gauge railway follows over 6km of the route of the abandoned Waterford-Dungarvan line. The line runs mostly along the picturesque banks of the River Suir between Kilmeadan and Waterford City offering panoramic views of the

Industrial locomotives

Name	*No*	*Builder*	*Type*	*Built*
—	LM179	Deutz (57121)	0-4-0DM	1960
—	LM183	Deutz (57127)	0-4-0DM	1960
—	—	M/Rail (60SP382)	4wDM	1969

River Suir, rolling farmland and mountains
Location: Kilmeadan station, Kilmeadan, Co Waterford on the R680.
Contact: Maria Kyte, Business Development Manager, Waterford & Suir Valley Railway Co, Kilmeadan Station, Kilmeadan, Co Waterford
Telephone: 00353 (0) 51 384058
Fax: 00353 (0) 51 876002
Internet address: *e-mail:* wsvr@waterfordchamber.ie
Web site: www.wsvrailway.ie
Access by public transport: Suirway bus service to Kilmeadan (schedule can vary)

Stock
Two carriages built specially for the railway. The steel coaches have approximately two thirds of the accommodation in open toastrack seating, the remainder being an enclosed saloon, accessed from an end veranda

Length of line: 6km, 3ft gauge railway
Catering facilities: Coffee shop at station
Souvenir shop: Kilmeadan
Car parking: On site
Length of track: 6km of track laid from Kilmeadan to Carriganore. The summer schedule will provide for a 12km round trip on the 6km of track
Public opening: Provisional schedule for 2006 is Easter to September — Monday to Saturday 11.00-16.00, and Sundays 12.00-17.00
Special events: Halloween Ghost Trips — October; Santa Trips — December
Facilities for disabled: Train carriages, ticket office, shop and toilets accessible wheelchairs

Steam Centre

West Clare Railway

County Clare

Originally closed in 1961, the West Clare Railway is being re-created at the triangular Moyasta Junction station where only the original station house survives. The line was made famous (or infamous) by the Percy French song called 'Are ye right there, Michael'
Location/headquarters: West Clare Railway, Moyasta Junction, Kilrush, Co Clare, Republic of Ireland
Telephone: 065 9051284
Internet address: *Web site:* www.westclarerailway.com
Chief Executive: Jackie Whelan
Access by public transport: On National Route N67 between Kilrush and Kilkee
Main station: Moyasta Junction

Locomotives

Name	*No*	*Builder*	*Type*	*Built*
Slieve Callan	5*	Dübs (2890)	0-6-2T	1892
—	—	RFS (101L)	4wDH	1989

*an original West Clare Railway locomotive undergoing restoration in England, due for completion during 2006

Rolling stock
2 carriages, with extra vehicles currently under construction

Car park: Located beside station
Length of line: 1.5 miles (3ft gauge), ongoing construction
On site facilities: Refreshments located in carriage beside station, Souvenir Shop and Museum located in Station House. The main depot is also located at Moyasta Junction
Period of public operation: Daily all year round, 10.00-18.00 (Sundays 12.00-18.00)
Facilities for disabled: Yes, including wheelchair
Membership details: Membership Secretary, c/o above address

Heritage Railway Association

www.heritagerailways.com

Company Limited by Guarantee and not having a share capital.
Registered in England No 2226245
(Registered Office: 2 Littlestone Road, New Romney, Kent TN28 8PL)
President: Dame Margaret Weston DBE
Vice Presidents: Ian Allan OBE, Allan Garraway MBE, Brian Simpson MEP

Friends of HRA Membership Secretary:
Ian Leigh, 206B Crowfield House, North Row, Milton Keynes, MK9 3LQ.
E-mail: ian.leigh4@btinternet.com

Corporate Membership Secretary:
Steve Wood, 15 Croftlands Drive, Ravenglass, Cumbria CA18 1SJ
Tel: 01229 717080 (weekends)
E-mail: woodsysteve@hotmail.com

Members of the Heritage Railway Association

UK Affiliate Members (not in the main part of the book)

Association of Community Rail Partnerships: Dr P. Salvenson, The Rail and River Centre, Canalside, Slaithwaite Civic Hall, Huddersfield HD7 5AB

Brookes No 1 Locomotive Co: Mr D. R. C. Moncton, 10 Blenheim Terrace, Woodhouse Lane, Leeds LS2 9HX

Edmondson Ticket Printing Co: Pat & Andrea Geall, Proprietors, 1 Winchester Drive, Muxton, Telford, Shropshire TF2 8SJ

English Welsh & Scottish Railways: Mr P Johnson, Loco Engineer, Toton TNMD, Toton Sidings, Long Eaton, Nottingham NG10 1HA

Europe Railway Heritage Trust: Mr M. Pease, 52 Marian Street, Blaengarw, Bridgend CF32 8AG

R. E. V. Gomm Ltd: Mr M. J. Tyler, Jayesco Works, 31 Commercial Street, Birmingham B1 1RJ

Guild of Railway Artists: Mr F. Hodges, Chief Executive Officer, 45 Dickins Road, Warwick CV34 5NS

Gullane plc: Mathew Way, Maple House, 149 Tottenham Court Road, London W1T 7NF

Lloyd's Railway Society: Mr Douglas Cooper, 24 Yew Tree Road, Southborough, Tunbridge Wells, Kent TN4 0BA

Locomotive Club of Great Britain: Mr R. L. Patrick, 8 Wolviston Ave, Bishopgate, York YO1 3DD

LocoRH200 DE No 424839: Mr B. Cunningham, 20 Ladybrook, Chapel Park, Newcastle upon Tyne

Marsh (UK) Ltd: Mr A. J. C. Brown, No 1, The Marsh Centre, London EC1 8DX

Rannoch Station Visitor Centre: Normanhurst Enterprises Ltd, 9 Burscough Street, Ormskirk, Lancs L39 2EG

Transport Trust: 202 Lambeth Road, London SE1 7JW

Westinghouse Signals Ltd: Helen Webb, PO Box 79, Pew Hill, Chippenham, Wiltshire SN15 1ND

Overseas Affiliate Members

Australian Railway Historical Society: Mr R. Jowett, New South Wales Division, 67 Renwick St, Redfern, NSW 2016, Australia

Puffing Billy Railway: Mr Mel Elliot, PO Box 451, Belgrave, Victoria 3160, Australia

Stoomscentrum Maldegem: Rik Degruyter, De Streep 19, B-8340 Damme-Sysele, Belgium

Stoompoorlijn Dendermonde-Puurs: Mr Jaak Serckx, Station Baasrode Noord, Fabrieksstraat 118, B-9200, Baasrode, Belgium

Additional Corporate Members not listed in the main part of the book

Aln Valley Railway Society:
Mr S. Manley, Alnwick Station, Alnwick, Northumberland NE66 2NP

Altrincham Electric Railway Preservation Society: Mr A. D. Macfarlane, 25 Prestbury Avenue, Timperley, Altrincham, Cheshire WA15 8HY

Battle of Britain Locomotive Preservation Society:
Mr J. Gartside, 66 Hawthorn Hill, Letchworth, Herts SG6 4HQ

Bridgend Valleys Railway:
Mr J. Leach, 10 Y-Wern, Bettws, Bridgend, Mid Glamorgan CF32 8RR

Britain's Great Little Railways: Mr M. B. Beevers, 64 Bullar Road, Southampton SO18 1GS

Britannia Locomotive Society:
Mr A. Sixsmith, 6 Vermont Grove, Peterborough PE3 6BN

Bulleid Society Ltd:
Mr A. J. Fry, 28 Houndean Rise, Lewes, Sussex BN7 1EQ

Caerphilly Railway Society Ltd: Mr A. Smith, 51 Worcester Crescent, Newport NP9 7NX

Camelot Locomotive Society: Mr P. W. Gibbs, 13 Clarendon Road, High Wycombe, Bucks HP13 7AW

Class 40 Preservation Society: Martin Walker, 2 Priory Court, Lindley, Huddersfield, West Yorkshire HD3 3NU

Class 45/1 Preservation Society: Mr N. Burden, 97 Richmond Park Crescent, Handsworth, Sheffield S13 8HF

Class 56 Group: Tim Dawe, 1 Stanley Avenue, Sutton Coldfield B75 7EQ

Cornish Steam Locomotive Preservation Society Ltd:
Mr M. Orme, 3 Jubilee Terrace, Goonhavern, Truro, Cornwall TR4 9JY

Cravens Heritage Trains:
Mr G. Thorp, 'Bachelors', Broad Street, Hatfield Broad Oak, Bishops Stortford, Herts CM22 7JD

Darlington Railway Preservation Society: Mr M. Bentley, 64 Dimsdale View East, Porthill, Newcastle under Lyme ST5 8HL

Dean Forest Locomotive Group:
Mr J. S. Metherall, 15 Sudbrook Way, Gloucester GL4 4AP

Darjeeling Himalayan Railway Society:
Mr P. K. Jordan, Lime Tree Lodge, Thorpe Road, Mattersley, Doncaster DN10 5ED

Devon Diesel Society Ltd: Mr D. Martin, 89 Osprey Park, Thornbury, Bristol BS35 1LZ

Diesel and Electric Group:
Mr J. E. Cronin, The Old Goods Shed, Williton Station, Williton, Somerset TA4 4RQ

Diesel Unit Preservation Associates Ltd: Mr M. Cornell, 24 Ashbury Drive, Marks Tey, Colchester, Essex CO6 1XW

Dolgarrog Railway Society:
Mr P. Smith, 84 Gorlan, Conwy LL32 8RR

East Essex Locomotive Preservation Society: Mr R. Moore 7 Woodbine Grove, Enfield, Middx EN2 0EA

Eastleigh Railway Preservation Society Ltd:
Neil Kearns, 38 Arundel Road, Boyatt Wood, Eastleigh, Hants SO50 4PQ

Eden Valley Railway Trust:
Ms G. Boyd, 1 Victoria Road, Barnard Castle, Co Durham DL12 8HW

EPB Preservation Group: Mr R. Baines, 73 Woodhurst Avenue, Petts Wood, Orpington, Kent BR5 1AT

Firefly Trust: Mr S. Bee, 9 Shenstone, Lindfield, West Sussex RH16 2PU

The Flour Mill: Mr W. A. Parker, Stowe Grange, St Briavels, Lydney, Glos GL15 6QH

Foxcote Manor Society:
Mr G. Heddon, 31 Lordsmill Road, Shavington, Crewe, Cheshire CW2 5HB

Gloucester Railcars Trust Ltd:
Mr M. Hancocks, 19 Abbots Road, Abbots Langley, Herts WD5 0AY

Glyn Valley Tramway Group:
David Norman, 4 Yew Tree Court, Gresford, Wrexham LL12 8ET

Great Western Heritage Trust:
Stephen Atkins, Dowsers Cottage, 25 High Street, Meysey Hampton, Glos GL7 5JT

GWR 813 Preservation Fund:
Mr P. Goss, 23 Hatchmere, Thornbury, Bristol BS35 2EU

Haig Colliery Mining Museum: John Greasley, Haig Colliery Mining Museum, Solway Road, Kells, Whitehaven, Cumbria CA28 9BG

Hampshire & Sussex Units Preservation Society: Mr C. Dann, 48 Hollybrook Park, Bordon, Hants GU35 0DL

Hastings Diesels Ltd:
Mr J. White, The Rail Engineering Centre, Bridgeway, St Leonards on Sea, East Sussex TN38 8AP

Heaton Park Electric Tramway: Roger Morris, 38 Wolsey Road, Sale, Cheshire M33 7AU

Holden F5 Steam Locomotive Trust: Steve Cooper, 4 Dukes Close, North Weald, Nr Epping, Essex CM16 6DA

Hull & Barnsley Railway Stock Fund: Mr A. E. Hallman, 6 Chequerfield Court, Pontefract, West Yorkshire WF8 2TQ

Kingdom of Fife Railway Association (The): Mr A. Sawson, 54 Townend Place, Kirkcaldy, Fife KY1 1HB

Lambton No 29 Syndicate: Mr J. M. Richardson, 509 Westgate Apartments,York YO26 4ZF

Lancashire & Yorkshire Railway Preservation Society: Mr E. Ring, PO Box 3593, Newport Pagnell MK16 9ZJ

Lincolnshire Coast Light Railway Historical Vehicles Trust: Mr H. L. Goy, 12 Giles Street, Cleethorpes DN35 8AE

LMS Carriage Association: David Winter, 42 Tandlewood Park, Royton, Oldham OL2 5UZ

Locomotive Owners Group (Scotland) Ltd: Mr H. Stevenson, 28 Hazeldean Avenue, Bo'ness, West Lothian EH51 0NJ

London & North Western Society: Mr R. J. Williams, 3 Chieveley Court, Emerson Valley, Milton Keynes MK4 2DD

Lynton & Barnstaple Light Railway: Mr D. Hill, 8 Long Lakes, Williton, Taunton, Somerset TA4 4SR

Maid Marian Locomotive Fund: Mr H. Johns, 139 Stoops Lane, Doncaster DN4 7RG

Market Drayton Railway Preservation Society: Mr R. Pitt, 1 Queens Drive, Newport, Shropshire TF10 7EU

Maunsell Locomotive Society: Mr J. S. Pilcher, 312 Riverside Mansions, Garnett Street, Wapping, London E1 9SZ

Merchant Navy Locomotive Preservation Society Ltd: Mr R. Abercrombie, 12 Inglewood Avenue, Heatherside, Camberley, Surrey GU15 1RJ

Midsomer Norton Station Project: John Baxter, 12 Huxley Close, Shrewsbury SY2 6JR

Modern Railway Society of Ireland: Mr D. Brian King, 4 York Avenue, Whitehead, Co Antrim, N. Ireland BT38 9QT

Moseley Railway Trust: Dr John Rowlands, 10 Braxfield Court, St Annes Road West, St Annes on Sea, Lancs FY8 1LQ

North Eastern Locomotive Preservation Group: Mr C. Hatton, 20 Sorrell Court, Marton, Middlesbrough TS7 8RZ

North Gloucestershire Railway Co Ltd: Mr R. H. Wales, 'Wellesbourne', Oakfield Street, Tivoli, Cheltenham, Gloucestershire GL33 8HR

North Somerset Railway Co Ltd: Mr D. G. Edwards, 40 Belvedere, Lansdown Road, Bath, Somerset BA1 5HR

Ongar Railway Preservation Society: Mr B. Ayton, 75 Highland Road, Nazeing, Essex EN9 2PU

Princess Royal Locomotive Trust Ltd: Mr George Bailey, The Gables, Whitecross, Hallatrow, Bristol BS39 6ER

Railway Vehicle Preservations Ltd: Mr Gordon Maslin, 14 Lawson Avenue, Stanground, Peterborough PE2 8PA

Red Rose Society: Mr G. Jones, Astley Green Colliery Museum, Higher Green Lane, Astley, Tyldesley, Manchester M29 7JB

Salisbury Steam Locomotive Preservation Trust: Mr E. J. Roper, 33 Victoria Road, Wilton, Salisbury, Wiltshire SP2 0DZ

Scottish Locomotive Preservation Trust Fund: Mr J. Shepherd, 29 Earlspark Avenue, Glasgow G43 2HN

Sir Nigel Gresley Locomotive Preservation Trust Ltd: Mr A. Pitt, 30 Barham Road, Stevenage, Herts SG2 9HX

South Wales Pannier Group: Mr J. Melhuish, 74 Coychurch Road, Bridgend, Mid Glamorgan CF31 2AP

Southern Electric Group: Mr B. Cakebread, 41 The Drive, Shoreham by Sea, West Sussex BN43 5GD

Southern Locomotives Ltd: Mr S. Troy, 16 Arcadia Road, Istead Rise, Meopham, Kent DA13 9EH

Southwold Railway Society (The): Mr J. Bennett, 1 Barnaby Green, Southwold, Suffolk IP15 6AP

Stanier 8F Locomotive Society Ltd: Mr G. Moon, 5 Orchid Fields, St Christopher's Way, Burnham on Sea, Somerset TA8 2NU

Steam Power Trust '65: Mr A. R. Thompson, The Station House, Penshaw, Houghton le Spring DH4 7PQ

Stephenson Locomotive Society: Mr B. F. Gilliam, 25 Regency Close, Chigwell, Essex IG7 5NY

Stratford on Avon, Broadway Railway Society: Mr G. Turner, Manor Lodge, Penelope Gardens, Manor Road, Wickhamford, Evesham, Worcs WR11 6SG

Suburban Electric Railway Association: Mr R. Davidson, 6 Coombfield Drive, Darenth, Dartford, Kent DA2 7LQ

Underground Railway Rolling Stock Trust: Mr D. C. Alexander, 13 Irvine Drive, Stoke Mandeville, Aylesbury HP22 5UN

Urie Locomotive Society: Mr A. Ball, 'Lavenham', Adams Lane, Selborne, Alton, Hants GU34 3LJ

Wainwright 'C' Preservation Society: Mr N. W. DeMaid, Flat 2, The Old Stable House, Bromley, Kent BR1 3JF

Weardale Railway Trust:
Mr G. Chatsfield, Stanhope Station, Bondisle, Bishop Auckland, Co Durham DL13 2YS

Western Locomotive Association: Mr H. Coates, 5 Rake End Court, Ridware, Rugeley, Staffs WS15 5RW

Worcester Locomotive Society Ltd: Mr A. T. Dowling, 9 Queens Court, Ledbury, Herefordshire HR4 9DN

1857 Society: Mr G. West, 21A Broad Street, Brigtown, Cannock, West Midlands WS11 3DA

4247 Ltd: Mr N. Powles, Station House, Station Road, Lower Heyford, Oxon OX6 3PD

48624 Locomotive Soc: G. Robb, 26 Old Gardens Close, Tunbridge Wells, Kent TN2 5ND

6201 Princess Elizabeth Society Ltd: Mr A. Harries, 1 Ormerod Close, Sandbach, Cheshire CW11 4HA

35006 Locomotive Co Ltd: Mr G. Chidley, 102 Anfield Court, Russell Terrace, Leamington Spa, CV31 1HD

71000 Duke of Gloucester Steam Locomotive Trust Ltd: Mr F. Reid, 2 Bodmin Avenue, Marthside, Southport PR4 9TU

8E Railway Association: Mr A. Ashurst, 149 St Mary Street, Latchford, Warrington, Cheshire WA4 1EL

LM2MT 46464 Trust: Mr I. Hopley, The Carmyllie Pilot Co Ltd, 6 Ninian Place, Portlethen AB12 4QW

44871 Sovereign Preservation Society: Mr D. Buchan, Clickham, Milnab Terrace, Crieff, Perthshire PH7 4ED

Applicant Organisations

Amman Valley Railway Society

Beamish Museum

Bury Port & Gwendraeth Railway Co Ltd

Colne Valley Railway Preservation Society

Darlington Railway Centre & Museum (see main section)

Deltic Preservation Society

Derwent Valley Railway (see main section)

Denbigh & Mold Junction Railway Heritage Centre Trust

Ecclesbourne Valley Railway

Epping Ongar Railway (see main section)

Gwendraeth Valley Railways Co Ltd

Lincolnshire Coast Light Railway

Llanelli & Mynydd Mawr Railway Co Ltd

Rhondda & Cynon Valleys Railway Society

Rudyard Lake Steam Railway (see main section)

Shipley Glen Tramway

Threlkeld Museum

Waltham Abbey Gunpowder Mills

Waverley Route Heritage Association

Britain's Great Little Railways

Brookside Miniature Railway:
(see main section)

Dragon Miniature Railway:
Mr B. Lomas, Wyevale Garden Centre, Otterspool, Marple, Cheshire SK6 7HG

Eastleigh Lakeside Railway:
(see main section)

Exmoor Steam Railway:
(see main section)

Fairbourne Railway
(see main section)

Haigh Hall Railway: Mr T. Sharratt, Haigh Hall Country Park, Haigh, Wigan, Lancs WN2 1PE

Little Giant Railways: Merton Hill Railway, Merton Abbey Mills, London SW19 2RD

Moors Valley Railway (see mainsection)

Mull Rail (see main section)

Perrygrove Railway:
(see main section)

Road, Rail & Waterway: Mr J. Shackell, 27 Witney Road, Duckington, Witney, Oxon OX8 7TX

Rudyard Lake Railway:
(see main section)

Shibden Miniature Railway: Shibden Park, Listers Road, Halifax, W. Yorks HX3 6XG

Swanley New Barn Railway:
Mr P. Jackson, New Barn Lane, Swanley, Kent

Weston Miniature Railway:
Mr R. Bullock, Marine Parade, Weston-super-Mare, Somerset

INDEX

Heritage Railway Association

Anyone interested in nationwide railway preservation can become a Friend of the Heritage Railway Association.

Benefits include receiving a copy of the *Heritage Railway Journal,* published three times a year, and a copy of the Annual Report, which details the work of the Association during the year. There is the opportunity of attending various business meetings, weekend meetings, which include visits to member railways, and seminars. This gives an opportunity to learn more about the preservation movement.

There is the opportunity to purchase *Railways Restored* at a reduced price and to purchase an Inter-Rail pass which allows visits to member railways at a concessionary price.

Current annual subscription is £17.63 (non UK £17.63),

For further information, please contact the Private Membership Secretary, or send this form (or a photocopy) to:
Ian Leigh, 206B Crowfield House, North Row, Milton Keynes, MK9 3LQ.
E-mail: ian.leigh4@btinternet.com

Application Form to become a Friend of the Heritage Railway Association

Name
....

Address
....

....

....

Post Code
....

Telephone
....

Subscription enclosed
....

Donation enclosed
....

Railways

HERITAGE RAILWAYS 2006

NATIONAL TIMETABLE OF SCHEDULED SERVICES

Heritage Railways Timetable and Directory

This timetable has been produced by *Railways Illustrated* and Ian Allan Publishing Ltd and was printed by Ian Allan Printing Ltd of Hersham, Surrey.

NOTES TO THE TIMETABLE

Throughout the Timetable, the 24 hour clock is used.

Days of operation are shown on the grid or at the head of most entries. Timetable information is also provided.

Many trains have on board refreshment facilities. These are not shown herein as availability may vary according to staffing conditions and seasons of the year.

For details of Wine and Dine, Thomas the Tank Engine, Santa Specials and other out-of-the-ordinary facilities, please enquire of the appropriate railway company for details.

Telephone and fax number, postal address and www. address (website) of each railway operator is shown at the head of each entry so that specific enquiries can be made direct.

The entries are mostly in alphabetical order but in some cases there has been a slight variation to meet space requirements.

DISCLAIMER

This timetable has been compiled from information received from operating companies and is believed to be accurate. However, neither the publisher nor HRA accept any responsibility for any loss, damage or delay which may be caused by variances between this brochure and actual operations or any other cause.

Where there are exceptions to the normal operations of running, dates are shown in *italics* and throughout the timetable **Santa Specials** are denoted by the letters SS.

MARKS OF QUALITY

Some railways excel in certain fields, and in this timetable special merit markings are applied as has been thought appropriate. The symbols represent individual quality; a double symbol represents excellence. Winners in the 2005 Ian Allan Independent Railway of the Year Awards are highlighted.

 Award winner 2005

 Interesting Rolling Stock

On-board catering

On-shore catering

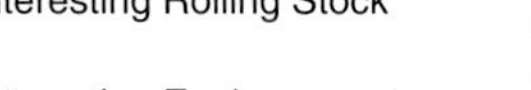 Interesting Engines

 Interesting Stations and Signals

 Big Engines

 Loos

 Views from the train

INDEX TO TIMETABLES

* Narrow Gauge Railway. † 2005 Heritage Railway of the Year Award Winner.

AVON VALLEY RAILWAY

Bitton Station, Bath Road, Bitton, Bristol BS30 6HD **0117 932 5538**

Fax: 0117 932 5935 Web: www.avonvalleyrailway.org

Trains run on **January** 1; **March** 26; **April** 2, 4-6, 8, 9, 11-17, 23, 29 and 30; **May** 1, 6, 7, 14, 19,20 and 27-31; **June** 1, 4, 10, 11, 17, 18 and 25; **July** 2, 9, 15, 16, 22, 23, 26, 27, 29 and 30; **August** 1-3, 5, 6, 8-10, 12, 13, 15-17, 19, 20, 22-24 and 26-31; **September** 2, 3, 10, 17 and 24; **October** 1, 7, 8, 15, 22, 24-26 and 29; **November SS** on 26; **December SS** on 2-4, 9, 10, 16, 17 and 22-24.

Timetable

Bitton	dep	11.00	12.15	13.30	14.45	16.00
Bitton	arr	12.00	13.15	14.30	15.45	17.00

BALA LAKE RAILWAY

The Station, Llanuwchllyn, Bala, Gwynedd LL23 7DD **01678 540666**

Fax: 01678 540535 Web: www.bala-lake-railway.co.uk

Trains run on **April** 4, 5, 8, 9, then daily from **April** 11 until **September** 30 ***EXCEPT April*** *24 and 28;* ***May*** *5, 8, 12, 15, 19, 22 and 26;* ***June*** *5, 9, 12, 16, 19, 23, 26 and 30;* ***September*** *4, 8, 11, 15, 18, 22, 25 and 29*, then on **October** 1, 3, 4, 10, 11, 17, 18 and 24-26; **December SS** on 9 and 10.
Timetable: Trains leave Llanuwehllyn at 11.15, 12.50 14.25, 16.00 and from Bala at 11.50, 13.25, 1500, 16.35. These times apply to most of the season but services are limited in off-peak period.

BATTLEFIELD LINE

Shackerstone Station, Shackerstone, Leicestershire CV13 6NW **01827 880754**

Fax: 01827 881050 Web: www.battlefield-line.railway.co.uk

Please phone for Timetable Information.

★★★BLUEBELL RAILWAY

Sheffield Park, Uckfield, East Sussex TN22 3QL **01825 720800**

Fax: 01825 720804 Web: www.bluebell-railway.co.uk

Trains operate on **January** 1, 2, 7, 8, 14, 15, 21, 22, 28 and 29; **February** 4, 5, 11-19, 25 and 26; **March** 4, 5, 11, 12, 18, 19, 25 and 26; daily from **April** 1 until **October** 31, then **November** 4, 5, 11, 12, 18, 19, 25 and 26; **December** 26-31 with **SS** on **December** 2, 3, 9, 16 17 and 20-24.

Timetable: Trains leave Sheffiled Park at 11.00, 13.00, 15.00 in off peak and 11.00, 12.00, 13.00, 14.00, 15.00, 16.47 in the peak season. All trains call at Horsted Keynes and the round journey time is approximately 90 minutes.

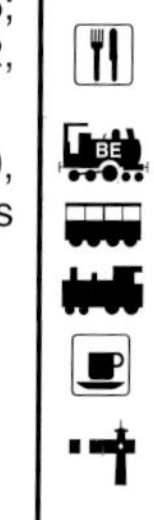

BODMIN & WENFORD RAILWAY

General Station, Bodmin, Cornwall PL31 1AQ **01208 73666**

Fax: 01208 77963 Web: www.bodminandwenfordrailway.co.uk

Trains run on **February** 11; **March** 18, 19, 22, 26 and 29; **April** 2, 4 and 5, then daily from **April** 9 until **September** 30, ***EXCEPT April*** *24, 27 and 28;* ***May*** *4, 5, 8, 11-12, 15, 18-20, 25 and 26;* then on **October** 1, 4, 8, 10, 11, 15, 17, 18 and 21-29; **November** 1 and 8; **December** 26, 27, 30 and 31 with **SS** on **December** 2, 3, 9, 10, 16, 17, 23 and 24.

Timetable A

Bodmin Parkway	dep	–	10.25*	12.40	15.48	
Bodmin General	arr	–	10.37*	13.00	16.00	
Boscarne Junction	arr	–	11.20	14.20	–	
Boscarne Junction	dep	–	11.30	14.30	–	
Bodmin General	dep	10.10*	12.10	15.10	–	
Bodmin Parkway	arr	10.22*	12.27	15.27	–	

Timetable B

–	10.25	12.40	14.40	16.40
–	10.37	13.00	15.00	17.00
–	11.20	13.30	15.30	–
–	11.30	13.38	15.40	–
10.10*	12.10	14.10	16.15	–
10.22*	12.27	14.27	16.32	–

Some trains call on request at Colesloggett Halt.

* Diesel Train (only runs on certain days).

BO'NESS & KINNEIL RAILWAY

Union Street, Bo'ness, West Lothian EH51 0AD **01506 825855/822298**

Fax: 01506 828766 **Web: www.srps.org.uk**

Trains operate on the following dates: **April** 1, 2, 8, 9, 14-17, 22, 23, 29 and 30; **May** 1, 6, 7, 13, 14, 20-22, 27, 28 and 30; **June** 1, 3, 4, 6, 8, 10, 11, 13, 15, 17, 18, 20, 22, 24, 25, 27 and 29; daily in **July** until **August** 27, **September** 2, 3, 9, 10, 16, 17, 23, 24 and 30; **October** 1, 6, 7, 14, 15, 21, 22, 28 and 29; **December** 30 and 31 and **December SS** on 2, 3, 9, 10, 16, 17, 23 and 24.

Timetable:							
	Bo'ness	depart	11.00	12.15	13.45	15.00	16.15
	Birkhill	arrive	11.17	12.32	14.02	15.17	16.32
	Birkhill	depart	11.35	12.42	14.20	15.35	16.40
	Bo'ness	arrive	11.52	12.59	14.37	15.52	16.57

BRECON MOUNTAIN RAILWAY

Pant Station, Merthyr Tydfil CF48 2UP **01685 722988**

Fax: 01685 384854 **Web: www.breconmountainrailway.co.uk**

Trains run daily from **March** 25 to **October** 29; ***EXCEPT March*** *27 and 31;* ***April*** *3, 7, 10, 24 and 28;* ***May*** *8, 12, 15, 19, 22 and 26;* ***September*** *18, 22, 25 and 29;* ***October*** *2, 6, 9, 13, 16 and 20;* **December SS** operate daily until 23; ***EXCEPT December*** *1.*

Timetable: Trains leave Pant at 11.00. 12.15, 13.30, 14.45, 16.00.

BURE VALLEY RAILWAY

Aylsham Station, Norwich Road, Aylsham, Norfolk NR11 6BW **01263 733858**

Fax: 01263 733814 **Web: www.bvrw.co.uk**

2006	1	2	3	4	5	6	7	8	9	10	11	12	13	14	15	16	17	18	19	20	21	22	23	24	25	26	27	28	29	30	31
Jan	M	M	M	M																											
Feb											A	A	A	A	A	A	A	A	A												
Mar				A	A						A	A						A	A						A	A					
Apr	A	A	A	A	A	A	A	B	B	B	B	B	B	D	D	D	D	B	B	B	B	B	B	B	B	B	B	B	B	D	
May	D	B	B	B	A	A	B	B	B	B	B	A	A	B	B	B	B	B	A	A	B	B	B	B	B	B	T	T	T	C	C
June	C	C	C	C	C	C	C	C	B	B	C	C	C	C	C	B	B	C	C	C	C	C	B	B	C	C	C	C	C	B	
July	B	C	C	C	C	C	B	B	D	D	D	D	D	D	D	D	D	D	D	D	D	D	D	D	D	D	D	D	D	D	D
Aug	D	D	D	D	D	D	D	D	D	D	D	D	D	D	D	D	D	D	D	D	D	D	D	D	D	D	D	D	D	D	D
Sept	C	C	C	C	C	C	C	C	C	B	B	B	B	B	B	B	B	B	B	B	B	B	T	T						A	
Oct	A						A	A						A	A						B	B	B	B	B	B	B	B	B		
Nov																									S	S					
Dec		S	S						S	S						S	S	S	S	S	S	S	S	S			M	M	M	M	M

T denotes Thomas events, S denotes Santa Specials, M denotes Mince Pie Specials, see local announcements.

Service A

Aylsham	dep	11.00	14.15
Wroxham	arr	11 45	15.00
Wroxham	dep	12.15	15.30
Aylsham	arr	13.00	16.15

Service C

10.10	11.30	12.45	14.15	15.25	16.30*
10.55	12.15	13.30	15.00	16.10	17.15
10.10*	11.30	12.45	13.55	15.25	16.30
10.55	12.15	13.30	14.40	16.10	17.15

* = diesel

Service B

Aylsham	dep	10.10	12.45	15.25
Wroxham	arr	10.55	13.30	16.10
Wroxham	dep	11.20	13.55	16.30
Aylsham	arr	12.05	14.40	17.15

Service D

09.30*	10.10	11.40	12.45	14.15	15.25	16.30*
10.15	10.56	12.25	13.30	15.00	16.10	17.15
10.30*	11.20	12.45	13.55	15.25	16.30	17.30*
11.15	12.05	13.30	14.40	16.10	17.15	18.15

Service M

11.00	14.15
11.45	15.00
12.15	15.30
13.00	16.15

CHASEWATER RAILWAY

Chasewater Country Park, Pool Road, Nr Brownhills, Staffs WS8 7NL01543 452623

Fax: 01543 452623 Web: www.chaserail.com

Trains run on **January** 1, 8, 15, 22 and 29; **February** 5, 12, 19 and 26; **March** 5, 12, 19 and 26; **April** 1, 2, 9, 15-17, 23, 29 and 30; **May** 1, 7, 14, 21 and 27-29; **June** 4, 11, 18, 21, 25 and 28; **July** 1, 2, 5, 8, 9, 12, 15, 16, 19, 22, 23, 26, 29 and 30; **August** 2, 5, 6, 9, 12, 13, 16, 19, 20, 23, 26-28 and 30; **September** 2, 3, 6, 9, 10, 16, 17, 23. 14 and 30; **October** 1, 8, 15, 22 and 29; **November** 5, 12, 19 and 26; **December** 26 and 31 with **SS** on **December** 2, 3, 9, 10, 16, 17, 23 and 24.

Timetable: Limited services during January and February. Trains run approximately every hour from Brownhills West returning from Chasetown 35 minutes later.

CHINNOR & PRINCES RISBOROUGH RAILWAY

Chinnor Station, Station Road, Chinnor, Oxon OX39 4ER 01844 353535

Fax: 01844 354117 E-mail: info@cprra.co.uk

Trains run on most Sundays and some Saturdays during the season.

CHOLSEY & WALLINGFORD RAILWAY PRESERVATION SOCIETY

Wallingford Station, 5 Hithercroft Road, Wallingford OX10 9GQ 01491 835067

Fax: 01491 826804 Web: www.cholsey-wallingford-railway.com

Trains run on **April** 15-17 and 30; **May** 1, 6, 7, 13, 14, 20 and 21; **June** 24 and 25; **July** 8 and 9; **August** 19 and 20; **September** 2, 3, 16 and 17; **October** 28 and 29; **December SS** on 2, 3, 9, 10, 16 and 17.

CHURNET VALLEY RAILWAY

Cheddleton Station, Station Road, Cheddleton, Staffs ST13 7EE 01538 360522

Fax: 01538 361848 Web: www.churnet-valley-railway.co.uk

Trains run on **February** 11, 12, 14 and 15; **March** 4, 5, 11, 12, 18, 19, 25 and 26; **April** 1, 2, 8, 9, 14-17, 19, 22, 23, 29 and 30; **May** 6, 7, 13, 14, 20, 21 and 27-29; **June** 1, 3, 4, 7, 10, 14, 17, 21 and 28; **July** 1, 2, 5, 8, 9, 12, 15, 16, 19, 22, 23, 25, 26, 29 and 30; **August** daily, **September** 1-3, 9, 10, 16, 17, 23, 24 and 30; **October** 1, 7, 8, 14, 15 and 21-28; **December** 27 and 31 with **SS** on 2, 3, 6, 9, 10, 13, 16, 17, 20, 23 and 24.

Timetable: Train service is approximately hourly with augmented running on Bank holidays and high season days. Travel time 13 minutes between Froghall and Consall and 7 minutes from Consall to Cheddleton and vice versa.

COLNE VALLEY RAILWAY

Castle Hedingham, Halstead, Essex CO9 3DZ 01787 461174

Web: www.colnevalleyrailway.co.uk

Operations take place on **March** 5, 12, 19 and 26; **April** 14-17, 23, 29 and 30; **May** 1, 7, 14, 21 and 27-31; **June** 4, 11, 17, 18, 24 and 25; **July** 2, 9, 16, 23, 26, 27, 29 and 30; **August** 1-2, 5, 6, 8-10, 12, 13, 15-17, 19, 20, 22-24 and 26-31; **September** 2, 3, 5, 6, 9, 10, 17, 24 and 30; **October** 1, 3-5, 7, 8, 15-22, 24-26 and 29; **December SS** on 3, 9, 10, 16, 17 and 22-24.

Please phone for details as to which trains are operating by steam, diesel and Thomas.

CLEETHORPES COAST LIGHT RAILWAY 01472 604657

Lakeside Station, Kings Road, Cleethorpes, North East Lincs, DN35 0AG

Fax: 01472 291903 Web: www.cleethorpescoastlightrailway.co.uk

Trains run on **January** 1, 8, 15, 22 and 29; **February** 5, 12-19 and 26; **March** 4, 5, 11, 12, 18, 19, 25 and 26; daily from **April** 1 until the end of **August**; **September** 1-10, 16, 17, 23, 24 and 30; **October** 1, 7, 8, 15 and 21-30; **November** 1-5 and **December** 26-31 with **SS** on **December** 2, 3, 8-10 and 16-23.

Off Peak

Lakeside	dep	10.30*	11.10	10.50	12.30	13.10	13.50	14.30	15.10
Kingsway	dep	10.45*	11.25	11.05	12.45	13.25	14.05	14.45	15.25
Lakeside	dep	15.50	16.30	17.10*					
Kingsway	dep	16.05	16.45	17.20*					

Peak Season

Lakeside	dep	10.30	11.00	11.30	12.00	12.30	13.00	13.30	14.00
Kingsway	dep	10.45	11.15	11.45	12.15	12.45	13.15	13.45	14.15
Lakeside	dep	14.30	15.00	15.30	16.00	16.30	17.00*		
Kingsway	dep	14.45	15.15	15.45	16.15	16.45	17.10*		

CORRIS RAILWAY SOCIETY

Station Yard, Corris, Machynlleth, Mid Wales SY20 9SH 01527 542580

Web: www.corris.co.uk

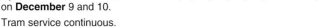

Corris Railway operating days 2006, **April** 14-23, 29 and 30; **May** 1. 7, 14, 21 and 27-31; **June** 1-4, 11, 18 and 2 5 ; **July** 1, 2, 8, 9, 15, 16 and 22-30; **August** 5, 6, 12, 13 and 19-28; **September** 2, 3, 10, 17 and 24; **October** 28

CRICH TRAMWAY VILLAGE

Crich, Matlock, Derbyshire DE4 5DP 01773 854321

Fax: 01773 854320 Web: www.tramway.co.uk

Open and operating from **February** 11-26; **March** 4, 5, 11, 12, 18, 19, 25 and 26; then daily from **April** 1 until **October** 29; **November** 4, 5, 11, 12, 18, 19, 25 and 26; **December** 2, 3, 16, 17 and **SS** on **December** 9 and 10.

Tram service continuous.

DARTMOOR RAILWAY

Okehampton Station, Station Road, Okehampton, Devon EX20 1EJ 01837 55637

Fax: 01837 54588 E-mail: info@dartmoorrailway.co.uk Web: www.dartmoorrailway.co.uk

Trains operate at weekends and Bank Holidays throughout the year from Okehampton to Meldon and Samford Courtenay. Also daily during the summer holidays, half terms, Easter and Whit week. Special events such as Santa Specials and Easter Specials.

DEAN FOREST RAILWAY

Forest Road, Lydney, Gloucestershire GL15 4ET 01594 845840

Fax: 01594 845840 Web: www.deanforestrailway.co.uk

Trains run on **March** 25*, 26*, **April** 2, 7*T, 8*T, 9*T, 10*T, 14-17, 22*, 23*, 30; **May** 1, 7, 14, 21, 27, 28, 29; **June** 1-4*T, 5*T, 7, 9, 10, 11, 14, 17, 18, 21, 24*, 25*, 28; **July** 1, 2, 5, 8, 9, 12, 15, 16, 19, 22, 23, 26, 29, 30; **August** 1, 2, 3, 5, 6, 8, 9, 10, 12, 13, 15, 16, 17, 19, 20, 22, 23, 24, 26, 27, 28, 29, 30, 31*T; **September** 1*T, 2*T, 3*T, 6, 9, 10, 13, 16, 17, 20, 23*, 24*, 27, 30; **October** 1, 8, 15, 22, 29; **December** 3*S, 9*S, 10*S, 16*S, 17*S, 23*S, 24*S.

* = Special event with revised service.

T = Days out with Thomas.

S = Santa Specials.

DIDCOT RAILWAY CENTRE

Great Western Society, Didcot, Oxfordshire OX11 7NJ 01235 817200

Fax: 01235 510621 Web: www.didcotrailwaycentre.org.uk

Open Saturdays and Sundays all year. Daily **February** 11-19; **April** 1-17; **May** 27-**June** 4; **June** 24-**September** 3; **October** 21-29; **December** 27-**January** 1 2007. Opening times weekends and Steamdays March to October 10.00-17.00, other dates 10.00-16.00. Last admission 30 minutes before closing time. **Closed *Christmas Day and Boxing Day*.** Refreshment room – Souvenir and Book shop – Relics display. Children under 12 must be accompanied by an adult.

EAST KENT RAILWAY

Station Road, Shepherdswell, Kent CT15 7PD 01304 832042

Web: www.eastkentrailway.com

Trains operate on **March** 26; **April** 14-17; 23 and 30; **May** 2, 7, 14, 21 and 27-29; **June** 4, 11, 18 and 25; **July** 2, 9, 16, 23, 29 and 30; **August** 5, 6, 13, 20 and 26-28; **September** 3, 10 and 17; **October** 28 and 29; **December SS** on 3, 9, 10, 16, 17 and 22-24.

Please phone to establish which service is operating on date of travel.

Timetable: First departures are at 11.30 and then at various intervals. Round trip takes 37 minutes.

★EAST LANCASHIRE RAILWAY

Bolton Street Station, Bolton Street, Bury, Lancs BL9 0EY 0161 764 7790

Fax: 0161 763 4408 Web: www.east-lancs-rly.co.uk

Trains run on **January** 2, 7, 8, 14, 15, 21, 22, 28 and 29; **February** 4, 5, 11, 12, 18, 19, 25 and 26; **March** 4, 5, 11, 12, 18, 19, 25 and 26; **April** 1, 2, 8, 9, 12-23, 29 and 30; **May** 1, 3-7, 10-14, 17-21, 24-29 and 31; **June** 1-4, 7-11, 14-18, 21-25 and 28-30; **July** 1, 2, 5-9, 12-16, 19-23 and 26-30; **August** daily ***EXCEPT*** *1, 7, 8, 14, 15, 21, 22 and 29,* then on **September** 1-3, 6-10, 13-17, 23, 24 and 30; **October** 1, 7, 8, 14, 15, 21, 22, 28 and 29; **November** 4, 5, 11, 12, 18, 19, 25 and 26; **December SS** on 2, 3, 9, 10 and 21-24.

Timetable: Varies considerably during operating season and intending passengers are advised to phone for the current situation before travelling.

EAST SOMERSET RAILWAY

Cranmore Station, Shepton Mallet, Somerset BA4 4QP 01749 880417

Fax: 01749 880764 Web: www.eastsomersetrailway.com

Trains operate on **March** 5, 12, 19 and 26; **April** 1, 2, 8, 9, 15, 16, 22, 23, 29 and 30; **May** 1, 6, 7, 13, 14, 20, 21 and 27-29; **June** 3, 4, 7, 10, 11, 14, 17, 18, 21, 24, 25 and 28; **July** 1, 2, 5, 8, 9, 12, 15, 16, 19, 22, 23, 26, 29 and 30; **August** 2, 3, 5, 6, 9, 12, 13, 16, 17, 19, 20, 23, 24, 26-28, 30 and 31; **September** 2, 3, 9, 10, 16, 17, 23, 24 and 30; **October** 1, 7, 8, 14, 15, 21, 22, 25, 28 and 29; **November** 5, 12, 19 and 26; **December SS** on 2, 3, 9, 10,

EMBSAY & BOLTON ABBEY STEAM RAILWAY

Bolton Abbey Station, Bolton Abbey, Skipton, N. Yorks BD23 6AF 01756 710614

Fax: 01756 710720 Web: www.embsayboltonabbeyrailway.org.uk

Trains operate on **March** 5, 12, 19, 25 and 26; **April** 1, 2, 8, 9, 14-23, 29 and 30; **May** 1, 6, 7, 13, 14, 20, 21 and 27-31; **June** 1-4, 6, 10, 11, 13, 17, 18, 20,24, 25 and 27; **July** 1, 2, 4, 8, 9, 11-13, 15, 16, 118-20, 22, 23, 25-27, 29 and 30; **August** daily; **September** 2, 3, 5, 9, 10, 12, 19, 23, 24, 26 and 30; **October** 1, 7, 8, 14, 15 and 21-29; **November** 5, 12; **November SS on** 19 and 26; **December SS** on 2, 3, 9, 10, 16, 17 and 22-24; **December** 26,

Timetable

Embsay	dep	10.30	12.00	13.30	15.00	16.30*
Bolton Abbey	arr	10.45	12.15	13.45	15.15	16.45*
Bolton Abbey	dep	11.10	12.40	14.10	15.40	17.10*
Embsay	arr	11.40	13.10	14.40	16.10	17.20*

EXBURY GARDENS STEAM RAILWAY

The Estate Office, Exbury, Southampton, Hants SO45 1AZ **023 8089 1203**

Fax: 023 8089 9940 **Web: www.exbury.co.uk**

Trains run daily from **March** 1 to **November** 5. **December SS** on 9, 10 and 16-19.

FAIRBOURNE & BARMOUTH STEAM RAILWAY

N.W.C.L.R. Ltd, Beach Road, Fairbourne, Gwynedd LL38 2EX **01341 250362**

Fax: 01341 250240 **Web: www.fairbournerailway.com**

Trains run daily from **February** 11-16 and 18-22; **April** 1, 2, 8-27, 29 and 30, then daily during **May, June, July, August** and **September** ***EXCEPT May*** *5, 12, 19 and 26;* ***June*** *9, 16, 23 and 30;* ***July*** *7 and 14;* ***September*** *8,15, 22 and 25-30;* then on **October** 7, 8, 14, 15, 21-26, 28 and 29; **December SS** on 9 and 10.

Timetable:

Fairbourne	dep	11.30	12.50	15.10
Penrhyn Point	dep	12.10	14.00	16.00

★★★FFESTINIOG RAILWAY

Harbour Station, Porthmadog, Gwynedd LL49 9NF **01766 516000**

Fax: 01766 516005 **E-mail: enquiries@festrail.co.uk**

Trains run daily throughout the year from **February** 11 to **October** 29, ***EXCEPT February*** *20, 21 and 24-28;* ***March*** *3-7, 10-14, 17, 20, 21, 24 and 31;* **December SS** on 9, 10, 16 and 17.

Two trains per day operate in the off peak augmented to a more or less hourly service in the peak months. All trains call at intermediate stations Tan-y-Bwlch 40 minutes after leaving Porthmadog.

FOXFIELD STEAM RAILWAY

PO Box 1967, Stoke-on-Trent, Staffordshire ST4 8YT **01782 396210**

Fax: 01782 396210 **E-mail: enquiries@foxfieldrailway.co.uk**

GARTELL LIGHT RAILWAY

Common Lane, Yenston, Templecombe, Somerset BA8 0NB **019630 370752**

Fax: 01963 373915 **Web: www.glr-online.co.uk**

Trains operate on April 17; **May** 1 and 29; **June** 25; **July** 30; **August** 6, 13, 20, 27 and 28; **September** 24; **October** 29; **December SS** on 16 and 17.

Standard service operates every 45 minutes throughout the day and in the high season every 15 minutes from 10.30 until 16.30 inclusive. Return journey time 22 minutes.

GOLDEN VALLEY LIGHT RAILWAY

c/o Butterley Station, Ripley, Derbyshire DE5 3QZ **01773 747674**

Fax: 01773 570721 **Web: www.midlandrailwaycentre.co.uk**

Trains run on **March** 4, 5, 11 and 12; **April** 1, 2, 8, 9, 14-23, 29 and 30; **May** 1, 6, 7, 13, 14, 20, 21 and 27-31; **June** 1-4, 10, 11, 17, 18, 24 and 25; **July** 1, 2, 8, 9, 15, 16 and 22-31; daily in **August**; **September** 1-4, 9, 10, 16, 17 and 24; **October** 1, 7, 8, 14, 15, 21, 22, 28 and 29; **November** 4.

Trains leave Butterley at 12.30 and every three-quarters of an hour until 16.15. Return journey 25 minutes.

GWILI STEAM RAILWAY

Bronwydd Arms Station, Bronwydd Arms, Carmarthen SA33 6HT **01267 230666**

Web: www.gwili-railway.co.uk

Trains run on **April** 14-18 and 30; **May** 1, 7, 14, 21 and 28-31; **June** 1-4, 7, 11, 14, 18, 21, 25 and 28; **July** 2, 5, 9, 12, 16, 19, 23-28, 30 and 31; daily during **August**, ***EXCEPT August*** *5, 12, 19* then on **September** 3, 10, 17 and 24; **October** 27-29; **December SS** 9, 10, 16, 17 and 20-24.

Timetable: Please phone for details.

★★GLOUCESTERSHIRE WARWICKSHIRE RAILWAY

The Railway Station, Toddington, Glos GL54 5DT **01242 621405**

Web: www.gwsr.com

2006	1	2	3	4	5	6	7	8	9	10	11	12	13	14	15	16	17	18	19	20	21	22	23	24	25	26	27	28	29	30	31
Mar				B	B						B	B						B	B						B	C					X
Apr	X	X		B	B	B		A	A		B	B	B	A	A	A	A	B				A	A						A	A	
May	A					A	C						A	A						A	C						X	X	X	X	X
June	X	X	X	X				B		A	A				B		A	C				B		T	T				B		
July	A	C				B		A	A				B		A	C				B		A	A		B	B	B		A	A	
Aug	B	B	B		A	C		B	B	B		A	A		B	B	B		A	C		B	B	B		A	A	A	B	B	B
Sept		A	C				B		X	X				B		A	C						A	A						T	
Oct	T						B	B						B	B						B	B		B	B	B		B	B		
Nov				X	X													B	B						B	B					
Dec		S	S						S	S						S	S					S	S	S		B	X	B	B	B	B

T denotes Thomas events, X denotes special events, see local announcements.

Service A

Toddington	dep	10.30	11.30	12.30	13.30	14.30	15.30	16.30
Cheltenham	arr	11.01	12.01	13.01	14.01	15.01	16.01	17.01
Cheltenham	dep	11.15	12.15	13.15	14.15	15.15	16.15	17.15
Toddington	arr	11.51	12.51	13.51	14.51	15.51	16.51	17.46

All trains call at Winchcombe 9 minutes after leaving Toddington and 21 minutes after leaving Cheltenham.

Service B

Toddington	dep	10.30	12.15	14.30	16.15
Cheltenham	arr	11.02	12.47	15.02	16.47
Cheltenham	dep	11.20	13.05	15.20	17.00
Toddington	arr	11.53	13.38	15.53	17.33

Service C

Toddington	dep	10.30	11.35	13.15	14.25	15.30	16.30
Cheltenham	arr	11.03	12.08	13.47	14.58	16.02	17.02
Cheltenham	dep	11.20	12.25	14.10	15.15	16.15	17.15
Toddington	arr	12.00	12.58	14.51	15.54	16.54	17.47

★★GREAT CENTRAL RAILWAY

Great Central Road, Loughborough, Leicestershire LE11 1RW **01509 230726**

Fax: 01509 239791 **Web: www.gcrailway.co.uk**

2006	1	2	3	4	5	6	7	8	9	10	11	12	13	14	15	16	17	18	19	20	21	22	23	24	25	26	27	28	29	30	31
Jan	X	X					A	A						A	A						A	A						X	X		
Feb				A	A						A	A						T	T						A	A					
Mar				A	A						A	A						A	A						X	X					
Apr	A	A						A	A					B	A	X	X	X	B	B	B	A	A			B			X	X	
May	X		B			A	A			B			X	X			B			A	A			B			T	T	T	B	B
June	B		A	A		B	B	B		X	X		B	B	B		A	A		B	B	B		A	A		B	B	B		
July	X	X		B	B	B		A	A		B	B	B		A	A	B	B	B	B	B	A	A	B	B	B	B	B	X	X	
Aug	B	B	B	B	A	A	B	B	B	B	B	A	A	B	B	B	B	B	A	A	B	B	B	B	T	T	T	T	B	B	
Sept		A	A			B			A	A			B		X	X	X			B			A	A			B			A	
Oct	A						X	X						A	A						T	T			B			A	A		
Nov			X	A	A						A	A						A	A						S	S					
Dec		S	S						S	S						S	S				S	S	S	S	X	X	X	X	X	X	X

X denotes special events, S denotes Santa Specials, see local announcements.

Service B

Loughborough Central	dep	11.00	13.00	15.00	19.30
Leicester North	arr	11.28	13.28	15.28	20.30
Leicester North	dep	11.45	13.45	15.45	20.50
Loughborough Central	arr	12.13	14.13	16.14	22.15

Service A

Loughborough Central	dep	09.30	10.15	11.15	12.15	13.15	14.15	15.15	16.15	17.35	19.00	19.30	20.45
Leicester North	arr	09.58	10.43	11.43	12.43	13.53	14.47	15.47	16.43	18.03	19.27	20.30	21.12
Leicester North	dep	10.00	11.00	12.00	13.00	14.05	15.00	16.00	17.00	18.15	19.45	20.50	21.30
Loughborough Central	arr	10.26	11.26	12.26	13.26	14.43	15.26	16.26	17.26	18.41	20.12	20.00	20.09

GREAT ORME TRAMWAY

Conwy Tourism Services, 1-2 Chapel Street, Llandudno LL30 2SY 01492 575275

Web: www.greatormetramway.com

Open: Late March – Late October 2006, 10.00 to 18.00 every day (17.00 in October).

Frequency: Every 20 minutes – on the hour, twenty past and twenty to the hour (trams are able to run every 10 minutes during the peak season).

Journey time: The journey is split into two sections: lower section and upper section. Each section takes approximately 8-10 minutes to complete. Passengers then have to change at the Halfway Station, where there is a tramway exhibition and a chance to view into the Winding House, before boarding the tram to the summit.

GROUDLE GLEN RAILWAY

29 Hawarden Avenue, Douglas, Isle of Man IM1 4BP 01624 622138

E-mail: tbeard@manx.net

Trains run on **April** 16, 17 and 30; **May** 7, 14, 21 and 28; **June** 4, 11, 18 and 25; **July** 2, 5, 9, 12, 16, 19, 23, 26 and 30; **August** 1, 2, 6, 8, 9, 13, 15, 16, 20, 22, 23 and 27; **September** 3, 10, 17 and 24; **December** 26 and **SS** on **December** 17, 23 and 24.

Standard service operates between 11.00 and 16.30 and **SS** between 11.00–15.30.

HAYLING SEASIDE RAILWAY

20 Jasmond Road, Cosham, Portsmouth PO6 2SY 02392 372427

E-mail: haddock@jasmond.fsnet.co.uk

Trains run weekends and Wednesdays (market day) all year round and during school holiday periods. **December SS** on 9, 10 and 16-24.

Timetable: First train leaves Beachlands at 11.00 and then every 45 minutes (summer) and 15.30 (winter).

★★ISLE OF WIGHT STEAM RAILWAY 01983 882204

The Railway Station, Havenstreet, Ryde, Isle of Wight PO33 4DS

Fax: 01983 884515 Web: www.iwsteamrailway.co.uk

Trains run on **March** 19, 23, 26 and 30; **April** 2, 6, 9, then daily until **September** 30 ***EXCEPT April*** *10, 21, 22, 24-26, 28 and 30;* ***May*** *2, 5, 6, 8, 9, 12, 13, 15, 19, 20, 22 and 26;* ***September*** *18, 19, 25 and 26.* Autumn services run on **October** 1, 5, 8, 12, 15, 19 and 22-29; **December** 26 and 31 with **SS** on **December** 2, 3, 9, 10, 16, 17 and 20-24.

Services start at approximately 11.00 with trains running to Wootton and then returning via Smallbrook Junction back to Havenstreet and vice versa. Return journey approximately one hour. Various times are available and intended passengers should phone for details or turn up at Havenstreet where trains leave in both directions.

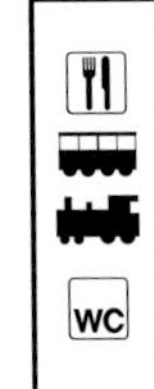

KEITH & DUFFTOWN RAILWAY

Dufftown Station, Dufftown, Banffshire, Scotland AB55 4BA 01340 821181

Web: www.keith-dufftown.org.uk

Trains run on **April** 14-16, 22, 23 and 27-30; **May** 1, 6, 7, 13, 14, 20, 21, 27 and 28; **June** 2-4, 9-11, 16-18, 23-25 and 30; **July** 1, 2, 7-9, 14-16, 21-23 and 28-30; **August** 4-6, 11-13, 18-20 and 25-27; **September** 2, 3, 9, 10, 16, 17, 23, 24, 29 and 30; **December SS** on 16 and 23.

Timetable

Dufftown	dep	11.25	14.00	15.50
Keith Town	arr	12.03	14.38	16.28
Keith Town	dep	12.15	14.50	16.40
Dufftown	arr	12.53	15.28	17.18

★★★KEIGHLEY & WORTH VALLEY RAILWAY

Haworth Station, Keighley, West Yorkshire BD22 8NJ 01535 645214

Fax: 01535 647317 Web: www. kwvr.co.uk

Trains run on **January** 1, 2, 7, 8, 14, 15, 21, 22, 28 and 29; **February** 4, 5, 11, 12 and 18-26; **March** 4, 5, 11, 12, 18, 19, 25 and 26; **April** 1, 2, 8-23, 29 and 30; **May** 1, 6, 7, 13, 14, 20, 21, 27-31; **June** 1-4, 10, 11, 17, 18, 20-22, 24, 25 and 27-29; daily during **July** and **August, September** 1-3, 9, 10, 16, 17, 23, 24 and 30; **October** 20-22; **November** 4, 5, 11, 12, 18, 19, 25 and 26; **December** 26-31 with **SS** on **December** 2, 3, 9, 10, 16, 17, 23 and 24.

Timetable: In the high season trains run approximately every three-quarters of an hour from Oxenhope and Keighley. During the off peak six trains operate per day. Please check details at any station.

★KENT & EAST SUSSEX RAILWAY

Tenterden Town Station, Station Road, Tenterden, Kent TN30 6HE 0870 06006074

Fax: 01580 765654 E-mail: enquiries@kesr.org.uk Web: www.kesr.org.uk

Trains operate on **March** 18, 19, 25 and 26; **April** 1-17, 22, 23, 29 and 30; **May** 1, 3, 4, 6, 7, 10, 11, 13, 14, 17, 18, 20, 21, 24, 25 and 27-31; **June** 1-4, 7, 8, 10, 11, 14, 15, 17, 18, 21, 22, 24, 25 and 27-29; **July** daily *EXCEPT* 3, 7, 10, 14, 17 and 21; **August** daily; **September** 1-7, 9, 10, 12-14, 16, 17, 19-21, 23, 24 and 30; **October** 1, 7, 8, 14, 15 and 20-29; **November** 4 and 5; **December SS** on 2, 3, 9, 10, 15-17 and 20-24; also

KIRKLEES LIGHT RAILWAY

Park Mill Way, Clayton West, Near Huddersfield HD8 9XJ 01484 865727

Fax: 01484 865727 E-mail: trains@thekit.wanadoo.co.uk

Trains depart from Clayton West station on the hour. Arrive Shelley turntable approx 25 minutes past the hour. Depart Shelley 30 minutes past the hour. Arrive Clayton West approx 50 minutes past the hour.
Summer opening times – trains hourly from 11.00 until 16.00 daily from 30th May to 5th September.
Winter opening times – trains hourly from 11.00 until 15.00. Open every weekend and school holidays.

LAKESIDE & HAVERWAITE RAILWAY CO LTD

Haverthwaite Railway, Ulverston, Cumbria LA12 8AL 01539 531594

Fax: 015395 30503 Web: www.lakesiderailway.co.uk

Trains run daily from **April** 8 until **October** 29, Gala days on **November** 10 and 11, and **December SS** on 2, 3, 9, 10, 16 and 17.

Timetable: Please phone for details.

LAUNCESTON STEAM RAILWAY

01566 775665

St Thomas Road, Launceston, Cornwall PL15 8DA

Trains run daily **May** 28 until **September** 15, ***EXCEPT June*** *2, 10, 17 and 24;* ***July*** *3, 8, 15, 22 and 29;* ***August*** *5, 12, 19 and 26;* ***September*** *2 and 9.*

Timetable: Launceston depart 11.00, 11,50, 12.45, 14.00, 14.45, 15.35, 16.30 returning from Newmills 20 minutes later.

LEIGHTON BUZZARD RAILWAY

Page's Park Station, Billington Road, Leighton Buzzard LU7 4TN 01525 373888

Fax: 01525 377814 Web: www.buzzrail.co.uk

Trains operate on **March** 12, 19 and 26; **April** 2, 9, 12, 14-17, 23, 29 and 30; **May** 1, 7, 14, 21, 27-29 and 31; **June** 1, 3, 4, 7, 11, 14, 18, 21, 25 and 28; **July** 2, 5, 9, 12, 16, 19, 23, 26 and 30; **August** 1-3, 5, 6, 8-10, 12, 13, 15-17, 19, 20, 22-24, 26-28; **September** 3, 17 and 24; **October** 1, 7, 8, 15, 22, 25 and 29; **December SS** on 2, 3, 6, 9, 10, 13, 16, 17, 20, 23 and 26-28.

Trains run from Page's Park to Stonehenge Works at frequent intervals during the day. Travel time is 25 minutes each way. Round trip takes approximately 70 minutes.

LLANBERIS LAKE RAILWAY

Rheilffordd Llyn Padarn, Llanberis, Gywnedd, Wales LL55 4TY 01286 870549

Fax: 01286 870549 Web: www.lake-railway.co.uk

Trains run on **January** 31; **February** 7, 14, 19-26 and 28; **March** 7, 14, 20-23 and 27-30; then daily from **April** 2 until **October** 31, ***EXCEPT April** 7, 8 and 22; **May** 6, 13 and 20; **September** 9, 16, 23 and 30; **October** 6, 7, 13,14, 20, 21, 27 and 28,* then on **November** 1-3 and 5; **December SS** on 9, 10, 16 and 17.

Timetable: Trains operate from Llanberis at 11.00 until late afternoon. Please check which service operates on day of travel. In the high season trains run approximately half-hourly.

★★LLANGOLLEN RAILWAY

The Station, Abbey Road, Llangollen, Denbighshire LL20 8SN 01978 860979

Fax: 01978 869247 Web: www.llangollen-railway.co.uk

Trains run on **January** 1, 2, 8,15, 22 and 29; **February** 5, 12 and 18-26; **March** 4, 5, 10-12, 18, 19, 25 and 26; **April** 1, 2, 8-23, 25-27, 29 and 30; daily from **May** 1 until **October** 8, then **October** 10-12, 14, 15 and 21-31; **November** 1-5; **December** 27-31 with **SS** on **December** 2, 3, 9, 10, 16, 17 and 20-

MIDDLETON RAILWAY

The Station, Moor Road, Hunslet, Leeds LS10 2JQ 0113 271 0320

Web: www.middletonrailway.org.uk

Trains run on **April** 15-17, 22, 23, 29 and 30; **May** 1, 6, 7, 13, 14, 20, 21, 27 and 28; **June** 3, 4, 10, 11, 17, 18, 24 and 25; **July** 1, 2, 8, 9, 15, 16, 22, 23, 29 and 30; **August** 5, 6, 12, 13, 19, 20 and 26-28; **September** 2, 3, 9, 10, 16, 17, 23, 24 and 30; **October** 1, 8, 15, 22, 28 and 29; **November** 5, 12, 19 and 26; **December SS** on 2, 3, 9, 10, 17, 18, 23 and 24.

Timetable: Diesel services operate from 13.00-16.00 and steam services from 11.00-16.20. Please phone before travelling.

MID-HANTS RAILWAY (Watercress Line)

The Railway Station, Alresford, Hampshire SO24 9JG 01962 733810

Fax: 01962 735448 Web: www.watercressline.co.uk

Trains run on **January** 1, 2, 7, 8, 14, 15, 21, 22, 28 and 29; **February** 4, 5, 11-19, 25 and 26; **March** 3-5, 11, 12, 18, 19, 25 and 26; **April** 1, 2, 8-17, 22, 23, 29 and 30; **May** 1, 6, 7, 9-11, 13, 14, 16-18, 20, 21, 23-25, 27-31; **June** daily ***EXCEPT** 5, 9, 12, 16, 19, 23, 26 and 30;* **July** daily ***EXCEPT** 3, 7, 10, 14, 17, 21, 24, 28 and 31*; **August** daily; **September** 1-3, 5-7; 9, 10, 12-14, 16, 17, 19-24 and 30; **October** 1, 7, 8, 14, 15 and 21-29; **December** 30 and 31 with **SS** on **December** 2, 3, 9, 10, 16, 17 and 21-24.

Timetable

Alton	dep	–	10.50	11.55	12.50	13.55	14.50	15.55
Alresford	arr	–	11.24	12.29	13.24	14.29	15.24	16.29
Alresford	dep	11.00	11.43	13.00	13.43	15.00	15.43	–
Alton	arr	11.41	12.24	13.41	14.24	15.41	16.24	–

MID-NORFOLK RAILWAY

The Railway Station, Station Road, Dereham, Norfolk NR19 1DF 01362 690633

Fax: 01362 698487 Web: mnr.org.uk

Trains run on **Janaury** 1; **February** 25; **March** 5, 12, 18,19, 25 and 26; **April** 1, 2, 8, 9, 14-17, 22, 23, 29 and 30; **May** 1, 6, 7, 10, 13, 14, 17, 20, 21, 24 and 27-31; **June** 1-4, 7, 10, 11, 14, 17, 18, 21, 24, 25 and 28; **July** 1, 2, 5, 8, 9, 12, 15, 16, 19, 22, 23, 26, 27, 29 and 30; **August** 2, 3, 5, 6, 9, 10, 12, 13, 16, 17, 19, 20, 23, 24, 26-28, 30 and 31; **September** 2, 3, 6, 7, 9, 10, 13, 16, 17, 20, 23, 24, 27 and 30; **October** 1, 4, 7, 8, 11, 14, 15, 18, 21, 22, 25, 28 and 29; **November** 5, 12 and 19; **December SS** on 3, 9, 10, 16, 17 and 22-24.

Timetable: Trains run from Dereham to Wywondham Abbey with three services on most days but only two on the shoulder months. First train operates from Dereham mid-morning. Journey time 40 minutes each way.

★MIDLAND RAILWAY – Butterley

Butterley Station, Ripley, Derbyshire DE5 3QZ **01773 747674**

Fax: 01773 570721 **Web: www.midlandrailwaycentre.co.uk**

2006	1	2	3	4	5	6	7	8	9	10	11	12	13	14	15	16	17	18	19	20	21	22	23	24	25	26	27	28	29	30	31
Jan	X	X						A							A						A	A						A	A		
Feb				A	A						A	A						A	A	A	A	A	A	A	A	A					
Mar				T	T						T	T							A							C					
Apr	A	A						X	X	A	A	A	A	B	B	B	C	A	A	A	A	A	A						X	X	
May	X					B	B				B		A	A						X	X						T	T	T	T	T
June	T	T	T	T						A	A		X	X	X		A	C				B		X	X				B		
July	A	B				B		A	C				B		A	B						X	X	A	A	A	A	A	T	T	T
Aug	T	T	T	T	T	T	A	A	A	A	A	A	C	A	A	A	A	A	C	C	A	A	A	A	A	X	X	X	A	A	A
Sept	A	A	A	A			B		A	C				B		X	X							A							
Oct	C						X	X						T	T						B	B	A	A	A	A	A	X	A		
Nov				X	A							A						S	S						S	S					
Dec		S	S				S		S	S				S		S	S			S	S	S	S	S			X	X	X	X	X

X denotes special events, S denotes Santa Specials, T denotes Thomas events, see local announcements.

Service A

Butterley	dep	11.15	12.30	14.00	15.15
Swanwick Jctn	arr	11.45	13.09	14.39	15.54
Swanwick Jctn	dep	11.50	13.15	14.45	16.00
Butterley	arr	11.54	13.19	14.49	16.15

Service B

10.30	11.30	12.30	14.00	15.15
11.00	12.09	13.09	14.39	15.54
11.05	12.15	13.15	14.45	16.00
11.09	12.19	13.19	14.49	16.04

Service C

Butterley	dep	10.30	11.00	11.30	12.05	12.40	13.45	14.25	15.15	16.15
Swanwick Jctn	arr	11.00	11.28	12.09	12.42	13.19	14.24	15.04	15.54	16.54
Swanwick Jctn	dep	11.05	11.45	12.15	12.55	14.00	14.40	15.40	16.00	17.00
Butterley	arr	11.09	11.49	12.19	12.59	14.04	14.44	15.45	16.04	17.15

MULL RAIL

Old Pier Station, Craignure, Isle of Mull, Argyll PA65 6AY **01680 812494**

Fax: 01680 300595 **Web: www.mullrail.co.uk**

Daily April 1 to **October** 28. The high season trains run approximately every half-hour from 11.10 until 17.00. During off peak there are 4/5 per day. Please phone for up-to-date information.

HERITAGE RAILWAYS AWARD WINNER 2005

★★NORTH NORFOLK RAILWAY (The Poppy Line)

Sheringham Station, Sheringham, Norfolk NR26 8RA **01263 820800**

Fax: 01263 820801 **Web: www.nnr.co.uk**

Trains run on **February** 4, 5, 11-19, 25 and 26; **March** 4, 5, 11, 12, 18, 19, 25 and 26; daily thereafter from **April** 1 until **October** 29, ***EXCEPT April*** *3, 7, 24 and 28;* ***May*** *5, 8, 12 and 19;* ***September*** *25 and 29;* ***October*** *2, 9, 13, 16 and 20* then on **November** 4, 5, 11, 12, 18, 19, 25 and 26; **December** 26-31 with **SS** on **December** 2, 3, 6, 7,9,10, 16, 17 and 20-24.

Timetable

Sheringham	dep	09.30	10.30	11.15	12.00	12.45	13.30	14.15	15.00	15.45	17.00
Holt	arr	09.50	10.53	11.38	12.23	13.08	13.53	14.38	15.23	16.08	17.19
Holt	dep	10.00	11.15	12.00	12.45	13.30	14.15	15.00	15.45	16.20	17.30
Sheringham	arr	10.20	11.39	12.24	13.09	13.54	14.39	15.24	16.09	16.41	17.48

NENE VALLEY RAILWAY

Wansford Station, Stibbington, Peterborough PE8 6LR **01780 784444**

Fax: 01780 784440 **Web: www.nvr.org.uk**

2006	1	2	3	4	5	6	7	8	9	10	11	12	13	14	15	16	17	18	19	20	21	22	23	24	25	26	27	28	29	30	31
Jan	A	A						D							D							A							D		
Feb					D						AT	AT		AT	AT	AT		AT	AT			A				A					
Mar					A						A	A						AT	AT							A					
Apr	C	C						C	C		A	A	A	A	BT	BT	BT					C	C						BT	BT	
May	BT					C	C						C	C			A			C	C			A			BT	BT	BT	A	A
June	A	A	C	C			A		A	C	C			A			X	X			A		AT	AT	AT			A			
July	C	C			A			X	X			A			C	C			A			C	C		A	A	A	A	C	C	
Aug	A	A	A	A	BT	BT		A	A	A	A	B	B		A	A	A	A	B	B		A	A	A	A	BT	BT	BT	A	A	A
Sept		C	C						X	X						C	C			A			C	C			A			X	
Oct	X					X	X	X						D	D						AT	AT		A	A	A		AT	AT		A
Nov																										S					
Dec		S	S			S			S	S			S		S	S	S			S		S	S	S			D	D	D	AT	AT

X denotes special events, S denotes Santa Specials, T denotes Thomas in steam, see local announcements.

Where Thoms assists with the normal service the timetable number is shown followed by T.

Service A

Wansford*	dep	11.00	12.45	14.30
Peterboro NV	arr	11.45	13.30	15.15
Peterboro NV	dep	12.00	13.45	15.30
Wansford	arr	12.26	14.11	15.56

Service C

11.00	12.45	14.30	16.15
11.45	13.30	15.15	17.00
12.00	13.45	15.30	17.15
12.26	14.11	15.56	17.41

Service B

Wansford*	dep	10.30	11.40	12.50	14.00	15.10	16.20
Peterboro NV	arr	11.15	12.25	13.35	14.45	15.55	17.05
Peterboro NV	dep	11.30	12.40	13.50	15.00	16.10	17.20
Wansford	arr	11.56	13.06	14.16	15.26	16.36	17.46

Service D

11.30	12.30	13.30	14.30
11.50	12.50	13.50	14.50
12.00	13.00	14.00	15.00
12.20	13.20	14.20	15.20

• Trains go via Yarwell Junction though passengers cannot leave or join the train there.

All trains call at Ferry Meadows (35) minutes and Orton Mere (40) minutes after leaving Wansford and Orton Mere (6) minutes and Ferry Meadows (11) minutes after leaving Peterborough NV.

NORTHAMPTON & LAMPORT RAILWAY

Pitsford & Brampton Station, Pitsford Road, Chapel Brampton, Northampton NN6 8BA **01604 820327**

Trains run every Sunday and bank holiday March 5 to October 19 hourly except periods when they run every 45 minutes.

Please contact the railway for further details and special events.

★★PAIGNTON & DARTMOUTH STEAM RAILWAY

Queens Park Station, Torbay Road, Paignton, Devon TQ4 6AF **01803 555872**

Fax: 01803 664313 **Web: www.paignton-steamrailway.co.uk**

Trains run daily from **April** 8 until **October** 29 ***EXCEPT April*** *24, 26 and 28;* ***May*** *3, 5, 8, 10, 12, 15, 17, 19, 22, 24 and 26;* ***October*** *2, 4, 6, 9, 11, 13, 16, 18 and 20*; then **SS** on **December** 9, 10, 16, 17 and 22-24.

Standard service which is augmented in the peak season, when trains run every 45 minutes.

Timetable:

Paignton	dep	10.30	12.15	14.15	16.15
Goodrington		10.35	12.20	14.20	16.20
Churston		10.45	12.30	14.30	16.30
Kingswear	arr	11.00	12.45	14.45	16.45

Kingswear	dep	11.15	13.00	15.15	17.00
Churston		11.30	13.15	15.30	17.15
Goodrington		11.40	13.25	15.40	17.25
Paignton	arr	11.45	13.30	15.45	17.30

★★★NORTH YORKSHIRE MOORS RAILWAY

Pickering Station, Pickering, North Yorkshire YO18 7AJ 01751 472508

Fax: 01751 476970 Web: northyorkshiremoorsrailway.com

2006	1	2	3	4	5	6	7	8	9	10	11	12	13	14	15	16	17	18	19	20	21	22	23	24	25	26	27	28	29	30	31
Jan	A	A	A																												
Feb											A	A	A	A	A	A	A	A	A												
Mar											A	A						A	A						A	A					
Apr	B	B	B	B	B	B	B	B	B	B	B	B	B	D	C	D	D	C	C	C	C	X	X	B	B	B	B	B	C	D	
May	D	B	B	B	X	X	X	B	B	B	B	B	B	B	B	B	B	B	X	X	X	B	B	B	B	B	C	D	D	D	D
June	D	C	C	C	C	C	C	C	B	B	B	B	B	B	B	B	X	X	B	B	B	B	B	B	B	B	B	B	B	B	
July	C	C	C	C	C	C	C	X	X	C	C	C	C	C	C	C	C	C	C	C	C	C	D	D	D	D	D	C	C	D	D
Aug	D	D	D	C	C	D	D	D	D	D	C	C	D	D	D	D	D	C	C	D	D	D	D	D	C	C	D	D	D	D	D
Sept	C	C	C	C	C	C	C	B	T	T	C	C	C	C	B	B	C	B	B	B	B	B	B	C	B	B	B	B	X	X	
Oct	X	B	B	B	B	B	B	B	B	B	B	B	X	X	X	B	B	B	B	B	C	C	C	C	C	C	C	X	X		
Dec		S	S						S	S						S	S						S	S							

S denotes Santa Specials, X denotes Special events, T denotes Thomas events, see local announcements. No service in November.
NOTE: For train service after October, please see Winter timetable where available.

Service A

Pickering	dep	11.15	12.15	14.15	15.15
Grosmont	arr	12.20	13.20	15.20	16.20
Grosmont	dep	10.45	12.45	13.45	15.45
Pickering	arr	11.55	13.55	14.55	16.55

Service B

10.15	11.15	13.15	14.15	16.15
11.20	12.20	14.20	15.20	17.20
09.45	11.45	12.45	14.45	16.45
10.55	12.55	13.55	15.55	17.55

All services call at intermediate stations: Levisham (18), Newton Dale (29) and Goathland (46) minutes after leaving Pickering and Goathland (15), Newton Dale (33) and Levisham (46) minutes after leaving Grosmont.

Service C

Pickering	dep	10.15	11.15	12.15	13.15	14.15	15.15	16.15	–
Grosmont	arr	11.20	12.20	13.20	14.20	15.20	16.20	17.20	–
Grosmont	dep	09.45	10.45	11.45	12.45	13.45	14.45	–	16.45
Pickering	arr	10.55	11.55	12.55	13.55	14.55	15.55	–	17.55

Service D

Pickering	dep	10.15	11.15	12.15	13.15	14.15	15.15	16.15	17.15
Grosmont	arr	11.20	12.20	13.20	14.20	15.20	16.20	17.20	18.20
Grosmont	dep	09.45	10.45	11.45	12.45	13.45	14.45	15.45	16.45
Pickering	arr	10.55	11.55	12.55	13.55	14.55	15.55	16.55	17.55

PEAK RAIL PLC

Matlock Station, Matlock, Derbyshire DE4 3NA 01629 580381

Fax: 01629 760645 Web: www.peakrail.co.uk

Trains operate on **January** 2, 8, 15, 22 and 29; **February** 5, 12, 19, 21-22 and 26; **March** 5, 12 and 26; **April** 1, 2, 8, 9, 14-18, 22, 23, 29 and 30; **May** 1, 6, 7, 13, 14, 20, 21 and 27-31; **June** 3, 4, 7, 10, 11, 14, 17, 18, 21, 22, 24, 25, 28 and 29; **July** 1, 2, 5, 8, 9, 12, 13, 15, 16, 19, 20, 22, 23, 27, 29 and 30; **August** 1, 5, 6, 8-10, 12, 13, 15-17, 19, 20, 22-24 and 26-31; **September** 2, 3, 6, 7, 9, 10, 13, 16, 17, 20, 23, 24 and 30; **October** 1, 7, 8, 14, 15, 21, 22, 25, 26, 28, 29 and 31; **November** 5, 12, 19 and 26; **December SS** on 2, 3, 9, 10, 16, 17, 23 and 24.

★★★RAVENGLASS & ESKDALE RAILWAY

Ravenglass Station, Ravenglass, Cumbria CA18 1SW 01229 717171

Fax: 01229 717011 Web: www.ravenglass-railway.co.uk

Trains run on **January** 1, 2; **February** 4, 5, 11, 12 and 18-26; **March** 4, 5, 11 and 12 then daily from **March** 18 until **October** 29 and on **November** 4, 5, 11, 12, 18 and 19; **December** 26-31 with **SS** on **December** 2, 3, 9, 10, 16 and 17.

Timetable: Three different timetables operate during the season with first trains leaving Ravenglass at 10.30 (earlier service at peak periods). Services operate normally on approximately hourly basis with additional trains in the high season and four trains a day only in off-peak. Intending passengers should enquire which services are available.

★★ROMNEY, HYTHE & DYMCHURCH RAILWAY

New Romney Station, New Romney, Kent TN28 8PL **01797 362353**

Fax: 01797 363591 Web: www.rhdr.org.uk

Trains run on **January** 1, 2, 8, 15, 22 and 29; **February** 5, 11-19, 25 and 26; **March** 4, 5, 11, 12, 18, 19, 25 and 26; then daily from **April** 1 to **October** 1, then on **October** 7, 8, 14, 15 and 21-29; **December** 30 and 31 with **SS** on **December** 2, 3, 9, 10, 16, 17 and 20-24.

Timetable: The pattern of services is irregular and intending passengers are recommended to check the services operating on their day of travel. Journey time from New Romney to Dungerness is 25 minutes and from New Romney to Hythe 35 minutes.

★★★SEATON TRAMWAY

Harbour Road, Seaton, Devon EX12 2NQ **01297 20375**

Fax: 01297 625626 Web: www.tram.co.uk

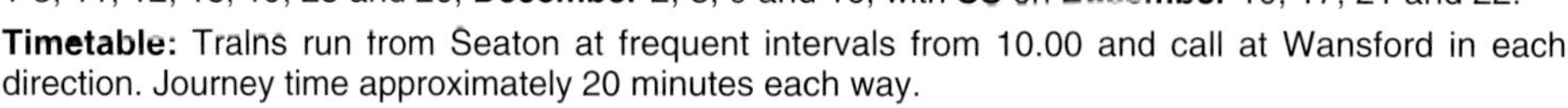

Trams operate on **January** 14, 15 and 28; **February** 11 and 18-26; **March** 4, 5, 11, 12, 18, 19, 25 and 26 and every day from **April** 1 until **October** 31, ***EXCEPT September** 1, 2*; then on **November** 1-5, 11, 12, 18, 19, 25 and 26; **December** 2, 3, 9 and 16; with **SS** on **December** 10, 17, 21 and 22.

Timetable: Trains run from Seaton at frequent intervals from 10.00 and call at Wansford in each direction. Journey time approximately 20 minutes each way.

★★★SEVERN VALLEY RAILWAY

01299 403816

The Railway Station, Bewdley, Worcs DY12 1BG **Fax: 01299 400839** **Web: www.svr.co.uk**

2006	1	2	3	4	5	6	7	8	9	10	11	12	13	14	15	16	17	18	19	20	21	22	23	24	25	26	27	28	29	30	31
Jan							A	A						A	A						A	A						A	A		
Feb				A	A						A	A	A	A	A	A	A	X	A						A	A					
Mar				A	A						A	A						X	X						B	B					
Apr	D	D						B	B	B	B	B	B	B	B	D	D	B	B	B	B	B	B						B	D	
May	D					T	T	B	B	B	B	B	T	T	B	B	B	B	B	B	B	B	B	B	B	B	B	D	D	B	B
June	B	B	C	B	B	B	B	B	B	C	B	B	B	B	B	B	C	B	B	B	B	B	B	X	X	B	B	B	B	B	
July	X	X	B	B	B	B	B	C	B	B	B	B	B	B	C	B	B	B	B	B	B	C	B	B	B	B	B	B	X	X	B
Aug	B	B	B	B	C	B	B	B	B	B	B	C	B	B	B	B	B	B	C	B	B	B	B	B	B	C	D	D	B	B	B
Sept	B	T	T	B	B	B	B	B	T	T	B	B	B	B	B	B	B	B	B	B	B	X	X	X	B	B	B	B	B	B	
Oct	B						B	X						X	X						B	B	B	B	B	B	B	X	X		
Nov				A	A						A	A						A	A						A	A					
Dec		S	S						S	S						S	S			S	S	S	S	S		X	X	X	X	X	X

X denotes special events, S denotes Santa Specials T denotes Thomas events, see local announcements.

Service A

Kidderminster	dep	10.45	12.00	13.15	14.30	16.25
Bridgnorth	arr	11.54	13.09	14.24	15.36	17.27
Bridgnorth	dep	11.15	12.30	13.45	15.00	16.15
Kidderminster	arr	12.26	13.42	14.57	16.03	17.18

Service B

		★				
10.30	11.45	12.15	13.05	14.20	15.35	16.50
11.44	12.56	13.31	14.13	15.31	16.42	18.02
			★			
11.05	12.15	13.35	14.15	14.50	16.05	17.25
12.13	13.27	14.44	15.20	16.00	17.13	18.30

Service C

Kidderminster	dep	10.00	10.30	11.15	12.45	13.30	14.15	15.00	16.50
Bridgnorth	arr	11.02	11.45	12.30	13.59	14.44	15.29	16.14	18.02
Bridgnorth	dep	11.05	11.50	12.35	13.20	14.50	15.35	16.40	17.25
Kidderminster	arr	12.22	13.07	13.52	14.37	16.07	16.46	17.50	18.30

Service D

Kidderminster	dep	09.55	10.30	11.15	12.00	12.45	13.30	14.15	15.00	15.45	16.30
Bridgnorth	arr	11.00	11.45	12.30	13.14	13.59	14.44	15.29	16.14	16.59	17.44
Bridgnorth	dep	11.05	11.50	12.35	13.20	14.05	14.50	15.35	16.20	17.05	17.50
Kidderminster	arr	12.22	13.07	13.52	14.37	15.22	16.07	16.52	17.37	18.18	18.56

SITTINGBOURNE AND KEMSLEY LIGHT RAILWAY

PO Box 300, Sittingbourne, Kent ME10 2DZ **0871 222 1568**

Web: www.sklr.net

Trains run on **April** 2, 9, 14-17, 23 and 30; **May** 1, 7, 14, 21, 28, 29 and 31; **June** 4, 11, 18 and 25; **July** 1, 2, 9, 16, 23, 26 and 30; **August** 2, 6, 9, 13, 16, 23, 26, 28 and 30; **September** 3, 10, 17, 23 and 24; **December SS** on 2, 3, 9, 10, 16, 17, 23 and 26.

Trains leave Sittingbourne at 13.00, 14.00, 15.00, 16.00 and Kemsley Down 13.35, 14.35, 15.35, 16.35. Journey time 15 minutes. In the high season additional trains run leaving Sittingbourne at 11.00 and 16.00 and Kemsley Down at 11.35 and hourly thereafter until 16.45.

SNOWDON MOUNTAIN RAILWAY

Llanberis, Caernarfon, Gwynedd LL55 4TY **0870 458 0033**

Fax: 01286 872518 Web: www.snowdonrailway.co.uk

Daily Service – from **mid-March** to **October** 31 (subject to weather conditions). There is no fixed timetable. Rocky Valley or Clogwyn are the destination from **mid-March** until the end of **April**. The Summit Station is the destination between early **May** and the end of **October**.

★★SOUTH DEVON RAILWAY

The Station, Buckfastleigh, Devon TQ11 0DZ **0845 345 1420**

Fax: 01364 642170 Web: www.southdevonrailway.org

Trains run on **January** 1 and 2; **March** 18, 19 and 25-31; daily thereafter from **April** 1 until **October** 29, then on **November** 4; **December** 30 and 31 with **SS** on **December** 3, 9, 10, 16, 17 and 20-23.

Timetable: Standard service which is augmented during August with trains every 45 minutes.

Buckfastleigh	dep	10.45	12.15	14.15	15.45
Totnes	arr	11.15	12.45	14.45	16.15
Totnes	dep	11.30	13.00	15.00	16.30
Buckfastleigh	arr	12.00	13.30	15.30	17.00

SOUTH TYNEDALE RAILWAY

The Railway Station, Alston, Cumbria CA9 3JB **01434 381696**

Talking Timetable: 01434 382828 Web: www.strps.org.uk

Services operate from **April** 1 until **September** 30, ***EXCEPT April*** *18-21 and 24-28;* ***May*** *2-5, 8-12, 15-19 and 22-26;* ***June*** *5, 7, 9, 12, 14, 16, 19, 21, 23, 26, 28 and 30;* ***July*** *3, 7, 10 and 14;* ***September*** *4, 6, 8, 11, 13, 15, 18, 20, 22, 25, 27 and 29;* then on **October** 1, 7, 8, 14, 15, 21, 22, 24-26, 28 and 29, with **SS** on **December** 2, 3, 9, 10, 16, 17 and 21.

Trains leave Alston at 11.00 and then at more or less hourly intervals until 15.30 in the off-peak season and

SPA VALLEY RAILWAY

West Station, Royal Tunbridge Wells, Kent TN15 8BB **01892 537715**

Web: www.spavalleyrailway.co.uk

Trains operate on **January** 1 and 2; **March** 25 and 26; **April** 1, 2, 5-8, 12-17, 22, 23, 29 and 30; **May** 1, 6, 7, 13, 14, 20, 21, 27-29 and 31; **June** 1-4, 10, 11, 17, 18, 24 and 25; **July** 1, 2, 8, 9, 15, 16, 22, 23 and 26-30; **August** 2-6, 9-13, 16-20, 23-28, 30 and 31; **September** 1-3, 9, 10, 16, 17, 23, 24 and 30; **October** 1, 7, 8, 14, 15, 21, 22

Timetable: Mid-week and low season

Augmented services operate at weekends

Tunbridge Wells West	dep	11.00	12.15	14.15	15.30
Groombridge	arr	11.16	12.31	14.31	15.46
Groombridge	dep	11.35	12.50	14.50	16.05
Tunbridge Wells West	arr	11.53	13.08	15.08	16.23

STRATHSPEY RAILWAY

Aviemore Station, Dalfaber Road, Aviemore PH22 1PY **01479 810725**

Fax: 01479 812220 **Web: www.strathspeyrailway.co.uk**

Trains operate daily from **April** 1 until **October** 29 ***EXCEPT April*** *3, 4, 7, 10, 11, 18, 21, 24, 25 and 28;* ***May*** *2, 5, 8, 9, 12, 15, 16, 19, 22, 23, 26 and 30;* ***October*** *2, 3, 6, 9, 10, 13, 16, 17, 20, 23, 24 and 27;* then on **December** 27 and 31; **December SS** on 10, 16, 17, 23 and 24.

Timetable

Aviemore	dep	–	10.30	12.20	14.45	16.25
Broomhill	arr	–	11.15	13.05	15.30	*

Broomhill	dep	*	11.30	13.20	15.40	17.30
Aviemore	arr	10.15	12.05	13.55	16.15	18.05

* Runs to and from Boat of Garten only.

SWANAGE RAILWAY

Station House, Swanage, Dorset BH19 1HB **01929 425800**

Fax: 01929 426680 **E-mail: davidagreen@orange.net**

Trains operate March 4, 5, 11, 12, 18, 19, 25 and 26; Daily **April** 1 until **October** 29; **November** 4, 5, 11, 12, 18, 19, 25 and 26, **December** 26-31 with **SS** on **December** 2, 3, 10, 11, 16, 17, 23, and 24. All trains stop at intermediate stations Harmans Cross and Corfe Castle.

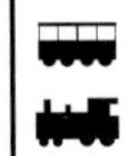

★TALYLLYN RAILWAY

Wharf Station, Neptune Road, Tywyn, Gwynedd LL36 9EY **01654 710472**

Fax: 01654 711755 **Web: www.talyllyn.co.uk**

Trains run daily in **February** from 11-22 inclusive and then on **March** 5, 12, 19 and 26-31. Daily services start on **April** 1 and operate until **November** 4 and on **December** 16 with **SS** on **December** 22-24.

Timetable

Tywyn (Wharf)	dep	10.30	11.40	13.55	15.00
Nant Gwernol	arr	11.25	12.32	14.47	16.12
Nant Gwernol	dep	11.35	12.45	15.00	16.22
Tywyn (Wharf)	arr	12.55	14.05	16.15	17.15

All trains call at intermediate stations: Rhydyronen (12) and Dolgoch Falls (31) minutes after leaving Tywyn and at Dolgoch Falls (10) and Rhydyronen (25) minutes after leaving Abergynolwyn.

TEIFI VALLEY RAILWAY

Henllan Station, Henllan, Newcastle Emlyn, Ceredigion SA44 5TD **01559 371077**

Fax: 01559 371077 **E-mail: elizabeth.perry1@tesco.net**

With some exceptions which should be checked trains run on most days between May and October. Trains run from 11.00 and 12.00 and hourly from 13.30-16.30.

VALE OF GLAMORGAN RAILWAY COMPANY

Barry Island Station, Romanswell Road, Barry, Vale of Glamorgan **01446 748816**

Fax: 01446 749018 **Web: valeglamrail.co.uk**

Trains run on **April** 14-17, 22, 23, 29 and 30; **May** 1, 27-29; **June** 10, 11, 17, 18, 24 and 25; **July** 1, 2, 8, 9, 15, 16, 22, 23, 29 and 30; **August** 5, 6, 12, 13, 19, 20 and 26-28; **September** 2, 3; **October** 29 and 31; **November** 5; **December SS** on 3, 9, 10, 16, 17, 22 and 23.

Timetable: Trains run from Barry Island from 11.00 and approximately at hourly intervals. The last train is at 16.15 from Barry Island.

VALE OF RHEIDOL RAILWAY

Park Avenue, Aberystwyth, Ceredigion SY23 1PG **01970 625819**

Fax: 01970 623769 Web: www.rheidolrailway.co.uk

Trains run daily from **April** 14 until **October** 28, ***EXCEPT April*** *21, 23, 24 and 28;* ***May*** *5, 7, 12, 14, 19, 21 and 26;* ***June*** *4, 11, 18 and 25;* ***September*** *3, 8, 10, 15, 17, 22, 24 and 29;* ***October*** *1, 2, 6, 8, 9, 13, 15, 16, 20, 22, 23 and 27.*

Timetable

Aberystwyth	dep	10.30	14.00
Devil's Bridge	arr	11.30	15.00
Devil's Bridge	dep	12.30	16.00
Aberystwyth	arr	13.30	17.00

Augmented services in August and certain specific dates providing additional trains at 12.15 and 15.45 from Aberystwyth.

WELLS & WALSINGHAM LIGHT RAILWAY

Wells-next-the-Sea, Norfolk NR23 1QB **01328 711630**

Trains run daily from **April** 14 until **October** 31 with departures fromf Wells at 10.30, 12.00, 14.00, 15.30 and from Walsingham at 11.15, 12.45, 14.45, 16.15. Augmented service operates in August with departures from Wells at 10.15, 11.45, 13.30, 15.00, 16.30 and from Walsingham at 11.00, 12.30, 14.15, 15.45, 17.15. There is a limited service in October and early autumn with departures from Wells at 11.00, 12.45, 14.30 and from Walsingham at 11.45, 13.30, 15.15. The journey time in each direction is 30 minutes.

★WELSH HIGHLAND RAILWAY (CAERNARFON)

c/o Ffestiniog Railway, Harbour Station, Porthmadog, Gwynedd LL49 9NF

Tel: 01766 516000 Fax: 01766 516005 E-mail: enquiries@festrail.co.uk

Trains run on **January** 1 and 2; **February** 11-19, 21-23, 25 and 26, then daily from **April** 9 until **October** 29, ***EXCEPT October*** *2, 6, 9, 13, 16 and 20;* **December SS** on 9, 10, 16 and 17.

The timetable varies during the season and enquiries should be made regarding specific journeys. Journey time between Caernafron and Rhyd Ddu is 65 minutes each way and the round trip takes 2 hours 30 minutes and trains call at intermediate stations Dinas and Waufawr 15 and 30 minutes respectively after leaving Caernarfon.

★WELSHPOOL & LLANFAIR LIGHT RAILWAY

The Station, Llanfair Caereinion, Powys SY21 0SF **01938 810441**

Fax: 01938 810861 Web: www.wllr.org.uk

Trains operate on **April** 8-23, 29 and 30; **May** 1, 6, 7, 13, 14, 20, 21 and 27-31; daily from **June** 1 until the end of **September**, ***EXCEPT June*** *5, 9, 12, 16, 19, 23, 26 and 30;* ***July*** *3, 7, 10, 14, 17 and 21;* **September** *4, 8, 11, 15, 18-22 and 25-29*; then on **October** 1, 7, 8, 14, 15 and 21-29; **December SS** on 9, 10, 16 and 17.

Standard services operate at 11.15 and 14.15 from Welshpool. Augmented service in high season.

WENSLEYDALE RAILWAY PLC

Leeming Bar Station, Leases Road, Leeming Bar, Northallerton, North Yorkshire DL7 9AR **01677 425805**

Fax: 01677 427029 Web: www.wensleydalerailway.com

Trains run on **January** 1, 2, 7, 8, 14, 15, 21, 22, 28 and 29; **February** 4, 5, 11, 12, 18 19, 25 and 26; **March** 4, 5, 11, 12, 18, 19, 25 and 26; **April** 1, 2, daily from **April** 8 until **October** 29 ***EXCEPT April*** *24-28*, then on **November** 4, 5, 11, 12, 18, 19, 25 and 26; **December SS** on 2, 3, 9, 10 and 16-24.

Timetable: Leeming Bar depart 10.35, 12.35, 14.35 and from Redmire 11.35, 13.35 and 15.35 with additional trains in the peak season at 16.35 from Leeming Bar and Redmire at 17.35.

★★★WEST SOMERSET RAILWAY

The Railway Station, Minehead, Somerset TA24 5BG **01643 704996**

Fax: 01643 706349 Web: www.West-Somerset-Railway.co.uk

Services operate January 1 and 2; **February** 11, 12, 14-16, 18, 19 and 26; **March** 4, 5, 11, 12, 18, 19, 23, 26 and 28-30, then daily from **April** 1 until **November** 2, ***EXCEPT April** 3, 4, 7, 10, 24 and 28; **May** 8, 12, 15, 19 and 22; **October** 2, 9, 13, 16, 20 and 30;* and then **December** 27-31 with **SS** on **December** 2, 3, 9, 10, 16, 17 and 22-24.

Timetable: Four different timetable services operate during the season and prospective travellers are recommended to check as the service does not follow a set pattern. First trains start mid-morning from Minehead and Bishops Lydeard with last trains leaving Minehead and Bishops Lydeard late afternoon. Most services operate throughout the line from Minehead and Bishops Lydeard and vice versa although some trains in the off peak season run between Minehead and Williton. Journey time is 1 hour 45 minutes in each direction. There are normally 4 or 5 trains a day with services augmented in the high season to 6 trains a day.

All trains call at intermediate stations: Dunster (6), Blue Anchor (14), Washford (23), Watchet (32), Williton (43), Stogumber (54) and Crowcombe (64) minutes after leaving Minehead and at Crowcombe (15), Stogumber (23), Williton (35), Watchet (44), Washford (52), Blue Anchor (60) and Dunster (67) minutes after leaving Bishops Lydeard.

HERITAGE RAILWAY OF 2005

Congratulations to **North Norfolk Railway** adjudged by this Heritage publication as:

Heritage Railway of the Year 2005

on the basis of its great progress in all departments.

Apart from dispensing merit marks for specific aspects of the various heritage railways we are awarding 1, 2 and 3 stars to those railways that are particularly worthy of recognition.

★★★ stars go to leading companies who offer professional service in all departments.

★★ stars go to the best of the rest.

★ star goes to the up-and-coming.

Cover image: Resident on the 2005 Heritage Railway of the Year Award Winner, the North Norfolk Railway, during summer 2005 was No 34081 *92 Squadron*, seen here following arrival at Holt. *Alan C. Butcher*